THE LONDONDERRYS

Books by H. Montgomery Hyde

The Rise of Castlereagh

The Russian Journals of Martha and Catherine Wilmot (with the Marchioness of Londonderry)

More Letters from Martha Wilmot: Impressions of Vienna (with the Marchioness of Londonderry)

The Empress Catherine and Princess Dashkov

Air Defence and the Civil Population (with G. R. Falkiner Nuttall)

Londonderry House and its Pictures

Princess Lieven

Judge Jeffreys

Mexican Empire

A Victorian Historian: Letters of W. E. H. Lecky

Privacy and the Press

John Law

The Trials of Oscar Wilde

Mr and Mrs Beeton

Cases that Changed the Law

Carson

The Trial of Craig and Bentley

United in Crime

The Strange Death of Lord Castlereagh

The Trial of Sir Roger Casement

Sir Patrick Hastings: His Life and Cases

Recent Developments in Historical Method and Interpretation

Simla and the Simla Hill States Under British Protection

An International Case Book of Crime

The Quiet Canadian

Oscar Wilde: The Aftermath

A History of Pornography

Norman Birkett

Cynthia

The Story of Lamb House

Lord Reading

Henry James at Home

Strong for Service: The Life of Lord Nathan of Churt

The Other Love

Their Good Names

Stalin: The History of a Dictator

Baldwin: The Unexpected Prime Minister

Oscar Wilde: A Biography

British Air Policy between the Wars 1918–1939

Crime Has Its Heroes

Solitary in the Ranks: Lawrence of Arabia as Airman and Private Soldier

AT THE COURT AT WYNYARD,

The 19th day of October, 1903.

PRESENT,

THE KING'S MOST EXCELLENT MAJESTY
IN COUNCIL.

HIS MAJESTY in Council was this day pleased to declare the Most Honourable Charles Stewart, Marquess of Londonderry, K.G., Lord President of His Majesty's most Honourable Privy Council, and his Lordship having taken the oath of Office, took his place at the Board accordingly.

A. W. FitzRoy

H. MONTGOMERY HYDE

THE LONDONDERRYS

A Family Portrait

HAMISH HAMILTON

LONDON

First published in Great Britain 1979
by Hamish Hamilton Ltd
Garden House 57–59 Long Acre London WC2E 9JL

Copyright © 1979 by Harford Productions Ltd

British Library Cataloguing in Publication Data
Hyde, Harford Montgomery
   The Londonderrys.
   1. Londonderry, Marquesses of
   I. Title
   929.7'2   CT439.L/

   ISBN 0-241-10153-0

Printed in Great Britain by
Western Printing Services Ltd, Bristol

For Mairi and Alastair

Contents

Illustrations

Between pages 236 and 237

Acknowledgments

I AM UNDER a profound sense of obligation and gratitude to Lady Mairi Bury, first, for suggesting that I should write the story of her family, and secondly, as her parents' literary executrix for putting at my disposal the private correspondence and papers of the seventh Marquess of Londonderry and his wife together with those of other members of the family. This material, formerly preserved at Mount Stewart, the family's Ulster home, has since been deposited by Lady Mairi in the Public Record Office of Northern Ireland in Belfast. Also in that office are the Castlereagh Papers, the great collection of public and private correspondence formed by the second Marquess previously kept at Londonderry House in London, subsequently transferred to Mount Stewart for safety at the beginning of the Second World War, and recently acquired by the Government of Northern Ireland when the greater part of Mount Stewart house passed into the possession of the National Trust of Northern Ireland.

In this connection, Mr Brian Trainor, Dr Anthony Malcomson, and other members of the staff of the Northern Ireland Public Record Office have rendered me the greatest assistance, and I am most grateful to them for their help with the Castlereagh and Londonderry Papers and other collections in their custody. I would also like to thank Mr J. E. C. Lewis-Crosby, Secretary of the National Trust of Northern Ireland and Miss Daphne Cunningham, the Trust's resident staff member at Mount Stewart, for help in various ways, notably with photographs of the house and its pictures. I would similarly wish to thank Mr Gervase Jackson-Stops of the National Trust in London.

From Alastair, the present Marquess, and his wife Doreen, as from his late parents and grandparents, and other members of the Londonderry family, I have received in the course of my work over many years abundant hospitality and innumerable kindnesses which I can never adequately repay. Lord Londonderry, who is deeply interested in his family's history as well as in maintaining Wynyard Park, the historic family property on Teesside, has deposited a mass of private papers in the Durham County Record Office, of which the principal are those of the third Marquess and his wife Frances Anne, also the correspondence of Theresa, wife of the sixth Marquess, and the earlier Vane-Tempest papers. I am indebted to Mr K. Hall, the Durham County archivist and his staff for facilitating my researches there, as well as to Lord Londonderry for permission to quote from the papers in Durham and also from his father's papers and letters in my own possession as well as those still preserved at Wynyard and those in the Northern Ireland Public Record Office of which he controls the copyright. Lord Londonderry has also kindly made available to me the unique collection of old photographs recently discovered in a darkroom at Wynyard and published by him in *The Londonderry Album* last year.

I wish to thank Her Majesty the Queen for graciously allowing me to quote from a letter from her grandfather King George V to the seventh Marquess of Londonderry when the office of Governor-General of Canada was offered to Lord Londonderry in 1931.

In addition my thanks are expressed to the following individuals and institutions for permission to use material in their custody and for generous assistance in other ways: Mr Hugh Alexander Boyd; the Brotherton Library, University of Leeds (Edmund Gosse Papers); Cambridge University Library (Baldwin Papers); Chartwell Trust and Dr Martin Gilbert (correspondence of Sir Winston Churchill with the 7th Marquess of Londonderry); Mr Alan Heesom; Hertfordshire County Record Office, St Albans (letters from the 7th Marquess of Londonderry to Lady Desborough); Lady Holman; the late Earl and Countess of Ilchester; Lord Jessel; the late Miss Nancy Kinghan; Miss Anita Leslie; the Rt Hon. Malcolm MacDonald, O.M. (letters from Ramsay MacDonald to Lady Londonderry); Mrs Dorothy Gies McGuigan; Sir Robert Mackworth-Young; Mr Brian Masters; Mr Duncan Morison; Mr Alan Muntz; Mrs Eileen O'Casey (letters of Sean O'Casey); Mr Michael Pick; the late (8th) Viscount Powerscourt (family papers and pictures); Rhodes House, Oxford (Cecil Rhodes Papers); Public Record Office, Kew (Cabinet Papers, Air Ministry records and Ramsay MacDonald Papers); Miss Betty Roberts; the Royal Military Academy Library, Sandhurst; Mr Rodney Searight; Mr Christopher Sinclair-Stevenson; the Soane Museum, London (correspondence and drawings of George Dance); the Society of Authors (letters of George Bernard Shaw); Sotheby Parke Bernet & Co.; Mr Michael Stanley; Miss Dorothy Stroud; Viscount Trenchard (Trenchard Papers); the Countess Waldegrave; Miss Judith Wilson; the Yale Centre of British Art (Paul Mellon collection); and Mr Kenneth Young.

Finally, I cannot thank my wife enough for all her help during my researches and for typing and retyping the various drafts of this work with such patience and care.

Westwell House   H. M. H.
Tenterden
Kent
February 1979

Prologue

THIS IS THE story of a remarkable family, part Irish and part English, originally Scottish, holding titles in both the Irish and United Kingdom peerages, whose members have made substantial contributions to the national life in the fields of politics, diplomacy, the army, travel, society and sport, besides being land and coal owners on a considerable scale. They have distinguished themselves in a variety of ways and like many members of the Anglo-Irish aristocracy have produced some notable eccentrics. Robert Stewart, who was raised to the lowest rank in the Irish peerage as Baron Londonderry in 1789, ended up as a Marquess eighteen years later, a record advancement, due in his case to powerful family and political influences. He was born in 1739 and died in 1821. Nor has the family lacked physical courage. The second, third and fourth Marquesses all fought duels with pistols—in fact the third Marquess fought two.

The second Marquess (1769–1822), better known by his courtesy title of Viscount Castlereagh, was successively Chief Secretary for Ireland, President of the India Board, Secretary for War, Foreign Secretary and Leader of the House of Commons, and latterly Prime Minister in all but name. He had previously refused a United Kingdom peerage as he preferred to remain in the House of Commons. A year later he committed suicide as the result of a mental breakdown caused by overwork and possibly also blackmail.

Castlereagh's younger half-brother Charles, the third Marquess (1778–1854) was known as the 'Soldier' or the 'Fighting Marquess' from his pugnacious character, which extended beyond the military field of battle. He served as Adjutant-General to the British Expeditionary Force under the Duke of Wellington in the Peninsular War and in other campaigns against Napoleon before turning diplomatist, notably as ambassador to Austria at the time of the Congress of Vienna. By this time he had received a United Kingdom Barony as Lord Stewart and shortly afterwards married, as his second wife, the wealthy heiress Lady Frances Anne Vane-Tempest, who owned extensive estates and collieries in the north-east of England. After his second marriage, the third Marquess adopted the surname Vane in place of Stewart and henceforth signed himself 'Vane Londonderry'. As a coal owner he sank several pits in the neighbourhood of Seaham and built the harbour there to facilitate the export of his wife's coal. His eldest daughter Frances Anne Emily by his second wife married the seventh Duke of Marlborough. Duchess Fanny, as she was always called, thus became the mother of Lord Randolph Churchill and the grandmother of Sir Winston.

Frederick, the fourth Marquess (1804–1872), the third Marquess's only child by his first wife Catherine, daughter of Lord Darnley, was known in his younger days as 'Young Rapid' when he was something of a rake. He sat in the House of Commons as Lord Castlereagh for County Down for a quarter of a century and held junior office in the governments of the Duke of Wellington and Sir Robert Peel. He also undertook an enterprising and adventurous expedition to the Middle East and afterwards wrote an interesting account of his travels there. He eventually suffered a mental breakdown like his uncle Castlereagh, but unlike him ended his days quietly in a mental home in Hastings. He married a good-looking widow, Lady Powerscourt, who, influenced by Cardinals Wiseman and Newman, became a Roman Catholic. She and her husband had no children, so that on his death the Londonderry and Castlereagh titles passed to his half-brother Henry who thus became the fifth Marquess (1821–1884).

The fifth, sixth and seventh Marquesses all began their careers as soldiers, since in those days they were able to combine soldiering with politics. Henry, the third Marquess's eldest son by Frances Anne, was known by his courtesy title of Viscount Seaham during his father's lifetime, and from his father's death in 1854 to the death of his half-brother Frederick, the fourth Marquess, in 1872, as Earl Vane. He was perhaps the least conspicuous member of the family, although he was a keen yachtsman and Vice-Commodore of the Royal Yacht Squadron. In the main, however, he lived quietly with his wife Mary Cornelia on her Welsh estate Plâs Machynlleth in Merionethshire, which she had inherited from her father. But in 1867, Henry emerged from his comparative obscurity, when he was commanded by Queen Victoria to head a special mission to St Petersburg to invest the Tsar Alexander II with the Garter, an occasion on which the equivalent Russian Order of St Alexander Nevsky was conferred upon him by the Tsar. He was a suitable choice as special ambassador, since his parents had been the guests of Alexander's father Tsar Nicholas I in the Russian capital after the third Marquess had been appointed ambassador to Russia in 1834 but had resigned the appointment in circumstances which will be described later. Also, the fifth Marquess was already known personally to the new Russian Emperor, who had visited London as guest of the third Marquess and his wife in 1839 when he was Tsarevich, and the Cesarewitch handicap race at Newmarket had been founded in his honour.

In 1889, five years after his father's death, the sixth Marquess (1852–

LONDONDERRY FAMILY PEDIGREE

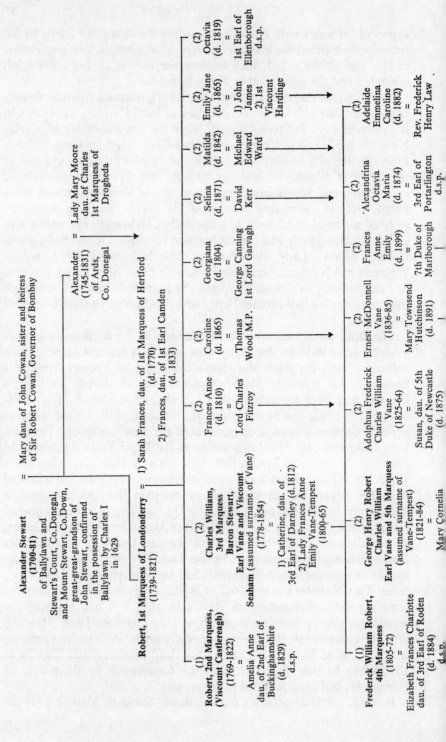

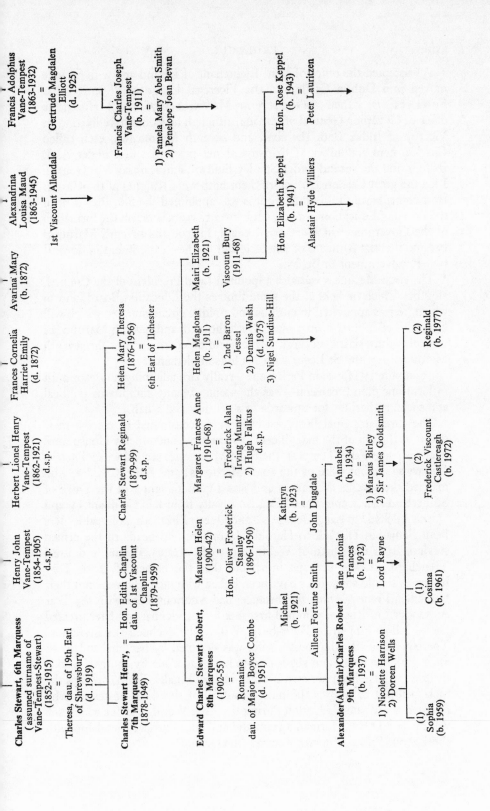

Charles Stewart, 6th Marquess (assumed surname of Vane-Tempest-Stewart) (1852-1915)
=
Theresa, dau. of 19th Earl of Shrewsbury (d. 1919)

Henry John Vane-Tempest (1854-1905) d.s.p.

Herbert Lionel Henry Vane-Tempest (1862-1921) d.s.p.

Frances Cornelia Harriet Emily (d. 1872)

Avarina Mary (b. 1872)

Alexandrina Louisa Maud (1863-1945)
=
1st Viscount Allendale

Francis Adolphus Vane-Tempest (1863-1932)
=
Gertrude Magdalen Elliott (d. 1925)

Francis Charles Joseph Vane-Tempest (b. 1911)
=
1) Pamela Mary Abel Smith
2) Penelope Joan Bevan

Charles Stewart Henry, 7th Marquess (1878-1949)
=
Hon. Edith Chaplin dau. of 1st Viscount Chaplin (1879-1959)

Charles Stewart Reginald (1879-99) d.s.p.

Helen Mary Theresa (1876-1956)
=
6th Earl of Ilchester

Mairi Elizabeth (b. 1921)
=
Viscount Bury (1911-68)

Hon. Elizabeth Keppel (b. 1941)
=
Alastair Hyde Villiers

Hon. Rose Keppel (b. 1943)
=
Peter Lauritzen

Edward Charles Stewart Robert, 8th Marquess (1902-55)
=
Romaine, dau. of Major Boyce Combe (d. 1951)

Maureen Helen (1900-42)
=
Hon. Oliver Frederick Stanley (1896-1950)

Margaret Frances Anne (1910-68)
=
1) Frederick Alan Irving Muntz
2) Hugh Falkus d.s.p.

Helen Maglona (b. 1911)
=
1) 2nd Baron Jessel
2) Dennis Walsh (d. 1975)
3) Nigel Sundius-Hill

Michael (b. 1921)
=
Ailleen Fortune Smith

Kathryn (b. 1923)
=
John Dugdale

Alexander (Alastair) Charles Robert 9th Marquess (b. 1937)
=
1) Nicolette Harrison
2) Doreen Wells

Jane Antonia Frances (b. 1932)
=
Lord Rayne

Annabel (b. 1934)
=
1) Marcus Birley
2) Sir James Goldsmith

Sophia (b. 1959)
(1)

Cosima (b. 1961)
(1)

Frederick Viscount Castlereagh (b. 1972)
(2)

Reginald (b. 1977)
(2)

1915) accepted the office of Lord Lieutenant of Ireland and with his wife moved into Dublin Castle and the Viceregal Lodge in Phoenix Park. Forty years later their son the seventh Marquess (1878–1949) refused the office of Governor-General of Canada, although he would have liked to be Viceroy of India. Both the sixth and seventh Marquesses, each called Charles, held a number of British Cabinet posts, the first under A. J. Balfour and the second under Stanley Baldwin and Ramsay MacDonald. Like the great Castlereagh before them both were Knights of the Garter. By a coincidence the sixth Marquess was appointed the first President of the Board of Education in 1902, while twenty years later, on the formation of the Government of Northern Ireland, his son the seventh Marquess became the first Minister of Education in the new experiment in devolutionary government in Belfast.

The sixth Marquess was also appointed Lord President of the Council, an office which he held at the same time as the Education Board, and to which he was appointed in curious and unique circumstances, which will be described in their proper place. Both the sixth and seventh Marquesses were also enthusiastic racehorse owners and breeders. In 1921 the seventh Marquess won the St Leger with his horse Polemarch.

Londonderry House in Park Lane—really two adjoining houses rebuilt to form one grand mansion—was the scene of many sumptuous political and social gatherings for upwards of a century and a half.

The three principal hostesses who were accustomed to receive their guests at the top of the magnificent staircase in Londonderry House were Frances Anne Vane-Tempest, the third Marquess's second wife; Theresa Chetwynd Talbot, wife of the sixth Marquess; and Edith Chaplin, who married the seventh Marquess and was a granddaughter of the Duke of Sutherland. They entertained English royalty from King William IV and Queen Adelaide to King George VI and Queen Elizabeth, political leaders from Benjamin Disraeli to Harold Macmillan, and heads of the armed services from the Duke of Wellington to Sir Henry Wilson and Lord Trenchard. It was perhaps inevitable that the names of these Tory hostesses should sometimes have been linked with men who were not their husbands. Frances Anne, for instance, had a curious affair with the Tsar Alexander I of Russia, who had first met her in Vienna, and later pressed her to follow him to St Petersburg. Wisely she declined the invitation. Theresa, the sixth Marquess's wife, was detected by her husband in an affair with one lover, and she is said to have had a son by another, who is believed to have been her own brother-in-law. Finally, Edith, perhaps the most brilliant as well as the most beautiful of the three hostesses, who founded the Women's Legion during the First World War for which she was made a D.B.E., formed a romantic and controversial friendship with the Labour Prime Minister Ramsay MacDonald.

Edith's husband, the seventh Marquess, whose career she promoted with all her characteristic vigour and talents, resigned from the Government of Northern Ireland in 1926 to look after his coal mining interests in Durham. Two years later he entered the British Cabinet as First Commissioner of Works under Baldwin, and largely due to his wife's influence with MacDonald, on the formation of the National Government in 1931, he was appointed Secretary of State for Air. When Baldwin became Prime Minister for the third time in June 1935, Londonderry was made Lord Privy Seal and Leader of the House of Lords, posts which he held for only a few months before he was abruptly 'dropped' altogether by Baldwin. That was the end of his political career, although he subsequently made several private visits to Germany with the object of promoting a better understanding with that country and was entertained by Hitler and Goering there. Looking back in moments of despondency during his long retirement from public life he was sometimes inclined to think that he had 'let down' his ancestors.

Yet when the final verdict of history is rendered, it may well be that the much criticised seventh Marquess will be worthily ranked with his ancestor Castlereagh, architect of the Anglo-Irish Union, War Minister and Foreign Secretary during the Napoleonic Wars, and leading exponent of the policy of diplomacy by conference. For it was Charles Vane-Tempest-Stewart, seventh Marquess of Londonderry, who strove hard and successfully to preserve the nucleus of the Royal Air Force when all military aviation was under attack by the advocates of disarmament at Geneva. Furthermore, he set up the official British departmental committee which initiated and developed the discovery of radar. He also promoted the designs of the famous Hurricane and Spitfire fighters which were to play a decisive part in the Battle of Britain in 1940, as indeed his kinsman Sir Winston Churchill has generously acknowledged.

A century ago, in the time of the fifth Marquess, the Londonderrys owned 27,000 acres in Ireland and 23,000 acres in England and Wales with a rent roll of over £100,000 a year, in addition to lucrative coal mines, five large country houses, and a magnificent London mansion. Today, taxation, death duties and other forms of penal legislation have radically changed the incidence of this type of landed ownership. The London mansion has vanished; the present Marquess lives in a wing of Wynyard Hall, the only one of the five country houses still in the possession of the family, where he runs what is left of the historic Wynyard estate; Seaham Hall is a hospital; Plâs Machynlleth and its grounds now belong to the local town council; Garron Tower, on the Antrim coast, which belonged for a time to Frances Anne's great-grandson Sir Winston Churchill, is a seminary for Catholic priests; while Mount Stewart, with its superb gardens laid out

by Edith Lady Londonderry overlooking Strangford Lough and the
Mourne mountains, has been taken over by the National Trust. All the
tenants on the Irish estates became the owners of their holdings under
the Irish Land Purchase Act early in the present century. The Seaham
coal mines were nationalised after the last war, and the remarkable stone
colliery offices with Frances Anne's arms carved on the front and her
personal flag flying above, which so impressed Disraeli when he visited
Seaham Harbour in 1861, are now occupied by the police as their area
headquarters.

In 1977, Edith Lady Londonderry's youngest daughter Lady Mairi
Bury, to whom Mount Stewart had been left by her father, formally
transferred the house and most of its precious contents to the National
Trust, retaining a few rooms for her own use, so that she could carry out
her father's wish that she should spend at least part of each year in the
place where she had been born and brought up and where she had later
run a very successful racing stud. Like other National Trust properties,
the house is now open to the public. One room is specially devoted to
memorabilia of the great Lord Castlereagh, which include the chairs
used by the plenipotentiaries at the Congress of Vienna as well as Castlereagh's library and photocopies of his private papers.[1] Personal mementoes
of the seventh Marquess are also preserved here. The pictures comprise
numerous family portraits and include the famous equestrian picture of
Hambletonian by George Stubbs, which is reproduced with others in the
Londonderry collection in this book. With the gift of Mount Stewart the
Trust also obtained a substantial endowment designed to ensure the
preservation of this unique national heritage for the benefit of posterity.

[1] The originals are preserved in the Public Record Office of Northern Ireland in
Belfast.

CHAPTER I

THE STEWARTS

I

THE FIRST MARQUESS'S father Alexander Stewart owned a small landed property called Ballylawn, near Moville, in County Donegal, which had been granted to his great-great-grandfather John Stewart, at the time of the Plantation of Ulster by Scottish settlers in the reign of King James I.[1] Alexander Stewart, who was born in 1700 at Stewart's Court, as the family residence at Ballylawn was called, served his apprenticeship in the linen industry in Belfast, subsequently migrating to London, where he did business with France and Flanders. For a short time he represented Londonderry City in the Irish House of Commons. In 1737, he married his cousin Mary Cowan, who had inherited a large fortune from her brother Sir Robert Cowan, Governor of Bombay. The trustees of her marriage settlement recommended that a part of her fortune, which consisted of East India Company stock, should be sold and invested in real estate. After looking round for several years for suitable properties, Alexander Stewart and his wife learned that there were two extensive manors in County Down, Newtownards and Comber, consisting in all of sixty townlands, which were for sale and might be expected to yield a satisfactory return on the capital investment. The sale for £42,000 by the impecunious owner, Robert Colville, was completed in 1744.

Robert Colville also owned Galgorm, a property in County Antrim near Ballymena, and there was a rumour at the time that Alexander Stewart intended to purchase this as well. It seems likely that he did so, preferring to draw the rents instead of living there and to concentrate on developing the property in County Down. Bernard Ward, later the first Lord Bangor, whose family owned Castle Ward in the same County, wrote to his father, a King's Bench judge in Dublin, in 1744: 'Have you heard that Stewart is about purchasing the Galgorm Estate? If he gets that added to Newtown and Comber, he will not have less than £7,000 per annum in this neighbourhood which will give him a greater property than any commoner in this part of the world and give him opportunities enough of being troublesome.'

The Newtownards estate included an attractive demesne a few miles from the town overlooking Strangford Lough, the place then being called

[1] Further genealogical details are given in the Appendix.

Mount Pleasant. Here Alexander Stewart planned to build a country house. In the meantime he erected a temporary structure, of which little is known and of which practically nothing remains. His grandson Charles referred to it as 'an old barn, with a few rooms added'. At the same time he built another house for himself and his family in Newtownards and developed the town by laying out a large market place and erecting a Market House, as well as a considerable number of dwelling houses.

Newtownards was a corporation borough and returned one member to the House of Commons in Dublin, customarily elected by a small number of burgesses under the control of the local landed proprietor. Colville offered to transfer his interest in the borough to Stewart for £500, or £1,100 according to another account, which sum represented arrears of rent which were due to him. However, Alexander Stewart refused the offer, 'supposing it impossible', so we are told, 'that the borough should not necessarily fall into the hands of him who possessed the estate.' Colville thereupon disposed of his interest to his kinsman John Ponsonby, then head of the Irish Revenue Board. It is possible that if Alexander Stewart, who was then living in Dublin, had gone immediately to New-townards, he might have defeated Ponsonby's interest in the corporation, since most of the burgesses were tenants on the Newtown estate. But Ponsonby, who probably anticipated this move on Stewart's part, got there first and either by promises of places in the Revenue Department or by direct money bribes persuaded the burgesses to vacate their seats in the corporation which he proceeded to fill with subservient non-residents. Residence was then usual but not invariably necessary for members of municipal corporations, and after Stewart had unsuccessfully challenged Ponsonby's action in the courts Ponsonby promoted a Bill in Parliament putting the legality of non-residence beyond dispute, the legislation in question being known as the Newtown Act.

Some years later the Ponsonby family sold the borough to James Alexander, later first Earl of Caledon and ancestor of Field Marshal Earl Alexander of Tunis. 'We dined at Newtownards,' wrote a visitor in 1787, 'and the same day Nabob Alexander was entertaining, under the noses of the Stewarts, his burgesses for the borough for which he paid £10,000.'

Thus Alexander Stewart lost the parliamentary control of Newtownards borough. He also failed to get elected M.P. for Belfast which he would very much like to have been, but he was unable to reach an accommoda-tion with the Donegall family who controlled the representation there. However, he had the satisfaction of seeing his son Robert become Member for County Down.

2

As a young man the future Marquess of Londonderry was sent by his Presbyterian father under the care of a tutor to study 'literature' at the University of Geneva, and later to make the Grand Tour when he had his portrait painted by the well known German artist Antony Raphael Mengs, afterwards director of the Vatican school of painting. Robert Stewart was in his early twenties when he returned from his Continental travels and fell in love with Lady Sarah Seymour-Conway, the teenage daughter of the Earl (later Marquess) of Hertford, a rich landowner and borough proprietor in County Down, who had an income from his Irish estates alone of £15,000 a year. In 1765, Lord Hertford was appointed Lord Lieutenant of Ireland, and Robert Stewart attended the viceregal court in Dublin where he continued to press his suit for the hand of the viceroy's daughter. Having satisfied himself as to the means of his daughter's suitor, Lord Hertford gave his consent to their engagement, and the couple were married with fitting ceremony in the Chapel Royal of Dublin Castle on 3 June 1766, the bridegroom being twenty-six years old and the bride eighteen. A few months later Lord Hertford wrote to his son-in-law from London that he had obtained an Irish peerage for him as Baron Ardes [sic] without any knowledge or solicitation on Stewart's part, adding that it would not be gazetted until Hertford had heard from him. This honour, had he accepted it, would have given Robert Stewart a seat in the Irish House of Lords, although he was only twenty-seven years old at the time. But in fact he declined it, as it was his ambition to represent County Down in the Irish House of Commons, which was to be realised not long afterwards.

Meanwhile he and his wife lived in his father Alexander's Dublin house No. 28 Henry Street.[1] In due course they had two sons. Alexander the elder died when he was a little more than a year old. The younger whom they called Robert was destined to become Lord Castlereagh and at different periods perhaps the most unpopular man in his native Ireland as well as in England. Before the end of the same year Lady Sarah Stewart was again pregnant, but a few months later some unexpected complication occurred and she died on 17 July 1770. Five years later, by which date he had entered the Irish House of Commons, Robert Stewart married as his second wife Lady Frances Pratt, eldest daughter of the Lord Chancellor Earl Camden. By her he had eleven more children, three sons and eight daughters, all of whom, with the exception of three who died young, grew to adulthood and found suitable wives and husbands.

---

[1] Later demolished with other houses in the same street to make way for the General Post Office.

Charles, the eldest son of this marriage, was thus Castlereagh's half-brother: he was to succeed him as third Marquess of Londonderry on Castlereagh's tragic death in 1822.

A few years after her marriage Lady Frances Stewart was the victim of a 'melancholy adventure' while on a visit to one of her father's estates in Kent, where she was reputed to have been robbed in the park and to have come home 'quite naked'. Many things were said at the time and Horace Walpole heard it whispered in the Mayfair salons that it was 'a sudden fit of lunacy' with which she had been afflicted. But Mr Walpole was sure that the reports of the affair were exaggerated. Whatever was the explanation, the incident changed the course of her life. Henceforth she lived in relative seclusion at Mount Stewart 'in the bosom of her family'. Nevertheless visitors were agreeably impressed by her manners and hospitality. 'The more I have known her,' said the popular aristocrat Lord Charlemont, 'the better I have loved her, the surest test of real value.' His friend Dr Alexander Haliday was equally enthusiastic. 'On a certain evening,' wrote Haliday to Charlemont in 1796, 'I had the pleasure of seeing her dance with such grace and spirit in the midst of her whole brood of eleven most amiable creatures whom she has brought up, or is bringing up, in a manner which does her infinite honour—it was a delightful sight.' It should be added that she treated her stepson Castlereagh as if he were one of her own children, and he in turn always regarded her as his mother.

In the year after his first wife's death, Robert Stewart entered the Irish House of Commons as Member for County Down, which he continued to represent for the next dozen years, thus establishing the tradition by which members of the family periodically represented this county, first in Dublin and later at Westminster. He was returned by the 'independent' or 'county' interest backed by the local Whigs and Dissenters as opposed to the 'official' or 'court' interest of the Hill family which received the support of the Tories and High Churchmen, and whose head the Earl of Hillsborough (later Marquess of Downshire) wielded the greatest influence in County Down, being the absolute proprietor of six boroughs and partly controlling a dozen more, besides being the wealthiest landowner in the county and its Lord Lieutenant as well as one of the Secretaries of State in the Government in Whitehall. Indeed the political feud between the Stewarts and the Hills was to continue for several generations and through successive elections, and it was due to the Hillsborough influence that the Earl's eldest son Lord Kilwarlin defeated Robert Stewart at the election in 1783, an influence which according to Lord Charlemont was characterised by bribery on a large scale, besides which Kilwarlin and his friends persuaded the returning officer to close the poll prematurely while many of the supporters of Robert Stewart, 'whose honesty was almost proverbial,' (according to Charlemont), were on their way to Downpatrick to register their votes, having been delayed by stormy weather.

As befitted a county Member of Parliament, Alexander intended that his son Robert should live at Mount Pleasant, or Mount Stewart as it was to be renamed when the temporary structure was gradually replaced by a more permanent dwelling. However the work of construction seems to have proceeded at a very leisurely pace during Robert's term as M.P. between 1771 and 1783. Of the original house with its additions very little survives today with the exception of parts of three rooms on the ground floor of the west wing, although its plan was largely to determine the form of the larger building and extensions which followed at intervals. Shortly after his father's death, Robert Stewart commissioned the Dublin architect James Wyatt to design a completely new house for him, but all that was done from Wyatt's designs was the building of a stable block, the rest of Wyatt's plans being abandoned in order to meet the enormous cost of the parliamentary elections which Robert's eldest son, the future Lord Castlereagh, was obliged to incur in following his father as M.P. for County Down.

While these operations were going on, Robert Stewart used to accommodate his growing family and on occasion his guests in a series of stone and slate cottages or 'cabins' on the shore of Strangford Lough close to what was slowly taking shape as Mount Stewart house. Among the visitors at this period was Robert's father-in-law Lord Camden who wrote that 'my apartment is a snug cabin upon the shore of a vast arm of the sea, and commanding a very fine and extensive prospect', an opinion already endorsed in the year 1776 by the traveller Arthur Young who remarked upon the row of neat cabins 'in the neighbourhood of some new plantations where Mr Stewart intends to build'. As he looked across Strangford Lough, Lord Camden was particularly struck by the 'amazing variety of islands, creeks and bays which appear among cultivated hills in the most picturesque manner'. Incidentally Camden, who continued to visit Mount Stewart until well advanced in age, was a great favourite with his daughter's large family, and it was at his prompting that her stepson the younger Robert, later Lord Castlereagh, was sent to Cambridge while Charles went to Eton. 'I will teach Charles to respect England and to love Ireland,' he told his daughter, 'for I wish both countries united by as strong a tie as your family and mine whose interests can never be divided though you are personally separated by the sea.'

Alexander Stewart, Robert's father, died at his home in Newtownards in 1781; the house later became the Londonderry Estate Office. His widow, the Cowan heiress, survived him by seven years. A contemporary described him as 'a man of polite and pleasing manners, a clear and comprehensive understanding and principles truly liberal in politics and religion . . . It is true he had no small share of ambition; but it was an ambition to raise his family to honour and influence in his country for his country's good.' In this he may be said to have succeeded handsomely.

3

Robert Stewart's political advancement after he had lost his seat in the Irish House of Commons was largely due to his connection with the powerful Whig family of which Earl Camden was head, and into which he had married in 1775. Eleven years later Robert Stewart became a Privy Councillor of Ireland. In 1789, he was raised to the Irish peerage as Baron Londonderry, which entitled him to sit in the Irish House of Lords in Dublin. In 1795, the year in which his brother-in-law the second Earl Camden became Lord Lieutenant of Ireland, he was created Viscount Castlereagh and a year later Earl of Londonderry, which enabled his eldest son Robert to be styled by the courtesy title of Castlereagh. His final step in the peerage, to Marquess, came in 1816 in recognition of his son Castlereagh's diplomatic achievements as Foreign Secretary in Paris and Vienna. He was one of the twenty-eight Irish Representative Peers created by the Act of Union between Great Britain and Ireland, which gave him a seat for life in the United Kingdom House of Lords at Westminster. However he rarely came to London, preferring to spend his time managing his Ulster estates and helping to bring up his large family by his second wife. According to his son Charles, later third Marquess, he was a popular and indulgent landlord.

Although this has been contested by his enemies, there is some evidence that he reduced the rents on his Ards estate when times were hard and he also encouraged the custom known as Ulster tenant right which prevailed in the north of Ireland and guaranteed a measure of security of tenure to tenant farmers unlike other parts of the country.

In the original Mount Stewart house, which the first Marquess completed in 1782, the entrance was on the west side through an attractive hall, flanked by a library-cum-sitting room on the right and a dining room on the left. In 1804 he proposed to entrust the work of rebuilding and enlarging what later became the west wing of the house to a skilled carpenter from Belfast named John Ferguson. However, Castlereagh persuaded his father to obtain designs from the well known London architect George Dance, Professor of Architecture at the Royal Academy and perhaps best known for his rebuilding of Newgate prison. The result at Mount Stewart was that the original entrance hall became a music room, and the entrance was moved to the north side of the house, while the music room and the two adjoining rooms were connected, in Dance's words, by 'very large folding doors so as occasionally to lay all the three rooms into one'. Londonderry was 'much afraid my carpenters will blunder in the executing of them, and as I mean they should be of mahogany I should like to have them finished in the neatest and best manner'. And so they were, together with other embellishments in the architect's characteristic neo-classical style, including a grand staircase leading from an inner hall to the bedrooms on the first floor. Actually the work was carried out by Ferguson, and in the library the veneered window shutters when closed revealed mock book backs, an ingenious addition which cost the first Lord Londonderry the sum of £14 7s 7d, according to the account rendered in 1805.

Dance had visited Ireland in 1795 when Frances Lady Londonderry's brother the second Lord Camden was Lord Lieutenant and the architect was on intimate terms with her sister Lady Elizabeth Pratt, 'a merry maid' who never married and is thought by some to have been Dance's mistress; it is very probable that he visited Mount Stewart at the time with the viceregal party. But it does not appear that he ever came in a professional capacity, being content to leave the execution of his plans in 1804 to Ferguson. However, he gave some useful advice with his drawings. The larger rooms should not exceed fifteen feet in length and twenty-two feet in width because of the 'difficulty in stiffening the timber in the floors.' Also, he proposed to erect 'a coach porch or portico at the entrance', which was to be on the north-west and which would be 'both ornamental and extremely convenient at night and bad weather to drive under'.

Londonderry accepted Dance's plans subject to some qualifications, such as that the bedrooms on the first floor should be higher than the architect had proposed.

> I acknowledge the proportion may be less pleasing as to the look of the building without [he wrote to Dance], but I like airy sleeping rooms, which are particularly eligible in case of illness, and as stones and mortar are not scarce with us, the additional expense is insignificant. I [would] make the walls very thick and substantial, which you will perceive from the ground plan, and as I mean this to be a permanent dwelling which may be added to when our present home fails . . . I wish to finish and complete every part of the new work in a substantial and neat plain manner, for which reason I shall certainly have the porch of firestone as the sketch you sent me was to be of wood.

A quarter of a century later, after the first Marquess and his son Castlereagh were both dead, Mount Stewart house, with generous help from the third Marquess's second wife, born Lady Frances Anne Vane-Tempest, was completed to the designs of the Irish architect William Vitruvius Morrison, the remaining old temporary buildings being demolished and the permanent structure being roughly trebled in size, while the present entrance on the north front with its large imposing Ionic colonnade and *porte-cochère* was constructed so as to lead into another hall and a sculpture gallery. At the same time Morrison removed the fluted Doric columns of Dance's original 'coach porch' to the new south front facing Strangford Lough.

Some mention must be made of the first Marquess's favourite architectural creation, the Temple of the Winds, built in 1782–3 on a hill above Strangford Lough to the designs of James ('Athenian') Stuart and executed by John Ferguson of Belfast, having been inspired by the famous octagonal temple in Athens and erected on the site of an ancient druidical cemetery about half a mile from the house. It remains one of the finest, if not actually the finest, neo-classical buildings of its kind in Ireland today. There was a cellar underneath for storing wine, and after dinner— as a rule eaten much earlier than today—the family would go there to drink port or claret, particularly when they had guests to the meal. Dr Haliday was one visitor who enjoyed the wine and post-prandial talk. 'I could have stayed,' he confessed on one occasion when he was called away from one of these gatherings to a patient. 'An honest wine glass is the well at the bottom of which squats truth.'

It is in the exquisitely decorated room with its marquetry floor in the Temple of the Winds that one particularly associates the first Marquess as well as in the library of the house which he built on the shore of Strangford Lough. When, early in 1821, his younger son Charles, by then British ambassador in Vienna, heard the news that he was dying, Charles wrote to his elder brother the Foreign Secretary: 'When we consider the life of our excellent and inestimable parent, and his course during the last twenty or thirty years in Ireland, he may be deplored as a national loss as well as the greatest calamity that can befall his children. Indeed, my dearest Castlereagh, when I contemplate in my mind the scene at Mount Stewart and the breaking up of that house, it is a sort of wreck of veneration that is replete with anguish.'

A year later, the first Marquess's widow Frances, Lord Camden's daughter, left Mount Stewart and retired to what in a later age the writer A. C. Benson called 'the dreary and loathsome town of Hastings', but which was then a fashionable watering place. There she died in 1833. Her eight surviving children all made 'good' marriages, one daughter Amelia marrying Field Marshal Viscount Hardinge and the youngest Octavia becoming the wife of Edward Law, Lord Ellenborough and future Governor-General of Canada.

4

Robert Henry Stewart, second Marquess of Londonderry, generally known by the courtesy title of Lord Castlereagh, who succeeded to the

Marquessate a little more than a year before his death, was the first Marquess's only surviving son by his first wife. He is the best known member of the family in British history and for that reason his career is only briefly summarised here. Born on 18 June 1769 (the anniversary of the Battle of Waterloo) at his father's Dublin house, he was brought up at Mount Stewart and educated at the Armagh Royal School and St John's College, Cambridge, which he left without taking a degree in order to make a brief Grand Tour of Europe prior to entering politics. In August 1786, when he was eighteen, he narrowly escaped drowning in Strangford Lough when the boat in which he was sailing with a companion over-turned in a sudden squall and he was only saved by the foresight of his tutor and the estate agent who happened to be looking out across the Lough from the Temple of the Winds and organised their rescue after they had been in the water for over an hour.

In 1790, at the age of twenty-one, the Hon. Robert Stewart (as Castle-reagh then was) was elected M.P. for County Down, after a relatively costly election which amounted to not less than £30,000. This, coupled with the necessity for Lord Londonderry to provide dowries for seven of his daughters on their marriages, crippled the family finances and delayed the completion of Mount Stewart for many years. Certainly, so far as Castlereagh was concerned, the expenditure was justified since his rise in Irish politics was rapid, being facilitated by the appointment of his brother-in-law the second Earl Camden as Lord Lieutenant of Ireland. Thus Castlereagh became Chief Secretary to the Lord Lieutenant, and afterwards he served in successive British Cabinets, eventually becoming Prime Minister in all but name. Indeed he was offered the Premiership by King George IV in 1821, but declined the offer.

As Chief Secretary to the Lord Lieutenant at the time of the rising of 1798, Castlereagh earned the soubriquet of 'Bloody', since he was blamed, quite unjustly, for the military excesses with which the rising was suppressed. Even his English political opponent Henry Brougham exposed the baselessness of this charge when he wrote in his *Historical Sketches* that 'Lord Castlereagh uniformly and strenuously set his face against the atrocities committed in Ireland and that to him, more than perhaps anyone else, was to be attributed the termination of the system stained with blood'.

The English Prime Minister William Pitt the Younger and his cabinet colleagues decided that the best policy was to abolish the corrupt Irish Parliament, in which Catholics were never allowed to sit and were only given the vote in 1793, and to unite the Parliament in Dublin with the Westminster assembly, to be followed by a full measure of Catholic Emancipation. At the same time, as part of the proposed Act of Union, Pitt agreed with Castlereagh that it was only fair to compensate the borough proprietors and others who had bought seats in the Irish House of Commons for large sums of money; hence the oft-levelled charge against Castlereagh that he had carried the Act of Union through the Irish Parliament by 'bribery'. After a prolonged struggle during which the measure was first rejected by the Irish House of Commons, the Act of Union was passed in Dublin and Westminster and became law on 1 January 1801. Under it one hundred Irish Members were elected to the House of Commons at Westminster and 28 so-called Irish Representative peers were chosen from the body of the Irish peerage to sit for life in the British House of Lords.

In 1802, Castlereagh entered the British Cabinet where he remained, with two short breaks, until his death twenty years later. He had the advantage of serving under the younger Pitt in his last ministry, first at the India Board and then at the War Office, and in these posts he played an important part in the conduct of the war with France. At the War Office, where he continued to serve after Pitt's death, his principal achievement was the decision to send his friend Sir Arthur Wellesley, later Duke of Wellington, to command the expeditionary force during the Peninsular War. A Cabinet intrigue shortly afterwards, in 1809, provoked a duel with his colleague the Foreign Secretary George Canning, in which the latter was wounded. Both ministers resigned from the Government.

In 1812, Castlereagh re-entered the Cabinet as Foreign Secretary which post he combined with the leadership of the House of Commons, since the Prime Minister Lord Liverpool was in the Lords. It was largely owing to Castlereagh's firmness and energy at this period that the conflict with France was terminated and Europe was saved from the lasting domination of Napoleon. At the same time, at the Congress of Vienna in 1814 and the Peace of Paris in 1815, he insisted that the conquered country should be treated reasonably and humanely. 'It is not our business to collect trophies,' he said, 'but to try if we can to bring the world to peaceful habits.'

Castlereagh also enunciated his great political ideal of diplomacy by conference when he persuaded the Great Powers

to renew at fixed intervals, either under their own auspices or by their representative Ministers, meetings consecrated to great common objects and the examination of such measures as at each of these epochs shall be judged most salutary for the peace and prosperity of the nations and for the maintenance of the peace of Europe.

These words, which he caused to be incorporated in the Treaty of Vienna, laid the foundation of all future schemes of international government. Three such meetings took place during Castlereagh's lifetime, and he was preparing to attend another in August 1822 when his mind gave way under the overwhelming pressure of work.

There is some evidence that at the time of his death in 1822 Castlereagh was being blackmailed for an alleged homosexual offence and that he had allowed himself to be entrapped into a compromising position with an individual whom he took to be a woman but who turned out to be a young man dressed in women's clothes. However, the evidence is not absolutely conclusive, although there is no doubt that a few days before his suicide he told both King George IV and the Duke of Wellington that he had been 'accused of the same crime as the Bishop of Clogher', the Hon. Percy Jocelyn, an Irish prelate and brother of Lord Roden, who had been caught in the act with a private soldier at an inn in the Haymarket a few days previously. On the other hand, the great affection Castlereagh had for his wife makes it difficult to credit any alleged infidelities.

Lady Castlereagh's niece Lady Emma Edgcumbe, later Countess of Brownlow, was particularly attached to him and has left a charming picture of his domestic life. 'The calm dignity of his manner gave an impression that he was cold,' she wrote afterwards, 'but no one who had seen his kindly smile, or been greeted by his two hands stretched out in welcome, could have thought him so. When his sister-in-law, Lady Catherine Stewart, was taken ill during the absence of his brother Charles in the army, he attended upon her constantly, gave her with his own hands her medicines and was with her when she died. He liked the society of young people and, far from checking their mirth and their nonsense, he enjoyed and encouraged it with his own mirth and cheerfulness.'

At his widow's request the Prime Minister Lord Liverpool and the Dean of Westminster agreed that he should be buried in the Abbey. Unfortunately the funeral was marked by disgraceful cheering on the part of a small crowd outside the west door when the hearse appeared, since Castlereagh had been blamed for the repressive measures enacted by Parliament after the Napoleonic wars. Those inside the Abbey mistook the cheers as being for the Duke of Wellington. Otherwise the funeral went off decorously, all the diplomatic corps and many members of both Houses of Parliament and the government service assembling to pay their last respects. Castlereagh's brother Charles later erected a statue to his memory beside the grave.

'Well, this is a considerable event in point of size,' wrote Henry Brougham when he heard the news of the Tory leader's death. 'Put all their men together in one scale, and poor Castlereagh in the other—single he plainly weighed them down . . . Also, he was a *gentleman*. And the only one amongst them.'

5

On 9 June 1794, within a fortnight of his twenty-sixth birthday, Castle-reagh had married Lady Amelia (Emily) Anne Hobart, youngest daughter of John second Earl of Buckinghamshire, and heiress to her mother Caroline Conolly's fortune. They probably met through the Camdens or else through the bride's uncle Thomas Conolly, the 'Squire' of Castletown, Ireland's largest house. The bride was attractive and good-looking, four years younger than the bridegroom. The courtship was short and swift. 'You have left me, as far as I am myself concerned, nothing to wish for,' he wrote to her a few months before their marriage: 'you have given repose to all my disquietudes and opened prospects of happiness which give me a new interest in life.' He also sent her a beautiful miniature of himself painted by Richard Cosway and set in a gold locket which contained some strands of his hair. Robert's stepmother pronounced her 'truly amiable—her figure striking', a description borne out by her portrait as Juno which Sir Thomas Lawrence painted at the time of her marriage, but which, because it had been harshly criticised in the press, her own family refused to accept; instead she gave it to her husband and it is now in the Londonderry collection.

It was remarkable, in an age of prolific child-bearing and high infant mortality, that Castlereagh and his wife should have had no children. This gave rise to the malicious gossip that the husband was impotent. Indeed, during the Union debates in the Irish House of Commons, Castlereagh was taunted with his childlessness when the anti-Unionist member William Conyngham Plunket, later Lord Plunket, declaimed from the Opposition benches pointing at the Chief Secretary: 'I cannot fear that the Constitution which has been founded by the wisdom of sages and cemented by the blood of patriots and heroes is to be smitten by such a green and sapless twig as this.'

Nevertheless they were devoted to each other throughout their lives, although Emily sometimes showed jealousy of his quite innocent friendship with other women such as Princess Lieven and Mrs Arbuthnot, with whom he shared a common interest in politics. The fact remains that she was his constant companion and he could not bear being separated from her. Whenever they were parted by circumstances or his official duties, he wrote to her by every possible conveyance. 'I don't know what you feel,' he told her in one letter, 'but I am quite determined never to pass from one country to another even *for a day* without you. You know how little I am given to professions, but I really of late felt the deprivation with an acuteness which is only known to those who are separated from what they most love.' For her part she would follow him faithfully across Europe, and on these official journeys would cheerfully 'spend nights of cold, hunger and weariness in miserable lodgings without complaining or seeming to feel any inconvenience'. On one occasion during the Congress of Vienna she caused some surprise when she appeared at an important function wearing her husband's Order of the Garter in her hair.

As a 'patroness' of Almack's famous assembly rooms in King Street, St James's (later known as Willis's Rooms), she joined with her fellow committee members in scrutinising and rejecting candidates for admission. Since her town house, where she and her husband had lived since 1805, was at the north-east corner of King Street and St James's Square, almost directly opposite Almack's, it was very convenient for the assemblies and dances. She also did her share of entertaining for her husband and the other Tory leaders and M.P.s, though as a hostess she seems to have lacked the forceful personality which her sister-in-law Frances Anne and the wives of the sixth and seventh Marquesses were later to exert. However, Emily's receptions were a favourite meeting place for contemporary celebrities, while invitations to the less formal supper parties which she gave after the opera were much sought after.

The Castlereaghs were probably at their happiest when they were together at Cray Farm, which Castlereagh leased in 1811 for the life of himself and Emily, making extensive improvements to the property and building on to the house which was little more than a cottage when he first took it. Here Castlereagh raised a flock of merino sheep while his wife kept a small zoo. 'Lady Castlereagh had the good sense to lay aside her finery at Cray,' one foreign visitor noted. 'She was to be found in a muslin dress, with a large straw hat on her head, an apron round her waist, a pair of scissors in her hand, cutting away dead flowers.' Her zoo included an antelope, several kangaroos, emus and ostriches and a tiger which Lord Combermere had brought back from India for the Duke of Wellington and which Wellington had given to Emily. These animals would be proudly displayed by her, although the tiger did not welcome visitors. 'It seemed very vicious and growled at us,' noted Mrs Arbuthnot when she and her husband first saw it. As for the merino sheep, their master won several prizes with them at agricultural shows, including a particularly fine inscribed silver tea pot.[1]

At Cray the Foreign Minister and his wife would sometimes entertain informally members of the diplomatic corps and their wives. On 2 August 1820 Princess Lieven described one such entertainment in a letter to her lover the Austrian Chancellor Prince Metternich. The host insisted on waltzing with her—indeed she has been credited with having introduced the waltz into the English ballroom. 'We tried to be very gay,' she remarked, adding jocularly what 'hard work' it was 'to keep the Minister in revolution!' (It was still the Age of Revolution.) After a while the ballroom almost emptied, the younger couples having wandered off into the garden, where they apparently proceeded to disport themselves among the bushes and shrubberies. 'Englishwomen always astonish me, in spite of my long experience of the country,' commented the Princess. 'I should

---

[1] This is now in the possession of Lady Mairi Bury at Mount Stewart.

like to take their indiscretion for the height of *naïveté*; but, after all, they have husbands, and I confess myself baffled.'

At the time of her husband's death Emily was blamed in certain quarters for neglecting his health, but it is certain that she looked after him to the best of her ability. She took him down to Cray, kept him in bed and sent for the family doctor; she also took the precaution, apparently on their doctor's advice, of removing his razors. Unfortunately a small penknife was overlooked and it was with this that he severed his carotid artery, dying in the doctor's arms on the morning of 12 August 1822.

Amongst his possessions which she inherited under his will were the family diamonds, known as the Down diamonds and probably brought back from India by Sir Robert Cowan, the Governor of Bombay, whose sister married Castlereagh's grandfather Alexander Stewart. There were also Castlereagh's Garter insignia and some jewels presented to him by the allied monarchs at the time of the overthrow of Napoleon. In a letter which Castlereagh wrote to his wife four years before his death, he told her that he was leaving them to her, and in the event of a revolution in England, 'an event which in this happy country can hardly be apprehended' in contrast to the 'political events in other countries which have shaken private property', he begged her to sell them. 'If the occasion should not occur,' he went on, 'it is my wish that they should be considered as memorials in the family of the public transactions most of which you have shared with me as witness.' This desire was fulfilled after her death when they passed to Castlereagh's brother Charles and they have been worn ever since by successive Marchionesses of Londonderry.

In her later years Emily's good looks were marred by a distressing corpulence, so that when she sat for Lawrence a second time, in about 1820, she had grown so stout that it is difficult to recognise her as the same person as the 'Juno' of the earlier picture. In the later portrait she was painted wearing the Down diamonds, consisting of a waistband at least three inches wide and composed entirely of brilliants amounting to 1,225, scroll necklace and collet bracelet.

Emily remained in comparative seclusion for about eighteen months after her husband's death and although she subsequently reappeared in society her health had clearly begun to fail. She died on 12 February 1829 at 18 St James's Square within a week of her fifty-seventh birthday and was buried beside her husband in Westminster Abbey.

6

In the early nineteenth century Ministers of the Crown had much more latitude than their successors today in retaining official and semi-official papers as well as private letters written by and to them during their terms of office. Castlereagh left a mass of such papers, more than 10,000 at his death, going back to 1793, together with his father's family papers, to be dealt with by his executors, George Holford, M.P., who was an old friend, and his solicitor William Groom. On looking through them cursorily the executors refused to accept the responsibility of handing over the papers to the heirs-at-law on account of the number of state papers which were included, and so they deposited them all in the custody of the Court of Chancery. Both Castlereagh's widow and his half-brother Charles, who had succeeded as third Marquess of Londonderry, were anxious that some account of Castlereagh's life, public and private, should be written, based on the papers if they could be recovered from the Court. Eventually, after several years of tedious correspondence, Charles succeeded in getting possession of most of the papers from the Lord Chancellor, Lord Cottenham, only to find that there were numerous gaps, no doubt due to the removal of some of the more important state papers.

In 1827, while Emily was still alive, Sir Walter Scott was asked to undertake the official biography, but when the missing papers had been retrieved, he declined on the ground that he felt 'totally incapable of doing justice to the task'. Charles then turned to his son Frederick's tutor, the Rev. S. Turner, who agreed to take on the job. However, the prospective biographer had only time to arrange the papers in chronological order before he was appointed Bishop of Calcutta. He took a selection of the papers with him on the voyage to India, but unfortunately he was shipwrecked, so that a further portion of the archive was lost. Nevertheless, several thousands of documents remained, and these the third Marquess decided to publish more or less as they stood with a long introduction and a minimum of editing, and incidentally a mass of verbal inaccuracies, under the general title of *Memoirs and Correspondence of Viscount Castlereagh*, the first four volumes being devoted to Castlereagh's career as an Irish M.P. and later Chief Secretary to the Lord Lieutenant.

On the eve of the publication of the first four volumes, which was announced for 1848, Charles wrote to Queen Victoria asking if he could dedicate the whole work to her. Twenty years previously he had published his *Narrative of the Peninsular War*, based on his correspondence with his brother when the latter was War Minister and he himself was Adjutant-General, and he had by permission dedicated this work to the future King William IV. He consequently expected no difficulty from Queen Victoria in obtaining similar permission. To his surprise he met with a sharp rebuff which was communicated to him through the Lord Chamberlain, Earl Spencer. Apparently the Queen was particularly annoyed by what she considered the third Marquess's tactlessness in bringing out the volumes on his brother's Irish career in the very year which had witnessed another rising in that unhappy country.

Osborne 31 July 1848 . . . the Queen upon public grounds entertains the strongest objections to the publication of any biographical Memoirs of Statesmen who have been employed in the service of the Crown within so short a time after the public events and negotiations in which they have borne a part, and during the lifetime of many who have been employed either in the support or opposition to the line of policy adopted by the Government of the country during their administration.

Such a biography to be complete must include the publication of State Papers and other documents which might be detrimental to the public service to have published at so early a date.

As it is impossible therefore for Her Majesty to know how far, or whether in any degree, the proposed publication might be open to these important objections, and upon the general grounds above stated, I am commanded to inform you that the Queen cannot comply with the Marquess of Londonderry's request and sanction the dedication to Her Majesty of the proposed Memoirs.

Independently of these reasons which apply generally to recent biographies, the Queen considers the present moment of unhappy excitement in Ireland as peculiarly unsuitable for bringing so prominently before the public all the elements of the History of the Rebellion in Ireland, and its Union with Great Britain.

It was in vain for Londonderry to point out that there had been biographies of Wellington, Nelson, Lord Eldon and others published in recent years containing detailed correspondence. The Queen was adamant, and the work, which was held up for several months, eventually appeared without any dedication.

On the question of publication the Queen's arguments were strongly reinforced by the Foreign Secretary Lord Palmerston who pointed out to the Queen that if the documents were official they should first be submitted for consideration by the Secretary of State, and if private 'much circumspection ought to be used in regard to their publication in as much as they may contain events, which it might, for reasons connected with the public interest, be inconvenient or improper at the present time to publish'. There was, of course, no Official Secrets Act in those days, but Londonderry's solicitor warned him that he and his publishers would run the risk of prosecution for divulging state secrets if they went ahead with publication. However, with his customary *sang-froid* the third Marquess disregarded the warning on Wellington's principle of 'Publish and be damned!' and the publication duly proceeded, the twelfth and final volume appearing in 1853. The Tory essayist and politician John Wilson Croker, who had known Castlereagh, congratulated Londonderry 'on having got through your important and arduous task, which will do justice to your brother's memory and to your own good feeling, as well as ability', adding that he did not think 'you will have any complaint from the quarter you apprehend'. Croker was right. The authorities took no further action. Nor did the Queen bear the third Marquess any lasting ill-will. When she visited Ireland in 1849—the first of only two visits to this part of her kingdom during a reign of more than sixty years—he rode with her in her carriage through the streets of Belfast. However, three years later she showed considerable reluctance to confer the Order of the Garter upon him after the Duke of Wellington's death had created a vacancy among the Knights, telling the Prime Minister, Lord Derby, who had put his name forward, that she was 'of opinion that it would not be advisable on the whole to give the Garter to Lord Londonderry'. Nevertheless she was persuaded to the contrary by Prince Albert, to whom she could refuse nothing, and so the 'Soldier Marquess' not unfittingly became a Knight Companion of the oldest order of chivalry in the kingdom. The honour had previously been conferred upon his brother Castlereagh and it was also to be conferred upon both his grandson and great-grandson, the sixth and seventh Marquesses.

CHAPTER II

THE VANE-TEMPESTS

I

CHARLES WILLIAM STEWART, the first Marquess's eldest son by his second wife Lady Frances Pratt, was born on 18 May 1778 in a house which his father had taken in Mary Street, Dublin, close to the river Liffey; he was thus nine years younger than his better known half-brother Castlereagh, whom he was to succeed as third Marquess of Londonderry in 1822. Although he lacked his brother's superior intellectual qualities and his behaviour on occasion was less dignified, he was as brave as a lion and as a young man appeared the typical dashing cavalry officer calculated to win any maiden's heart. At Eton, he made a determined effort to save a schoolfellow Lord Waldegrave from drowning. In doing so he narrowly escaped with his own life, being seized by the hair and dragged unconscious by a boatman from the river after his friend had been drowned.

'Having dived without success nine times I made one more attempt,' young Stewart, then sixteen, wrote to a friend from Eton on 5 July 1794.

> Guess what my feelings were when having dived a little way I saw the Body just under me. I was then so exhausted with fatigue and had such a pain across my breast and was so shocked at this dreadful sight, when I was hopeless of doing good, that it entirely took away my senses. I sunk twice and was going down for ever (I suppose) again when a man in a boat which had been sent after Waldegrave took me up. I was carried home and was for a long time without life. At last the water that came up and other applications recovered me. I am now thank God perfectly well.
>
> If my endeavours had been crowned with success, my happiness would have been unbounded. As it is I only have to lament that such unhappiness was not allotted by Heaven to me and thank Providence for my own preservation. I am sure that I have been much overpaid for a mere act of duty in the testimonies of approbation that have been shown to me by Relations Friends and Schoolfellows.

On leaving school, he obtained a commission in the 18th Dragoons, serving successively in the Netherlands, on the Rhine and Danube, where he was struck by a bullet under the left eye in the course of a cavalry charge. 'I am in great hope that there is no reason for apprehending any bad consequences,' Castlereagh wrote at the time. 'Scars, if not too deep and destructive of shape, are a soldier's most becoming ornament, and it will animate and attach him more strongly to his profession.' Nevertheless his sight was seriously affected for a time. When he had recovered, his appointment as A.D.C. to his uncle Lord Camden when the latter became Lord Lieutenant of Ireland gave him a temporary respite from active service, but he was soon back with his regiment during the Rebellion in 1798. His subsequent advancement both military and political he owed largely to his brother Castlereagh, to whom he was deeply devoted. In 1803 he was made A.D.C. to King George III and a full colonel in the army. Meanwhile he had entered the United Kingdom Parliament, serving as Chief Secretary for Ireland and later as Under-Secretary for War between 1807 and 1809, when his brother was Secretary of State. But office work was irksome to him, and while still Under-Secretary he persuaded Castlereagh to let him go out to Portugal to command a hussar brigade in Sir John Moore's army corps. Here he particularly distinguished himself in the field, among other exploits surprising a French post with a handful of troops and capturing eighty prisoners. After Moore's death at Corunna, he became Adjutant-General of the British forces in the Peninsula under Sir Arthur Wellesley, future Duke of Wellington. In 1810, he received the thanks of the House of Commons in his place in the chamber for his bravery at the Battle of Talavera. A few months later he was promoted to the rank of Major-General, being then only thirty-two, after which he continued to serve in the succeeding campaigns until he was invalided home in 1812.

If one may judge from the three-quarter-length portrait of him by Sir Thomas Lawrence in hussar uniform with the Talavera medal and star, painted during the Peninsular War, Charles Stewart was a strikingly handsome individual, though he was considerably below the average height. In 1804 he married Lady Catherine Bligh, youngest daughter of the third Earl of Darnley; she was three years older than himself. They were married for barely eight years; and, since Charles was on active service in Portugal and Spain for the greater part of this period, they cannot have seen very much of each other. However they had one child, a son called Frederick, who later succeeded his father as fourth Marquess of Londonderry. On the subject of the Lawrence portrait, which is generally regarded as one of the artist's best, if not his very best, there is a story that while on leave in 1809 Charles sat for it unknown to his wife. Seeing a letter arrive one day from the War Office ordering his return to Portugal, she found out from the servants that he was at Lawrence's house. Ordering her carriage to take her there, she rushed into the studio where she fainted in her husband's arms. When she had recovered, he made the artist lead her up to the picture, and on seeing it she was so surprised and delighted that she involuntarily dropped on one knee and kissed the artist's hand.

Lady Catherine Stewart died quite suddenly during the night of 10–11 February 1812. The news was broken to her husband by Wellesley, who

had had it in the first instance in a private letter from Edward Cooke, the
Permanent Under-Secretary at the War Office. She had 'a small knob or
protuberance in the middle of her head', which had been imperfectly cut
in the previous year so that she was determined to have another operation
to remove it. This was successfully performed by Astley Cooper, the
leading surgeon of his time and a future President of the Royal College.

> It was trifling and the wound was healing, when she imprudently went airing in an
> open carriage and twice into a cold bath. These imprudences brought on a sudden
> and violent attack of the Erysipelas on the head and throat with violent fever. The
> disorder took a dangerous form. Lightheadedness followed and continued with
> intervals. She felt her danger, took leave of her family, and at length exhausted
> expired about 2 o'clock on Monday with tranquility and ease.

In a letter to his brother from Castlereagh, which Cooke enclosed with
that to Wellesley, Castlereagh exonerated Charles from anything he could
have done to save his wife's life had he been at home. 'Don't let an
additional pang affect your mind from an idea that you have, in serving
your country, contributed in the slightest degree to her irreparable loss,'
he wrote to him.

> She was never in better health and spirits than before this fatality occurred, and had
> learnt in the attachment she bore you to reconcile herself to your absence without
> suffering it to prey upon her health . . . Your dearest boy, consigned to my care,
> under an appeal which adds to every natural tie, will be cherished by Lady C and
> myself with a tenderness that can leave you no anxiety at the moment from his
> welfare. He is under my roof, and that I trust is a sufficient pledge to you on this
> subject.

Later in the same month, Castlereagh, who had recently refused a
United Kingdom peerage, rejoined the Cabinet as Foreign Secretary—he
had been out of office for three years following his duel with Canning—
and he was to hold this post combined with that of Leader of the House
of Commons for the remainder of his life. It was a fortunate coincidence
for his younger brother who benefited considerably in consequence. In
1813 Charles was made a Knight of the Bath and was despatched by
Castlereagh to the Court of Berlin on special liaison duty with the Prussian and Swedish armies. Prince Bernadotte of Sweden was being heavily
subsidised by Britain both in men and supplies, and it was General Sir
Charles Stewart's duty to see that the British Parliament got value for its
money, particularly as Bernadotte had not shown himself, in Stewart's
words, 'disposed to spill Swedish in drawing French blood'. That he
should have succeeded in keeping Bernadotte up to the mark while
remaining on good terms with him, with beneficial results for the allies,
showed that as a special ambassador Stewart possessed some diplomatic
ability. Soon, to his satisfaction, he was able to resume his military career,
being conspicuous as a cavalry commander in the subsequent fighting,

gaining Russian, Prussian and Swedish decorations and undaunted by another severe wound.

The following year saw him with his brother at Allied Headquarters in France during the closing stages of the war against Napoleon, and he entered Paris with the victorious armies in March 1814. Further honours followed in the shape of being sworn a Privy Councillor and advanced to G.C.B., as well as being raised to the United Kingdom peerage as Baron Stewart of Stewart's Court and Ballylawn in the County of Donegal. In August 1814, Castlereagh appointed him ambassador to Austria. In Vienna he thus assisted his brother and afterwards Wellington in the negotiations at the celebrated 'dancing' Congress which was suddenly broken up by the news of Napoleon's escape from Elba and landing in France. Both the table on which the Treaty of Vienna was signed in January 1815, and the chairs used by the allied sovereigns, ambassadors and plenipotentiaries at the congress as they sat round the conference table, were subsequently presented to Stewart and his brother and thus passed into the possession of the Londonderry family. After Napoleon was finally defeated and overthrown at Waterloo, Stewart again accompanied the allied sovereigns to Paris, before returning to his diplomatic post in Vienna, which he was still holding three years later when he made the acquaintance of his second wife Lady Frances Anne Vane-Tempest.

For a man in his forty-first year, as he was in 1818, his record could hardly be regarded as anything but distinguished. Granted that he owed his position, notably as ambassador, to his brother's influence, there is no doubt that Lord Stewart, as he had now become, displayed considerable skill in it. The Duke of Wellington, for instance, who was never particularly partial to him though outwardly they always remained on friendly terms, had to admit that he was 'very fit' for his post. Indeed the Duke told the diarist Charles Greville that in his opinion Lord Stewart 'was an excellent ambassador, procured more information and obtained more insight into the affairs of a foreign court than anybody, and that he was the best relator of what passed at a Conference, and wrote the best account of a conversation of any man he knew'. Anyone who troubles to read Stewart's despatches at this period cannot fail to endorse this straightforward estimate.

On the other hand, Charles Stewart, particularly after his wife Catherine's death, had a reputation for gallantry in the boudoir as well as on the field of battle, judging by the stories which were common gossip about his behaviour during the Congress of Vienna. His vanity and conceit, not to mention his eccentricity—he loved to dress up in splendid uniforms—led the Viennese to nickname him the 'Golden Peacock' and also 'Lord Pumpernickel'. Thanks to the painstaking care with which the Austrian secret police kept distinguished foreigners under observation and reported their movements to the Chancellor, Prince Metternich, we have an exact record of all the houses at which the British Ambassador called, especially at night, and how long he spent in each. For instance, he had many clandestine meetings with Metternich's former mistress the Duchess of Sagan, whose acquaintance he had made in Prague while recovering from a wound he received in the battle of Kulm; after she had broken with the Chancellor she transferred her affections to Stewart who gave her a fine horse and once accompanied her on horseback to an inn in the Semmering mountains where they spent the night together. In the course of one of the Ambassador's nocturnal visitations in the capital, he got into an angry altercation with two hackney-cab coachmen on the Danube Bridge, which ended in the cabbies belabouring him with their whips, leaving his Lordship lying bruised and battered in the gutter.

On another occasion we learn that the gay ambassador, after a gala performance at the Opera, whilst waiting to leave the building, happened to find himself immediately behind a certain Countess's good-looking young daughter on the grand staircase. There was a great crush, and taking advantage of it, according to a bystander who witnessed the incident, Lord Stewart was 'guilty of an act of impudent familiarity, which he might have found to his cost could only be washed out with blood'. To be precise he pinched her in a tender part of her body. Indeed, not being content with one pinch, he is said to have given her several. At all events, his behaviour, which was more amorous than diplomatic, produced an instant reaction. 'Without being in the least disconcerted,' so the account goes, 'the young, handsome and innocent girl quietly turned round and gave him a good box on the ears as a warning to leave innocence and beauty alone.' He pleaded drunkenness for his behaviour and indeed he was known to be a heavy drinker at this time, as were many of his military contemporaries.

One evening in February 1818, Stewart, who was in London on leave from Vienna, was invited by his friend Lady Antrim and her second husband Edmund Phelps, whom she had recently married and who had taken the Antrim family name of MacDonnell, to dine at their house in Bruton Street. Although in the social scale Phelps was somewhat beneath his wife, who was a Countess in her own right—his father was an auctioneer in Plymouth and his mother was a milliner in the same town; also he was reputed to have a wife already living whom he had married in Demerara and who had borne him a son—the marriage was quite successful. In fact Mr MacDonnell was accepted in Ulster where his wife's property was situated and he became High Sheriff of Antrim. He also got on reasonably well with his thirteen-year-old stepdaughter, Frances Anne, who was his wife's daughter by her first husband Sir Henry

Vane-Tempest, Bart.; the latter had died in 1813, having appointed his widow and his sister Mrs Angelo Taylor her guardians. Since Frances Anne was heiress to an immense fortune, including productive coal mines in Durham, she was made a ward in chancery until she came of age.

Some brief mention should be made of Frances Anne's father. The son of a parson, the Rev. Sir Henry Vane, first baronet, of Long Newton, Co. Durham, the second Sir Henry had inherited the vast estates of his uncle John Tempest of Wynyard and Brancepeth Castle in the same county on condition that he added the surname Tempest to his own of Vane which he accordingly did on John Tempest's death in 1794. The Tempest heir was a noted sportsman, devoted to hunting, racing and cockfighting, in addition to succeeding his uncle as M.P. for Durham City, pursuits which took up so much of his time that his only legitimate child Frances Anne grew up largely with servants, grooms and stable boys, since her mother also seems to have been away from home a good deal, no doubt with her family in Ireland. Her only playmate was Jack Vane, a natural son of her father, who was eight years older than herself. 'Our thus being thrown together was ill-judged,' Frances Anne commented afterwards, 'and the way he was brought forward was not in good taste.'

Harry Vane-Tempest, as he was generally known in the neighbourhood, owned a string of racehorses, with which he carried off many prizes, and of which the most celebrated was Hambletonian, which he had bought as a four-year-old, after it had already won the Doncaster Gold Cup and the St Leger. Hambletonian thereupon proceeded to win the Doncaster Gold Cup again and in the same week also won the Newmarket Craven Stakes. He was only beaten once when he ran off the course at the beginning of a race at York, so that it was hardly a race at all. Hambletonian's most celebrated achievement was the match against Mr Joseph Cookson's horse Diamond for three thousand guineas, which was run over the Beacon course at Newmarket in 1799, Hambletonian winning by half a neck and giving his opponent three pounds, the weights being 8 st 3 lbs. The horse, which was buried under a mound at Wynyard, was painted by George Stubbs, who showed him being rubbed down after the match. For years the picture, generally regarded as one of the best the artist ever painted, hung in the library at Londonderry House, whence it was sent to Mount Stewart for safety at the beginning of the Second World War.

To return to Frances Anne Vane-Tempest and Lord Stewart. The ambassador accepted Lady Antrim's dinner invitation and in this way he met Frances Anne for the first time. According to her, he said little and there was no one else there apart from her mother and step-father. 'When my mother asked me what I thought of him,' Frances Anne noted in her diary afterwards, 'I said not much, that he seemed finnikin and looked as

if he had false teeth.' So much for first impressions. After this she sometimes found him in her mother's house in the mornings and 'began to
think his manner pleasing'.

In spite of the difference in their ages—Stewart was old enough to be
Frances Anne's father—Lady Antrim thought her friend the ambassador
would be a suitable husband for her daughter and she encouraged the
match. However, Frances Anne's other guardian Mrs Angelo Taylor took
an immediate dislike to the prospective suitor and did everything she
could to prevent the marriage, appealing to the Lord Chancellor Lord
Eldon. After the Chancery court had eventually ruled in favour of the
match, she threatened to appeal to the House of Lords on the grounds,
among others, of Lord Stewart's loose morals, alleged insanity in his
family, and the fact that Stewart wished to marry her for her money. (Her
annual income was in the region of £60,000.) With regard to the last
charge, at any rate, there was no substance in it, since Stewart had an
income of his own of £18,000 a year, so that he could hardly be called a
fortune hunter. Mrs Taylor also seems to have considered Stewart's
family by no means the equal of the Tempests of Wynyard and the Vanes
of Long Newton, since Sir Piers Tempest had fought with Henry V at
Agincourt and Sir Henry Vane was Secretary of State in the reign of
Charles I.

Her aunt Mrs Taylor's opposition only made Frances Anne more eager
to marry Lord Stewart should he propose to her. He did so in her mother's
house on 9 April 1818 and she accepted him. Immediately afterwards
Mrs Taylor's Chancery action began and continued for three months,
during which time Frances Anne was only allowed to see her fiancé
provided that her governess was present. 'This is insufferable,' she wrote
to him, her hand trembling with rage. Eventually, after a further delay,
Mrs Taylor gave in and withdrew her notice of appeal to the House of
Lords. The Vane-Tempest family lawyers then drew up a stringent
marriage settlement under which, although the husband became tenant
for life of his wife's estates, the trustees were empowered to suspend the
husband's authority if they considered that he had acted imprudently in
his management of the estates, especially the collieries, as indeed they
were to do on one occasion. Nor was the husband allowed to sell any
portion of the landed property unless he made good the sale by the
purchase of land or government stock of equivalent value.

After these formalities had been completed, Charles and Frances Anne
were married by special licence in her mother's London house by the
Bishop of Exeter on 3 April 1819. The Castlereaghs lent the bridal couple
their house at Cray Farm for the honeymoon. 'She is not a beauty,' wrote
the Foreign Secretary of his new sister-in-law, 'but she is extremely well
looking, mild and intelligent . . . and for her time of life, she seems to have

a great deal of decision and character. The situation in which she is placed will require a large share of both.'

2

The journey to Vienna was accomplished by easy stages and took three months, the travellers stopping on the way at Paris, Geneva, Munich and Salzburg. In the French capital, where Frances Anne was presented to the restored Bourbon King Louis XVIII and met the various members of the diplomatic corps, she found the formal dinners very boring. They were a foretaste of what lay in store at the end of the journey. 'I was delighted with the shops in Paris,' she noted, 'but I cannot say I was happy.'

> Charles was kindness itself to me, every wish was forestalled and every want gratified. He was very affectionate and good to me, but many little things vexed me. People were always telling me some uncomfortable story, referring to former times and other attachments. I knew I was not his first love, and this reflection had always been a corroding one. Besides he had a son, not mine, and I had at that time no chance of children.

However, she was mistaken in the latter surmise, since by the time they reached Geneva 'to my great joy', as she put it, she found herself pregnant. By the time they had crossed the Semmering pass and reached St Polten, she felt sick. But, as this town was only four posts from Vienna, Charles thought they should push on. They arrived at the British Embassy in Minoreten Platz on 10 October, by which time she was quite ill. The embassy residence struck her as magnificent as well as comfortable, but further than that she was in no mood to appreciate the beauties of Viennese architecture. The cause was soon apparent, as shortly after her arrival she had a miscarriage. 'This made me both ill and very unhappy,' she wrote in her journal, 'and for some months I continued in wretched health and worse spirits. This accident, I believe, laid the foundation for my dislike of Vienna.'

At first she went out little in Viennese society on account of the state of her health. Nevertheless she quickly got to know the embassy staff, including the chaplain, the Rev. William Bradford, and his quick-witted Irish wife Martha, who had recently arrived and who had a good opportunity of observing Frances Anne at close quarters. ''tis plain she is not free from caprice,' noted Martha Bradford, 'and 'tis equally plain that she is a complete spoiled child with fine natural qualities and excellent abilities, and with a quickness of perception and sense of the ridiculous which makes her at once entertaining to a degree and perhaps a little dangerous.' On Christmas Day there was a large party at the Embassy, and on this occasion Mrs Bradford expressed her opinion of the ambassador as well as his wife. 'Certainly Lady Stewart is a most lively clever and agreeable creature . . . Lord Stewart has very pleasing good natured manners, and they dote on each other of course.'

Unfortunately Stewart's manners were not invariably everything that could be desired, at any rate in an ambassador. At a ball which he and his wife gave in honour of King George III's brother, the Duke of Cambridge, one of the guests was the Archduchess Charles, the Austrian Emperor's sister-in-law, who happened to be very fond of dancing. Some time before the ball was due to end, the hostess complained of feeling indisposed and went off to bed followed by her husband, without apparently a word of apology to the Archduchess. A little later the ambassador sent word by a servant to the musicians to stop playing, but the band leader ignored the order and the music went on. Eventually the ambassador appeared in person and peremptorily ordered the musicians to stop. This time they did so, whereat the Archduchess remarked to her partner, 'I think 'tis time for me to retire!' The embassy servants escorted her to her carriage, the attachés apparently not knowing what they should do. The result was that for some time afterwards the Imperial family pointedly absented themselves from the British Embassy functions, including one which Frances Anne gave for the Russian Tsar Alexander I and the other delegates who were on their way through Vienna for the Congress of Laibach (now Liubljana) in Slovenia towards the end of 1820. Before the ball the Tsar paid a formal call at the embassy. It was the first time that Frances Anne had met him, and he was so impressed by her that he stayed for an hour.

When he first caught sight of her, the Tsar gave a startled sign of recognition, which has a curious explanation. In 1818, while she was engaged to Charles, Frances Anne sat to Lawrence for her portrait, as Charles's first wife had done. However the artist had not finished the portrait when he was asked to go to Aix-la-Chapelle and paint the delegates. Among them was the Tsar, who noticed the unfinished portrait on an easel in the artist's studio and asked who the sitter was and whether he could buy the picture. Lawrence had promised Lord Stewart that he would not reveal her identity, so he told the Tsar that the lady was a 'Miss Stephenson' and that the picture was not for sale. Nevertheless the Tsar insisted on having the canvas placed in front of him while his own portrait was being painted, since, as he subsequently confessed, he 'felt a sort of foreboding that the person whose picture was before him was fated to have an influence over his destiny and cause him much disquiet'. And so it was that the Tsar recognised 'Miss Stephenson' as Lady Stewart.

The year 1820 was a busy one for the ambassador, since George IV had succeeded his father in January. The new king was determined to divorce his wife Caroline, who had been living abroad for many years, mostly with her Italian courier, who was also reputed to be her lover. The evidence against her had to be collected in northern Italy which was then Austrian territory, and it fell to the ambassador to discharge this unpleasant task and transmit the results to the new monarch's lawyers in England. Then Charles had to go off to the Congress of Troppau (now Opava) in Silesia as an observer before it was adjourned to Laibach. These absences irritated Frances Anne, and the indulgent Castlereagh excused his brother from attending the adjourned congress, since there had been a fire in the embassy which had caused Frances Anne considerable nervous shock, besides which she was again pregnant and the child was expected during the session of the Laibach Congress.

The child arrived somewhat later than expected, on 26 April 1821, and it was a son. 'Certainly the moment when I found myself the mother of a boy was the happiest I ever experienced before or since,' Frances Anne wrote in her journal. 'It was the largest, finest, and prettiest baby ever seen. Paris, Brussels, London and Vienna had been ransacked for my layette, which was magnificent and cost £2,000. Three nurses were sent from England, a monthly nurse, a wet nurse and a head nurse. I was myself very ill. The milk fever was violent and I was long recovering.'

The christening, which took place in the embassy six weeks later, was a gorgeous affair, the infant being baptised by the embassy chaplain and the sponsors being King George IV, Castlereagh and Lady Antrim, for whom the Austrian Chancellor Prince Metternich and the child's parents stood proxy respectively. Martha Bradford subsequently wrote an amusing and perceptive account of the ceremony, at which the infant was given five names, George Henry Robert Charles William—the first after the King, the second and third after the child's two grandfathers, and the last two after his father. The latter gave Frances Anne a set of pearls which cost £10,000 and which she wore for the first time on this occasion with a 'profusion of diamonds in her hair', while her husband was 'in full hussar uniform, yellow boots and all, not to mention a gold chain clasped with a ruby and an emerald set in diamonds, and a diamond serpent which he always wears'. At the proper time, Martha Bradford's account continues, 'the proxies renounced in the babe's name all the pomps and vanities of this wicked world, while the unconscious little innocent was dressed in blue satin, Brussels lace and surrounded with every vanity and pomp which money could purchase. The entire scene was theatrical but of the very first order'.

The Stewarts' intention had been to leave for England immediately after the christening, which would allow six weeks, plenty of time, in which to reach London for the Coronation of George IV. But the journey had to be postponed for several weeks, since the child was vaccinated, a somewhat daring experiment for those times, and then caught a bad cold, after which the wet nurse 'failed' and the child became quite ill. By the time he recovered it was too late to reach London for the Coronation. In fact they did not reach Calais until the beginning of August, making the crossing to Dover in the first steam packet to be employed on that route. The passage was 'rough and boisterous' and took five hours, so that it was late in the evening when their vessel steamed into Dover harbour. On disembarking, Stewart found a letter from his brother Castlereagh inviting them all to spend a few days at his farm in Kent before going on to London. 'You will find Cray made very comfortable and ample room for George Henry and his nurses,' he wrote, 'so don't fail to come to us.'

As things turned out, Castlereagh was not at Cray to welcome his brother and sister-in-law, since he had to accompany the King on his state visit to Dublin. (It was on this occasion that the rapturous welcome which Castlereagh received from the Dublin crowds made him observe that he had 'grown as popular in 1821 as unpopular formerly, and with as little merit; and of the two, unpopularity is the more convenient and gentlemanlike'.) But Emily was at the farm, and also Frederick, now a schoolboy at Eton, who had been given special permission to come up to Lawrence's studio in London to sit for his portrait. 'You know I am heavily in your debt and there seems no settlement to our account,' Stewart wrote to the artist at the time, 'and yet how can I refuse what will give me the greatest pleasure in life—to have your painting of my boy?'

After they had spent a few days at Cray Farm, where they admired Lady Castlereagh's zoo, Charles, Frances Anne and the baby Henry and their large retinue proceeded on their way to London and thence to Wynyard, Frances Anne's property near Stockton which she had inherited from her father. 'Our boy meanwhile was quite recovered and as strong as he was, intelligent and beautiful,' noted his mother. 'At Wynyard, we entirely papered, painted and furnished the old home, and after great expense and trouble made it fit to receive 40 people.' Their first visitor was Charles's mother, the Dowager Lady Londonderry, who struck Frances Anne as 'a very active, clever person, with no other signs of age but extreme deafness'; she had been staying at Harrogate before finally settling in Hastings.

It was during this visit that Charles learned that Sir Ralph Milbanke, a Yorkshire baronet, who had represented County Durham for many years in the House of Commons and had recently retired, contemplated selling his property at Seaham twenty miles away on the coast since it was heavily mortgaged. He had thought of constructing a harbour at Seaham for the coal-carrying trade and in 1820 had gone as far as employing an engineer to draw up a plan. But he abandoned this idea in the face of his financial difficulties, and he decided to put up the property for auction including the manor house Seaham Hall. It was in this house that in 1815 Lord

Byron had married Arabella Milbanke, the owner's only daughter. The
Stewarts learned of some of the Byronic legends originating from the
poet's stay in the house, when he galloped his horse on the beach and
practised pistol shooting at bottles in the garden. Once when Lady Milbanke's favourite dog Prim died and she was very upset, her husband told
her not to make such a fuss over a dead dog. Lady Milbanke thereupon
appealed to her future son-in-law for an epitaph and quick as a flash
Byron replied:

> Alas! poor Prim
> I'm sorry for him;
> I'd rather by half
> It had been Sir Ralph.

The sale took place on 13 October 1821, and Stewart secured the whole
Seaham estate for £63,000. Though admittedly something of a speculation,
this purchase was to prove a very profitable investment in the course of
time. For one thing, he reckoned that by building a railway from the
pits to Seaham and a harbour there, his wife would save about £10,000 a
year in river and port dues, since the coal had first to be conveyed down
the river Wear to Sunderland, where it was reloaded into larger vessels
for the onward sea voyage to its eventual destination. Part of the purchase
money was raised by a charge on the Irish property, to which Castlereagh
was agreeable. 'I think you will be enabled to work through your difficulties, if you firmly resist building or buying houses until all is square,'
Castlereagh wrote to his brother. 'It will certainly be a service rendered
to Lady Stewart's interest to have so largely added to her landed estate,
which I am sure you will have a peculiar pride in having accomplished
after all her devotion to you.'

However, the question of having a London house had to be considered,
and whilst they were looking round for one they took the Duke of St
Albans', No. 21 St James's Square, at what Frances Anne rightly described as 'the immense rent of £500 a month'. Besides this, Frances Anne
was again pregnant, and they wished to be close to the Castlereaghs, who
were only two doors away at No. 18, for the child's birth. When Princess
Lieven called, Frances Anne took her up to her bedroom, where the
Princess noticed an enormous bed surmounted by a Baron's coronet hung
about with heavy draperies, held up at the four corners by gilt figures of
Hercules. Here, on 15 April 1822, Frances Anne was delivered of a girl,
'born the most diminutive object you have ever seen', who was to grow
up to marry the seventh Duke of Marlborough. She was christened by the
Bishop of Lincoln on 18 May, her father's birthday, 'with a great deal of
vulgar ostentation', as Princess Lieven remarked, and there was a large
party of over thirty including the Duke of Wellington as well as Prince
Lieven and his wife. The great bed, 'with backcloth and lamp hanging

from the canopy', according to Princess Lieven, 'was transformed into an altar before dinner and a sideboard after, and back into a bed at the end of the festivities. The whole town came to see the farce'.

A few days later Charles signed the title deeds for the purchase of Holdernesse House at the corner of Park Lane and Hertford Street, together with the adjoining house in Hertford Street, with the intention of joining them together and rebuilding them so as to form one grand mansion. He also purchased the garden ground on the opposite side of Park Lane, but this plot passed to the London County Council after the thoroughfare was widened in the middle of the nineteenth century. The whole purchase, which was paid for by raising money on Frances Anne's estate, cost £43,000. A further £200,000 was spent in due course on the conversion and interior decoration by the architects Benjamin and Philip Wyatt. This included a ballroom, picture and sculpture gallery, banqueting hall and a magnificent staircase. It continued to be known as Holdernesse House until the death of Frances Anne's stepson the fourth Marquess in 1872, when her eldest son Henry succeeded to the Londonderry titles. The building was then renamed Londonderry House, and was so known for the next ninety years, after which it was sold to a property developer for half a million pounds and pulled down to make way for a modern hotel.

Charles and Frances Anne left London with their two children on 18 July 1822 to return to Vienna. By this date Castlereagh was showing signs of considerable mental strain, but Charles put this down to a quarrel which had broken out between the Foreign Minister's wife and the King's mistress Lady Conyngham and had in turn led to one lady refusing to be present at any official function if the other was also there.

Nevertheless Castlereagh went ahead with his plans to attend the next European Congress which it was intended should be held in Verona in October. When they said good-bye, Castlereagh told his brother that he looked forward to seeing him in Vienna *en route* for the Congress. A few days later he wrote to Prince Metternich confirming his plans and telling the Austrian Chancellor of 'the very great pleasure' with which he was looking forward to 'our approaching meeting'. At this date the British Foreign Minister was to all outward appearances his customary cheerful and confident self. Yet, within the next fortnight, his mind gave way completely. In the ensuing tragedy, he not only put an end to his own life but to his brother's diplomatic career as well.

3

Since Castlereagh had no children, his Irish titles passed to his half-brother who now became third Marquess of Londonderry, while the latter's only son Frederick by his first wife became the new Viscount Castlereagh. On learning the appalling news of his brother's suicide, Charles immediately drafted a letter of resignation as ambassador to the Prime Minister with the intention of returning home immediately, his action being prompted by the fact that his late brother's successor at the Foreign Office was his hated rival George Canning. However, as he had already agreed to attend the Congress of Verona as ambassador, he consented to stay on until he should be officially recalled. Meanwhile Frederick came out to Vienna to give his father the details of the tragedy and funeral. He also brought word that the Duke of Wellington was to attend the Verona Congress as the principal British plenipotentiary.

A week or two later the Tsar Alexander arrived in Vienna with a large retinue. During the next month, before he went on with the Austrian and British delegations to Verona, Alexander spent all his spare time with Frances Anne. Indeed on the day after his arrival he sent a message to the embassy saying he would like to call on Lady Londonderry. 'Charles said I was very ill and had not even been able to pay my duty to the Emperor or Empress of Austria,' Frances Anne noted at the time, to which the Tsar's aide replied that 'His Imperial Master knew I was not well and therefore begged I would not dress myself or be under any ceremony, as he would come and see me in my bedroom if I were not up'. He duly appeared at four o'clock without a single attendant and stayed for two hours talking in French to Frances Anne and her husband, expressing sympathy over the late British Foreign Minister's death, and playing with the children whom he coaxed and kissed, though when he took Henry in his arms the child 'began to scream dreadfully'. At the same time, Frances Anne remarked that 'nothing could be kinder, indeed I might say affectionate than the Emperor was'.

By the time they were due to leave for Verona, Charles had learned that his successor as ambassador was to be Wellington's youngest brother Sir Henry Wellesley, later Lord Cowley. The Verona Congress was the last of the experiments in international Government which the dead Castlereagh had largely inspired, and in spite of the poor accommodation which the town provided it was attended by two emperors, three kings, three reigning grand dukes, one cardinal representing the Pope, one viceroy, three foreign secretaries, twelve ministers and twenty ambassadors.

Before they left for Verona, Frances Anne received the Tsar alone and they continued to meet in this way in Italy. By now the Russian Emperor had become strongly attracted to Frances Anne. Soon they were exchanging gifts, the Emperor giving her jewellery and Frances Anne giving him books and a despatch case with a curious lock which he had seen and admired in her bedroom. Of course these visits could not remain a secret for long, particularly as they were observed by Metternich's secret police.

Many people, including Princess Lieven, took it for granted that the beautiful young Marchioness of Londonderry had become the Tsar's mistress. But there is no evidence whatever that this was so, and it is unlikely in view of Alexander's known austere way of life. However there is no doubt that he did form a very strong sentimental attachment to Frances Anne and he would have liked her to visit him in St Petersburg, while he for his part promised to come and stay at Wynyard.

Their final parting, which was long and tearful, took place in Venice, which many of the delegates had travelled to see after the Congress broke up in December. She told him that she was expecting another child and he promised to be godfather. Their final embraces were so passionate that after a while the Emperor evidently could stand the strain of parting no longer, since he rushed from the room. Afterwards Frances Anne wrote:

> In truth I loved him, and though my affection for Charles was unshaken, my admiration and gratitude increased by the unbounded confidence he placed in me. I was engrossed in a new and overpowering feeling. Indeed it was hardly possible to learn oneself loved by such a man as the Emperor Alexander, who combined everything that could please the eye, fascinate the ear, flatter the vanity and captivate the heart, and yet remain cold and insensible . . . Indeed when Memory recalls this too highly gifted and all perfect being at my feet, kneeling before me and covering my hands as he was wont with kisses, so far from wondering at my weakness I can only rejoice and wonder we came out of the ordeal innocent of guilt.

Since his successor in the Vienna embassy had now been formally appointed, Charles did not go back to the Austrian capital but made arrangements to return direct to England while continuing to correspond with Lord Liverpool on the subject of the customary recognition of a retiring ambassador's services. The Prime Minister offered to advance Charles a step in the United Kingdom peerage to Viscount, but the ex-ambassador pressed for an earldom with special remainder to his son Henry by Frances Anne. The matter hung in the balance for several weeks, but eventually Liverpool agreed to the double step, prompted it seems by Wellington so as to keep Charles quiet. Thus, the third Marquess of Londonderry in the Irish peerage became Earl Vane and Viscount Seaham in the United Kingdom peerage with the special remainder as requested. The news of this unusual award, which was gazetted on 28 March 1823, reached Charles and Frances Anne when they were in Rome. Frances Anne was naturally delighted since it carried a courtesy title for Henry. 'My boy, therefore, became Viscount Seaham,' she wrote afterwards, 'and thus my favourite object was attained after much trouble and negotiation as a reward for Charles's services.'

The family returned to England in June 1823 and Frances Anne's expected child was born in the following month at Holdernesse House. She had a difficult time at the birth, her labour lasting for twenty-six hours, and she was most disappointed when the result turned out to be a girl as she had greatly hoped for a boy whom she intended to call Alexander after the Tsar. However Alexandrina served equally well for the girl and as promised the Tsar was godfather. There was only a small christening party as the social season was over: indeed Prince Lieven had to interrupt his holiday in Brighton and come up to London to act as proxy for the Tsar.

Not content with his double step in the peerage, the third Marquess wrote to the Prime Minister claiming a pension of £2,000 a year as an additional reward for his diplomatic services. 'He has above £20,000 a year of his own and married a woman with £60,000 a year,' remarked one of the Foreign Office permanent secretaries. Mrs Arbuthnot correctly surmised that Lord Liverpool would refuse it, which he did, minuting the request, 'This is too bad!'

The request subsequently became a subject of gossip in official circles and was actually introduced in a debate in the House of Lords, although Londonderry was not mentioned by name.

The third Marquess's behaviour was characterised by other peculiarities. 'The Marquess has the bewildered air of an insane person,' John Cam Hobhouse, later Lord Broughton, remarked in 1824; 'the Marchioness looks like the young Lady Holland without her talents.' In the same year he fought a duel with a young cornet in his regiment named Battier. Londonderry was Colonel of the 10th Hussars and, when Battier complained that one of his fellow officers had criticised his horsemanship, Londonderry on making inquiries remarked in the mess that evidently Mr Battier could not ride and he had better go to the riding school for instruction. Battier immediately called out his colonel. In accepting the challenge, Londonderry acted contrary to military discipline, and the Duke of York as Commander-in-Chief of the army was anxious to try him by general court martial but was persuaded by the Duke of Wellington to let the matter drop. In the event the duel was fought with pistols. The cornet fired first, but his weapon either missed its aim or else flashed in the pan. The Marquess thereupon asked that he should be given another pistol, which Battier refused, and an apparent reconciliation ensued, though for some unknown reason the cornet afterwards threatened to horsewhip Londonderry's second, Sir Henry Hardinge. 'He is so contemptible and pusillanimous a wretch,' Londonderry told his sister-in-law Emily, 'I only regret the necessity there was for an old worn out soldier measuring himself against such an antagonist.'

Fifteen years later, the Marquess fought another duel, this time with the Irish patriot M.P. Henry Grattan who had said in the House of

Commons that he would not put it past the Tory Ladies of the Royal Bedchamber to murder Queen Victoria by drugging Her Majesty 'in a long and endless sleep'. Londonderry thereupon stigmatised this suggestion as 'base and infamous', an expression which Grattan demanded that Londonderry should withdraw. On the Marquess's refusing to do so, Grattan sent him a challenge. This Londonderry might have ignored, since his words were uttered in Parliament and he could have pleaded privilege. However he preferred to waive his rights and to meet Grattan on Wimbledon Common. Grattan fired first and missed, whereupon the Marquess fired in the air. Grattan's second then proclaimed that honour had been satisfied and, according to one newspaper account, 'the affair terminated to the satisfaction of all parties'.

Nor was this the first time that the Marquess had used intemperate language in Parliament. Shortly after Liverpool's resignation as Prime Minister in 1827, when he was succeeded by Canning, destined to die after only a few months in office, Londonderry declared in the course of a debate that Canning had been intriguing for the job ever since Castlereagh's death five years previously. He also alluded to the Canning Ministry's association with the Whigs as a 'disgusting state of concubinage' and he went on to describe the Ministry as 'a sort of rubbish'. This prompted a Whig peer to hit back neatly by remarking, in a veiled reference to the renovation of Holdernesse House and Wynyard, that 'anyone who was practically acquainted with building houses must know that what was sent away was rubbish'.

On another occasion in the House, according to the contemporary diarist Charles Greville, when another speaker tried to raise a point of order, 'this put Lord Londonderry in such a fury that he rose, roared, gesticulated, held up his whip, and four or five Lords held him down by the tail of his coat to prevent his flying on somebody'.

The Whigs' determination under the Premiership of Lord Grey to bring in a comprehensive measure of parliamentary reform made Londonderry particularly vituperative on the Opposition benches whatever subject was under discussion. On 14 September 1831, for instance, Lord Holland, the Whig minister and statesman, noted in his diary that 'Lord Londonderry made one of the most foolish and offensive harangues, breathing hatred, malice and all uncharitableness towards France, and affording Grey an opportunity of bearing testimony to her good faith and the cordial understanding subsisting between us'. When the Reform Bill was before Parliament, he became the object of popular animosity being 'struck . . . one day on his arm with a stick and another on his head with a brick bat, in consequence of his imprudent defiance and threat of carrying pistols about him'. In January 1832, when William IV was staying with Queen Adelaide at the Pavilion at Brighton, the 'Soldier Marquess', who had requested an audience, was invited to dine, upon which Lord Holland commented:

> I was told that Londonderry, arriving late to dinner, had his audience of the King afterward; that for near an hour he was extremely dull and prosy, and then grew so violent and frantic with the reform Ministry and politics foreign and domestic that the King, who had borne all in patient silence, said at length, 'And now My Lord you had better go and see your Mother', old Lady Londonderry being at Brighton.[1]

Meanwhile the restoration and decoration of Holdernesse House, which had been virtually gutted and rebuilt, the demolition of most of the old house at Wynyard and its rebuilding on a grandiose scale to the designs of the Wyatts, the enlargement of Mount Stewart on a considerable scale by the architect William Vitruvius Morrison, the complete refurnishing of Seaham Hall, and finally the great project for the construction of Seaham Harbour, absorbed immense sums. As early as 1825 the annual interest on loans and mortgages was £13,000, while other outgoings in the shape of family annuities and contributions to the trust fund amounted to a further £22,000. This may not seem an excessive burden to a man whose income with that of his wife was over £80,000 a year, but their surplus income seems to have been rapidly eroded by household and other expenses. For example, it cost £200 a month to maintain Wynyard. Yet the housekeeper Mrs Pellett's wages only amounted to ten shillings a week, while the housemaids received seven shillings. According to an inventory made in 1841, Wynyard was equipped with 68 mattresses, 136 pairs of blankets, 602 towels, 80 damask table cloths, 463 napkins, 910 pieces of china, and 600 pieces of silver.[2]

First of a long line of distinguished visitors to Wynyard, who included Prince Louis Napoleon, George III's daughter the Duchess of Gloucester, his brother the Duke of Cambridge, Sir Thomas Lawrence, Sir Walter Scott and Sir Robert Peel, was the Duke of Wellington. He arrived in September 1827 and had a tremendous local reception. During his visit he laid the foundation stone of what was intended to be an arch, in the words of the inscription on it, 'to commemorate his visit to his friend, Charles third Marquess of Londonderry, who served as his Adjutant-General during his Campaigns in the Peninsula'. (The design was later changed and the intended arch became an obelisk, which is still a landmark in the neighbourhood.) The Duke also spent a night at Seaham Hall, where the

[1] Frances Dowager Marchioness of Londonderry was eighty-one at this date. She died in the following year in Hastings where she had settled on leaving Mount Stewart. She was buried in Bayham Abbey, the Camden family home in Kent.

[2] Most of the silver, including the third Marquess's ambassadorial plate ordered from the royal silversmiths Rundell, Bridge & Rundell and made by Paul Storr, is now on permanent loan to the Brighton Corporation and on display at the Pavilion. Each article of the ambassadorial plate bears the royal coat-of-arms of King George III and the arms or crest of Lord Stewart, as he then was.

plan of the projected harbour was explained to him, and he was taken to
see some of his hostess's coal mines. However, in spite of this attention
and hospitality, Wellington did not include Londonderry in his Government which he formed a few months later. 'The arrangement was not
precisely what you would have wished for,' he wrote to his old companion-
in-arms, 'but you will observe we cannot form a ministry as we do a
dinner or a party in the country. We must look to its stability and its
capacity to carry on the King's business in Parliament, and carry with it
the respect of the country, and of Ireland, and of foreign nations.' However, as a small consolation the new Conservative Prime Minister gave
Charles's eldest son Frederick Castlereagh the junior office of a Lord of
the Admiralty.

4

Holdernesse House, which had been opened with a grand banquet and
ball in 1825, was to remain the centre of political entertainment, over
which Frances Anne presided as hostess for the Tory party, for upwards of
forty years. Her private gatherings were no less distinguished. In May
1830, for instance, she gave a particularly splendid fête to celebrate the
baptism of her youngest daughter Adelaide, called after the Queen, who
came with King William IV. The Archbishop of York performed the
baptismal ceremony, while the Queen stood sponsor in person for the
baby girl and, we are told, 'presented a valuable silver-gilt cup and salver
of the most chaste manufacture in commemoration of the occasion'. But,
alas for the vanity of human wishes. Lady Adelaide Vane, the child for
whom these magnificent preparations took place, proved a disappointment
to her parents when she grew up, since instead of marrying a Duke like
her eldest sister, she eloped in 1852 with her brother's tutor, a lowly
commoner, and married him.

Another of Frances Anne's great parties at Holdernesse House was
given after a military review in Hyde Park, in which her husband's
regiment played a prominent part, during Queen Victoria's Coronation
celebrations. The young Benjamin Disraeli, who had just been returned
to the House of Commons and was consequently present in the Abbey,
noted that Frances Anne 'blazed among the peeresses' and 'looked like an
Empress.'[1] Frederick, with whom Disraeli was friendly, had introduced the
aspiring young politician to his stepmother, who put his name on her
invitation list for parties and receptions. 'Dizzy' watched the review from
the drawing room of his future wife's house at the corner of Grosvenor
Gate and Park Lane, and afterwards went to Holdernesse House. He
wrote to his sister next day:

[1] He was later to portray her, thinly disguised as the Marchioness of Deloraine, in
his novel *Sybil*.

The Londonderrys after the review gave the most magnificent banquet at Holdernesse House conceivable. Nothing could be more *recherché*. There were only 150
asked, and all sat down. Fanny was faithful and asked me, and I figure in the
Morning Post accordingly. It was the finest thing of the season. Londonderry's
regiment being reviewed, we had the band of the 10th playing on the staircase: the
whole of the said staircase (a double one) being crowded with the most splendid
orange-trees and Cape Jessamines; the Duke of Nemours, Soult, all the 'illustrious
strangers', the Duke of Wellington and the very flower of fashion being assembled.
The banquet was in the gallery of sculpture; it was so magnificent that everybody
lost their presence of mind. Sir James Graham said to me that he had never in his
life seen anything so gorgeous. This is the *grand seigneur* indeed, he added.

As we have seen, the third Marquess's violent and uncompromising
opposition to the cause of parliamentary reform made him extremely
unpopular in the country. During the debates on the Reform Bill the
windows of Holdernesse House were broken by the mob and he was
refused post-horses on his journeys to Wynyard when his identity
became known. However, he endeared himself to the new Conservative
leader Sir Robert Peel, so that when the King abruptly dismissed Lord
Melbourne and the Whigs and summoned Peel to form a government in
1834, the new Prime Minister offered Londonderry the St Petersburg
embassy which he accepted and immediately ordered two beautifully
embossed seal boxes from the court silversmiths to contain the seals which
it was customary to attach to the ambassador's letters of credence. But
Londonderry's record on the Reform issue had not been forgotten, and
when the Irish members, who held the balance between the two main
parties in the House of Commons, threatened to vote against the Government unless the appointment were withdrawn, Londonderry immediately
forestalled the possibility by resigning; the two beautiful silver seal boxes
were never used.

The Londonderrys now proceeded to travel extensively, first to
Nicholas I's court at St Petersburg, then in Europe, the Middle East and
Africa. They were in Rome in February 1841, when a fire broke out at
Wynyard due to an overheated flue connected with the conservatory, as a
result of which two-thirds of the mansion were destroyed, though some
of the furniture and the most valuable pictures were saved. The house
was rebuilt on an even grander scale than before.

Because of Londonderry's voluntary resignation of the St Petersburg
embassy appointment in 1835, Peel felt that he was 'entitled to some fair
offer' when he (Peel) returned to Downing Street with an increased
majority six years later. But this was vetoed by Queen Victoria. 'The
Queen is strongly of the opinion that Lord Londonderry should not be
employed in any post of importance,' she wrote to Peel on 9 September
1841, 'as this would, in her opinion, be detrimental to the interests of the
country.' In fact, on Wellington's advice, the Prime Minister had already

offered Londonderry the Vienna embassy on the ground that Metternich, who was still Austrian Chancellor, knew him well from his service there twenty years previously and this could 'prevent him from doing mischief'. However, Peel was saved from any possible embarrassment with the Queen, since Londonderry rejected the offer 'with disdain', for the reason that his own former secretary of embassy in Vienna, Robert Gordon, had likewise turned it down. If he was to take an embassy, Londonderry told the Prime Minister, it must be Paris or nothing. But Paris was out of the question on account of Londonderry's known pro-Russian sympathies, and Londonderry, after complaining that he was 'no longer considered of importance by those I have *loyally* served', went off to nurse his disappointment. Frederick Castlereagh, though offered junior office once more, declined it on this occasion, 'not wishing to be placed in the invidious position of once again being a member of a government which his father believed had insulted him'. Instead he decided to make an extended foreign trip to the Middle East.

Eventually Londonderry's desire for office was unexpectedly satisfied when the Lord Lieutenancy of Durham became vacant on the death of the Duke of Cleveland in 1842. Since the Lord Lieutenancy was in the Prime Minister's patronage, Peel offered it to Londonderry, who promptly accepted it after the Queen had signified her agreement. Evidently she did not consider the office was of a nature in which its holder could do much harm. But she could hardly have been pleased when the new Lord Lieutenant proceeded to appoint staunch Tories as clerks of the peace and magistrates, which he was empowered to do. However, Londonderry had a point in seeking to check the power of the Whig magistrates to license their political supporters to sell spirits and beer to a thirsty electorate. For example he claimed that in the borough of Sunderland alone the whole bench of ten magistrates 'were all Whigs, and they would not grant a licence to a public house to any but their own party'.

Besides Wynyard, Seaham Hall and Mount Stewart, the Londonderrys had a small arcadian house near Richmond called Rosebank, described by Disraeli as 'a thatched cottage on the banks of the Thames—surrounded by groves of the flowers which gave it a name, and where, to render the romantic simplicity complete, Lady Londonderry, in a colossal conservatory, condescended to make tea from a suite of golden pots and kettles'. It was at Rosebank that the Londonderrys were giving an afternoon party when the news was received that Peel, then in opposition, was dying as the result of a fall from his horse on Constitution Hill in June 1850. Disraeli, who was among the guests, afterwards described the scene:

> Lord Londonderry was restless and absorbed: he foresaw the revolution which the death of Peel might occasion in parties. He pressed my hand with affectionate anxiety, asked many questions, and, full of intrigue, showed, as usual, his cards. I

missed him at the fête. He reappeared towards the end. He came up and whispered
to me. It was hopeless. He had actually galloped to London, called at Whitehall,
and galloped back, while his band was still playing, and his friends still sipping ices.

Londonderry, although he favoured Protection, was very friendly with
Sir James Graham, Peel's leading Free Trade supporter in the House of
Commons, and at Disraeli's prompting Londonderry made overtures to
Graham with a view to forming a united Conservative front by combining
the Protectionist and Free Trade (Peelite) wings of the party against the
Whigs. The negotiations which Londonderry conducted eventually came
to nothing, as Disraeli's interesting letters to Frances Anne reveal. Con-
sequently, when Disraeli had his first short spell of office as Leader of the
House of Commons and Chancellor of the Exchequer in 1852, it was
without the support of the Peelites, who gradually became fused with the
Whigs to form the Liberal party.

The Londonderry collieries, taking into account the new pits sunk at
Seaham, were paying off: in the decade after 1844 the gross annual profits
averaged £33,400, and in 1854, the year Londonderry died, the working
profit was over £60,500. Women and girls were now forbidden by law to
work underground, while the employment of boys was restricted to those
above the age of twelve. Government inspectors were also appointed to
inspect the mines periodically. Londonderry strongly opposed the employment of these inspectors in an open letter to the press, in which he commented disparagingly on the 'disgusting pictorial woodcuts' showing
women and girls at work in the mines with which the Royal Commission's
Report had been illustrated. This drew a scathing anonymous reply
from Charles Dickens in the Radical *Morning Chronicle*, from which the
following is a characteristic extract:

> The 'disgusting pictorial woodcuts' which accompanied the report still haunt the
> nobleman of taste, who complains that 'they were seen in the *salons* of the Capital,
> and that the ladies were all enlisted in the cause of their own sex, thus represented
> in so brutal a manner.' And to be sure it was a sad depravity of taste to pity them,
> and in the very worst taste for any lady or gentleman to look into the rooms at
> Wynyard Park and see those brutal forms reflected in the glittering plate and
> polished furniture, and even bordering in fantastic patterns the pages of the bankers
> book of the most noble the Marquess of Londonderry in account with Coutts & Co.

In fact, conditions in the Londonderry mines were considerably better
than in many others in the country, and various amenities were provided
for the pitmen in the shape of free medical treatment at the local infirmary
and practically free education for their children at schools which were
built and maintained by Frances Anne, who also defrayed the cost of the
necessary school books and paid the masters' salaries. Other children in
the neighbourhood, whose fathers were not employed in the pits, could

even take advantage of these educational facilities. Frances Anne also built a miners' hall for meetings and recreation, and finally—a great innovation for those times—she started a needlework guild for the free distribution of warm clothing for the miners, their wives and children and old people. It is noteworthy that this guild was still in operation when the mines were nationalised after the Second World War. Both Frances Anne and her husband were proud of their collieries, which were managed by the able engineer John Buddle, and after his death by a most experienced mining hand, George Elliott, who began work in the Londonderry pits as a trapper boy and rose through all the various grades to be manager-in-chief of all the Londonderry collieries, eventually becoming M.P. for North Durham and being knighted. He had the welfare and safety of the miners very much at heart.

Londonderry liked to think of himself as a benevolent employer, who was occasionally obliged to visit his displeasure on the miners when they behaved in ways of which he did not approve, such as going on strike and forming a trade union. Nevertheless he realised how much he owed to their industry. When his eldest son by Frances Anne, Henry Lord Seaham, came of age in 1842, Londonderry took him to meet the miners and see the pits which he was one day to control. 'It is now more than twenty years since I first came amongst you,' Londonderry told the pit-men, 'and if any of you look around and see the increase of the great power which this district wields in the mining community—that Stewart's Wallsend is always at the head of the market—where you have thus placed your proprietor, by the sweat of your brow, the first man in the coal trade, is it possible I should look on you without feelings of gratitude?'

The original Seaham Harbour, which cost over £118,000 to construct, had been completed in 1831, and five years later 373,000 tons of coal were being exported in Londonderry's ships. Several extensions were made to the harbour in subsequent years. For long there was a story current on the north-east coast, and which continued as late as 1928 when Seaham Hall became a hospital, that Londonderry had boasted that by his operations at Seaham he 'would make the grass grow in the streets of Sunderland'. The story is completely without foundation. On the contrary, in responding to the toast of 'Success to Seaham Harbour' at a dinner which Frances Anne gave in Seaham Hall to mark the opening of a new harbour extension, her husband made the forthright statement that 'Sunderland need never fear any rivalry from Seaham'. He went on, in jocular mood, to allude to 'a circumstance connected with his family to show that *Seaham* could never injure *Sunderland*'. The allusion was to the courtesy titles of his eldest son by Frances Anne (Viscount Seaham) and his eldest grandson, the Earl of Sunderland, son of their eldest daughter the Marchioness of Blandford, who eventually became Duchess of Marlborough. As a further gesture of goodwill to the neighbouring port, Londonderry promoted the construction of a railway linking the two towns, and in fact one of his last public appearances was when, in the face of a biting north-east wind, he cut the first sod of the Londonderry, Seaham and Sunderland railway on 8 February 1853.

Frances Anne and her husband were also instrumental in constructing the harbour at the village of Carnlough on the Antrim coast in Ulster on the property which she had inherited from her mother Lady Antrim. At the same time she determined to build a castle on the nearby Garron Point. The object of these undertakings, to which was added a good inn in Carnlough still known as the Londonderry Arms, was to provide employment following the terrible famine when the potato crop failed for two successive years. As Frances Anne put it in the inscription which she had engraved in the limestone rock below the castle, she undertook the building, 'being connected with this province by the double ties of birth and marriage and being desirous to hand down to posterity an imperishable memorial of Ireland's affliction and England's generosity in the year 1846–7, unparalleled in the annals of human suffering'. The castle, which Frances Anne called Garron Tower, and which, as well as Mount Stewart, she was to visit with her husband during most summers, later passed out of the possession of the family; it was for many years an hotel and is now a Catholic college of higher education. At one time it belonged to Frances Anne's great-grandson Winston Churchill who visited it in 1926. The inscription on the limestone in the road below can still be seen, except for the words 'and England's generosity', which have been obliterated by local Nationalist sympathisers.

Garron Tower was described at the time of its completion, as 'a castellated mansion built after the style of the 15th century'. The building formed two sides of a quadrangle, with a high octagonal tower, the east side fronting an overhanging cliff with a sheer drop of nearly 300 feet to the sea. The grand hall and staircase were decorated with the old arms and flags, including the colours of the 18th and 25th Light Dragoons and the 10th Hussars, all three of which regiments the 'Soldier Marquess' had commanded. On the first landing was a huge stained-glass window, showing the owner's illustrious ancestor Sir Harry Vane receiving the accolade of knighthood on the battlefield of Poitiers in 1356. The drawing room and dining room had very fine oak doors, with wood-carving specially executed by Austrian craftsmen imported for the purpose. Outside there was a portcullis, and along the cliff-top an embattled rampart over half a mile long, with embrasures and bastions mounted with cannon. Frances Anne also laid out a rose garden and planted an eucalyptus tree which today is one of the oldest in the British Isles. This remarkable structure, which cost less than £4,000, was ready for occupation in the summer of 1850, and a great housewarming took place, at which the guest of honour was the then Lord Lieutenant of Ireland, the Earl of Clarendon, whose arrival was greeted with the traditional salute of twenty-one guns, the echoes reverberating among the surrounding mountains and headlands. 'I hope you are well and happy in your tower, a true Lady Chatelaine,' wrote Disraeli to the proud mistress of Garron. 'What are you going to do with Ireland? They ought to make you Queen. It is the only chance left . . .'

One action of the third Marquess deserves honourable mention, since it may seem surprising that he and his wife should have interested themselves in the fate of one so remote from the worlds in which they lived as an Arab sheik. The sheik was Abd-el-Kader, Emir of Mascara. For fifteen years he had waged a great fight against the domination of Algeria by France, proving himself a courageous leader and a chivalrous opponent. Eventually, in 1847, he had been obliged to surrender to the French, which he did on the understanding that he would be allowed to retire and live in Egypt or Palestine. Contrary to this promise the sheik and his family were taken to France and held captive in a château on the Loire. Londonderry, who like many others in England felt that his treatment was a shocking violation of the terms of the sheik's surrender and showed that a Moslem could not rely on the word of Christians, made strong representations to the French king Louis Philippe, to whose son the sheik had in fact given himself up. But it was not until after the Revolution of 1848 had removed Louis Philippe from the throne of France that anything effective could be done. Londonderry now took up the case with the President of the new Republic, Louis Napoleon, later the Emperor Napoleon III, whom both the third Marquess and his wife had often entertained in his days of exile. At the same time Londonderry was granted permission from the French military authorities to visit Abd-el-Kader in prison.

The upshot of Londonderry's intercession was that the French President, accompanied by his War Minister, went to see the sheik in his prison and released him on the spot, after the sheik had sworn an oath on the Koran never to return to Algeria. He first settled at Broussa in Asia Minor. Shortly afterwards he came to London to thank the Londonderrys and he stayed at Holdernesse House where he presented them with his portrait and other gifts. It need only be added that the third Marquess's confidence in him was fully justified, since some years later when Abd-el-Kader was living in Damascus his prompt action saved the lives of many Christians when the Druses of the Lebanon revolted.

Early in 1854 Londonderry was shocked to learn that Britain and France had become allies against the Russian Tsar, his old friend and host Nicholas I. He learned the news of the outbreak of the Crimean War when he was in bed in Holdernesse House suffering from influenza. The influenza turned to pneumonia, and he died on 6 March 1854. After lying in state in the private chapel at Wynyard, his remains were buried in the Vane family fault in Long Newton Parish Church, the black funeral horses being the same as had drawn the Duke of Wellington's hearse sixteen months previously to St Paul's when the third Marquess was one of the pall-bearers.

The gallant old warrior's death occupied a good deal of space in the obituary and editorial columns of the newspapers at the time, and his services, or, as some held, his disservices, which he had rendered to the country were set out in considerable detail. But even those journals which had not seen eye to eye with him in politics, and which had disapproved of some of his more eccentric acts, were united in doing justice to the more endearing features of his character. One of these was the Liberal *Daily News*, which published a long notice from the pen of the philosophical radical Harriet Martineau. 'He was always ingenuous, always brave, and meaning to be kind,' wrote Miss Martineau.

He bore admirably the destruction by fire of his noble seat, Wynyard; and one of our latest recollections of him is one of the pleasantest,—his persevering intercession with the French Emperor for the release of Abd-el-Kader. There will be mourning in Broussa when the tidings of his death arrive there. There will be regret in many quarters in the remembrance of his large hospitalities, and his genuine goodwill towards his serfs on the one hand, his imperial friends on the other, and all between who would take him as he was.

No doubt, his last view of the world was a stare of astonishment that his country should go to war with his Russian idol. He has escaped the yet greater amazement of finding his idol vulnerable. One who knew him well remarked, on finishing his book of travels [*Recollections of a Tour in the North of Europe*], that 'his heaven is paved with malachite.' It is well that the notion was not cruelly broken up in an old man's mind; but the Tsar has lost in him one English admirer and champion. As for us, we feel some regret in parting with one of our last Peninsular heroes, and one who, with all his foibles, intellectual and social, was never wanting in frankness and manliness which give its best nobleness to nobility itself.

5

It must be rare, if not unique, in the history of the British peerage, that two sons of a peer should each inherit separate peerages on their father's death, the younger son holding a higher rank than the elder in the House of Lords. But so it was with the third Marquess of Londonderry and his sons Frederick and Henry. In 1854, Frederick Lord Castlereagh, the elder, succeeded to his father's Irish titles as fourth Marquess as well as to his United Kingdom barony, while the third Marquess's second son Henry Lord Seaham succeeded by special remainder to the United Kingdom Earldom of Vane. Both brothers were thus entitled to sit in the

House of Lords by virtue of their United Kingdom creations, Frederick as Baron Stewart and Henry as Earl Vane. Since both brothers were married it was anticipated that the Londonderry line would be carried on through Frederick. No one could imagine at this time that Frederick would die childless and as a result his younger half-brother Lord Vane would eventually inherit his Irish titles and become fifth Marquess.

Frederick William Robert Stewart, fourth Marquess of Londonderry, was the only child of the third Marquess and his first wife Lady Catherine Bligh, youngest daughter of John third Earl of Darnley. The Hon. Frederick Stewart, as he was then styled, was born on 7 July 1805 in South Street, Grosvenor Square. He was only seven years old when he lost his mother, and he was looked after by his uncle Castlereagh, the Foreign Secretary, and Lady Castlereagh, while his father was serving in the army overseas, before he went to Eton in 1814. When his father became the third Marquess in 1822, Frederick succeeded to the courtesy title of Lord Castlereagh. Four years later, when he had barely attained his majority, his family's influence secured his return as one of the two M.P.s for County Down, which he continued to represent for the next quarter of a century.

'Cas', as he was known to his friends, or 'Young Rapid', for his tendency to social dissipations, made an initially good impression at Westminster. When he could be persuaded to speak, he did so wittily and well and it seemed at one time that he might be marked out for high political office. When Wellington formed his ministry in 1827, Frederick's father was annoyed at his eldest son being passed over as well as himself and gave vent to his displeasure widely and loudly. In the result, when there was a minor government reshuffle in June 1829, Mrs Arbuthnot spoke up for young Frederick, as she recorded in her diary:

> I urged Lord Castlereagh upon the Duke and represented that, though his father was behaving so ill, still that the young man had done nothing and that he had claims and that he was clever and that it was hard to set him down as an idler merely because, having nothing to do, he did nothing. Added to which, at the funeral of the late Lord Londonderry, Lord Liverpool, while they were still in the Abbey, told Lord Castlereagh that he considered that he had the greatest claims on the Government from the name he bore and that, if he ever wished for political office, he had only to come to him and he might depend upon it he would consider him as his first object.
>
> The Duke told me he would consider of it, and he agreed with me that it would certainly be better to have a Tory than one of the Canningites.

A few days later the Duke offered Castlereagh the post of Lord of the Admiralty and he accepted it much to Mrs Arbuthnot's satisfaction. However, she felt he was 'so flighty' in spite of his cleverness that she doubted that he would 'do very much'. In the event he did not have much chance to prove his worth, as Wellington's government fell sixteen months later. Frederick's only other chance came towards the end of 1834, when Peel appointed him Vice-Chamberlain of the Household, otherwise a Tory Whip in the House of Lords, but this office only lasted a few months, since Peel resigned in April 1835 to be replaced by a Whig government under Lord Melbourne. Such was Frederick's brief experience of political office, though he had become a Privy Councillor in February 1835. But, if he made no lasting mark in politics, 'Young Rapid' was a delightful companion, very popular with all classes of society and always full of boyish jokes and good humour. He was a member of Lady Blessington's social and literary circle, which included Count D'Orsay, who was married to her stepdaughter, and other 'dandies', and it was in her house in Seamore Place, Mayfair, that he first met Disraeli, with whom he became friendly, particularly after Lady Blessington moved to Gore House, Kensington in 1836. 'Dizzy' was often a guest at the 'very recherché' parties which Frederick gave at his house, No. 37 Grosvenor Square. 'What delicious little suppers after the Opera!' Disraeli wrote in his diary. 'Castlereagh ever gay, a constant attendant . . .' It was at a fancy dress ball during the London season of 1835 that Disraeli met Frances Anne for the first time through her stepson. 'Lady Londonderry, as Cleopatra, was in a dress literally embroidered with diamonds from top to toe,' he remarked. 'It looked like armour and she like a rhinoceros.'

Frederick not only liked the opera but a particular performer there in the summer season, the famous Italian soprano Giulia Grisi, for whom Bellini had written *I Puritani*. Frederick first met her when she was performing at Covent Garden, paying her a great deal of attention which continued for some time after she married her French husband Count Gerard de Mélcy in 1836. He took to riding up and down on horseback in front of her house and finally addressed a letter to her in affectionate language which her husband intercepted. The irate Count found Frederick at home on his return from Ascot races, and challenged him to a duel, although Frederick apologised handsomely and admitted that he had not received the least encouragement from the opera singer. However, the Count stated that the insult to his wife could not be settled by any verbal excuse, and after their respective seconds had argued about the choice of weapons, the Count preferring swords to which Frederick admitted he was 'not accustomed', pistols were eventually decided upon. Accordingly the principals met at Wormwood Scrubs at ten o'clock one morning in June 1838. In the resulting exchange, Frederick was severely wounded in the wrist. Indeed, had it not been for the position of his arm when he received his adversary's shot, he might well have been fatally wounded. However, he made a good recovery.

Four years later Frederick had another narrow escape, when a boat on which he was travelling up the Nile ran aground on a sandbank and capsized, and he was only saved from drowning by the prompt action of his companion Dr Tardrew who threw him a rope and dragged him to safety through the window of the after cabin which he smashed as the boat was practically full of water. They were all shivering with cold, when responding to 'baksheesh' some of the Arab crew dived into the hold to see if any brandy which Frederick knew to be there could be recovered. 'After a good deal of ducking and diving,' Frederick recalled afterwards, 'two bottles were produced, which, drenched to the skin as we were, probably proved our salvation. This supply we distributed to our fellow sufferers, and did not find any religious scruples interfering.' After being twenty hours under water, the baggage and stores were recovered by the divers, and soon the sandy beach at the river's side was strewn with a miscellaneous collection of rice, coffee, candles, gunpowder, books, medicines, bedding, clothing, crockery and cooking utensils, all saturated with water and in various stages of decomposition. Eventually every article was recovered, but some were damaged beyond repair, including the knives, scissors and needles which they had taken out from England as presents. In gratitude to Dr Tardrew for saving his life, when he got home Frederick persuaded his father to appoint him regimental surgeon to the 2nd Life Guards.

Frederick had sailed from Southampton with Tardrew and a Maltese artist of German extraction named Schranz in November 1841 on a voyage to Egypt and the Holy Land which lasted twelve months and which was to take him to Damascus and back and involve him in many adventures and curious experiences, including a fight with Bedouin tribesmen who attacked their caravan, visiting the Mosque of Omar in Jerusalem disguised as a Moslem pilgrim—discovery of his identity would have meant death—and having two long interviews with the celebrated Mehemet Ali, the founder of modern Egypt, who was now the Sultan's nominal viceroy but in reality the independent ruler of Egypt.

Immediately after the accident to the boat, which occurred near Philae, Frederick and his party sailed up stream in another vessel, which they had managed to hire, to Abu Simbel to see the great figures cut in the rock and the temples which have since been submerged. Frederick took the opportunity of cutting his name and the date—'Castlereagh 1842'—on the wall of one of the temples which his great-great-great-nephew, the ninth and present Marquess, was able to photograph over a century later when he visited the site just before the flooding.

While he was in Cairo, Frederick met the English artist John Frederick Lewis, whom he commissioned to paint a picture of himself and his party which was to include their guide Sheikh Hussein and 'our factotum' Mahmoud, their dragoman. The agreed price for the painting was two hundred guineas, a high though not unreasonable sum for a major work by an artist of Lewis's reputation. 'You will exercise your discretion as to place, person and details,' Castlereagh wrote to him on 10 May 1842. Castlereagh was about to visit the ancient monastery of St Catherine on Mount Sinai, or convent as it was known, although it was exclusively inhabited by monks. Since Lewis had recently returned from there, and Castlereagh had been impressed by some of his sketches, this was the chosen scene of the water-colour painting *Frank Encampment in the Desert of Mount Sinai*, which, though apparently executed, or at any rate made the subject of a preliminary sketch, in 1842, was not publicly exhibited until 1856 at the Water Colour Society in London when it drew quite extravagant praise from Ruskin. 'I have no hesitation in ranking it among the most wonderful pictures in the world,' wrote Ruskin in the same year; 'nor do I believe that, since the death of Paul Veronese, anything has been painted comparable to it in its own line.'

The picture not only shows Castlereagh and his whole entourage, with the monastery in the background, but sitting on a chair behind his master is Castlereagh's cairn terrier Dusty, whose name is also carved on the temple wall at Abu Simbel. In the past the central figure in the picture has been mistaken for another Oriental traveller, Lord Prudhoe, later fourth Duke of Northumberland. But it has now been proved beyond all reasonable doubt that he is Frederick Lord Castlereagh, who had become fourth Marquess of Londonderry by the time the picture was first put on exhibition. Incidentally Sheikh Hussein was the subject of a separate portrait. 'The Sheikh has been sitting for his picture, much against his will, as it is forbidden by the Koran,' Frederick noted in his diary just before they left Cairo in May 1842. 'So that it was only by the gift of a pair of pistols that he has been prevailed upon to allow himself to be immortalised by Lewis.'

At one time the Turkish viceroy Mehemet Ali ruled an empire stretching from Khartoum to the borders of Anatolia, but a revolt of the Syrians against his rule, which they found more oppressive than the direct rule of the Sultan, coupled with the intervention of the Great Powers, notably Britain and France, who wished to support Turkey against Russian encroachment on the one hand and on the other to preserve the balance of power, left him in the end with little more than Egypt and Nubia, since he was deprived of his other spoils of war including Syria. When Frederick told him that he had heard that it was unsafe to travel in Syria, Mehemet Ali defended his Syrian policy vigorously. 'I spent more money upon Syria than years will repay,' he remarked. 'I drained Egypt to keep it in order. You might have gone securely from one end of it to the other. It is no affair of mine now. But you may tell Lord Palmerston and Lord Ponsonby, if ever you see them in England, that I know they wished to do me all the harm in their power; but I now thank them, for, instead, they have done me good. They have taken away a great source of anxiety, and have enabled me to do more for this country.'[1]

Political topics being exhausted, the viceroy turned to other questions, and whenever there was a pause in the conversation he would say to Frederick, 'Tell me something.' He talked of the difference of rank in England and said he could not understand why the term 'lord' was applied to all peers except dukes; nor could he understand the difference between substantive and courtesy titles such as that borne by his guest who could sit in the House of Commons as Lord Castlereagh and not in the House of Lords. Frederick gave the best answers he could. There is no doubt that Mehemet Ali took quite a fancy to Frederick, since he gave a dinner for him the day before he embarked for home at Alexandria and after he and his party had succeeded in reaching Damascus without mishap. During the tour the artist Schranz filled several volumes with water-colours of the places they had visited.[2]

In those days, before M.P.s were paid, their constituents seldom objected to their members' prolonged absence travelling. During his visits to the constituency, Frederick sometimes stayed at Mount Stewart, which he was eventually to inherit on his father's death. There is a revealing letter in the Downshire papers from Frederick to Lord Hillsborough, afterwards fourth Marquess of Downshire, which from internal evidence was probably composed soon after Frederick's return from his travels in the Middle East; it is undated but written from Downpatrick, the county town, possibly when an election was pending, and it contains one allusion to a Down Conservative Association meeting which suggests that Frederick's recent year abroad may have been brought up.

My dear H,

I am delighted that you intend to try and go to Bangor. What a bore it is! but after all these things do good to ourselves and the cause.

I wish you were in better form. I am afraid from what Jocelyn tells me you are not doing the right thing. You are dancing and living well, whereas you should live low and *never sweat* because perspiration takes all the effect of the medicine away. I am an old hand at these matters . . .

The association concern was disposed of before I arrived here and squashed as it deserved, nem con.

[1] Lord Palmerston was Foreign Secretary and Lord Ponsonby was British ambassador in Constantinople during the troubles with Mehemet Ali. In 1840, Palmerston characteristically threatened Mehemet Ali that if he did not conform to British policy he would 'just be chucked into the Nile'. In July 1841, Mehemet Ali was recognised as hereditary pasha of Egypt under the definite suzerainty of the Sultan.

[2] Frederick subsequently gave these paintings, which he had specially commissioned, to his wife, the former Lady Powerscourt. The present writer, acting for the 7th Marquess of Londonderry, purchased the collection from the 8th Viscount Powerscourt in 1935, and they are now at Mount Stewart.

Francis Forde has been drunk every night, and last night having been appointed President was carried off at 11, before we left the dining room.

I was very ill yesterday from the surfeit of brandy and water.

Thine ever,
Castlereagh

The Jocelyn mentioned here was Lord Jocelyn, eldest son of the third Earl of Roden, and brother of the widowed Elizabeth Lady Powerscourt, whose husband, the sixth Viscount, had died in 1844. Two years later she married Frederick when she was thirty-six. She already had three sons by Powerscourt and no doubt she looked forward to presenting her second husband with a son and heir. But, by the time she became Lady Castlereagh, she was apparently incapable of further child-bearing, since they had no children.

In 1845, Frederick became Lord Lieutenant of County Down, but knowing that, when his father's health began to decline, he might succeed him, he did not continue as M.P. for the county after 1852. Four years later, after he had become fourth Marquess, he was created a Knight of St Patrick, in recognition of his long parliamentary service. In the years following his marriage he spent a good deal of time at Powerscourt, since his wife's eldest son, the new Viscount, was only ten when his mother married again and Elizabeth wished to be with him and her two other sons as much as possible, and under her late husband's will she was entitled to the use of the place during her lifetime. This suited Frederick, who greatly liked the beautiful Georgian mansion with its views of the Wicklow mountains and sporting facilities in the 34,000-acre estate which rivalled Mount Stewart. 'I am heart sick of London,' he wrote to his step-mother Frances Anne from White's Club on 14 July 1854. 'I hate the pent up feeling of the town after so much country as we have had . . . and I quite long to be off. We shall I hope be at Powerscourt by the 24th but till then I feel like a prisoner of state.'

Also, when he came into the Mount Stewart property on his father's death, as he complained to Frances Anne, the place had become very run down, and he had to spend money on repairs and improvements. These were carried out during the next year or so and the house made habitable, but in the meantime Powerscourt was always available.

Frederick got on well with his stepmother, as their correspondence indicates. For example, when going through her late husband's papers, she came on an important document which she sent to Frederick. This was a letter from Edward Cooke, the Permanent Under-Secretary for War, to Charles describing the Cabinet intrigue to remove Castlereagh which led to the famous duel with Canning. In a letter from the Powerscourt mansion thanking her, he wrote:

The letter from Cooke is very remarkable and most interesting to me as I had always heard the history of these times discussed as a boy in a manner discreditable to Lord Camden and other members of the Cabinet of that day who certainly threw overboard Castlereagh in the basest manner and helped Mr Canning in his futile scheme for his overturn and dismissal. You can well understand *now* if you never did before the violent animosity which made my father give up Vienna in spite of the King and the Duke.

In 1855, Frederick's wife had become a convert to the Roman Catholic faith, influenced largely by Cardinals Wiseman, Manning and Newman, with all of whom she carried on a long correspondence. Fortunately this made no difference to her relations with her husband, who was deeply devoted to her, while for her the creed which she had embraced was to prove a great and lasting consolation during the last ten years of Frederick's life which were clouded by distressing mental illness. She built the Catholic chapel and school in Newtownards and for long was remembered with affection and sympathy by her co-religionists. At the same time her husband constructed the great tower on Scrabo Hill overlooking the town in his father's memory.

It is perhaps worth mentioning that Frederick was a very keen salmon fisherman and deer stalker in days when these sports were only just beginning to come into fashion. In the autumn of 1845 he was a member of a syndicate which took the fishing on the river Lochy and its tributary the Spean in Inverness. One of the syndicate was John Bright, who had recently been returned as M.P. for Durham on the Free Trade ticket. There is a pool at Spean Bridge which had to be fished from a precipitous rock. Frederick liked to recall how Mr Bright, who in spite of his Lancashire blood affected a kilt, slipped off the rock and fell into the pool where he was gaffed by the Highland gillie and pulled out by the tail of his kilt. As for deer stalking Frederick was an old hand at the sport, having indulged in it as a young man in Germany. After he succeeded his father as fourth Marquess, he used to take the forest of Glenisla in Forfarshire from Lord Airlie, and between 1851 and 1856, when he and his friends had it, he made the great collection of stags' heads which adorned the Central Hall at Mount Stewart for many years until most of them were dispersed early in the present century.

Frederick's mental trouble first manifested itself about the middle of 1862. 'I am so grieved also for your husband,' Lady Londonderry's parish priest wrote on 11 March of the following year—'so terrible an affliction. May it please God to deal with him mercifully.' On 21 March Cardinal Manning wrote to her: 'I do not ask about Lord L. knowing what your answer must be.' A few weeks later, when Manning was in Rome, he wrote again:

I have just come from an audience with the Holy Father who spoke very kindly of you, and I begged a special blessing for you which he gave me to convey to you . . .

Lady Campden has told me of your letter, and I fear that you have been suffering much on your dear husband's account. God has been pleased to give you a mournful and lone life of many blessings: but it is a sign of His great love for you: and no one but you can know what are all the circumstances of grief and pain which surround you daily.

Frederick was medically certified as being of unsound mind and removed to White Rock Villa, an infirmary on the site of the present White Rock Pavilion overlooking the promenade and the sea at Hastings. Only one letter from Elizabeth Lady Londonderry has survived from this period. It was written in April 1868 from her house in Grosvenor Square to another priest, the Rev. C. McGhee, and it shows how her faith sustained her at this difficult period.

Whenever I have heard you I always think of a story I once heard of a man standing outside a Cathedral looking up at the fine painted window. He could see nothing but a complex mass of columns. When he got inside how great was his surprise to see such beauty of design, all harmony and loveliness. So it is with many outside the Catholic Church. They see but the reality as it is, and nothing will convince them that their notice of a Catholic belief is a literally mistaken one calculated to engender strife and ill feeling . . .

Frederick died at White Rock Villa on 25 November 1872, the causes on the death certificate being given as bronchitis (four weeks), 'wasting away' (six months), besides his mental condition which had been previously certified. Apparently the only person present at his death was a female nurse named Ann Devereux, who was unable to write, so that she made her mark on the certificate which was accepted.

Frederick's widow, who survived him by twelve years, died on 2 September 1884 in her London house at 22 Upper Brook Street. She was buried beside her husband in Newtownards.

6

'Here begins a new and sad era dating from the fatal March 6th, 1854.' With these words Frances Anne prefaced the collection of her late husband's obituary notices, which she had specially bound in an album. Although she could not be called an old woman at this date—she was fifty-four—nevertheless it was inevitable that her life should undergo some change, however comfortably off she was left, having the use for life of Holdernesse House, Wynyard and Seaham Hall, as well as becoming the absolute owner of the collieries, and Garron Tower on her Antrim estate. Her various married children invited her to live with them and the Disraelis offered her the hospitality of their home. 'I wish I could have gone to you, but it is impossible,' she wrote to Mary Anne Disraeli from Holdernesse House. 'I have refused so many kind offers, and above all have excused myself to my children, who would feel hurt if I had been tempted to look for sympathy and consolation with any but them. The Portarlingtons—who urged my living with them—the Seahams—who want me to go to Wales—and to all I have said I have neither energy nor courage to leave my own hearth, sad and lonely as it is.'

It was not long after her husband's death that Frances Anne began to take up various interests with a zeal which astonished her stepson Frederick. 'I wish I had your energy and activity,' he wrote to her a few months after the 'Soldier Marquess's' death. 'I wonder at your work, for you never seemed as if you would rouse yourself to great exertion. I am sure it suits you for you look better and younger by many years than I have seen you before all this weight was on you.'

One of Frances Anne's first acts during her widowhood was to ask her friend Lord Ravensworth to design a sepulchral chamber at Wynyard worthy of her late husband. This Ravensworth duly did, constructing the mausoleum beside the chapel, engraving in letters of gold the twenty-five battles in which the 'Soldier Marquess' had fought, together with all his insignia, uniforms, numerous orders and decorations, and other memorabilia, notably the sword and cuirass of the French Colonel de la Motte, whom he fought single-handed and disarmed at the engagement at Fuentes d'Onoro during the Peninsular War in 1810. Ravensworth, who was something of a poet and had translated the Odes of Horace into English lyric verse, was also commissioned by Frances Anne to compose suitable verses which she had inscribed on the tombstones of her various dogs which adorn the grounds of Wynyard and Garron Tower.

Frances Anne erected two other memorials to her late husband. One was a church in Seaham. The other was an equestrian statue in Durham City, locally known as 'the wooden horse'. The statue was commissioned from a Milanese sculptor named Gaetano Monti, and Frances Anne is said to have paid him £2,000 in advance for it. After it had been completed but before it had been delivered, Monti was declared bankrupt, with the result that Frances Anne was obliged to pay a further £1,000 to obtain possession of the statue, a transaction which caused her to express herself in very strong language.

For the unveiling, Frances Anne invited Disraeli and his wife among others to stay at Seaham. He subsequently wrote the following description of his visit:

Seaham Hall,
December 8, 1861

. . . This is a remarkable place, and our hostess is a remarkable woman. Twenty miles hence she has a palace (Wynyard) in a vast park, with forest rides and antlered deer, with all the accessories of feudal life. But she prefers living in a hall on the shores of the German Ocean, surrounded by her collieries and her blast furnaces, and her rail roads, and the unceasing telegraphs, with a port hewn out of the solid rock, screw steamers and four thousand pitmen under her control. One day she dined the whole 4,000 in one of the factories.

In the town of Seaham Harbour a mile off, she has a regular office, a fine stone building with her name and arms in front, and her flag flying above; and here she transacts, with innumerable agents, immense business—and I remember her five-and-twenty years ago, a mere fine lady: nay, the finest in London! But one must find excitement if one has brains . . .

The idea of building the blast furnaces had occurred to Frances Anne by reason of the demand for her coal by neighbouring iron masters for use in smelting iron ore. About twenty acres were set aside for the purpose roughly a mile to the south of Seaham Harbour, near the village of Dawdon. Four furnaces were planned, each to be capable of smelting 200 tons of iron a week, the necessary fuel being provided by 120 coke ovens. The foundation stone of the first furnace was laid by Frances Anne on 12 December 1859, 'in the ardent hope', so ran the inscription of her own composition, 'that this undertaking will add to the prosperity of this town, of which one lamented laid the first stone, and who was permitted to see it rise to importance, with prayers that the success which was permitted to crown his great conception may be extended to our humble endeavours'. After the ceremony Frances Anne entertained 150 guests to a luncheon in the newly constructed ballroom at Seaham Hall, which together with other additions and improvements to the old house had cost her £15,000. But no doubt she thought the expenditure fully justified in view of the profits being made by the collieries and the blast furnaces when they were completed ten months later. Once asked if she did not mind the smoke from the furnaces affecting her comfort in Seaham Hall, she replied that she did not as she knew 'they were making money' for her.

When she asked to see the furnaces in operation, the railway carriage, which had not been used since the visit of the Duke of Wellington to the collieries in 1827, was got ready and newly painted. Unfortunately the paint had not sufficiently dried before her Ladyship sat down, with the result that her shawl stuck to the paint and the paint stuck to her shawl. 'This untoward circumstance,' in the words of the railway engineer, 'aroused the indignation of her Ladyship.' The harbour engineer, who happened to be the culprit, we are told, 'was not condemned to death, but what was to him equally severe, he being ordered never to show his face again to her Ladyship, and this request he religiously kept until the end of his days'.

Besides Henry, Fanny, Alexandrina, and the unfortunate Adelaide, Frances Anne had two other children, Adolphus, born in 1825, and Ernest, born in 1836. She also had eighteen grandchildren, of whom eleven were the offspring of Fanny Duchess of Marlborough. Naturally she took an interest in their progress, though with her own children she could be haughty and formal. For instance, Henry used to tell a story of how as a young man he came home unexpectedly (presumably to Holdernesse House) and, on going to see his mother, was greeted with the words 'Who asked you to come?' He replied, 'No one.' 'Then you can go away again,' she told him. And so he did—in the same cab that had brought him there. When invited to stay at Wynyard, she would send to meet him at the station a dog-cart, an open conveyance drawn by a single horse, in which he was liable to be drenched in wet weather. However, after he had got married and was living at Plâs Machynlleth, she arrived in state in a coach and six horses to stay with him and her daughter-in-law. On leaving the Plâs, she is reported to have said condescendingly, 'I am so glad to have been able to visit you in your *little* house.' Since it contained forty-eight rooms, it could hardly be called little, even by Victorian standards, but it certainly was by Frances Anne's.

One of the first things Henry did on succeeding his father as Lord Vane in 1854 was to add by Royal Licence the name Tempest to the name Vane which his father had adopted, so that his two sons were known respectively as Lord Henry Vane-Tempest and Lord Herbert Vane-Tempest. Perhaps not to be outdone by his wife Mary Cornelia, who was sometimes heard to murmur, 'the blood of Welsh Princes runs in my veins,' Henry considered that the Tempests deserved mention since they had a pedigree of twenty-four descents and one of them had fought at Agincourt.

Adelaide, the youngest daughter, had now been forgiven for her runaway marriage with the tutor Rev. Frederick Law, who had secured a good living in Derbyshire; she was to be a great comfort to her mother in her last illness. However her favourite was her second son Adolphus (Dolly) who became a Lieutenant-Colonel in the Scots Guards and M.P. for Durham. After his father's death he continued to live mostly with his mother until his marriage, except when he was on active service in the Crimea and occasionally attending to his parliamentary duties which he does not seem to have taken very seriously. He took part in the siege of Sebastopol, for which he received the Crimean Medal and Clasp. 'Lady Londonderry is in despair about her son Lord Adolphus Vane who is now in the trenches,' wrote Disraeli on 2 September 1855. 'The trenches are so near the enemy that we lose forty *per diem* by casualties! *Casualties*, she says, and truly what a horrible word to describe the loss of limb and life!' Fortunately Dolly came through the campaign unscathed and received a conquering hero's welcome when he visited his constituency. But the rigours of two Crimean winters had seriously undermined his health, and towards the end of 1857 he suffered what it is charitable to describe as a nervous breakdown. In the following year he fell in love with Lady Susan Clinton, a girl fourteen years younger than himself. She was the only daughter of the fifth Duke of Newcastle, who had been War

Minister during the earlier part of the Crimean campaign, and the unfortunately divorced Lady Lincoln. Susan's friends and her governess Miss Dennett begged her to break off the affair, but she was so infatuated with Dolly that she was determined to marry him as soon as she was of age and legally free to do so. Accordingly she left her father's London house one April morning in 1860 and went off to meet Dolly at St Mary's Church, Bryanston Square.

Lord Clarendon wrote an interesting account of what happened, emphasising that Frances Anne, whom he described as 'a hard old devil', had told the Duke of Newcastle who had remonstrated with her that she was 'convinced that the marriage would promote the happiness of her son which was all she had to do with'.

> He [the Duke] asked Miss Dennett to go with her to the Church, but most strangely would not allow her a carriage or his servants to call a cab for her. Lord Adolphus was to send a carriage to the corner of the square (his mother having refused hers or to be at the wedding) but did not, and Miss Dennett was obliged to get some woman in the street to call a cab and lend her the money to pay for it, as neither she nor Susan had 6d! Not a soul at the Church but [Susan's brother the Earl of] Lincoln who gave her away, and a W. Wood, a cousin of A. Vane's. He trembled so much during the ceremony that they expected a fit.
>
> The old Lady afterwards gave a sort of breakfast at Holdernesse House, to which she asked a few people, and then the ill-fated couple set off for Brighton. What a chapter in the history of the *haute société* of England.

The honeymoon seems to have been a stormy one. It was reported that 'Adolphus Vane has gone mad again and threw a decanter and knives and forks at her [his bride]'; yet she wrote to her sister the Duchess of Marlborough that she 'never had so happy a week in her life'. A few weeks later the Duke of Newcastle wrote: 'I hear accounts of her behaviour worthy of the wife of such a blackguard,' and again, a day or two afterwards, 'Lord A was on the verge of another attack yesterday—he is probably under restraint today.' In March 1861, Dolly was arrested for creating a disturbance in Coventry Street, and when brought up at Marlborough Street Police Court was remanded on bail for a medical examination. He was afterwards removed to a mental hospital, and in the circumstances the charges against him were dropped. Meanwhile Lady Susan went to stay with her mother-in-law, but according to Lord Clarendon 'they have not exchanged a word for weeks'. Clarendon added that Dolly had been 'regularly mad and is so still' and that 'the doctors say he will recover and may stand one more attack but not two'.

Contrary to medical opinion, Dolly survived several more of these 'attacks', although each succeeding outburst seems to have been worse than the last. However, he recovered when he heard that his wife was pregnant, and after she had been delivered of a son, on 4 January 1863, sent a telegram to his mother at Wynyard, saying he was sorry to learn that she too had been ill and adding that no doubt she would like to know that 'my wife is safe with a boy, both doing well'. Unfortunately he had another relapse a few days later and the doctor telegraphed to Frances Anne that it was 'necessary for Lady Susan's safety to remove Lord Adolphus immediately'. On 31 January the Duchess of Argyll wrote to Lord Dufferin:

> Lady Susan Vane is very ill, perhaps dying—she was confined and doing well. He had one of his delirious fits, and tossed his baby to the ceiling. She thought he had killed it, and became very ill—then rallied—then worse again. It is very horrible—but how can one think death an evil for one so wedded?

Shortly after this, on medical advice, Dolly sailed for America in search of health, but returned after four months worse than ever, 'quite maniacal' and behaving 'like a wild animal', in the early part of 1864. He died on 11 June. 'I forgot to tell you,' wrote Queen Victoria to her daughter from Windsor at this time, 'that poor Susan Vane's husband died . . . I believe in a struggle with four keepers when he burst a vein in his throat. She is left penniless . . . He tried to kill her last week and also the child—so that I believe it is to her a real release too.'

Poor Lady Susan, who could hardly be blamed for becoming an opium addict, survived her husband by eleven years. Their son Adolphus Vane-Tempest joined the Durham Light Infantry and later went on the stage where he had a fair success, though he never succeeded in becoming a star. He died in 1932, a few weeks short of his seventieth birthday, having married and had two sons, the elder of whom, Francis, was for some years heir presumptive to the Londonderry Marquessate before the present Marquess was born.

Frances Anne's third son, Ernest, who was a leap year baby—he was born in Holdernesse House on 29 February 1836—was also a cause for anxiety as he grew up. When he was eighteen, he left his tutor and enlisted in the army as a private soldier. A commission was then obtained for him as a cornet in the 2nd Life Guards and he was posted to the regimental depot at Windsor. Here, one night in September 1855, he visited the local theatre and forced his way into the actresses' dressing room. When he refused to leave the manager sent for the police. On the arrival of a constable Ernest left the dressing room and catching sight of the manager threw him down a flight of stairs, where fortunately his fall was broken by the stage prompter who happened to be standing there and caught him in his arms. Whereupon Lord Ernest assaulted the manager again, striking him in the face with his fists as he lay on the floor. Ernest subsequently received a summons to appear before the Windsor bench of magistrates on a charge of assault. However, the magistrates, on hearing the evidence, somewhat surprisingly decided that the assault was not of a sufficiently 'aggravated' nature to justify them in committing him to the next Quarter Sessions for trial and they accordingly imposed the maximum fine of £5.

Frederick did his best to defend Ernest with Frances Anne, telling her in 1855 that he had dined with him in the officers' mess and did not think he was 'misbehaving' any more. However, he added, 'they all go to Pratts. Powerscourt was not a week in the regiment before he was a member. So are all the young men of the day. I believe they vote White's a bore and a fogey's nest. I am told that Pratts is not the *mauvais sujet* it used to be. They certainly congregate to play billiards and smoke, but I expect they would do this elsewhere if not there'.

After the Windsor Theatre escapade Ernest was transferred to the 4th Dragoon Guards and went out to the Crimea just as hostilities ended. Shortly after his return he was involved in a disgraceful 'ragging' of another cornet in the regiment, so bad that Ernest was placed under close arrest, and at the subsequent Court of Inquiry he and the others who had joined in the 'ragging' were found guilty of 'conduct unbecoming officers and gentlemen' and were dismissed the army. Ernest then went abroad where he lived for some years presumably on an allowance from his mother paid on condition that he remained there. There is only one subsequent reference to him in Frances Anne's papers in the shape of a telegram to her solicitors in 1863: 'Lord E has not been in England nor has he an idea of coming.' Whether he was sent for, with the other members of the family, at the time of his mother's last illness is not known. She died at Seaham Hall on 20 January 1865, three days after her sixty-fifth birthday, and her remains were buried in the family vault at Long Newton. Ernest did not attend the funeral. But some financial provision was made for him under Frances Anne's will, and not long afterwards he came back to England where, it is only fair to record in his favour, he married into a respectable Durham family and had one son. Ernest died in 1885. His grandson Charles Vane-Tempest joined the Durham Light Infantry in the First World War, subsequently transferring to the Royal Flying Corps, and died in 1917 of wounds received in action.

7

It remains to touch briefly on the subsequent fortunes of Frances Anne's other three children, Henry, Alexandrina and Fanny.

As Lord Seaham, Henry was M.P. for North Durham from 1847 until his father's death in 1854 removed him to the Lords as Earl Vane. Writing to Frances Anne in April 1851, Disraeli, who now led the Tory Opposition in the Commons to Lord John Russell's Whig administration, expressed disappointment at a lost opportunity of defeating the Government on a hostile amendment to the Budget which he had moved. 'But the annoying thing is,' he went on, 'that disheartened and misled by the enemy, enough of our good men were absent to have gained the victory. Among them, I am sorry to say, were the two sons of your great house—I did not much count on Castlereagh, but I am, for many reasons, annoyed about Seaham. However, we must forget it . . . In fact the enemy was in our power, had not some of our friends mistaken their wooden guns for well-proved ordnance . . . We shall certainly try to knock up the Government again.' Disraeli and his Tory following succeeded fairly soon. In fact, less than a year after his letter to Frances Anne, he found himself in Lord Derby's Cabinet as Chancellor of the Exchequer and Leader of the House of Commons. Nor did he forget Frances Anne's eldest son when he eventually reached 10 Downing Street.

One of Henry's first actions on succeeding his half-brother Frederick as fifth Marquess in 1872 was to change the name of the family house in London, which he had inherited along with Mount Stewart, Wynyard and Seaham Hall, from Holdernesse House to Londonderry House. In 1876, the magazine *Vanity Fair* published a cartoon of him accompanied by a brief biographical notice signed 'Jehu Junior' in which the writer remarked that, having got married, the Marquess had 'taken to his estates as a business, to yachting as an occupation, and to snuff as a pleasure'. The notice went on:

> Although a strong and reliable Conservative, always ready to do his duty hand-somely by his Party, he has taken little part in the public discussion of the affairs of his country. He has consequently never had a place or a ribbon offered to him that he could accept; and though honoured with the Order of St Alexander Nevski in Russia, he has not even received the Order of the Bath in his own country.

This statement is not strictly speaking true. Although Henry had been given no English order or decoration, Disraeli shortly after he became Prime Minister recommended the Queen to confer the Irish Order of St Patrick upon him. In 1874, the Prime Minister wrote in a letter to Lady Bradford 'I have given the Patrick to Lord Londonderry, the son of a *grande dame* who was kind to me when I was a youth, though she was a tyrant in her way. But one remembers only the good in the departed . . .' One of Disraeli's last acts before surrendering the Premiership to Mr Gladstone in 1880 was to appoint the fifth Marquess of Londonderry Lord Lieutenant of Durham, a post which he held until his death.

Appropriately for one who had begun his career as a subaltern in the 1st Regiment of Life Guards and ended it as Colonel of the 4th Battalion of the Durham Light Infantry, the fifth Marquess raised a volunteer corps of his own: this was the Seaham Artillery Volunteer Brigade, of which he became Colonel Commandant. *Vanity Fair* considered this a matter for particular congratulation, as also that he had recently been elected Vice-Commodore of the Royal Yacht Squadron at Cowes. 'Withal he is urbane, accessible and hospitable,' the journal concluded its notice, 'though on occasion he knows how to exert his dignity.'

Except when he was sailing at Cowes and elsewhere, the fifth Marquess lived with his wife at Plâs Machynlleth, only visiting his own estates when business demanded. However he and his wife did entertain Prince and Princess Christian of Schleswig-Holstein along with Duchess Fanny and the Duke of Marlborough and their son Lord Randolph Churchill at Wynyard in 1870 and also the Prince and Princess of Wales and the German Chancellor Bismarck in 1883. Visits to London were usually for some special occasion, as when Disraeli invited them to a dinner at No 10 Downing Street which he gave in honour of the Russian Special Envoy Count Ignatiev who came to London in March 1877. The Prince of Wales, who according to the Prime Minister invited himself to the dinner, was placed between Mary Cornelia and Madame Ignatiev. 'The fine ladies, who had heard that Madame Ignatiev was even finer than themselves and gave herself airs, determined not to yield without a struggle,' wrote the Prime Minister afterwards. 'Lady Londonderry staggered under the jewels of the three united families of Stewart and Vane and Londonderry, and on her right arm, set in diamonds, the portrait of the Emperor of Russia—an imperial present to the great Marchioness. Madame Ignatiev had many diamonds, and a fine costume, but paled before this.'

'Mummy Londonderry', as Mary Cornelia was known to her children and grandchildren, was by all accounts a gentle and lovable person, who would go to any amount of trouble to help a friend or protégé. For example she wrote several times to Lady Hardwicke, the wife of the Postmaster General and also to the Minister himself in an attempt to get a man named Thornton a job as a postman in London, describing him as 'respectable and trustworthy' and 'also a Teetotaller! which in my opinion is a great recommendation'. However, Mr Thornton was over thirty and it seems that his age disqualified him, though he was appointed a 'letter carrier' in Birmingham—the difference seems more apparent than real.

The fifth Marquess and his wife had six children, three boys and three girls. The eldest son Charles, who was born on 16 July 1852 and was eventually to succeed his father as sixth Marquess, was known as Lord Seaham from the time of his grandfather's death in 1854 to that of his half-brother Frederick's in 1872. When his father became the fifth Marquess, it was announced that his eldest son would in future use the courtesy title of Castlereagh which went with Londonderry, instead of Seaham which went with Vane. After leaving Eton, he spent a year in the National University of Ireland before matriculating at Christ Church, Oxford. In 1875, when he was twenty-three, he married Lady Theresa Chetwynd Talbot, eldest daughter of the 19th Earl of Shrewsbury, Premier Earl of England. Three years later, after contesting two expensive elections without success, Lord Castlereagh was returned at a by-election in County Down by a large majority over the Liberal candidate. 'We have had a great victory in County Down,' wrote Alfred Baldwin at the time to his son Stanley, who though only a schoolboy was already eagerly lapping up political news. The victory resulted in the victor being selected, no doubt by the ever-mindful Disraeli, for the task of moving the Address of Thanks for the Queen's Speech which, in the words of *Vanity Fair*, he did 'with much modesty and good taste'. In the same issue of the journal which carried his cartoon, well matching his father's which had appeared three years before, 'Jehu junior' wrote of the young M.P.:

> He has good natural talents, no excessive amount of application, and none of that devouring ambition which wears men out before their time. His prospects are of the most brilliant kind, and if he should show a disposition to do so, he will certainly become one of the subaltern officers of that Conservative Party which his father has done so much to support.

In fact, as will be seen, he was to rise far above the position of a subaltern in the Party.

The fifth Marquess died suddenly, as the result of a stroke at Plâs Machynlleth on 6 November 1884, aged sixty-three. His widow also died there on 19 September 1906. Neither of their two other sons, Henry and Herbert, ever married. Henry, the elder, who served in his father's old regiment and also in the Seaham Volunteers, predeceased his mother, dying in 1905. Lord Herbert Vane-Tempest, who lived on at Plâs Machynlleth after his mother's death, entertained King George V and Queen Mary there on the occasion of the investiture of the Prince of Wales at Carnarvon Castle in July 1911. During the week-end the royal party motored over to Aberystwyth where the King laid the foundation stone of the new National Library of Wales.

'Bertie' Vane-Tempest was an intimate friend of both King George V and his father. He was well known for his wit, which was of the kind that both sovereigns appreciated. Indeed he is the author of the oft-told sally when Edward VII informed Lord Herbert that he proposed to make a mutual friend a member of the Royal Victorian Order. 'Serve him right, sir; serve him right!' was the swift rejoinder which amused the King greatly. Bertie was in one scrape or another from his schooldays at Eton, when he once overturned a grocer's cart full of groceries into Barnes Pool, and he liked to recall escapades such as when he rode in the Meath Hunt Cup, actually falling off at the last fence and clambering on again to be first past the winning post. It came as a tremendous shock to his friends and relations when he and his valet were killed in a railway accident in Wales in January 1921.

Frances Anne's second daughter, Alexandrina, was twenty-four when she married Henry third Earl of Portarlington in 1847. Like her sister-in-

law Elizabeth Lady Londonderry, Frederick's wife, she too became a
convert to the Roman Catholic faith. She died in 1874 at Emo Park, her
husband's Irish estate and was buried there. Finally there was Duchess
Fanny who had in 1843 married John seventh Duke of Marlborough,
when he was Marquess of Blandford, although his father did not approve
of the match. He succeeded to the Dukedom and Blenheim Palace in 1857.
It could hardly be said that Duchess Fanny did not do her duty as a wife
and mother since she bore her husband eleven children, five sons and six
daughters (the third son, whom she adored, was Lord Randolph Churchill). Yet she survived her husband who died in 1883 and all her sons,
including George the eighth Duke who died in 1892 and Randolph who
died in 1895. Like her mother at Wynyard, Duchess Fanny ruled Blenheim with a firm hand, and we learn from one of her daughters-in-law that
'at the rustle of her silk dress the household trembled'. In 1876 she accompanied her husband to Dublin on his appointment as Viceroy, a post which
he did not particularly want.

During the Marlboroughs' third year in the Viceregal Lodge there
was an exceptionally wet summer, in which the potato crop again failed,
the grain would not ripen and the turf could not be dried. Duchess Fanny,
whose grandson Winston described as 'a woman of exceptional capacity,
energy and decision', threw herself wholeheartedly into the work of
famine relief, and as a result of her endeavours she was able to raise
£135,000. Furthermore, the administration of the fund and the provision
of food, clothing and fuel which it was instrumental in providing for the
poor and destitute was, in her grandson's words, 'entirely free from sectarian or party influence, Roman Catholics and Protestants being equally
represented on the Committee'.

However, for her part, Duchess Fanny does not seem to have been as
attached to Winston as she was to his father, nor did she relish the idea of
this particular grandson becoming Duke of Marlborough, since Winston
was actually heir presumptive for a short time between Randolph's death
in January 1895 and the birth of a son to the ninth Duke in September
1897. But she did write to Winston from time to time and in 1898 he sent
her the script of his novel *Savrola* which she criticised for a want of
interest in the plot. 'It is clear you have not yet attained a knowledge of
women,' she added, 'and it is evident you have (I am thankful to see) no
experience of Love!' She also castigated him for acting as a special correspondent for the *Morning Post* while he was a serving officer in the
army, 'for I fear it has laid you open to the charge of breaking your
word'.

By this date her great-grandson, later the tenth Duke of Marlborough,
had been born to the ninth Duke and his wealthy American wife Consuelo
née Vanderbilt. But Duchess Fanny was less easy in her mind about the

future, when Consuelo visited her for the first time a few months after her marriage. Consuelo, who described her grandmother-in-law as having 'large prominent eyes, and aquiline nose, and a God-and-my right conception of life', has left a characteristic account of their meeting:

> The Duchess was seated in an armchair in the drawing-room of her house at the corner of Grosvenor Square where she had lived since her widowhood. Dressed in mourning with a little lace cap on her head and an ear-trumpet in her hand, she bestowed a welcoming kiss in a manner of a deposed sovereign greeting her successor. After an embarrassing inspection of my person, she informed me that Lord Rosebery had reported favourably on me after our meeting in Madrid. She expressed great interest in our plans and made searching inquiries concerning the manner of life we intended to live, hoping, she said, to see Blenheim restored to its former glories and the prestige of the family upheld.
>
> I felt that this little lecture was intended to show me how it behoved me to behave. Then fixing her cold grey eyes upon me she continued, 'Your first duty is to have a child and it must be a son, because it would be intolerable to have that little upstart Winston become Duke. Are you in the family way?' Feeling utterly crushed by my negligence in not having insured Winston's eclipse and depressed by the responsibilities she had heaped upon me, I was glad to take my leave.

One letter which Duchess Fanny particularly treasured was from Queen Victoria thanking her for her work in raising such a substantial sum for famine relief in Ireland. Not long before her death she handed the letter to her grandson the ninth Duke to be placed in the family archives. 'I may seem a useless old woman now,' she remarked as she did so, 'but this letter will show you I was once of some importance and did good in my day.'

The awesome Duchess, Lady of the Royal Order of Victoria and Albert, survived her seventy-seventh birthday by one day. She died at No 50 Grosvenor Square on 16 April 1899 and was buried at Blenheim.

CHAPTER III

VICTORIAN SUNSET AND EDWARDIAN AFTERGLOW

I

LADY THERESA SUSEY HELEN CHETWYND TALBOT, who married the sixth Marquess of Londonderry when he was Lord Castlereagh, was born on 6 June 1856 at Ingestre, the Talbot family seat in Stafford-shire. Her father, then Viscount Ingestre, M.P., succeeded his father as 19th Earl of Shrewsbury and 4th Earl Talbot in 1868. The Talbots were among the oldest families in the country, an ancestor Richard de Talbot being mentioned in Domesday Book, while the Earldom of Shrewsbury, dating as it did from 1442 thus made Theresa's father the Premier Earl of England. Theresa's maternal grandmother, also called Theresa, was one of the eight illegitimate daughters of the second and last Viscount Newcomen, a partner in a well known firm of merchant bankers in Dublin which did considerable business with the East Indies. In fact, the elder Theresa, who later became Countess of Eglinton, had been born in Calcutta and was to share with her sisters in her father's considerable fortune. At the same time the Shrewsburys were substantial landowners in Cheshire, Shropshire and Staffordshire, where they possessed two seats, Ingestre, near Stafford, and Alton Towers, near Stoke-on-Trent.

Theresa, who was the eldest daughter, had two sisters Guendolin and Muriel, and one brother, Charles, who later became the 20th Earl. They were a happy family, and since their father had been a keen Conservative M.P., they grew up in a strong Tory political atmosphere. 'I began liking politics when I was only ten years old,' wrote Theresa, looking back in old age. One of her 'greatest earlier griefs' was when her father, who was M.P. for South Staffordshire, was beaten at the General Election of 1867. However he got in again shortly afterwards for Stamford, which was something of a Talbot pocket borough. But he represented Stamford for only a few months, since his father's sudden death in 1868 removed him to the Lords. Another early girlhood recollection was of being taken by her father to see Lord Palmerston's funeral procession to Westminster Abbey one October day in 1865. 'I remember both the day before and the day after,' Theresa wrote, 'he [my father] gave me a short sketch of what he was like and his politics, and he always spoke of him as a thorough Englishman and sportsman.'

She also remembered her father taking her to Stafford House 'to see Garibaldi, the Italian patriot, and explaining to me about the States of Italy, the oppression, and the wish of Italy to be a free and separate Kingdom'. Harriet, the Dowager Duchess of Sutherland, had offered Garibaldi the hospitality of the Sutherland family's famous town house, and invited all and sundry of her friends to meet him, including Palmerston, who duly came. However, the Queen was somewhat concerned at the old guerilla's triumph and the matter was raised in Cabinet. Theresa was all for the Duchess, who stood her ground although she was a Liberal, and refused to ask Garibaldi to leave. Afterwards Theresa wrote:

> Harriet Duchess of Sutherland was a character with which I must say I had great sympathy, as after all it is always much better and more agreeable to meet people who have done something, or tried to do something than the ordinary ruck of individuals who are pleased to sit and do nothing. She was a very beautiful woman herself, a widow, and a daughter of Lord Carlisle.
>
> When the presence of Garibaldi rather embarrassed the Government, someone asked: 'How can we get rid of Garibaldi?' So a wit remarked: 'Marry him to the Duchess of Sutherland.' The objection was then raised: 'But he [Garibaldi] has a wife already!' Answer: 'Never mind, get Gladstone to explain him away,' the latter sentence showing what a casuist the Liberal was supposed to be.

Theresa 'came out' in 1873, being one of a crowd of débutantes who were formally presented to Queen Victoria at one of her 'Drawing Rooms' in Buckingham Palace. 'It was a very frightening moment when my train was taken away from me, and I followed Mother into the throne room,' she wrote to her sisters next day. 'The Queen was so gracious and kissed me so nicely that I forgot my fright.' Incidentally, daughters of peers were kissed by the Queen on these occasions, while commoners were expected to kiss the Queen's hand.

The first ball she went to was a few weeks later at Stafford House. By this time Duchess Harriet was dead and her successor as hostess and Duchess (and also as Queen Victoria's Mistress of the Robes) was Anne Countess of Cromartie in her own right, having been so created by the Queen with special remainder to her second son, as well as being Duchess of Sutherland. In the event there was a considerable family discussion as to whether Theresa should go to the ball at all. As she wrote to her sisters:

> You can imagine all the reasons for and against my going. Father, as usual, of course, was for it, and Mother, I think, was in favour but wondered very much what everybody would say—not 17—what would people think, and after all there would be plenty of time. But I put all my will in trying to get there, and I went ... I wore my white tulle dress and a bouquet of gardenias ...
>
> First of all, the house is splendid, the front hall rather dark. I was shivering with excitement and my bare shoulders, which made me feel very awkward. We went through a passage which is splendid, bigger than any staircase either of you have ever seen, as I think neither of you came here when Father brought me to look at Garibaldi. We began to go up it ... Mother knew everybody. I really could not help

laughing at the remarks, 'Is that your daughter?' 'I didn't know you had a daughter out.' 'How like her grandmother!' 'Really at your age (37) it seems impossible you should have a daughter out!'

As she told her sisters, Theresa was 'divided between wanting to see celebrated people, of which there seemed to be no end, listening to the comments as you know how sharp my ears are, and wondering if I should get a partner at all. It was rather upsetting to find that I was expected to stand glued to the floor in front of Mother until someone asked me to dance, and as I did not know a single man in the room except some old ones, and some politicians, I felt I was not going to have a very good chance'. However, she eventually found plenty of partners, including 'a very suave young man', who someone jokingly told her was a dangerous Radical. He turned out to be Lord Castlereagh. As for her, like her father, she was already a staunch Tory, since she spotted Mr Gladstone in the throng and dubbed him a 'horrible wretch'. Her mother, her two aunts Lady Pembroke and Lady Brownlow, and 'of course' the Princess of Wales she thought were 'the most beautiful people' she saw at the ball. 'I shall always remember Stafford House as the first big house I have been to.' And well she might, since Queen Victoria had once remarked on taking leave of the Duchess of Sutherland after a visit to her, 'I am returning from your palace to my house.'

She was unusually absorbed in politics for a débutante, as can be gathered from the same letter:

> I have seen Mr and Mrs Disraeli. He is quieter than ever, I think, and she jolly as usual. He was very kind. Father took me down to the House of Lords again. I wish our side was in Office, because I'm afraid we shall only be asked to one Court Ball now, and as we are coming home the day after tomorrow, and not coming back till June, I shall probably miss it . . .
>
> I am to go to the House of Commons tomorrow and Father says he will take me to peep again at the door, and see Mr Gladstone and Mr Disraeli sitting opposite to one another. What fun it will be when the sides are changed, as I hope they will be some day.

In fact they were changed a few months later; in the following January when Gladstone dissolved Parliament, the Conservatives were returned with a large majority, and Disraeli became Prime Minister on 20 February 1874.

Lady Theresa Chetwynd Talbot and Lord Castlereagh were engaged to be married in the summer of 1875. The match was arranged in the sense that their respective families approved of it, although it is doubtful whether they were deeply in love with each other. It was announced that the marriage should take place on 2 October in the private chapel of Alton Towers. At first there was some question of the ceremony being strictly private owing to the death in September 1875 of the bridegroom's aunt Susan Vane, the unfortunate Adolphus's widow. Eventually it was decided that all who desired should be allowed to be present, so that in the event upwards of a thousand tenants on the Shrewsbury estates made the journey to Alton Towers. The best man was Lord Helmsley, eldest son of the first Earl of Feversham, while the bride was attended as brides-maids by her two sisters Guendolen and Muriel. It was obvious that the best man took a strong fancy to the younger bridesmaid Lady Muriel, since they were married just over a year later.

Meanwhile the Castlereaghs took Kirby Hall at Bedale in Yorkshire as a country house and also a London house at 76 Eaton Place. Their first child, a girl called Helen Mary Theresa, but always known in the family as 'Birdie', was born on 8 September 1876, the chief sponsor at her christening being Queen Victoria's son Prince Leopold, later Duke of Albany. On 13 May 1878 the Castlereaghs had a son, Charles Stewart Henry, who was born in Eaton Place. And, in the same month, Lord Castlereagh was returned after two expensive and unsuccessful attempts to get into Parliament, the first for Durham in 1874 and the second for Montgomery in 1877, as Conservative M.P. for County Down in a by-election in which he defeated his Liberal opponent by a large majority.

Shortly afterwards, both being keen riders to hounds, the Castlereaghs acquired a house called The Hall at Langham, near Oakham, in the Cottesmore country. Here their second son and last child Charles Stewart Reginald was born on 4 December 1879. It was rumoured at the time, and it has been generally acknowledged since in the family, that Reginald's father was not Lord Castlereagh, later the sixth Marquess of Londonderry, but his wife's brother-in-law Lord Helmsley. It is noteworthy that there never had been a Reginald in the Londonderry family, Lord Helmsley's second name was Reginald, and his only son by his wife Lady Muriel, who had been born a few months previously, was also called Reginald. According-ing to another hearsay account, Reginald's father was none other than the Prince of Wales, who is said to have seduced Theresa at a shooting party. Whether Charles Castlereagh had any suspicions that Reginald was not his son is a question on which no direct evidence exists, although the fact that he allowed seven weeks to elapse before registering the birth and himself as the father as required by law may be regarded as evidence of his reluctance to satisfy this legal requirement. However, if one may judge from other associations in her life, Theresa was more highly sexed than her husband. She also quickly blossomed into a very beautiful, sexually attractive, clever and ambitious wife, which served a useful purpose when her husband inherited the Londonderry Marquessate.[1]

[1] The 6th Marquess also inherited his father's sporting land agent, Mr Newton Wynne Apperley, whose grandfather Charles Apperley was the well known writer on hunting who had the pseudonym 'Nimrod'.

His succession naturally involved his taking his place in the Upper House, where he sat as Earl Vane, although he was customarily referred to by the superior title of his Irish peerage. Then, just as his father had added the surname Tempest to that of Vane, so the sixth Marquess by Royal Licence dated 3 August 1885 further added the original name of Stewart to that of Vane-Tempest for himself and his children, thus becoming Vane-Tempest-Stewart, although his brothers remained Vane-Tempest. At the same time he received permission to quarter the arms of Vane-Tempest with those of Stewart, together with the family motto 'Metuenda corolla draconis' which may be freely translated as 'Beware of the dragon's crest'.

He was a wealthy man of property by the standards of his times. In the words of *Vanity Fair*, 'socially he is a good fellow, a pleasant companion, and a very fine host who "does" his guests royally'. His generosity to his guests, particularly his female guests, was indeed legendary. Once, when one of his horses won a race, he presented every lady in the house party with a diamond brooch. No wonder he and Theresa were particular favourites of the Prince and Princess of Wales, later King Edward VII and Queen Alexandra, whom they entertained in state no less than eight times between 1890 and 1903, six at Wynyard, once at Machynlleth and once at Mount Stewart, not to mention sundry banquets and other parties at Londonderry House.

By all accounts the sixth Marquess was friendly, simple and unaffected, with a fine sense of public duty, and with none of his wife's *hauteur*. One friend with whom he habitually corresponded was the poet and man-of-letters Edmund Gosse, who became Librarian of the House of Lords in 1904. The following characteristic letter from Londonderry to him written in his own hand is undated and probably belongs to an earlier period when Gosse, who had a poorly paid and inferior post in the Board of Trade, was supplementing his income by lecturing at Cambridge. Gosse had been able to find a copy of a book which Londonderry had lost, and the Marquess was profuse in his thanks to Gosse for his trouble.

> You are a really true and kind friend for I know what trouble you must have taken to find an original 'Spirit of the Nation'. It was truly kind of you and I cannot tell you how *very very* much I appreciate it.
>
> I was very vexed losing my old copy, and now your kind action in replacing it has not only given me great pleasure but shows me what a truly kind friend I possess. I trust for the future that this 'affectionate friend' will drop the 'Lord' whenever he writes his old 'Irish pal'. I cannot tell you how touched I am.

The Spirit of the Nation, it should be explained, was a collection of Irish patriotic ballads and songs, which had appeared in *The Nation*, the journal started by Charles Gavan Duffy in 1842 and suppressed seven years later for allegedly advocating rebellion. One of the verses which it contained

denounced the Act of Union and the role played in its passing by Londonderry's ancestor.

> How did they pass the Union?
>   By perjury and fraud;
> By slaves who sold their land for gold,
>   As Judas sold his God;
> By all the savage acts that yet
>   Have followed England's track—
> The pitchcap and the bayonet,
>   The gibbet and the rack.
> And thus was passed the Union,
>   By Pitt and Castlereagh;
> Could Satan send for such an end
>   More worthy tools than they?

2

Theresa Londonderry was such a remarkable character in her way that
she deserves some further mention. 'Lady Londonderry was a wonderful
woman, with her masculine brain and warm feminine temperament,'
wrote her Irish Catholic friend Lady Fingall. 'The best and staunchest
friend in the world, she would back you up through thick and thin. In love
with Love, she was deeply interested in the love affairs of her friends, and
very disappointed if they did not take advantage of the opportunities she
put in their way. She used to say of herself: "I am a Pirate. All is fair in
Love and War", and woe betide any one who crossed her in either of
these!' At her house parties at Wynyard the bedrooms were conveniently
allocated in the interests of her female friends and their lovers. She is
easily recognisable as 'Lady Roehampton' in Vita Sackville-West's novel
The Edwardians.

Lady Fingall's view of Theresa was endorsed by the novelist E. F.
Benson in his 'Victorian peep-show' *As We Were*:

> She revelled in personal splendour, she frankly and unmitigatedly enjoyed
> standing at the head of her stairs when some big party was in progress, with the
> 'family fender', as she called that nice diamond crown gleaming on her most comely
> head, and hugging the fact that this was her house, and that she was a marchioness
> from top to toe and was playing the part to perfection . . . She liked violence and
> strong colour, and sweeping along with her head in the air, vibrant with vitality. She
> did not plot or plan or devise, she 'went for' life, hammer and tongs, she collared
> it, and scragged it and rooked it like a highwaywoman in a tiara, trampling on her
> enemies, as if they had been a bed of nettles—and occasionally getting stung about
> the ankles in the process—incapable of leniency towards them, or of disloyalty to
> her friends . . .
>
> She lived on a plane of high-pitched sensation of the most catholic kind: sailing
> a small boat in a gale of wind, the twelve o'clock Communion at St Paul's Cathedral,
> the state-coach in which she attended the opening of Parliament, a loud noise on
> the organ, all these were of the quality which gave her sustenance.

'I am a good friend and a bad enemy,' she once admitted to Margot Asquith, with whom she remained socially friendly although they were opposed politically.

Only once did Margot get the better of her, and that was when she was Miss Tennant before her marriage to the future Liberal Prime Minister. At this time she scarcely knew Theresa, who was eight years older, and the occasion was a dinner party when the conversation became general after the gentlemen had joined the ladies. Theresa began talking about books, mentioning *Studies in Italy* by John Addington Symonds, and this led to a discussion on style, in the course of which Theresa asked the younger woman whether she admired Symonds's style. Margot replied that she did not, although she liked some of his books.

Theresa appeared to take exception to Margot's remark and, according to Margot, the Marchioness, after disagreeing with a lofty shake of her head, inquired in a challenging manner:

'I should be curious to know, Miss Tennant, what you have read by Symonds!'

Suspecting that a trap was being laid for her, Margot replied coolly: 'Oh, the usual sort of thing.'

'Have you by any chance looked at *Essays, Suggestive and Speculative*?' asked Theresa, visibly annoyed.

'Yes, I've read them all,' was the confident reply.

'Really! Do you not approve of them?'

'Approve?' queried Margot. 'I don't know what you mean.'

'Do you not think the writing beautiful?' Theresa retorted. 'The style, I mean.'

'I think they are all very bad,' answered Margot, 'but then I don't admire Symonds's style.'

Feeling confident that she could crush this audacious critic, Theresa observed sarcastically: 'I am afraid you have not read the book.'

This gave Margot the opportunity of coming back with a superb riposte. 'I am afraid, Lady Londonderry, that you have not read the preface. The book is dedicated to me. Symonds was a friend of mine and I was staying at Davos at the time he was writing those essays. He was rash enough to ask me to read one of them in manuscript and write whatever I thought upon the margin. This I did; but he was offended by something I scribbled. I was so surprised at his minding that I told him he was never to show me any of his unpublished work again, at which he forgave me and dedicated the book to me.'

In her autobiography, which came out in the early 1920s, and was considered in some quarters at the time to be rather indiscreet, although it reads tamely enough today, Margot referred to Gladys Lady de Grey as Theresa's 'rival' and her 'social antagonist' but felt inhibited from giving any details of their inimical relationship. Writing half a century later, in her book *Edwardians in Love*, Anita Leslie experienced no such inhibition and gave an account which is substantially correct but not altogether accurate in every particular. This, then, is what really happened between these two great society beauties.

About the year 1884, when Londonderry succeeded to the Marquessate, his wife began to have an affair with Henry Cust, a member of the Brownlow family, a future M.P. and editor of the *Pall Mall Gazette*; he was five years younger than Theresa, thus being twenty-three or twenty-four at this time. As a young man about town Harry Cust already had the reputation of being something of a lady-killer and he soon became irresistible to women, that is married women, and he was to have numerous affairs in subsequent years. Theresa returned his passion and unfortunately for her and unwisely for him she wrote him a number of love letters which he kept. While he was dallying with Theresa he started another affair with the widowed Lady Herbert who married Lord de Grey, eventually becoming Marchioness of Ripon. Gladys, judging by her portraits, was a woman of exceptional beauty, tall and dark who, according to a contemporary 'made any woman near her look pale'.

Cust was in the habit of receiving his lady friends in his bachelor rooms and he gave Gladys a key which she used on one occasion when he was out. Becoming suspicious that he was 'carrying on' with someone else besides herself, she rummaged amongst his belongings and her search revealed Theresa Londonderry's indiscreet missives, in which she was said to have made some derogatory remarks about her husband. At all events Gladys removed the letters and it is said that she read choice extracts from them to some of her friends including Anita Leslie's grandmother, Lady Leslie, *née* Jerome, sister of Lady Randolph Churchill. Eventually, tiring of this exercise, she is supposed to have tied up the letters in a sealed package and given them to one of her household with instructions to take the package to Wynyard and see that it was placed in Lord Londonderry's hands. Allegedly this was done with the result that Londonderry 'had it out' with his wife, who pleaded for forgiveness. According to Anita Leslie, who got the story from her grandmother, Lord Londonderry, who may well have known of his wife's affair with Lord Helmsley, refused to speak to her in private, his only communications being in public when the occasion demanded.

No doubt it took Londonderry some time to get over his wife's infidelity. But there is absolutely no evidence that he never again spoke to her in private, each going their separate ways. The Londonderry family papers make this quite clear, just as they provide no substance for the story that when he was dying she sent him a message and he refused to see her. On the contrary, he forgave her and thereafter they were very close, particularly politically, working together in the anti-Home Rule campaign in Ulster, and she was heartbroken when he died at the relatively early age of sixty-two. Of course, it may well be that after Reginald's birth they ceased to have physical relations and slept in separate rooms. This must have resulted in a sense of sexual frustration for Theresa and she found it necessary to find an outlet for her natural desires, hence her affair with Harry Cust and possibly others. At Wynyard she slept in a bedroom on the ground floor in the front of the house, and there is a legend that when she was alone she used to leave the window unbolted so that the game-keeper whose name was Houliston could visit her.

There is also a story that Londonderry consoled himself with several lady friends, the one to whom he was most devoted being Violet de Trafford, wife of Sir Humphrey, the third baronet. Sir Almeric Fitzroy, the Clerk of the Privy Council, who met her at a dinner party in London, liked her very much. 'Indeed she struck me as singularly unspoiled,' he wrote in his diary: 'there was a gentleness, a sympathy, and a joyousness about her outlook that I was hardly prepared for.' Eventually Lord Londonderry's attachment to her became so talked about that Theresa took steps to quiet the chattering tongues: she took Lady de Trafford for a drive in her carriage at the most fashionable hour in Hyde Park so that all their friends could see what good terms they were on.

Another married woman and society belle to whom Londonderry paid some attention, as did many others, was Ettie Grenfell, whose husband Willie later became Lord Desborough (they were the parents of the soldier-poet Julian). Ettie used to go racing at Newmarket with Lord London-derry, and she records that on one occasion she was driven round the town by him in his coach—he was a great 'whip'—'the greatest fun; terrific bear-fight; Lord L in my bed!' By a curious coincidence she was to become the closest political confidante that Londonderry's son Charley Castlereagh had with the sole exception of his wife Edith. There is some evidence that after 1891 Ettie took on several lovers, of whom Londonderry may or may not have been one. However Charley Castlereagh was no more than what is colloquially called a 'pen-pal'.

As for Theresa and Margot Asquith, they remained socially friendly until after Asquith became Prime Minister. In the early years of the century when the Conservatives were in office, Londonderry wrote a note to Herbert Gladstone, the Opposition Whip, asking for a list of the Liberal Front Bench with the names of wives, daughters, etc. 'Lady L is giving a party next Friday,' he added, 'and I want to send them cards.' But relations became strained during the Home Rule struggle, and Theresa and Margot were never on speaking terms again, although after London-derry's death early in 1915 Margot held out an olive branch which, according to a letter she wrote at the time to Lady Leslie, was rejected.

If you know Nellie Londonderry you can tell her I am *deeply* hurt and even profoundly shocked that she should not have jumped at the opportunity I gave her when Londonderry died to be nice with me. *Never* again ought a woman like Nellie to go to the Communion Service at St Paul's and dare say she is at peace with all men when I am kneeling a little further down (before the same altar praying to the same God). I wrote her a simple and very dear kind letter expressing what I felt of sympathy for her, saying that of course the Past would always be the past as far as we were concerned. No woman could have got a nicer letter.

How easy for her even if she still wants to give way to a naturally vulgar revengeful nature to acknowledge my letter but she never has written *one line*.

But then, in Margot Asquith's eyes, 'there was nothing wistful, reflective or retiring about Lady Londonderry. She was keen and vivid, but crude and impenitent'. Certainly with her enemies, as she had once told Margot, there was 'no kiss-and-make friends' about Theresa. It was a trait which she was to carry with her to the grave.

3

On 25 July 1886, Lord Salisbury became Conservative Prime Minister for the second time, following the rejection of Gladstone's Home Rule Bill for Ireland by the House of Commons in the previous month after some ninety Liberals led by Joseph Chamberlain had gone into the Opposition Lobby, henceforth calling themselves Liberal-Unionists. Among the more important appointments which the new Prime Minister had to make was that of Lord Lieutenant of Ireland. It was a great and historic office, since as viceroy the Lord Lieutenant represented the sovereign, he was responsible for the peace and security of the kingdom, and he exercised the prerogative of mercy as well as considerable patronage; besides which, he was the official leader of Irish Society. Two days after becoming Prime Minister Salisbury offered the post to the thirty-four-year-old Marquess of Londonderry and he immediately accepted it; a few days later he crossed to Ireland and was sworn in at a meeting of the Irish Privy Council in Dublin Castle.

The Lord Lieutenant was surrounded with considerable state. There were sixteen paid members of his household, the majority of whom were appointed by him personally. They included a State Steward, Comptroller, Gentleman Usher, Chamberlain, Master of the Horse, four A.D.C.s, three Gentlemen-in-Waiting, Private Secretary, physician and surgeon. Their combined salaries amounted to a mere £3,500 but some of them like the State Steward had free living quarters in Dublin Castle. As State Steward Lord Londonderry appointed Lord Langford, an Irish representative peer, who had taken his seat in the House of Lords in the same year as the Lord Lieutenant and had thus become acquainted with him. Lord Langford succeeded Lord Fingall, a young Liberal Irish Catholic peer, who also became friendly with the Lord Lieutenant and coached Langford

in the important duties of his office, since the State Steward was responsible for sending out invitations to the various functions in the castle, and
the seating arrangements for state banquets and dinners, including guests'
order of precedence.

The Lord Lieutenant lived with his family in the Castle during the
short 'season', which began after Christmas and ended with a ball on St
Patrick's Night. The 'Presentation' of débutantes took place in the
Throne Room in the Castle during the 'season' when it was customary for
the Lord Lieutenant to kiss each débutante on both cheeks. Lord Londonderry's principal A.D.C. (unpaid) was his brother Lord Herbert Vane-
Tempest, who bore a remarkable resemblance to him and was sometimes
mistaken for the Lord Lieutenant, so that the débutantes had the pleasant
experience of curtseying and being kissed twice.

When the 'season' was over the Lord Lieutenant and his family and
entourage would move to the beautiful Georgian mansion in Phoenix
Park on the outskirts of the city, where he spent the remainder of the year
when he was not touring the country. The Viceroys—and doubtless
Londonderry was no exception—usually brought some of their best
pictures with them, much of their own furniture, and their own plate, so
that the guests at the Londonderry dinners no doubt ate off the exquisite
ambassadorial plate which had been ordered from the royal silversmiths
and made by Paul Storr for Lord Stewart's Vienna embassy.

The Lord Lieutenant received a salary of £12,000 a year, on which it
was impossible for a Viceroy without private means to live in view of the
levées, receptions, garden parties, lunches and dinners which he had to
give. 'The wealthy avoid the office,' Disraeli had complained, 'and the
paupers won't fit.' Londonderry with his ample private means was an
ideal choice. He also created a precedent by being the first member of an
Irish family to hold the office: hitherto it had been held by an English or
Scottish peer. On the other hand, his Castlereagh title was not likely to
endear him to the Nationalists, who could be expected to regard a descendant of 'Bloody' Castlereagh, the hated architect of the Act of Union, with
the reverse of affection. Apparently the reason why Londonderry was
offered the post was that Salisbury was anxious that Sir Michael Hicks
Beach, who as leader of the Tory Opposition when the Gladstone Government was in office had waged such a successful anti-Home Rule campaign,
should become Chief Secretary for Ireland. However, Hicks Beach
refused to go to Dublin unless an Irishman was appointed Viceroy, and
this, as W. H. Smith the Leader of the House of Commons noted on July
27, caused 'a little difficulty'. But the difficulty was quickly overcome and
the offer to Londonderry was made and accepted on the same day.

The Chief Secretary to the Lord Lieutenant, who in an earlier period
had played a relatively subordinate role in the government of Ireland,

had by this time become considerably more than the Viceroy's chief of staff, and although he carried out his duties subject to the Viceroy's nominal supervision, he was the principal instrument in the local administration and the execution of Cabinet policy. Usually, although not invariably, a member of the Cabinet, and always an M.P., he was responsible for getting all Irish legislation through the House of Commons, answering parliamentary questions, and dealing with the Irish members. The recesses as a rule he spent in Ireland, but when Parliament was sitting he necessarily had to spend most of his time at Westminster, leaving his nominal chief in Dublin to supervise the working of the Irish governmental machine from Dublin Castle. In Dublin there was a Permanent Under-Secretary, and other officials who were civil servants and formed the core of the Irish Office. It was a remarkable innovation to send over such an experienced politician as 'Black Michael', as Hicks Beach was nicknamed, since he had served as Chancellor of the Exchequer and Leader of the House of Commons in an earlier Salisbury Cabinet, and his action emphasised the new importance attached to the post which had too often in the past been regarded as a stepping stone to higher Cabinet office.

On 18 September 1886, a gloriously fine morning, the new Lord Lieutenant, with his Marchioness, made his state entry into the Irish capital, arriving by special train at Westland Row station from Kingstown, as Dun Laoghaire had been renamed to commemorate King George IV's visit with the then Lord Castlereagh in 1821 (it has since reverted to its old name).

Prior to 1885 it had been the custom for the new Viceroy to be met by the Lord Mayor and Corporation of the City at the station and thence escorted by them and a troop of cavalry to Dublin Castle. From there after various speeches of welcome and other formalities the viceregal party would proceed to the residence in Phoenix Park. But in 1885 the Dublin Corporation declined to meet the incoming Viceroy Lord Carnarvon, another Salisbury appointee, and henceforth the Lord Mayor and his colleagues stayed away. Consequently Londonderry had to be content to be received by the Commander in Chief of the forces, Major General Prince Edward of Saxe-Weimar, and the cavalry troopers and any others whom the Castle authorities could muster. The Lord Lieutenant and the Prince rode on horseback, with the Vicereine and the G.O.C.'s wife, the Lord Lieutenant's mother and other members of the family and staff, including his brother and principal A.D.C., driving in the carriages. But there was no popular demonstration of joy or welcome, although troops lined the streets and the 'loyalist' elements cheered the carriages as they passed and the students of Trinity College sang 'God Save the Queen' and shouted

'Castlereagh'; the Nationalists retorted by singing 'God Save Ireland' and shouting 'Home Rule'.

During the decade which had passed since Londonderry's aunt Duchess Fanny and her husband the Duke of Marlborough had inhabited the Viceregal Lodge, the Irish scene had undergone a marked change for the worse with the rise of the Nationalist leader Charles Stewart Parnell, the Land League and the Home Rule movement, accompanied by 'boycotting', evictions, cattle maiming and other forms of agrarian crime, including attacks on landlords and their agents. Lord Frederick Cavendish, who had been appointed Chief Secretary by Gladstone and was related to him, had been murdered on the very day he arrived in Dublin, as he walked through Phoenix Park with the Permanent Under-Secretary T. H. Burke, who was a Catholic and was also stabbed to death. The fact that the Lord Lieutenant, Lord Spencer, rode instead of walked through the park may well have saved him from a similar fate. Furthermore during Lord Spencer's viceroyalty there had been a particularly unpleasant homosexual scandal with its roots in Dublin Castle, involving a number of senior officials, which led to a series of prosecutions and trials. These were still being talked about when the Londonderrys took up residence in Dublin. Indeed the quip was going the rounds that, now that Spencer had resigned, he should be promoted a couple of steps in the peerage with a new title—Duke of Sodom and Gomorrah.

It is true to state that Londonderry performed all the duties of his office punctually and fairly, but with a Cabinet Minister as Chief Secretary he felt that it was his duty apart from his ceremonial obligations to leave the actual government of the country mainly to Hicks Beach and not to allow any possible divergence of political view to become apparent. Hence to a considerable extent Londonderry's viceregal policy was one of unselfish self-effacement in the interests of Queen and country. However it was not long before the Lord Lieutenant found himself at odds with the Chief Secretary, who was suspected of favouring the Nationalists at the expense of the landlords, not least because Londonderry was himself a considerable landlord in County Down. Indeed Hicks Beach went so far as to withhold from the landlords military and police protection in carrying out evictions. The Viceroy kept silence, at least in public, but the senior judge, Chief Baron Palles, plainly hinted that the Chief Secretary would find himself in jail if he persisted in this course. No doubt it was fortunate for Hicks Beach at this moment that he developed acute eye trouble, which led him to send in his resignation to Lord Salisbury.

To the general surprise and, it must be added, to the delight of the Irish Nationalists who expected to make short work of him, the Prime Minister appointed as successor to Hicks Beach his nephew, thirty-eight-year-old Arthur James Balfour, the author of several works on philosophy, whose delicate appearance had earned him the nickname of the 'Tiger Lily' among his fellow M.P.s at Westminster. Now was Balfour's great political opportunity and he grasped it with both hands. Passed as fit by his doctor, he immediately caught the mailboat train for Dublin, where he was sworn in to the office of Chief Secretary by the Lord Lieutenant whom he had described in a fragment of autobiography as 'long my friend and once my fag at Eton'. He then returned to Westminster to introduce the most comprehensive Crimes Bill which ever reached the statute book. The Act, which became law in July 1887, gave the Viceroy power to 'proclaim' any association as 'dangerous' and suppress it; the Executive could also 'proclaim' any district, with the result that criminal trials which would normally have been conducted there could be removed to another part of the country and take place before a 'special jury' with a property qualification in preference to the more usual 'common jury'. In addition the Act made certain offences such as conspiracy, intimidation, unlawful assembly and obstructing officers of the law punishable on summary conviction before a Resident Magistrate. This meant that these offences could henceforth be tried without a jury. Furthermore, witnesses could be compelled to give evidence in such a Court under oath, even though such evidence might tend to convict them as well as the accused. The rigour with which the new law was enforced showed Balfour's determination to combat political crimes, and under its operation about thirty Nationalist M.P.s were sent to prison. The new Chief Secretary's role soon resulted in his being generally known to the Nationalist camp as 'Bloody Balfour', while the rising young barrister Edward Carson, who became in effect Crown Prosecutor at the age of thirty-three, was popularly referred to as 'Coercion Carson'. Carson, with his strong Irish brogue and saturnine features, immediately impressed himself upon Balfour and still more upon the Viceroy and his wife, with whom he was to become on terms of intimate friendship. He was seen with increasing frequency at the Castle levées and the Viceregal Lodge parties.

Lord Fingall's beautiful young wife Daisy, who was a Liberal Home Ruler like her husband as well as a Catholic, has described the Londonderrys' viceroyalty as 'very magnificent' and she saw a good deal of it at fairly close quarters. 'I have often wondered why the Londonderrys should have been so good to me, rebel and Papist as I was,' she wrote looking back many years later. 'Sometimes I thought that they asked me to prove their broadmindedness. Anyhow their friendship was never failing and it made no difference that we fought over politics . . .' She also recalled one of the innovations on the social side:

> When Lord Londonderry came to Dublin Castle he hurried up the dinners. He hated food and he instituted short meals instead of the immensely long ones to which we had been accustomed. I believe half an hour was the time allowed for

dinner and the occasion was a poor one for a gourmet. A footman stood behind
nearly every chair and plates were often whipped away from the guests before they
had finished. If you stopped to talk, you would get nothing to eat at all. Lord
Londonderry must have cut down the number of dishes. He also instituted cold
entrées and it was a new idea to be offered cold ham at dinner.

One night I sat beside a Lord Mayor at a State Banquet. The Lord Mayor who,
no doubt, had been looking forward to his Viceregal meal, was a slow eater and
talker and while his head was turned towards me the footman took away his plate
and he was left looking in some surprise at the empty one put before him for the
next course. When he was offered cold ham his endurance gave out and he expressed
his feelings to me: 'I don't call this a dinner at all,' he said, 'I call it a rush,' and,
eyeing the ham disdainfully, 'cheap, too!'

It is difficult to get a clear idea of what Lord Londonderry was like at
this time, since the family papers contain no letters from him and there
are very few in other collections. Perhaps he did not much care for writing
letters. In a moment of anger, according to Lady Fingall, after some particularly brutal outrage, he described Parnell in one letter as a murderer.
But he toned down the phrase after his cautious and tactful Private
Secretary, John Mulhall, remarked: 'It would be better, your Excellency,
to say that he *connived* at murder.' Lady Fingall also paid the Lord Lieutenant an unconscious tribute, greater perhaps than she imagined, when
she wrote that, while Lord Londonderry was not an exceptionally clever
man, he always 'did the right thing by instinct'. As for Theresa, who was
'Nellie' to her friends and 'Guy' in the family circle, 'she was most
beautiful then, although not in her first youth' (she was thirty). According
to Daisy Fingall, 'if she had had a little more height she would have been
wonderful to look at, but she was too short for her regal beauty and rather
square in figure. Hers was a most dominant personality. She had the
proudest face I have ever seen, with a short upper lip and a beautifully
shaped determined chin'. This opinion is certainly borne out by contemporary photographs, as well as by her portrait in middle age painted by
John Sargent.

Perhaps it was this feature which so impressed the Shah of Persia,
Nasir-ed-din, when he met her during his state visit to England in 1889
and offered to buy her. 'I don't know if he inquired about her price,'
commented Lady Fingall on the incident. 'But I think if he had carried
through his purchase he would have found that he had met his match.'

1887 was the year of Queen Victoria's Golden Jubilee. 'Everything that
year was dubbed "Jubilee", from knights and babies to hats and coats.
"God Save the Queen" was heard ad nauseam on every conceivable
occasion, until the tune became an obsession.' This we learn from Lady
Randolph Churchill who stayed with the Londonderrys that year and
has given an amusing account in her reminiscences of a practical joke at
the Castle.

One morning, speaking of the Jubilee craze, I pretended that I had received as an advertisement a 'Jubilee bustle' which would play 'God Save the Queen' when the wearer sat down. This, of course, created much curiosity and laughter. Having promised to put it on I took my host into my confidence. An aide-de-camp was pressed into the service, and armed with a small musical-box was made to hide under a particular arm-chair. While the company was at luncheon I retired to don the so-called 'Jubilee wonder', and when they were all assembled I marched in solemnly and slowly sat down on the arm-chair where the poor aide-de-camp was hiding his cramped limbs. To the delight and astonishment of everyone the National Anthem was heard gently tinkling forth. Every time I rose it stopped; every time I sat down it began again. I still laugh when I think of it and of the startled faces about me.

In June, Prince Albert Victor, later Duke of Clarence, the elder son of the Prince of Wales, then aged twenty-three and generally known as Prince Eddy, together with his younger brother Prince George, afterwards King George V, visited Dublin and stayed at the Viceregal Lodge. In general the two Princes had a friendly reception from the Dublin people, who always liked pageantry and colour; the Nationalist elements kept quiet and there were no hostile demonstrations as there had been when Prince Eddy visited Cork with his parents three years before. A great deal was crowded into the four-day visit, which began with a dinner at the King's Inns where the Lord Chancellor Lord Ashbourne presided, and Prince Albert Victor was formally elected an Honorary Bencher in the presence of all the judges and Queen's counsel and about two hundred junior members of the Irish Bar. A ball followed in Leinster House, to which 1,800 ladies and gentlemen had been invited. However the Vice-reine was not present at either the ball or any of the other festivities or at the parties at the Viceregal Lodge where the guests were confined to the male sex on account of her absence. The newspapers did not state the reason, but it seems likely that her younger son Reginald had one of his periodic illnesses and she was with him at Seaham Hall, where it was thought that the sea air was beneficial for invalids.

The second day of the Princes' visit opened with a grand military review in the famous Fifteen Acres in Phoenix Park, nine regiments being represented including the 10th Hussars which was Prince Eddy's regiment and whose uniform he wore, although he was only a subaltern and had not yet attained field rank. The review was followed by a service in St Patrick's Cathedral to mark Queen Victoria's Golden Jubilee, after which Prince Albert Victor was invested a Knight of St Patrick. Since the dis-establishment of the Irish Church in 1869, the Order had been secularised and the Knights no longer had their stalls in St Patrick's Cathedral where investitures had previously taken place. Now the ceremony was conducted in St Patrick's Hall in Dublin Castle by the Lord Lieutenant, who was Grand Master of the Order. The Prince was duly girded with the sword and robed with the striking light blue ribbon and badge, insignia which were to disappear in mysterious circumstances from the castle ten years later; the culprits, although known to the police, were never brought to trial for lack of evidence. Prince Albert Victor also received an honorary degree at Trinity College, an Elizabethan foundation and a Protestant stronghold, and the other arrangements made for his entertainment included a visit to the Rose Show held in the agricultural grounds of the Royal Dublin Society at Ballsbridge. It was the only royal visit during the Londonderry viceroyalty and the second and last by the heir presumptive to the throne who was destined to die of pneumonia in 1892.

Since the Chief Secretary was in the Cabinet and the Viceroy was not, Londonderry continued to be content with the role of a constitutional sovereign, leaving it to Balfour to cope with the political problems, while he and his wife as leaders of local society diffused an amiable hospitality and carried out the somewhat boring duties expected of the Queen's official representative. Londonderry supported Balfour's idea of establishing a Catholic University, while his wife made a point of visiting Catholic schools and other denominational institutions. To one curious action in a country of horse-lovers he responded in character. The Nationalists, principally because many landlords were Masters of Hounds, decided to proscribe fox hunting, a short-sighted move, since in many parts of the country it merely deprived the poorer local folk of a useful means of supplementing their livelihood. The Viceroy showed what he thought of the ban by following hunts without any security protection and his gesture was generally applauded. Eventually the ban was rescinded and hunting continued throughout the country as before.

At the time he accepted the appointment of Viceroy, Londonderry had made it clear to the Prime Minister that, on account of the needs of a growing family and his interests as a landlord and colliery owner, he did not wish to serve beyond three years. Salisbury agreed and accepted Londonderry's resignation three years to a month from the date of his acceptance. Meanwhile his devotion to duty had been recognised by his being created a Knight of the Garter in 1888. The farewell ceremony took place in the Throne Room in Dublin Castle on 30 August 1889, when he declared:

> Now that the time has come for me to say farewell, let me assure you that it softens the pain of departure to think that it is only as Lord Lieutenant that I bid you good-bye, for connected as I am with Ireland by ties of birth, property and residence, it will often be the duty and the pleasure of Lady Londonderry and myself to again return to those whose kindness has made our term of office a period we shall ever look back to with grateful and happy recollections.

The viceregal party drove through the streets to Westland Row Station to entrain for Kingstown. On this occasion the cheering was a good deal louder and more prolonged than it had been on the Viceroy's arrival three years before, evidence of his increased popularity and his wife's supporting role as a hostess and social figure.

4

When the Londonderrys left Dublin, their three children were growing up. 'Birdie', the eldest, was ten and would soon be 'coming out'; a few years later she was to marry Lord Stavordale and eventually to become Countess of Ilchester.[1] Meanwhile the elder son Charley Castlereagh had gone to Mortimer Vicarage School, a preparatory school for Eton, near Reading. The headmaster, the Rev. C. L. Cameron, was a brother of the African explorer Verney Cameron, and he seems to have liked young Castlereagh, judging by one report which has survived and which complimented him on getting a prize in some unspecified subject. 'He certainly deserves credit for sustained industry,' the headmaster wrote to his father on 5 April 1890. 'He has been in all ways a good boy and has got on most happily. Next half he must throw himself with vigour into cricket as well as work, as it is really of much importance to a boy before he goes to Eton.' Evidently he did both as he appears as the second choice as captain in the school XI and in his last half was top of the school in work, being first in Class One. In 1892, when he was fourteen, he went to Eton where he was placed in the Remove, ending up three years later in the Army Class in the Upper School, since he had decided to be a soldier. No record of his time at Eton under the rule of the progressive but fearsome headmaster Edmond Warre seems to have survived, and we only have his own word for it that while he was there Castlereagh did not distinguish himself 'either in an intellectual or an athletic way'.

His principal recollections of this period were of politicians he met at Londonderry House during the holidays. Somewhat surprisingly these included the Liberal party leaders Mr Gladstone and Sir William Harcourt, since party political feelings over the Irish Home Rule issue were relatively mild compared with the bitterness which they later engendered, and many Liberals were invited to the receptions at Londonderry House. Gladstone impressed the Eton boy as 'being rather kindly, but very old, for he was eighty-four at the time.' Although she was the leading Tory political hostess of her day, Theresa Londonderry had friends among the Liberals, particularly Harcourt who often came to the house to discuss literature as well as politics; Theresa besides being widely read had

---

[1] She had previously turned down Lord Kitchener who proposed to her in 1899, since she felt that he was not in love with her but merely needed a wife for social reasons. Also he was 26 years older.

literary pretensions of her own which were to find expression in an excellent short book on her husband's ancestor the great Castlereagh, an abbreviated version of which had originally appeared in the *Anglo-Saxon Review* under the editorship of Lady Randolph Churchill.

The first time that Londonderry took his son to the House of Commons was in June 1894, shortly after the summer holidays had begun. The Liberals were in power. It was not a very exciting debate, on a vote for a railway in Uganda, but it was noteworthy as the last occasion on which Lord Randolph Churchill spoke. It was a pathetic performance on Lord Randolph's part since he repeatedly lost the thread of his argument and had to be prompted by Hicks Beach and Balfour, being as he was virtually a physical and mental wreck. His health rapidly deteriorated during a prolonged sea voyage undertaken shortly afterwards, and he was brought back to England to die in his mother Duchess Fanny's house in Grosvenor Square in January 1895. Thus his son Winston became for a short time heir presumptive to the Marlborough Dukedom. Winston, who was four years older than his cousin Castlereagh, had just passed out of the Royal Military College, which Castlereagh was to enter in January 1896, so that they narrowly missed each other.

The Royal Military College had been founded in 1802 and ten years later it was established on its present site at Sandhurst about thirty miles from London on the main Southampton road. Every half-year about 120 young men were accepted as cadets, and the course consisted of three terms spread over sixteen months. Examinations took place half-yearly in June and December, and they included military administration, military law, tactics, fortification, military topography, drill, gymnastics, riding and musketry. The cadets wore a uniform of blue serge, and for full dress one of scarlet and gold. Discipline was strict and the work was heavy— reveille at 6.30, first study at 7, breakfast at 8, parade at 9.10, further study from 10.20 to 1.50, luncheon at 2 (three-quarters of an hour), afternoon parade at 3, gymnastics from 5 to 6, and mess at 8. 'So you see,' as Winston Churchill told his father, 'there is hardly any time for writing or idling.' Much to Cadet Castlereagh's disappointment, polo was abolished during his time at Sandhurst on grounds of expense. But riding remained in the syllabus, and as might be expected from his having been taught to ride well from childhood this was his best subject and in the final examination he was awarded 200 out of 200 marks, thus winning the college riding prize for that half-year. His academic performances were not, however, particularly distinguished and his marks on the whole were considerably below what his cousin Winston's had been. His best subjects were tactics and military topography and his total marks for the first two examinations for these subjects were 153 and 177 respectively out of 1500, while in the final he did best in fortifications for which he scored 374 out of 600, this having been his worst subject in the first examination. At all events he passed out adequately if not with marked distinction.

Among his contemporaries was the Irish peer Lord Dunsany who even then showed signs of his future poetic talent by composing an appropriate parody of Kipling's *Road to Mandalay*, when they passed out. No doubt this appealed to Castlereagh, who shared Dunsany's sporting tastes:

> Let me somewhere loose in Ireland where a man may shoot a snipe,
> Where there ain't no standing orders and you needn't shoulder hype.
> Fear not it is now all over and at last we've got away,
> And we'll find some roads are rougher than the road to Camberley.

After leaving Sandhurst in June 1897, Castlereagh was commissioned three months later in the Royal Horse Guards (The Blues), one of the three regiments constituting the Household Cavalry. For the next few years, until he became adjutant of the regiment at the age of twenty-two, a post he was to hold for four years, he had what he truly called 'a delightful time', whether soldiering at Hyde Park Barracks, Windsor or at Aldershot with the Cavalry Brigade, hunting, playing polo and riding in point-to-point races. Shortly after he had been commissioned, he wrote to his mother from Hyde Park Barracks describing an incident which no doubt gave her pleasure:

> I went into the shop Dreyfous yesterday and told them to send me things to Londonderry House. The man (a Frenchman I think) said to me, 'You are not Lord Londonderry.'
> 'No,' I said.
> 'Well,' he said, 'you are not Lady Londonderry's son.'
> 'Yes,' I said.
> 'Oh, I never knew Lady Londonderry had a son as big as you, she is so pretty,' responded the Frenchman. So you have a great admirer there.

According to his bank account with Cox's, his mess bill was about £28 a month, while his subaltern's pay only amounted to £10 a month, and he had various sundry expenses to meet such as subscriptions to the polo club and flowers for ladies, so that he could not have managed without an allowance from his father, which seems to have been in the region of £1,200 a year. He also had to pay a groom, but his monthly wages did not exceed £6. 10s.

As a handsome and eligible subaltern in one of the élite regiments in the army, Lord Castlereagh was naturally in demand at Court balls and dances. Among the débutantes who 'came out' in the same year as he was commissioned was a beautiful and vivacious girl called Edith Chaplin, whose father, popularly known as 'Squire' Chaplin, combined sport with politics to a remarkable degree, being celebrated as a master of hounds and racehorse owner (his horse Hermit won the Derby in a snowstorm in

1867), as well as being a staunchly Conservative M.P. and having sat in the Cabinet as the minister successively responsible for agriculture and local government. Unfortunately, his wife, Lady Florence Leveson-Gower, eldest daughter of the third Duke of Sutherland, died after they had been married for less than five years, so that their daughter Edith was largely brought up by her Sutherland relations since her father was busy with his sporting and political interests.

Charley Castlereagh and Edie Chaplin were immediately attracted to one another, and when she went off to Turkey on a holiday with her aunt Millicent Duchess of Sutherland early in 1899, Charley wrote giving her advice. 'Please be careful of the Sultan, he is a flighty man,' and again, from Aldershot on 4 April, 'My dear Miss Edie . . . I hope you are returning soon, and can't you quite make up your mind whether to join the harem or not.' He proposed at a ball during the following season and was accepted. A big wedding was planned for the autumn, but almost at the last moment it had to be postponed on account of the illness of Charley's younger brother Reginald, which took a serious turn in September.

Poor Reggie had been a sickly child, afflicted with a painful hip disease, so that it was evident from an early age that he would never be able to walk naturally.[1] Despite the affliction and the fact that he was reputedly Theresa's son by Lord Helmsley and not by her own husband, Reggie was always accepted as a member of the family and his mother was devoted to him, as also were Birdie and Charley, although Lord Londonderry's devotion may understandably have been less marked. Not being strong enough to be sent away to a boarding school, he was taught at home by a private tutor named McKendrick from Glasgow, who discovered that the boy had a remarkable scientific bent, which the tutor did his best to encourage. At the same time, his mother, who was a keen amateur photographer, showed Reggie how to use a camera, with which the boy quickly became proficient. The earlier pictures were taken at Wynyard by Theresa but most of the groups such as those showing the Prince and Princess of Wales, Lord and Lady Randolph Churchill, Mrs Keppel and Theresa herself and her husband were taken by Reggie. The negatives were developed in a special dark room fitted out with running water, a sink and the usual chemicals like hypophosphate. After Reggie's death the dark room remained shut up for more than a century and was only recently discovered by the present Marquess while exploring some of the

[1] According to the late Mrs Apperley, daughter-in-law of the 6th Marquess's land agent Mr N. W. Apperley, Lord Londonderry lost his temper on discovering the truth of Reggie's paternity, seized him as he was being nursed by his mother on her lap and threw him on the floor. This action, quite out of keeping with Lord Londonderry's generally acknowledged kindly character, is said to have been the origin of Reggie's hip complaint.

older and unused parts of the house. In the corner of the room stood a small pair of crutches which had belonged to Reggie. But in the pictures of him alone and with other members of the family taken by Theresa his lameness was often disguised.

Another of Reggie's interests was engineering, and there was nothing he enjoyed more than travelling with the driver in the cab of a locomotive on the railway which had been built in Frances Anne's time and which ran between Wynyard, Seaham and Sunderland. Before long he had become so familiar with the mechanics of the locomotive that he was able to drive the engine, spending the whole day on the line, eating a picnic lunch with the drivers and stokers, often returning to Wynyard or Seaham thoroughly begrimed, a condition to which his mother apparently made no objection, since this was taken as a sign that his health was improving and it was thought that he would soon be able to discard his crutches altogether. By the time he was fifteen he could drive the train single-handed and on one occasion did so with a number of distinguished passengers who included the Duke of Cambridge.

Unfortunately, although his hip trouble was improving, Reggie was stricken by another malady, tuberculosis. In 1897, a London specialist, James Donellan of Cavendish Square, was consulted and he recommended a voyage to a milder climate. Consequently the end of the year found him in Tenerife, which in those days was regarded, quite wrongly, as most suitable for consumptives. But Reggie's health did not improve, and after his mother had consulted her friend Cecil Rhodes, then Prime Minister of the Cape, he was despatched to the Kimberley Sanatorium where he spent the greater part of a year, after which he stayed with Rhodes as his guest, having the run of the Cape Premier's fine library and astonishing his host by his scientific knowledge. Meanwhile his health gradually deteriorated, and in May 1899 his mother journeyed out to South Africa to bring him home. On their return to England they went to Seaham Hall, since the mistaken view still prevailed that sea air was beneficial to consumptives. All that happened was that Reggie's coughing got steadily worse.

'You will be sorry to hear that Reggie is very weak,' his mother wrote to Rhodes on 8 September 1899 from Seaham Hall; 'he really is too good for this world—his patience is exemplary. Since I wrote I have had a great shock as my eldest boy's horse ran away with him and turned head over heels: he had a bad concussion but I am thankful to say he is all right. He is engaged to be married, which I am very glad of, to Harry Chaplin's girl who is pretty, nice and everything that could be wished.' On 14 September, Edith Chaplin wrote to her future mother-in-law: 'I can't tell you how much I feel for you just now. It is so hard for you, poor dear Reggie being so ill. You must be having a dreadful time, I am *so so* sorry.

I wish I knew what to say to cheer you up; the only thing he being so ill one can hardly wish him to continue in pain and suffering.'

On 25 September Charley Castlereagh wrote to his fiancée: 'I have not seen Reggie yet as I write, but he is awfully weak and on Saturday night went into a dead faint; for a short while he was quite given up. It was due to failure of the heart and they had to give him opium for the other complaint which of course is the worst thing possible for the heart.' Next day he wrote again: 'I only saw Reggie for a moment before dinner last night but sat with him for about ¾ hour today, but he gets weaker every day and now it is hardly possible to hear what he says.'

Three days later Reggie rallied slightly and Charley reported that he was 'much better', so that he concluded it was safe to go fishing in Perthshire. On 3 October he wrote to Edie Chaplin who was at Dunrobin Castle: 'We have got a new idea now of having the wedding earlier quietly about the week of 1 November, and then if anything did happen to poor Reggie just then it could be put off to the original date, but it is for you to decide . . .' Unfortunately Reggie's improvement did not last. By this time he had a nurse and Dr Donellan was also in attendance. Shortly after seven o'clock on the morning of 9 October, his strength gave way and it was clear that he was dying. His mother and sister, as well as the nurse and doctor, stayed by his bedside during the last hours. A message was sent to Lord Londonderry, who was at Wynyard, but he arrived too late, while Charley, who was also sent for, came down from Scotland in the afternoon.

Because of his fondness for Seaham, which dated from his days with the trains, Reggie asked that he should be buried there, and in accordance with his wishes the funeral took place privately three days later at Old Seaham Church. In tribute to his memory the local shops were closed for two hours while the service was taking place, blinds were drawn on windows, and a sizeable crowd turned out in the rain to pay their last respects to this talented and lovable young man. Six of the engine-drivers with whom he had spent so many hours of his youth carried his coffin to the grave, over which his mother later erected a large Celtic stone cross. Among the many wreaths and other floral tributes was a large spray inscribed from 'Cecil Rhodes to a young and esteemed friend'.

Among the letters of sympathy which Lord Londonderry received at Wynyard was one from Edward Carson, who had migrated from Dublin to London and was shortly to be appointed Solicitor-General. 'You always are such a good friend,' replied Londonderry. 'I know you will feel for us. Charley is well and in London. He and Miss Chaplin are the one bright spot.'

5

Charley Castlereagh and Edith Chaplin were married at St Peter's, Eaton Square, on 28 November 1899. The bride was given away by her father, who was then President of the Board of Agriculture in Lord Salisbury's Cabinet. On her arrival with her father at the church the Corporal-Major of the bridegroom's regiment stepped forward and presented her with a bouquet, tied with the Blues' colours. Officers and men of the bride-groom's squadron lined the nave on both sides. The best man was the bridegroom's close friend and fellow subaltern in the regiment Lieutenant Harold Brassey, destined to be killed in action in the First World War. The service was conducted by the Bishop of Rochester, assisted by the Vicar of Blankney and Lord Londonderry's private chaplain.

The wedding reception took place in Stafford House, where the bride's aunt Millicent Duchess of Sutherland received the guests at the top of the grand staircase. When the time came for the 'going away', the bride and her husband left by the famed great glass doors which were never opened except for a crowned head or a bride on her departure. The Sutherlands had placed Lilleshall, their Shropshire seat, at the couple's disposal, and the honeymoon was spent there. It concluded with a visit to Seaham Harbour where they received presents of two fine pieces of silver-plate and a silver punch bowl.

Since Charley Castlereagh was a serving officer, there was a chance that he would be sent to South Africa since the Boer War was then at its height, and in fact on the very next day a considerable contingent embarked at Southampton drawn from the regiments of the Household Cavalry. However, Charley's parents were able to pull strings to prevent his going off to the battle front and much to his disappointment he was ordered to stay behind with the rest of the regiment. 'I know I am a horrid beast to wish to have gone,' he told his wife, 'but it is the only ambition I have ever had . . . If I hadn't got you and had to stay behind I should hang myself I believe.'

After the honeymoon Charley had to return to his regiment, but he managed to get some leave in the New Year, for much of January and February, which he and his wife spent mostly hunting in Leicestershire, having taken a hunting box called The Cottage at Whissendine, a large strung-out village in Rutlandshire between Oakham and Melton Mowbray full of red brick houses but with magnificent views over what is perhaps the finest open hunting country in England. 'Tomorrow,' he wrote from Hyde Park Barracks to his wife at Whissendine on 7 March 1900, 'I have to escort the Queen from Paddington to Buckingham Palace which will be a most uncomfortable long trot on a rough horse. I do wish we could go at a slow canter instead.'

The occasion was part of the celebrations for the relief of Ladysmith, and Charley, who commanded the escort, rode beside the step of the Queen's carriage. When the cavalcade reached the Palace and took leave of Her Majesty in the main courtyard, the Queen asked one of her military aides who the young, fair, good-looking subaltern was in charge of the escort. When she was told, she turned round at the top of the steps leading into the Palace and bowed most graciously to him. Castlereagh always said it was most moving and done with perfect dignity. She was then over eighty. Shortly afterwards, on returning to Whissendine from a day's hunting to their traditional tea of bacon and eggs, the Castlereaghs found a letter which had just been delivered by a special messenger from the Queen commanding them to dine and sleep at Windsor that night, the letter no doubt having been brought on from some other address. 'We were terribly fussed,' Edith Castlereagh afterwards recalled, '—fussed at being unable to obey the command, and fussed at the idea of obeying it! However, shortly after, another command reached us giving us longer notice, and away we went.' She later described the visit:

> Queen Victoria always liked to see the children of her friends, and used to summon the newly married couples for inspection. The Queen was wheeled into the room in a chair she always used then, and after our presentations she was pushed along in it to the room in which she dined. We were the only guests, apart from the Household, and conversation was carried on in hushed tones round quite a small table, the Queen taking very little part. After dinner a circle was formed round her wheeled chair, and you were called to the centre for five or ten minutes. The chair was very low, and you had to bend down to speak to her Majesty. Although she was very frail physically, you were immediately struck by the alertness of her mind and the extraordinary manner in which she remembered and referred to relatives and incidents connected with both our families. This was the last occasion on which either of us saw Queen Victoria alive. In less than a year her long reign had ended.

Considering that he was the regimental adjutant, it is remarkable how much sport Charley was able to get in at this time, hunting, polo, deer stalking, fishing, shooting and so on, not to mention dinners with plenty to drink. 'I was damned ill yesterday,' he wrote to his wife on 19 April 1900: 'I had a sort of chill and a bad liver attack. I think I must have eaten too much . . . It always happens the same way that if I leave you behind, you never follow me. Something always happens to stop you coming, you really are rather a devil.' By this time Edith was pregnant, and we find her husband writing to her about a month later from Hyde Park Barracks: 'You must not be depressed and unhappy and you must not cry. Don't as it is not good for you . . . You know I love you: why do you write and ask me if I do? . . . Please don't be depressed or I shall give up being Adjutant.'

That autumn Edith spent much of her time at Wynyard while her husband was deer stalking at Dunrobin Castle, the Duke of Sutherland's

Scottish seat. On 26 September he wrote that he was going stalking with her brother Eric Chaplin. Eric's other sister Florence Chaplin was also staying at Dunrobin and in the evening there was some good humoured horseplay, encouraged by a beaker of 1796 brandy. 'We had a bit of a fight last night and I being somewhat tired got into Florence's bed, clothes and all (Florence was not in it) and remained until I was kicked out. I then unlaced Florence who would keep on betting me to begin at the bottom, so I did (with a damned good smack).' A few days later, before drinking the health of the Monarch of the Glen in more 1796 brandy: 'We had the devil of a day, 6 stags between us. Eric got 4. I could have got 2 more easily but spared them as I did not think they were big enough.'

Edith had decided to have her child in Stafford House and so she was installed there early in December. 'I can lunch with you at 1.30 if that will suit,' her husband wrote to her on the 6th. 'Telephone me if it will.' In fact the child was born that same day, a girl, which apparently so disappointed Lord Londonderry that he excused himself from attending the christening. But Theresa agreed to be one of the sponsors. 'Mama has graciously consented to be the brat's Goddam, so there's one for you,' the baby's father wrote from Wynyard a fortnight later. 'You must get the remainder.' Presumably the mother did so, since the baby daughter was duly christened Maureen Helen.

Queen Victoria died at Osborne on 22 January 1901, her reign having lasted more than sixty-three years. Lord Salisbury's Government, after consulting her eldest son and successor King Edward VII, decided to send a distinguished special ambassador formally to announce to the crowned heads of Europe and to the Sultan the Queen's death and the accession of the new sovereign. The individual chosen for this mission was the former commander-in-chief of the army Field Marshal Viscount Wolseley, and he took Castlereagh with him as his A.D.C. On their arrival by train in Vienna they were received with great formality and were driven to the Hofburg where initially they were to stay as the guests of the Austrian Emperor Franz Josef. On reaching the Burg Lord Wolseley sent his A.D.C. with one of the court officials to find out where their rooms were located in the great palace. Afterwards Charley Castlereagh sent his wife an account of what happened:

> I remember ascending the staircase and was greeted at the top by a domestic clothed in the Imperial livery. I noticed that this individual appeared to be somewhat familiar, but never having travelled abroad I was under the impression that this was probably the natural habit of the Austrians towards guests and foreigners. The official accompanied me the whole length of the corridor whilst I requested him to be good enough to show me the apartments which had been set aside for the use of Lord Wolseley and the mission. When we arrived at the end of the corridor, the functionary turned round and proceeded to walk me back along the same corridor. With each step we took his familiarity increased, until at length he insisted on taking

my arm, and in this manner we progressed until we arrived back again at the top of the stairs up which Lord Wolseley was advancing. By that time I had discovered what Lord Wolseley and the rest of his suite noticed at once, and with much amusement, that the functionary was most hopelessly drunk!

Shortly afterwards the mission moved to the Hotel Imperial, which was a good deal more comfortable than the old-fashioned rooms in the Burg. They also dined at the British Embassy. 'Sir William Plunkett is the ambassador,' Charley wrote to his mother 'and the attachés are not of a type to impress the Austrians.' Sightseeing included a visit to the arsenal and an inspection of Mannlicher rifles and carbines, which Charley felt would have special interest for his mother who, surprisingly enough for those days, was a crack shot with a rifle. But he did not think much of the horsemanship in the military riding school.

From Vienna they went on to Belgrade where they met King Alexander and Queen Draga of Serbia, both soon to be brutally murdered. 'At the British Legation in Belgrade there was a reception of the Serbian élite . . . At the banquet I sat next to a Serbian who next year is going to represent Serbia in London at the Telegraphic Congress. I hope that before that time he will take a bath or two as he smelt worse than anything you can imagine. This failing was unfortunately very common among the Serbians and Romanians.' However it did not apparently extend to the Queen of Romania, who wrote much under her pseudonym 'Carmen Sylva', and who gave the young A.D.C. a beautiful blue-and-gold native dress to take home to his wife. He wrote to his mother:

> *Pera Palace Hotel, Constantinople. 13 April 1901.*
> We have had a very nice time here and have been well taken care of by the old Turk. Yesterday we went to the Palace to see the Sultan Abdul Hamid . . . In the evening we dined at the Palace; our embassy, the English Embassy and their wives and a few leading pashas (the Sultan did not dine) making up the party. Mrs Willie James [the famous Edwardian hostess] who was staying with the ambassador came as a special favour and received the order of Shefatkat from the Sultan who was quite delighted with her; the embassy wives were furious as most of them had not been offered the order and those who had were not allowed to take it by the Government. Mrs James will never be allowed to wear it except as an ornament.

The Sultan, who took Mrs James to be the A.D.C.'s wife, having first asked his permission, kept plying her with cigarettes and sweetmeats, and was obviously much attracted to her. But the embassy wives really had little cause for jealousy, since Charley Castlereagh, as he subsequently told his wife, understood that the decoration which Mrs James had received was the Order of Chastity Second Class. Incidentally the Sultan kept 370 women in his harem in the Yildiz palace where he entertained the British party.

The tour ended at Athens, taking in Troy on the way, as well as the

Olympic Games and the Marathon Race, after which Lord Wolseley
embarked on a yacht at the Piraeus for a cruise, while the rest of the
mission returned home, having spent an interesting and rewarding five
weeks, particularly since the Sultan Abdul Hamid presented every member of the mission with a gold cigarette case studded with diamonds.

While Castlereagh was on his official round of the European capitals
with Lord Wolseley, Edith went off on a holiday to Spain with her uncle
and aunt, the Sutherlands. They went by train to Barcelona, where they
picked up the Duke's yacht and cruised round Spain, stopping at Algeciras
and Gibraltar, where they met the Duke of Marlborough, Lord Wimborne
and Winston Churchill, all cousins of her husband Charley, who were
dubbed 'The Three Musketeers'. They then continued the journey by
train, having to wait for some time at Bobadilla, the rail junction notorious
for such delays. Here Edith went for a walk with Winston Churchill,
noting afterwards in her diary that they 'found the country to consist
chiefly of smells—and swine!' Later when they met again at Granada, 'a
scene of revelry ensued where wine, added to Winston's wit, made things
go round. While these revels were proceeding, all our luggage had been
muddled up and put into the wrong rooms, even into those of strangers.
There was frightful confusion, lots of noises, and most amusing badinage'.
Next day they heard fragments of conversation between two ladies:

> First lady: Have you heard there is a troupe of music hall singers arrived here
> last night?
> Second lady: Music hall singers! Why, it's the Duchess of Sutherland's party!

There followed exclamations of astonishment and disbelief.

Edith Castlereagh left the yacht at Algiers and made her way to Paris,
where she met her brother Eric, a pioneer motoring enthusiast, who had
just acquired a 24 h.p. Morse. After visiting Versailles and Fontainebleau
'at forty miles an hour', they made for Le Havre, being stopped on the way
by the French police for speeding but allowed to go on when they said,
greatly to the gendarme's surprise, that their '*destination*' was '*Londres*'.
'This was in April, 1901,' Edith recalled long afterwards, 'when none, or
very few of our friends ventured in motors. Cars were very unreliable—
you never knew at what hour you might arrive—if ever.'

When they were in London and Charley was not on duty in barracks,
the Castlereaghs lived with Lord and Lady Londonderry at Londonderry
House, going down to Oakham for an occasional week end and for as
much hunting as they could fit in during the winter. 'There were drawbacks, it is true, in not having our own house in London,' Edith wrote
later, 'but any drawbacks were more than balanced by the opportunities
we had for meeting everyone in London or from the continent at Londonderry House. My mother-in-law's acquaintances ranged from crowned

heads and prime ministers to poets and sculptors and men of letters. She often sent for me to have tea with her in the drawing-room, but we never went there unless there was a message from her to say she wanted to see us. On the occasions on which King Edward used to pay her a private call you would see a small plain single brougham outside the front door, and we knew that the King was there, and if we found a message from her to go to the drawing-room we knew who her visitor was likely to be.'

It was after one of these royal visits that Lady Londonderry, who had dressed rather early for dinner, happened to go into the drawing room before her usual time and discovered one of the housemaids, duster in hand, sitting in all the chairs by turn. The housemaid had not heard her and Lady Londonderry, guessing the purpose of her behaviour, immediately pointed to a particular chair, saying: 'That is the chair the King sat in. Now have a good sit in it!'

At the larger royal parties there seems to have been an excess of guests, not to mention some 'gate-crashing'. One such occasion was the reception Lady Londonderry gave to celebrate the King's birthday on 26 June 1903. 'The crowd at Londonderry House was the densest I had ever seen at a London party,' Sir Almeric Fitzroy wrote at the time. 'The rooms upstairs were never full because a large section of the company had to remain in the hall, and a still larger body was collected in Park Lane and never entered the house. On his return from conducting Princess Christian to her carriage, Lord Londonderry was very nearly torn in pieces, and the struggle to get out of the house was one of superhuman difficulty. One girl fainted in the street and had to be laid out on the pavement, and one or two others collapsed inside the building.' Again, when the Londonderrys gave a ball for the young King of Spain Alphonso XIII, which was also attended by Edward VII, 'the two Kings did not hit off their arrival at the same moment,' according to Fitzroy, 'and our Sovereign waited for five or ten minutes in the hall, where many people brushed past him without noticing who he was. I understand that the fault did not lie with those who were responsible for the King of Spain's movements, as it had been arranged that the two Kings should reach the ballroom separately, but apparently King Edward thought better, and on his arrival determined to wait for the other'.

In the spring of 1902, Edith again found herself pregnant, and she and her husband established themselves in a house in Regent's Park, 21 Cumberland Terrace. It was from here that he hurriedly scribbled a pencilled note to Theresa on 18 November 1902:

My dearest Mother,
    Edith has just had a boy in about two minutes. Both doing well.
                                        Ever your loving son
                                        Charley

The Castlereaghs' son and heir was baptised in the following month in the Chapel Royal, St James's Palace. King Edward VII personally stood sponsor, and the baby was christened Edward Charles Stewart Robert, the ceremony being performed by the ninety-two-year-old Vicar of Seaham, the Rev. Angus Bethune, who had christened three generations of Londonderrys and had been private chaplain to Frances Anne. Afterwards the King presented the baby with a fine old gilt porringer as a christening gift.

Although the baby's last name was Robert, he was always called Robin. However, his grandmother Theresa favoured Robert, which for some reason his father always disliked. 'I hope you are not telling everyone that Robin is to be called Robert,' Charley wrote to his mother some time afterwards, 'as I hate the name of Robert and am quite regretting that he was ever christened Robert.' Yet it had been the great Castlereagh's Christian name.

6

There is no evidence apart from gossip that Theresa Londonderry was Edward VII's mistress at any time, either when he was Prince of Wales or later when he became King, although according to one story he and not Lord Helmsley was the father of her son Reginald. However, the King liked her as a friend and appreciated her rumbustious character. He also liked her husband and he particularly enjoyed the shooting parties at Wynyard, during one of which he held a specially convened meeting of the Privy Council in the house for the purpose of appointing his host Lord President of the Council. In 1890, he wrote from Wynyard:

> We had a wonderfully good day's shooting here, about 2,600 rabbits! and 408 pheasants. It is the biggest rabbit day, I think, I ever had. Herbert Bismarck [son of the German Chancellor] was out and although his gun went off occasionally when it was not intended, he did nobody any harm.

On this occasion the Prince of Wales was accompanied by his Danish Princess. Besides Count Herbert von Bismarck, who had recently resigned as German Foreign Minister at the same time as his father was 'dropped' by the Kaiser William II, the other guests included the host's brother Lord Herbert Vane-Tempest; also Londonderry's cousin Lord Randolph Churchill and his beautiful wife Jennie; two of the Prince's ADCs, the Duke of Montrose and Lord Coke, with their equally beautiful wives; Henry Chaplin, MP, President of the Board of Agriculture and a widower, whose daughter Edith was to marry the host's son Charley Castlereagh; James Lowther, M.P., a noted bachelor sportsman and close friend of Theresa Londonderry, who lived at nearby Wilton Castle, Redcar; and finally the Danish Minister in London, M. Christian de

Falbe, and his rich wife, who had inherited Luton Hoo, one of England's stateliest homes in Bedfordshire. In fact, it was in Madame de Falbe's boudoir at Luton Hoo that just over a year later the Prince's elder son Albert Victor, now Duke of Clarence, and heir presumptive to the throne, became engaged to Princess May of Teck, only to die of pneumonia a few weeks afterwards. M. de Falbe was described as a quick, pleasant man with a rather bald head and an imperial, *persona grata* with Princess Alexandra and, through her, with other adjacent members of the Royal Family.

The Privy Council was held at Wynyard on 19 October 1903 and put Sir Almeric Fitzroy to some personal inconvenience, since he complained that he had to travel five hundred miles in twenty-four hours at a time when he was particularly busy, 'in order to assist at a ceremony that will occupy ten seconds'. The appointment was occasioned by the resignation of the Duke of Devonshire,[1] along with Joseph Chamberlain and several other ministers who left the Government on the issue of tariff reform. Arthur Balfour, by this time Prime Minister, wished to appoint his uncle and predecessor Lord Salisbury Lord President, but according to Fitzroy the King thought that 'Londonderry would be a better choice'. And so it came about Fitzroy travelled from King's Cross to Thorpe Thewles, the nearest station to Wynyard, along with several others who were joining the house party, including the Duke of Devonshire, the retiring Lord President. Fitzroy noted in his diary at the time:

> Lord Londonderry and his son met us at the station, and on reaching Wynyard we found most of the party lingering over tea in the library. The King told me he would hold the Council immediately after dinner, and was much interested to hear that, so far as we had been able to trace, the last occasion on which a Council had been held in a country house belonging to a subject was in October 1625, when Charles I held one at Wilton, the Lord Pembroke of the day being his Chamberlain. Lady Londonderry was greatly excited over the event, and was particularly pleased to learn that the King desired the documents connected with the Council to be headed 'At the Court at Wynyard', which is indeed the old style.[2]

Immediately after the ladies had left the dining room the King called Fitzroy to him to say that the Duke of Devonshire would preside as usual. 'He will assist at his own funeral,' was how the King put it, in Fitzroy's words, 'with great good humour.' It is noteworthy that on this occasion

[1] The Duke of Devonshire, formerly Lord Hartington and nicknamed 'Harty-Tarty', was the elder brother of the ill-fated Lord Frederick Cavendish, who had been assassinated in Dublin in 1882. Originally a Liberal, he followed Joseph Chamberlain as a Liberal–Unionist. He had been Lord President since the formation of the Salisbury Government in 1895. Three times he declined the office of Prime Minister, fearing his acceptance would break up the Liberal Party on the Irish Home Rule issue.

[2] See frontispiece.

the King was not accompanied by Queen Alexandra, nor was the King's mistress Alice Keppel by her husband.

Sir Almeric Fitzroy returned to London next morning. 'His Majesty was very late for breakfast,' he noted, 'but no one waited for him, and he came in quite unconcernedly in the middle of the meal. He went out shooting about 10.30, and I took a walk in the gardens . . . before it was time to start [for London]. The surroundings of the place are heavy and unattractive, and the atmosphere gloomy with Middlesborough smoke.'

In 1893, Londonderry was prominent in opposing Gladstone's Second Home Rule Bill, which was rejected by the House of Lords, and he presided over the great meeting at which the political alliance between the Conservatives and the Liberal-Unionists led by Joseph Chamberlain was formally ratified. When the Conservatives returned to power two years later, Lord Salisbury offered Londonderry the post of Lord Privy Seal. This was declined, since Londonderry wished for an office with departmental responsibilities. In 1900 he entered the Government as Postmaster-General, and in 1902 he joined the Cabinet as first President of the Board of Education, although he felt diffident about his capacity for the post. 'Lord Londonderry, with Sir W. Anson as his lieutenant, may make an efficient President,' was Almeric Fitzroy's comment at the time of his appointment. 'At any rate he will be popular with his staff, and may be trusted to listen to advice.' However, his incursion into the debate on the Committee Stage of Mr Balfour's Education Bill in December 1902 was marked by what Fitzroy called a singular episode. 'He gaily met one amendment with an answer that was intended for another, and left the House in a state of complete obfuscation. However, he is so pleasant, and animated with such an obvious desire to do his duty as the Minister in charge of the department that no one takes him to task.' It may be added that he did not give up Education when he became Lord President of the Council, but contrived to combine both posts, using the Lord President's room for his departmental work, no doubt on account of its fine view over the Horse Guards Parade and the fact that it got all the afternoon sun.

Theresa Londonderry took a keen interest in her husband's departmental work, particularly when it affected County Durham, and she did not scruple to use her influence to this end. A few weeks after the Privy Council meeting at Wynyard, Almeric Fitzroy recorded in his diary:

23 November 1903. A curious scene was to be witnessed in the bow-window of the Lord President's room this morning. For more than two hours Lady Londonderry presided over a departmental consultation as to the steps to be taken in dealing with the Durham County Council in its treatment of the voluntary schools of the county. It is true the Lord President was nominally a party to the conference, but he remained at the end of the table in isolated dignity, while Lady L. held the Permanent

Secretary and the subordinate official immediately concerned in close communion.

The Bishop of Durham had appealed to Her Ladyship, and I am informed that she displayed the utmost quickness and mastery of detail in handling the subject, and a power of apprehension of principles that astonished the officials.

'It is certainly a new departure,' commented Fitzroy on this extraordinary confrontation, 'when a Minister's wife undertakes to look into matters of departmental administration in the very seat of her husband's authority, and leaves to him the simple functions of an interested listener.'

Another ceremonial duty which Londonderry performed was that of bearer of the Sword of State at the Coronation. This had been fixed for 26 June 1902. The celebrations began with a grand military review at Aldershot on the 16th, the Court having moved from Windsor to the damp and uncomfortable Pavilion two days previously. In the middle of the night of the 14th, the King was seized with violent internal pains and two doctors were hurriedly sent for. It was clear that he was seriously ill; however, in a well meant but misguided attempt to reassure the public who had heard disquieting rumours of the King's health, it was announced that he was suffering from an attack of lumbago and consequently would not be able to take the salute at the march past but that Queen Alexandra would deputise for him. Among the 31,000 troops taking part in the review were the North Down Rifles of which Lord Londonderry was Honorary Colonel. Since the officers particularly wished Londonderry to be with them, Charley rehearsed him, being, in his mother's words 'most anxious that his father would not salute like a volunteer, so took great pains to practise him'. At the review he rode a horse called Miracle which had been bred at Wynyard and, as the Queen subsequently told Theresa, he 'went by beautifully'. For her part Queen Alexandra carried off the situation perfectly, driving on to the parade ground in an open carriage in spite of the pouring rain. Immediately after the parade was over—it lasted two and a half hours—the Court returned to Windsor, the King and Queen making the journey in a slow horse-drawn carriage, with the doctors following discreetly behind in a second carriage. It was also Ascot week, and a large party had been invited including Theresa and her husband. 'I had always wished to go to Windsor for Ascot,' wrote Theresa at the time, 'and was delighted when the invitation came in the old fashioned way—to dinner Monday night and stay the week . . .'

'We are beautifully housed in the York Tower overlooking the long walk,' Theresa continued her account of her visit. 'The rooms are lovely, upholstered in yellow and gold . . . Horace Farquhar [Master of the King's Household] paid us a visit and told us the King was much better but would not dine.' Besides the household and the Londonderrys, the party included the Duke of Cambridge, Prince Arthur of Connaught, the Duke and Duchess of Portland, Lords Spencer, Cadogan, Pembroke and Clarendon, and from the diplomatic corps the Marquis de Soveral and Count Mensdorff.

> I had not dined at Windsor since April [1888] when the late Queen gave 'C' [Lord Londonderry] the Garter, but had been up to the Castle to lunch the day of the late Queen's funeral, and well remember my feelings at seeing what was virtually a ball supper with all the usual guests—only all in deep mourning and sad countenance . . .
>
> We assembled in the dark green drawing room and the Queen came into the room about five minutes late. We dined in the dining room where the gold Punch bowl is —a beautiful table all pink roses, Sèvres and low gold bowls and vases. In the middle of the wall is Constable's picture of the late Queen, a really beautiful conception of the Queen and Empress of India. It is lighted admirably. The Queen walked about and talked most of the evening, the Ladies and Gentlemen coming out of dinner together . . .
>
> I hear the King does not go to the races. I feel so sorry, but think him wise in view of next week.

Just before the party set off for Ascot, the King sent for Theresa. 'I was agreeably surprised to see him looking so well, though of course pulled down,' she noted. 'He seemed in excellent spirits and bore his disappointment well. He has a charming sitting room overlooking the East Terrace. I did and do feel for him, his first Ascot as King, and also having had to miss the racing, but it would not do to take any liberties considering next week.' After the racing, when another horse bred at Wynyard, Carbine, was so badly ridden, according to Theresa, that he was beaten by a neck for the Ascot Stakes, the party returned to the Castle for tea in the green drawing room. ('The Queen made jokes about it not being supposed to be right to have the gentlemen up to tea, but they came.') After dinner the Queen played bridge and talked about the ball which had been arranged for the Friday. But this had to be cancelled owing to the death of the King of Saxony. 'Really too unlucky and unfortunate and seems a bad omen,' noted Theresa. 'I have not seen the King again but hope to do so before I leave.' She did so just before her departure on the Saturday. 'I found him pale and weak, but he assured me he felt as if he had been ill but was now all right.' At this time the King was still determined to go through with the Coronation on the appointed day. 'I will go to the Abbey though it kills me,' he said repeatedly.

After they got back to Londonderry House, the Londonderrys went to two rehearsals in Westminster Abbey, at the second of which, two days before the Coronation was due to take place, Lord Londonderry was coached in his duties of carrying the Sword of State. During this rehearsal, Lord Esher, who was in charge of the arrangements, suddenly appeared and announced that the Coronation was postponed since at that moment

the King was undergoing an operation in Buckingham Palace for perityph-
litis.

To attempt to describe the horror, consternation and grief evinced by everyone
is impossible [Theresa Londonderry's account continues]. 'C' and I rushed off to
Buckingham Palace and waited to hear that the operation had gone off well. Since
that thank Heaven H.M. has progressed well, though of course he cannot be pronounced out of danger for 60 hours. I hear his pluck is marvellous and his one
thought was that the people would be disappointed. One wonder was that H.M. was
not kept in bed at the beginning of this chill as it evidently arose from fatigue. It is
horrible seeing all the decorations being pulled down, the streets crowded.

Friday [27 June]. Yesterday we went to St Margaret's for a service, most affecting,
Litany prayers, hymns and the first verse of the National Anthem on our knees. I
think everyone cried. Today we hear there is a slight increase of pain in the wound,
but this morning's bulletin is excellent. Everyone has a rather more cheerful view.
One cannot help wondering what the doctors were doing allowing the King to drive
much less walk. It seems incredible people should be so stupid, or really it is criminal. No one thinks or talks of anything else. There are immense crowds outside
the Palace. Large parties of country people perambulating everywhere. But one still
hopes for the best.

In fact, the doctors were not to blame, apart from Sir Francis Laking's
responsibility, after appendicitis had been diagnosed, in informing the
press that the King was suffering from a severe attack of lumbago. Laking
prescribed a 'low' diet and advised His Majesty to spend as much time as
possible in bed, which he certainly did during Ascot week, although he
did go out but did not attend the races. However, when he returned to
Buckingham Palace, he was examined by Laking and Sir Thomas Barlow
who told him that he would certainly die unless he submitted to an
operation without delay.

After considerable argument the King was persuaded to agree, and the
operation was carried out successfully by Sir Frederick Treves, lasting
forty minutes and being pronounced a complete success. His recovery
was remarkably rapid. A week or so later the Prince of Wales was astonished to see him smoking a cigar and reading a newspaper. After conferring
baronetcies on Laking and Treves for having saved his life, he embarked
on the royal yacht on 15 July for a convalescent cruise. About the same
time it was announced that the postponed Coronation would be between
8 and 12 August. In the event it took place on the 8th, by which date most
of the distinguished foreign visitors had returned home, but although the
ritual was somewhat shortened to spare the King from fatigue, the occasion lost nothing in its impressiveness and the popular enthusiasm was
undiminished. A portion of the gallery in the Abbey had been screened
off and reserved for the King's particular women friends: irreverently
referred to as 'The King's Loose Box', it accommodated a bevy of beauties
including the French actress Sarah Bernhardt, Lady Kilmorey, Lady
Londonderry, Mrs Arthur Paget and the reigning favourite Alice Keppel.

However the great day was to leave Theresa Londonderry with some unfortunate memories. Things began to go wrong as she was driving down Park Lane from Londonderry House in the family coach. Apparently she was alone, her husband having gone on independently so as to take up his position as bearer of the Sword of State. The horses drawing the coach became excited and the coachman had difficulty in controlling them as they plunged and reared. She thereupon leaned out of the window and ordered some people to get out of the way. Among them was a cab driver who is said to have shouted at her: 'Go and fuck yourself, you and your fucking Coronation!' This could hardly have put her in a good temper. But worse was to come. On reaching the Abbey her Ladyship thought it prudent to retire, in view of the long ceremony ahead, to the convenience which had been provided for the use of peeresses. She remained there so long that a queue of peeresses formed outside the door and as time passed their impatience became voluble. Suddenly Theresa's voice was heard calling for a pair of forceps. Could it be? After all she was forty-six. But no. A desperate message was sent to the nearest doctor in the Abbey, and he duly appeared with a pair of forceps. Theresa finally emerged looking slightly dishevelled and explained what had happened. As she had been readjusting her train, her tiara with the famous Londonderry jewels had fallen into the lavatory pan, and to retrieve it without damaging the stones nothing less than a gynaecological instrument had been required.

7

Although the King and Queen had been to Wynyard many times, they had never visited Mount Stewart. After the Coronation they toured Scotland and in the autumn the King visited the City of London, lunched with the Lord Mayor and Corporation and two days later went to St Paul's Cathedral for a service of thanksgiving for his restoration to health. Various foreign tours in the Royal Yacht were planned for the following year to places as far afield as Rome and Lisbon. As the royal programme filled up, Theresa despaired of ever seeing Their Majesties in Ulster. However, during the Royal Wedding Anniversary Ball at Buckingham Palace on 10 March 1903, the King assured Theresa that he and the Queen would visit Ireland in the summer and would spend a week-end at Mount Stewart. After 'C' had talked it over with the Lord Lieutenant Lord Dudley, Lord Knollys and other Court officials and finally with the King himself, it was arranged that Their Majesties should go first to Dublin and arrive at Mount Stewart on Saturday, 24 July, and finally visit Belfast on the 26th to unveil a statue of Queen Victoria outside the projected new City Hall and also open the Royal Victoria Hospital which the old Queen was expected to open had she been able to come to Belfast during her last Irish visit in 1900.

'We came over at Whitsuntide,' Theresa wrote afterwards, 'and looking over the house, which I always think one of the most delightful and comfortable in the world, the place looked extraordinarily shabby, and we felt that it must be tidied up for the great occasion. We first arranged the Billiard Room, which was not furnished, and made it a comfortable, living hall with chairs, writing tables, and flower baskets.[1] The drawing room we decided to leave as it was, only adding to it chair tops and cushions of the beautiful embroidery which is worked by the women in the Ards and in which the women of Mount Stewart particularly are most proficient.' Theresa and her husband decided to give the King their own rooms, which were on the ground floor and which incidentally possessed the only bath with running water in the house, a huge affair with a mahogany surround. The Queen was allotted the bedroom called 'Genoa' at the south-west corner of the first floor, having a beautiful view over the gardens and Strangford Lough, while the dressing room next door was turned into a sitting room for Her Majesty, decorated with yellow damask and the walls adorned with prints. An adjacent room, 'Geneva', was similarly done up 'in pretty pink and blue chintz' for Princess Victoria, who was to accompany her parents, while Theresa put on the bed 'my lovely Irish point lace quilt'.

A fortnight before the royal visit was due, disaster struck the Londonderrys. 'Edith Castlereagh is at the point of death,' Lord Esher wrote to his son on 14 July. 'She had a cold, took a Turkish bath on Saturday, and went for a motor drive afterwards. Now she is probably dying of double pneumonia. She is so strong and healthy that her chances are *worse* than those of a weaker and more nervous would be with this particular illness. They all lean on Millie her aunt the Duchess of Sutherland who brought her up. Castlereagh is hopelessly broken down. It will be a tragedy if she dies.' The double pneumonia was complicated by pleurisy. 'For eleven days her life hung in the balance,' Theresa noted afterwards, 'and I really cannot describe the agonies of mind we suffered during this terrible time. Thank Heaven, on Tuesday the 21st the doctor pronounced her out of danger, so being assured, humanely speaking, all would go well with her, we decided to continue the preparations for the visit . . .'

In fact the royal visit was a huge success from the moment the King and Queen alighted from the Royal Train on Newtownards station platform on the Saturday afternoon, 'both seemingly in the highest spirits and most gracious', to the moment when they embarked on the Monday evening from Bangor pier on a launch for the *Victoria and Albert* against

[1] The Billiard Room, in the centre of the south side of the house, then became the Smoking Room.

six lines of battleships. Although it rained on the Saturday afternoon, no one seemed to mind, and the crowds lining the road from Newtownards to Mount Stewart showed no lack of loyal enthusiasm. 'We had tea ready in the Billiard Room, and Their Majesties afterwards walked through the sitting rooms and expressed great approval.'

> I showed them the two historical things we had in the house. The Congress of Vienna chairs, of which we have 22. I think Their Majesties imagined I was drawing the long bow, but when I showed them the print of the Congress of Vienna with the chairs in it, they believed me and were very much impressed.
>
> I showed them the gold snuff box which was given to Robert, first Lord Castlereagh, when he was Chief Secretary for Ireland, with the Freedom of the City of Dublin. This is one of our most treasured possessions. When Mr Morley[1] was given the Freedom of the City of Dublin, he said in a speech that he believed that he was the only Chief Secretary that had received the Freedom of the City. We told him afterwards we should have sent him the snuff box to look at and to show him he was wrong, only we feared we should not get it back, owing to the company he kept!

Sunday was a fine day, with the sun shining brilliantly through the windows. At divine service in the private chapel, Dr Alexander, the Archbishop of Armagh and Primate of All Ireland, preached an eloquent sermon, in which, according to Theresa, he 'alluded to the bitter feuds that had torn this country in pieces, and said we should all strive for peace'. After the service Their Majesties called Theresa into their sitting room and gave her 'a most lovely bracelet, their two miniatures set in diamonds, with the Royal crown and cyphers, and green enamel shamrocks on the sides—it really is beautiful and the miniatures are most wonderful likenesses'. Afterwards Theresa took the Queen round the sea walk along the shore of the Lough.

> She came without a hat, much to the surprise of some of the people on the road, who could not take their eyes off her when they realised it was the Queen. One of those who saw her remarked to me afterwards, 'The Queen is terribly lovely,' which sounds peculiar, but 'terrible' is the strongest adjective they can use here, and it was used in a complimentary manner of course. The sea walk looked lovely, even more so than usual. There was a strong smell of sea weed and a sweet briar, the tide was high, and a beautiful view of the Mourne Mountains above Strangford, and Scrabo looked majestic at the head of the lough. There were masses of birds circling and crying, terns, brown and white gulls, cormorants and sand snipe. We walked in by the [entrance] Lodge, the Queen much pleased with the St John's wort which is a lovely flower, and the Australian laurels and hollies and silver firs, which just now are in beautiful foliage. We came into luncheon, during which the Royal Irish Constabulary played extremely well.
>
> In the afternoon we went in motors to Clandeboye and saw Lady Dufferin, Charley [Theresa's brother Lord Shrewsbury] driving the King and Queen and myself. We went a good pace, the whole country side turning out. The Queen's one idea was, Charley should not drive over a dog, and of course every one we met must

[1] John Morley (later Viscount Morley) was Liberal Chief Secretary for Ireland in 1886 and again from 1892 until 1895.

needs run right in front of the motor, but Charley was lucky in getting past them. We walked all over the house, and one could not help feeling how dear Lord Dufferin[1] would have enjoyed showing the King and Queen over the house and demesne. The King planted a tree in front of the house before he left.

After breakfast on the Monday morning which began with grey skies but brightened up later, there was 'the inevitable photograph'. Then the King and Queen each planted a copper beech on either side of the approach to the main entrance to the house. 'I chose those trees,' noted Theresa, 'as I feel they are longer lived than the conifers, as I hope and trust that Robert's [Robin's] grandchildren will see them beautiful trees.' 'Beautiful place,' Queen Alexandra wrote in the visitors' book, 'but very damp'. The royal party and their host and hostess thereupon set off for Belfast, where the King and Queen were received at the Belfast and County Down railway station by the Lord Mayor, who presented a loyal address from the City Council together with over fifty similar addresses from other bodies, in contrast to the Dublin Corporation which had refused by forty votes to thirty-seven to present any address at all.

Their Majesties were then driven across the river Lagan, where the ships lying at anchor were dressed overall; indeed the whole city, except for the Nationalist areas, was gaily and profusely decorated. Lord Londonderry, as Lord Lieutenant of the City as well as of County Down, headed the procession to the late Queen's statue. 'I was delighted at the tremendous reception he got from the inhabitants of Belfast who know him so well and whom he cares for so much,' his wife wrote afterwards. 'As he reached the statue the sound died away, and we could hear the surge of the cheers for the King and Queen, and no one knows what Belfast can do in the way of a reception until they see it, nor can they form any idea what the sound is like unless they hear it.' After the statue had been duly unveiled ('it really is a most perfect likeness'), Their Majesties went on to open the Royal Victoria Hospital. A luncheon in the Town Hall was followed by a visit to the show grounds at Balmoral, a southern suburb several miles from the City Centre, where there was a horse show.

Finally the King and Queen and the rest of the party returned to the railway station and completed the journey to Bangor by special train to embark on the *Victoria and Albert* in Belfast Lough. 'We drove down to

[1] The 1st Marquess of Dufferin and Ava, statesman and diplomatist, Viceroy of India and Governor-General of Canada, had died in the previous year. He was a great-grandson of the Irish dramatist and M.P. Richard Brinsley Sheridan. Writing to Lord Dufferin in 1846 his mother, *née* Helen Sheridan, reproved him for his careless spelling. 'The reason I tell you of it,' she remarked, 'is that a habit of inattention to that matter easily grows on one; and you might end by writing letters worthy of Lord Londonderry . . . My grandfather Sheridan always affirmed that no Irish peer could spell. Pray don't let his first great-grandson be a proof of his knowledge of the Irish ignorance.'

the pier and walked the length of it,' Theresa wrote afterwards. 'At the end of it the King and Queen and Princess Victoria took leave of us, and I honestly think I never was so sorry to part with guests in my life. They had been so gracious, so charming, and so pleased with everything, and so easily pleased.'

The Londonderrys dined on board the *Majestic*, the flagship of Admiral Lord Charles Beresford, who commanded the Channel squadron ('a nice rest after such an exciting day'), and after dinner watched the Royal Yacht steaming through the battleships, while the *Majestic* sent a message 'Bon voyage and good luck' by siren ('the effect of this was most weird and the sound kept echoing off the next battleship'), while the Royal Yacht answered with signal lights. 'The last we saw of her was melting away into the darkness to the northward, leaving behind her the illuminated fleet.' The King had invited Londonderry to accompany him on board the *Victoria and Albert* for the rest of her voyage round Ireland, but Londonderry, who was not a particularly good sailor, was glad to plead that he had to be in his place in the House of Lords next day to introduce an Education Bill.

'The visit is all over now,' wrote Theresa, 'and one cannot help longing and hoping that it is the first of many, and now that Their Majesties have paid this state visit, they will make this country an integral part of England and Scotland, and pay visits here without any ceremony, as they do the other side of the Irish Channel. Their loyal subjects of all classes will gladly welcome them.'

They were never to visit loyal Ulster again, but there were to be two more royal visits to the south, in 1904 and 1907, when the popular reception was as enthusiastic as before, particularly when the King went racing at Punchestown and Leopardstown in 1904 and when he and the Queen opened the International Exhibition in Dublin in July 1907.

8

It was a great disappointment to Theresa that her son and his wife should have missed the royal visit, but Edith's illness from which she was slowly convalescing made this impossible. Also the doctors recommended that she should go abroad for the winter and her husband was able to obtain leave to accompany her. India and the Far East were chosen for their tour. They travelled out on the same ship with the Viceroy, Lord Curzon, who had been home on leave because of his wife's illness. They were surprised at the warmth of his welcome when the ship reached Bombay. Indeed the Viceroy was surprised himself. 'I was given a great reception in Bombay,' he wrote to the Secretary of State at the time, 'scarcely inferior, if at all, to that which I had when landing under the full glamour of novelty six years ago.' The Castlereaghs began their tour by staying with the Governor of Bombay, Lord Lamington, at Government House on Malabar Point, and there followed visits to various rulers, the Maharajahs of Baroda and Rajputana, the Maharanee of Jodhpur and the Maharajah of Idar, Sir Pertab Singh, who presented Edith Castlereagh with a beautiful Arab horse. Sport, in which they were invited to participate, included polo and pig-sticking. Christmas they spent with Lord Curzon at the Viceroy's attractive country residence at Barrackpore, about fourteen miles from Calcutta, on the east bank of the river Hooghly. After early service Edith never forgot the breakfast under a gigantic banyan tree, 'with shoots like the legs of an octopus hanging down from the tree to the ground . . . the branches making a roof like a perfect umbrella'.

Next day the Castlereaghs returned to Calcutta with Lord Curzon and stayed there as his guests for the Viceroy's Cup, the great horse race of the year. On 28 December 1904, Edith wrote from Government House to her mother-in-law:

> We are having such a splendid time and I think what I have seen so far delightful. I love this country, its people and its climate and the lovely bright colours; the crowd at the races yesterday was most peculiar with all the different races, types and nationalities and their coloured clothes and head dresses looked so bright, very different to our sombre crowds at Epsom and Ascot. Nothing here is out of taste or vulgar, the natives themselves never appear out of place or to jar with their surroundings, and a great many of them, particularly the Arabs I saw in Bombay, are very fine looking high bred men with hooked noses and very short upper lips. I mention this as I know you appreciate it! !
>
> It is sad to reflect that all the above is being rapidly vulgarised by us. Wherever English influence steps in, a terrible mixture of European bad taste appears. The Maharajahs' new palaces are rapidly being filled with coloured glass chandeliers and maple furniture and anything gaudy and atrocious that they can find and that is unmistakably English. What a sad reflection!
>
> Lord Curzon is not very well and so depressed I am sorry for him. I only hope he will not stay on here too long as it is too much to expect anyone to do under the double strain. I don't think his health would stand it for long.

However, shortly after the Castlereaghs had begun the next stage of their journey, to Benares, the Viceroy received word that his wife's health had considerably improved and that she was coming out to India to join him. In Benares where they were the guests of the local Maharajah ('he is a very strict Brahmin and may not go to England'), the Castlereaghs went down the sacred Ganges in a boat, watched bodies 'being burned with wailing relatives sitting around', and the other tourist sights, which Edith described in a letter to her parents-in-law at home:

> *Benares, 3 January 1905* . . . We also saw a temple today called by vulgar globe trotters like ourselves the Monkey Temple . . . It swarms with monkeys which are sacred. They were quite tame and fed out of our hands . . . A young baby monkey in a tree by the river fell in. The river was full of crocodiles who at once swam after

it to eat it. The mother and father monkey and a friend sitting on neighbouring trees at once dived in; the mother took the baby in her arms and with the father one side and the friend on the other side, presumably to defend her, swam to shore. Meantime hundreds of other monkeys lined both banks of the river and hurled stones at the crocodiles to cover their friends' retreat. Eventually they all escaped. Wasn't it an extraordinary scene to have witnessed? It only shows how horribly human monkeys are.

We go from here to Lucknow on Thursday morning. Lord Curzon and Colonel Baring [the Viceroy's Military Secretary] have been too kind for words and we are travelling right through all these towns in a state carriage which waits for us everywhere and where possible we stay in guest houses belonging to the different Maharajahs whose states we pass through. So we are having a very easy time. We raced, rode, saw steeplechases, polo and cricket, danced, played tennis and every sort of romp all the time at Calcutta; as you can imagine it was the greatest fun.

They did not miss much. Their special coach took them in succession to Lucknow, Delhi, Agra, Amritsar, Lahore, Rawalpindi, Peshawar, whence they were able to explore the Khyber Pass and the North-West Frontier territory, which Charley was to revisit officially thirty years later as Air Minister. They then retraced their steps to Hyderabad and Madras and finally left India for Singapore, Hong Kong and Japan, where Edith amongst other experiences had one of her legs tattooed with a snake pattern. In Yokohama they found 'an eccentric English friend ensconced in the country, who had cut himself adrift from Europe. He was living out there as a native, with delight and happiness, enjoying life very much, and the companionship of a gifted Geisha'. Having now gone half-way round the world, they decided to complete the round and so crossed the Pacific to Vancouver, a rough voyage which took fifteen days but was otherwise uneventful, and so home via Toronto, Ottawa and New York.

By the time they got back to England Balfour's Conservative Government was nearing the end of its life and it seemed that a General Election must come fairly quickly. Charley's parents were both anxious that he should resign his commission in the Blues and go in for politics, following the family tradition. For the moment, however, Castlereagh was more interested in polo than politics. Nevertheless his father was adamant and, as he held the purse strings, Charley had no alternative but to obey and resign his commission. 'With a heavy heart my husband agreed,' Edith wrote afterwards, 'and I cannot think that I was any help to him in this decision. I much preferred the easy going soldiering life, but the fiat had gone forth. The difficulty was to find a seat near London, which was our ambition.'

Charley's father would have liked to see his son Member for County Down, but there was nothing available there. For weeks Charley haunted Conservative Central Office. The trouble was that by this time all the good seats already had candidates and what was left was chiefly in the category of forlorn hopes. He was interviewed at Chatham, Shrewsbury, and for a seat in London, but failed to be selected for any of them. Eventually the Home Secretary Aretas Akers-Douglas (later Lord Chilston), who was a Cabinet colleague of Charley's father and had an estate near Maidstone, suggested to Londonderry that there might be a chance at Maidstone where the prospective candidate had withdrawn for private reasons, although it was considered a reasonably safe Liberal seat.

Towards the end of November Castlereagh went off to Maidstone where the Conservative Executive interviewed him. To his surprise he was selected as prospective candidate at a full meeting of the local Conservative Association on 5 December. He thereupon set about 'nursing' the constituency as assiduously as he could, although time was very short. He was only twenty-eight and furthermore quite inexperienced politically; indeed he had only spoken once at a public meeting, at Seaham during the 1900 election.

Balfour had already resigned as Prime Minister and the formation of a Liberal Government under Sir Henry Campbell-Bannerman was a prelude to the General Election which was expected to be fought early in the New Year, mainly on the issue of Free Trade versus Protection, with the Irish Home Rule question in the background. Castlereagh began by asking his mother to persuade Edward Carson to come down and speak for him. 'Our meeting was a great success,' Carson wrote to Theresa Londonderry on 17 December, 'it was very full and many could not get in. Castlereagh was very well received and made a sensible short speech, not touching on fiscals and leaving the bulk of the evening for me. I was quite delighted with the way he met the people, and he was affable and jolly with them. I hope it may have been of some use . . .'

'I arrived here late last night and return to Maidstone shortly as I am officially adopted on Wednesday,' Castlereagh wrote on Christmas Eve to his mother from Springfield, the house in the hunting country near Oakham which he and his wife had taken on after their round-the-world trip. 'It will be a very near thing and there is a good chance, I think, as they like a lord. I wish we were together at Wynyard but we must hope for the best another year. I shall think of you tomorrow and we shall anyway be together in spirit.'

His mother replied that she would come down and help in any way she could during the campaign. 'It is splendid your coming down here and I am sure your presence will do no end of good,' the candidate replied from the Royal Star Hotel in Maidstone. 'Of course I will make out no programme for you but the fact of your being here and driving about, in fact giving the Maidstone people a show, will assist me a great deal . . . I do not think my polling day will be until the 15th or 16th [January] 1906. Of course it is a great thing for me though I shall be heartily sick of this vote cadging in a very short time.' Nevertheless he had no illusions about his chances, since his Liberal opponent was the sitting member Sir Francis Evans, a baronet and influential businessman, who had come to know the place intimately during the past five years, whereas the Conservative candidate's local knowledge was confined to a few weeks.

Edith returned to Maidstone with her husband. Afterwards Edward Hills, the Chairman of the Conservative Association, wrote of her:

> Endowed with great physical attraction and charm of manner, she was naturally a born electioneer. I have always held the opinion that the average voter is quick to discriminate between natural and assumed friendliness. Lady Castlereagh was always genuine: I have been with her in cottages in the poorest slums where the mother who tended her baby cared little for her visitor as a grand lady, but whose heart was touched by another mother's loving sympathy. Lady Castlereagh possessed another essential of the successful canvasser, viz. cheerfulness, and a happy sense of humour. The stern realities of a strenuous campaign were softened and hard facts became romance in the bright atmosphere of her presence.

Theresa Londonderry, when she appeared on the scene, was much more of the *grande dame* than her daughter-in-law. However, she proved an active canvasser and ready speaker. A few days before polling day, 'she sent down her big barouche with four horses and postillions', according to Mr Hills. 'This paraded the constituency and duly impressed those whom such display influences. I should think it was almost the last time when such an argument was brought to bear on an English electorate.' Nevertheless the Liberals were confident they would hold the seat, particularly as there were such marked signs of a strong Liberal trend throughout the country.

'Wish you every success,' the Conservative leader Arthur Balfour telegraphed the Conservative candidate on the eve of the poll. 'You bear a name which should rally all Unionists to your standard now that the Union is again in peril.'

The majority of the voters turned out on polling day and when the votes were counted in the Town Hall the Conservatives' delight can be imagined after the returning officer announced the result: Lord Castlereagh had defeated Sir Francis Evans by a mere 132 votes.

As Mr Hills was writing down the figures, Sir Francis Evans passed him and remarked pointedly, 'Yes, for the present.' 'Are you going to have a recount?' asked the Conservative Chairman. 'No!' said the Liberal, repeating the words, 'for the present.' This was a clear hint that Evans was thinking of presenting an Election Petition alleging irregular conduct or corrupt practices on the part of the Conservative victor, which was in fact what eventually happened.

The Election throughout the country was a landslide for the Liberals, who captured 377 seats, and their ranks were swelled by the addition of 53 Labour and 83 Irish Nationalists, whereas the Conservatives and

Liberal–Unionists together numbered only 157. Less than a fortnight later Sir Francis Evans filed his election petition, which contained ninety-seven allegations, comprising specific and general bribery by money, treating in public houses, distribution of free meat, illegal voting, and unlawful payments to voters for travelling expenses.

The trial of the petition was heard by Mr Justice Grantham and Mr Justice Lawrence, beginning on 8 May 1906 and lasting a week. Unfortunately Maidstone had a bad record for corrupt practices at elections, and Castlereagh was by no means sure that evidence would not be produced sufficient to unseat him. He had not made his maiden speech in the House of Commons when the trial opened, and he determined to make at least one speech there, so he hurried off from the court on the third day to the House where there was a debate on the Home Rule question. He was fortunate enough to catch the Speaker's eye and was called. Although extremely nervous, he spoke well and to the point and his remarks were on the whole well received. Indeed *The Times* mentioned him in a leading article next day, while Mr James Bryce, the Liberal Chief Secretary for Ireland, paid him a particular compliment when he replied to the debate. 'While disagreeing with the views expressed by the noble Lord,' he said, 'we on this side recognise the talent and grace with which his speech was composed and delivered.' Next morning, when Castlereagh returned to Maidstone for the continuation of the hearing of the petition, he was cheered on his arrival at the Court House, while Sir Francis Evans was greeted with hisses.

On the sixth day of the trial Lord Castlereagh went into the witness-box, where he was cross-examined at length by the petitioner's counsel H. F. Dickens, later Sir Henry Dickens, the Common Serjeant. Dickens made much play with the fact that Castlereagh had come down to Maidstone and addressed a meeting with Sir Edward Carson before he had been officially adopted as the Conservative candidate, although this was legal provided that the cost of the meeting had not been included in the candidate's election expenses. The following dialogue ensued:

> Mr Dickens: Was not the meeting held for the purpose of promoting your interests at the coming election apart from the interests of the Conservative party?
> Lord Castlereagh: The meeting was called together for the purpose of showing me to the constituency as the prospective candidate.
> Mr Dickens: Of advancing your interests, of ingratiating yourself with the people?
> Lord Castlereagh: How do you mean, 'ingratiating' myself? Do you suggest that I came down here to do the reverse?
> Mr Dickens (*much offended*): That is not a polite answer.
> Mr Justice Grantham (*to Counsel*): You asked for it, you know.

In the result the judges dismissed the petition, but each side had to pay its own costs, and these were heavy.

9

'I sat 8 hours all but 20 minutes in the House yesterday trying to take an interest,' Charley Castlereagh wrote to his mother on 25 October 1906. Stanley Baldwin, who entered the House at a by-election in 1908, criticised him to his (Castlereagh's) son Robin many years later for failing to make an impression, particularly when Home Rule became a vital issue, and for not speaking often enough at a time when the Conservative and Unionist Opposition was so depleted. In any event, he was returned again for Maidstone at both General Elections in 1910, although his majority in the second one fell to 70, and he continued to represent the constituency until he succeeded as seventh Marquess on his father's death in 1915. It is worth adding that in 1910 Castlereagh formed a 'ginger' group along with his cousin Lord Helmsley and Lord Hugh Cecil, 'The Triplets' as they were nicknamed, sitting on the Opposition Front Bench below the gangway, for the purpose of harrying the Government and the Nationalist members on Home Rule. Castlereagh was also one of the original Executive Committee of the Other Club, the famous political dining club which was founded by Winston Churchill and F. E. Smith in the same year and one of whose rules was that 'nothing in the rules of intercourse of the club shall interfere with the rancour or asperity of party politics'.

On 9 March 1910, the Castlereaghs' third child and second daughter was born in Londonderry House. There was a family argument as to what she should be called, Janet and Theresa being objected to, and according to Edith the argument continued right up to the church door. Eventually Margaret was chosen as a compromise, being suggested by Theresa, with Frances Anne as second and third names. 'Charley dislikes your name very much,' Edith told her mother-in-law a month later as she was on the point of leaving Oakham for London to see a doctor about her leg, the tattooed one which had apparently been giving her some trouble. 'I shall be sorry to leave the baby or for it to leave me. I think I appreciate her more than I did the others, the seven years waiting, I suppose!'

Edith Castlereagh was in the Highlands convalescing after Margaret's birth when King Edward VII died in May 1910 and so she missed the royal funeral. She also missed the Coronation of King George V and Queen Mary, as this took place on 22 June 1911, shortly before her third daughter Helen Maglona was born at Springfield. In September of the same year the Castlereaghs decided to revisit Canada through which they had passed briefly during their world tour six years previously. They sailed from Liverpool early in September 1911, and on the 21st Castlereagh wrote to his son Robin from Vancouver:

We had a very good voyage on the Canadian Pacific steamer and landed at

Quebec. We then took the train to Montreal and then on to Ottawa where we stayed one night with the Governor-General Lord Grey. After that we started to come here and it has taken us 5 nights and 4 days continuously travelling to get here.

The journey is a very interesting one: the first part goes through the agricultural lands growing wheat, oats, barley, and the second part of the journey through the Rocky Mountains. The scenery here is magnificent; the railway goes through the mountains 10,000 feet high and the tops all covered with snow. The highest point which the railway reaches is 5000 feet and to descend the line passes the terraces one above the other.

When you are a little older, you shall make the same journey. The engines would interest you very much; they are quite 3 times the size of the engines which we use on the railways at home and one engine draws an immense train of some 350 yards long.

We go on to Victoria tomorrow and then come slowly back along the C.P.R. to Toronto. We then go on the yacht with Uncle Strath [the Duke of Sutherland] to Quebec where we embark for home. This will be on the 3rd November.

'I am feeling extraordinarily well and enjoying every minute,' he wrote to his mother at the same time. 'The Greys are returning on the 6th October and I think they have had enough and are very pleased to be going. They have been here for over six years now. Lord Grey is a stout "Diehard" and cannot understand why there was not more excitement over the crisis.'[1]

1912 witnessed the crystallisation of the anti-Home Rule movement in Ulster, culminating in the signing of the Solemn League and Covenant in the Belfast City Hall by nearly half a million men and women pledged to resistance on 28 September 1912. Londonderry became Chairman of the Standing Committee of the Ulster Unionist Council, the body responsible for policy and in the last resort for the setting up of a Provisional Government. Winston Churchill, then First Lord of the Admiralty, had proposed to come over and address a public meeting on the Home Rule issue on 8 February 1912 in the historic Ulster Hall where his father Lord Randolph had delivered a rousing anti-Home Rule speech twenty-six years before. Prior to his visit Churchill wrote to Londonderry, who was his cousin, as well as his political opponent, warning him of 'the very grave and direct personal responsibility which will fall upon you if serious rioting occurs in Belfast on the occasion of my visit', adding that he would ask the Ulster Liberal Association to seek another venue for his meeting. ('It is not a point of any importance to me where I speak in Belfast.')

After consulting with Carson, who was staying with him at Mount Stewart, Londonderry made a dignified rejoinder:

[1] The 4th Earl Grey was a grandson of the great Whig Earl Grey of the Reform Bill The 'crisis' was produced by the Parliament Bill, which had passed into law that summer.

By selecting the Ulster Hall, with its historic traditions and the memories connected with your late father's visit in 1886, and the advice he then gave to the people of Ulster, I have no doubt you intended directly to challenge the genuineness of the oft-expressed determination of those who have made up their minds never under any circumstances to allow themselves to be degraded from their present position under the Imperial Parliament, and, so far as you could by a choice of locality, to falsely represent that those who are unalterably opposed to you were adherents of the policy you come to advocate. Against such an attempt, which was only the culmination of many acts of insult and arrogance towards the Loyalists of Ulster, the Ulster Unionist Council felt bound in the most emphatic manner to protest, with a full knowledge that peace and order could not be preserved if a meeting under such circumstances took place.

In the same month the Belfast magistrates granted an application from the local Orange Lodges and Unionist Clubs 'to practice military exercises, movements and evolutions'. This was the origin of the Ulster Volunteer Force, and, so that there should be no going back on the Liberal assurance to hold the meeting elsewhere, the Volunteers bivouacked in the Ulster Hall. In the end the meeting was held in a marquee in a football ground in the Nationalist quarter of the city and passed off without incident, although while he was driving to the meeting a hostile crowd tried to overturn Churchill's car and only desisted because his wife was sitting beside him.

Meanwhile, as the Home Rule Bill made its progress to the statute book, there were mass meetings throughout Ulster addressed by Londonderry, Carson, James Craig, Carson's lieutenant and designated successor as Ulster leader, Bonar Law and F. E. Smith, who earned the soubriquet of 'Galloper' for his performance on horseback at the meetings. Party political feelings engendered by the Parliament Act and the shadow of Home Rule had now become so bitter that members of the Opposition and their Unionist supporters refused to meet Liberals even on social occasions, which had generally been the practice in the past. Writing on 8 May 1912 to Edmund Gosse, whom he had helped to get elected to Grillion's, the well-known non-party dining club, Londonderry remarked: 'I have not dined at Grillion's for some time. I do not care about meeting the Government Members who are members.'

During the week before the signing of the Covenant, the leaders and others who had been invited, including Castlereagh, gathered at Craig's house, Craigavon, on the outskirts of Belfast. Castlereagh wrote to his wife on 23 September:

It is damnable here and I am bored to tears, nothing in the world to do; I am simply loafing about; as yet I have done nothing; tomorrow evening a meeting and the same on Thursday and then I sign on Saturday. I wish I had just come over for the signing; for all the good I have done or will do I might have been at Timbuctoo. I hate swelling the train of Carson and F.E.; there are so many anxious to do it. I have no news, I am bored here. I played golf this morning and I do the same this afternoon.

'Disaster,' he wrote again later the same day. 'Bonar Law goes to Wynyard and the parents are most anxious I shall be there. It is the usual thing, "Of course don't bother if you have arranged anything else but etc. etc." and then if I don't go it would be a grievance for years.' And again two days later:

> I have just had a wire from you to say no need to go to Wynyard. 'High words for a small stomach', but I really must go. It is a great nuisance. I wish there was no need for it, but under the circumstances I don't really see what else I can do. B.L. is going to be there and Pa has expressed a wish for me to be there, a definite wish, and also the Springfield accounts are coming in and they are very high. If I say I can't go, it is a grievance at once . . .
>
> This blasted week has put me all wrong. Never again do I undertake a week like this unless I am the central figure, and I fear that it interests me less and less. The cant and the humbug of the whole thing is really sickening.

In the event, Castlereagh crossed that night to Wynyard and returned with his father in time for the signing of the Covenant on the 28th, henceforth to be designated 'Ulster Day'. Carson signed first with a silver pen delivered to him for the occasion, followed by the six denominational Church representatives, while Castlereagh and James Chambers, M.P. for South Belfast, completed the first page, all pledging themselves together with upwards of half a million others 'to stand by one another in defending for ourselves and our children our cherished position of equal citizenship in the United Kingdom, and in using all means which may be found necessary to defeat the present conspiracy to set up a Home Rule Parliament in Ireland'.

During the Home Rule struggle Theresa naturally spent more time than usual at Mount Stewart—normally a few days at Christmas, Easter and Whitsun were all she and her husband managed. For instance, she noted in her diary that she arrived at Mount Stewart on 20 March 1913 and stayed for more than a month. 'Sailed every possible day. Cold weather and good breezes and sunshine.' At Whitsun she took Ronald MacNeill (later Lord Cushendun and a leading Unionist) from her boat *Red Rose*'s moorings opposite Mount Stewart to Portaferry and back, 'a delightful sail in brilliant sunshine'. Sometimes it was so rough that her passengers were seasick, but she sailed on bravely regardless of squalls and even gales. At Easter 1914 she expressed disappointment that her sailing had been curtailed 'owing to gales and Ulster Volunteers', no doubt because of the gun-running and preparations for the civil war which was generally expected to break out when the Home Rule Bill became law.

Meanwhile the Bill had continued to pass through its various parliamentary stages, being fought bitterly by Carson and his supporters, including

Londonderry in the Lords and Castlereagh in the Commons. By September 1913, it was obvious that it was only a matter of time before the Bill became law. Accordingly 500 delegates of the Ulster Unionist Council met in the Ulster Hall in Belfast to approve the setting up of an Ulster Provisional Government, as soon as the Bill reached the statute book. Before the meeting began, Carson implored his old friend Lord Londonderry, who was to preside, not to involve himself in an undertaking fraught with such danger to himself and his family. 'They can do little to me, therefore I have little to fear,' he told Londonderry. 'But you have great possessions, a great title, friendships at Court, a seat in the House of Lords. You have to consider the future of your son Charley. The Government, when they grow vindictive, as they will, may strike at you—and him. For these good reasons keep out of it! Let me do it by myself. It matters little to me, but I do not want you to be involved in this last and ultimate matter!' But Londonderry, to his everlasting credit, refused to hear of such a thing. With tears streaming down his face, he clasped Carson's hands and said he must never be asked to stand aside when his friends and when Ulster were going into danger. 'My dear Edward,' he said, 'if I was to lose everything in the world, I will go through with you to the end!'

The Council, with Londonderry in the chair, proceeded to delegate its powers to a Provisional Government consisting of seventy-seven members, with an executive 'Commission of Five', of whom Carson was Chairman. Departmental matters, such as finance, military affairs, education, law, customs and post office were delegated to special committees. At the same time an indemnity guarantee fund was opened to compensate members of the Ulster Volunteer Force for any loss or disability they might suffer as a result of their service, and the widows and any dependents of any who might lose their lives. Londonderry, Carson and Craig headed the subscription list with £10,000 each, and a quarter of a million sterling was guaranteed on the spot. 'Our duty,' Carson told the assembled delegates, 'is to guide and direct into the proper channels the methods of resisting the Home Rule Bill if the Government persist in forcing it upon us, and that is exactly what we are trying to do by setting up a Provisional Government . . . We may be coerced in the long run into submission, because of course they have got the Army and Navy . . . but if we are we will be governed as a conquered community and nothing else.'

During the next year Londonderry was as deep as ever in Unionist councils and co-operated with Carson in the arming of the Ulster Volunteers. The Government made various threatening noises by reinforcing the Army and the Fleet, hinting that Ulster would be coerced into accepting the Home Rule Bill, which passed through Parliament for the third time in the following summer. It was due to become law in September 1914, but the outbreak of the Great War put it into cold storage for the duration. Otherwise civil war might well have broken out in Ulster. Most of the Volunteers now flocked to join the colours; Charley Castlereagh, for instance, went off to France with the British Expeditionary Force. Theresa and her daughter-in-law also plunged themselves into war work. But things did not go well for Lord Londonderry during the following months. He grew very despondent on account of the war and the turn events had taken in Ulster. Also the fact that his only son and heir had gone off to the front preyed on his mind and he was convinced that he would not return.

In January 1915, he was at Wynyard, and towards the end of that month he caught influenza which quickly turned to pneumonia, which he made little or no attempt to survive. When his condition became critical, the doctor attending him advised that his family should be sent for.

Charles, sixth Marquess of Londonderry, died on 8 February 1915 at Wynyard aged sixty-two and was buried three days later in the family vault at Long Newton. Carson, who went to the funeral, subsequently described him as 'a great leader, a great and devoted public servant, a great patriot, a great gentleman, and above all the greatest of great friends'. These words were echoed by his widow. 'I don't think there was anyone more beloved or thought more of in the two counties in which he lived,' she wrote afterwards. 'Apart from his having served his Government and his country in the Cabinet, he lived absolutely the life of a country gentleman and was identified with every political movement, every philanthropic institution, and every sport in both counties [Durham and Down]. I don't think anybody in this world had more friends than he had.'

The new Marquess referred to his father at the time as 'the most unselfish and one of the very best of men . . . He was fearless and honest, high-principled, and with it all he had the softest, kindest nature that man ever had.' To his friend and close confidante Lady Desborough, he wrote from Wynyard on the day after his father's death:

> I can't bear to think of the world without him, without his loving help in everything I tried to do. I knew whatever happened I always had a friend ready always to believe me in the right and fight all my battles to the end. I have been carried all my life by him and I know it. And only 62, so young really. The Home Rule Bill broke his heart; he has never looked up since and his only interest now, as it was one of his chief interests, was to do everything for my and Birdie's success and happiness . . . No one has ever lost a truer friend, and affection of that quality is so rare in this world that we can none of us afford to lose it. He was the dearest and most loving Father any son has ever had.

Theresa's manifest grief at her husband's death must give the lie for good and all to the story that after the Cust affair they never spoke again to each other in private. 'I am able to walk in the open air all day,' she

wrote to her grandson Robin from Wynyard two months later. 'It is the
only thing one wants when one is really unhappy.'

Unfortunately she was obsessed with the idea that she had become
extremely poor, whereas her husband had left her legacies in his will
totalling £100,000. 'She is passing through a dreadfully sad time and the
continual thought that arrangements must be made is not conducive to
peace and quiet which she wants,' Charley wrote a few weeks after his
father's death. 'She stays at Wynyard until the end of the year which she
wants to do at present, and poor thing I think she dreads going to London.'

'You are under the impression you are a pauper,' he wrote to her on 23
April 1915. 'I wish I could put the idea out of your mind . . . I will have
some figures made out for you and you will see for yourself that there is
no need to think about money and making both ends meet, and there is no
one who requires specially providing for.'

When the time came for her to leave Wynyard, Theresa rented Lumley
Castle, near Chester-le-Street in the same county, from Lord Scar-
brough, moving in just before Christmas, which she spent there alone,
since she found that 'when one is terribly unhappy it is much better'.

CHAPTER IV

WAR AND IRISH POLITICS

I

WITH THE DECLARATION of war on 4 August 1914, Charley Castlereagh immediately thought of applying to rejoin his old regiment, which was to form part of the British Expeditionary Force. However, General William Pulteney, a friend of his parents who often stayed at Wynyard and Mount Stewart, was appointed a corps commander and, at Edith Castlereagh's suggestion, he offered her husband an appointment on his staff as A.D.C. with the rank of Captain. This Castlereagh accepted, sailing from Southampton with the General and some of his troops three weeks later. 'It was a dreadful moment saying good-bye to you,' Charley wrote to his wife from the boat which took them to Le Havre.

> I did not mind the other good-byes except that it never is pleasant to see people unhappy, but it was a fearful wrench letting you go off in the motor and seeing your sweet face looking so sad and the tears in your eyes: but I somehow feel you are always with me and I am sure, quite sure, that we never can be really separated, that really we are always together no matter what space lies between us . . . I hate the separation from you but it was bound to come in some form or the other and this for me is very pleasant and nice going with Putty.

Pulteney, familiarly known as 'Putty', had fought as a subaltern at the battle of Tel-el-Kebir and seen service in Africa as well as Egypt. More recently he had been a divisional commander in Ireland during the Home Rule crisis when he saw a good deal of the Londonderrys. 'Putty is here for his sound commonsense and capability of taking responsibility,' Charley told his wife in confidence when he reached the front and had taken the measure of his chief's abilities. 'As to strategy he knows nothing. Consequently the chief of the staff is General Du Cane, who really is a genius. He issues all the orders and arranges all the movements and Putty just acquiesces . . . Du Cane has impressed me very much indeed. Don't say this as I expect Putty will get all the credit and I hope he will. He is very charming, but I am bored with this bottle washing. However, when we really get fighting it may be more interesting.'

From Le Havre Pulteney and his staff went by train to Paris which they reached on 29 August and where Pulteney found that his corps consisted of only one division and a semi-independent infantry brigade; it was not to be reinforced for several weeks. Although they missed the battle of Mons and the consequent retreat southwards, they saw something of the fighting on the Marne, where the rapid German advance was forced to withdraw northwards. On 2 September Charley wrote to his wife from Lagny on the Marne, about seventeen miles from Paris:

> We are just here to see Sir John French. We have been retiring harried all the time by Uhlans. I believe I shot one at a thousand yards at least. Three were picked up in the wood and we had about a hundred shots from our guns at them. I took a rifle.
> This retiring is dreadfully disheartening. Don't quote this letter to anyone as I ought not to tell you all this.

Three days later he wrote again:

> Yesterday at Lagny we thought we were going to defend our line but later in the evening were ordered to retire at once so have arrived about ten miles south-east of Paris. We had such a good place to fight in yesterday but the stampede was continued. It is playing the devil with the men and the whole force will take a long time to get over the effects of the continual bolting. It may be part of some great plan but none of us seems to understand it. I only hope we do not get shut up in the defences of Paris.
> The French I fancy are useless. I do not believe they ever put up a fight. The thing is they really don't care. The only thing they do is to set up posts on our line of retreat and we are always challenged and besides this they dig holes in the road and put up barricades of carts. Our line has been from Compiègne south east, passing Lagny.

However the tide had already begun to turn for the Allies, who clinched their victory on 9 September 1914 with the capture of 38,000 prisoners and 160 guns. On the same day Castlereagh wrote to his wife from La Ferté:

> Well, we are on the advance but are now losing precious moments on the River Marne. Think of it, we have not got a proper bridging train, and we took good care to blow up all the bridges as we retired and I do not expect that we shall get over until tomorrow and then by a bridge higher up the river . . . I cannot see how the Germans can advance again. If only we had more and good cavalry we could give them a dreadful time, but we are so hampered by having no divisional cavalry to report on our front. We have employed cyclists and lost three the day before yesterday but they are not of the same value as cavalry. We had an airman sent to us today but their reconnaissance is of no value if they ascend higher than four thousand feet. This of course is well within range. I don't care about staff work. I am a combination of a footman and a clerk and no fighting.

'Charley is very well indeed and has put on so much flesh he can hardly get his belt on,' the General wrote to Edith Castlereagh on the same day. 'All our spirits have been much better since we began to advance. The depression of the retirement was very trying. I took good care to take the sheets off the bed the last two nights as Germans had slept there. The Germans had drunk all the champagne here the previous night.' Next day they crossed the river Marne and a few days later reached the Aisne where Pulteney and his staff established themselves in a château near Soissons, where they were to spend the next four weeks. It was during this period that the battle of the Aisne took place in which the British, mostly from Haig's First Corps, lost 10,000 officers and men.

While the engagement of the Marne, fought in four days of blazing summer heat, following the retreat from Mons, broke the legend of German invincibility, the result at the Aisne broadly speaking was the stabilisation of the western front, across which the two sides were to face one another for the next four years. Castlereagh sent his wife a series of letters while the Third Corps was fighting on the Aisne:

15 September. We are stopped by the Germans from crossing the river Aisne . . . We seem to be getting on very slowly. We are sadly lacking in heavy artillery and machine guns . . . Breakfast is never later than six and we lie down when and where we can. Always noisy, talking, buzzing of the telegraph instrument, motors driving up, the engine of the electric light making a terrific row; one gets used to sleeping in a barrage of noise . . . I can't believe that the war can go on for very long at this rate. I don't think either side could stand it; the gun-ammunition must fail some day I would say as the continuous bombardments mean an enormous quantity of ammunition.

Seely is a great nuisance here, he motors round and gives his opinion to everyone unasked . . . [1] Sir J. French is surrounded by an immense staff, they can't have anything to do at all.

16 September. The attack on the Guards Brigade yesterday—and I believe the Germans made 22 different attacks—must have been for the purpose of breaking through but I understand the footguards waited until the range was about 150 yards and just mowed them down in hundreds . . . We have been at this address for four nights and we have had a lot of casualties from shells. I accompanied Putty to the hospital this afternoon. A very sad sight, in truth the horrors of war. There is only a makeshift hospital and only the worst cases are kept there and there are some dreadful ones and they were suffering terribly.

17 September. There are any number of German stragglers about the woods, longing to be taken prisoner. Our Headquarters picks up some every day; an officer and a sergeant were found the other day in some stooks of oats. Our camp Commandant Colonel Rose saw what he thought was a nice pair of boots and when he tried to pick them up he found a German inside.

19 September. We are now entirely by ourselves on the line of the Aisne and we seem to be fixed here indefinitely. I don't quite know what the plan is unless it is that delay is the best weapon against the Germans. Today the shelling has practically ceased but the reason for this is unknown. I expect it is due to a westward movement of the Germans with the object of enveloping our left flank but the French are closing the same thing.

The North Irish Horse went out the other day with Freddie Guest[2] and another on French's staff to catch some Germans straggling in a wood. After a certain

---

[1] J.E.B. ('Jack') Seely, later Lord Mottistone, had resigned as War Minister over the 'Curragh Mutiny' in March 1914. He commanded a cavalry brigade in France during the war.

[2] Later Air Minister. See below, p. 142.

amount of time one of the N.I. Horse opened fire at 170 yards on Freddie Guest. When he found out his mistake, he ran forward and said 'Sure I'm glad I didn't strike ye!'

24 September. Seely told me Winston [Churchill] was at Dunkirk . . . He sent me a message. Winston I suppose came over to get a medal; he is entitled to one if he sets foot on French soil I believe.

The thing that has most impressed me here has been the aeroplane service. A splendid lot of boys who really don't know what fear is. The Germans shoot shrapnel at them and you see the aeroplane like a dragon fly in the air and then a lot of puffs of white smoke which are the shells bursting. Luckily the shots are very wide and so far none has been brought down.

26 September. How much better I should have done if I had remained in the Army, and done the staff college instead of stagnating for eight years in the House of Commons. It is very irritating to see people in important positions, no better than me, and to feel that I am a sort of mixture of a footman and a clerk and this I shall remain as I see no prospect of doing anything else.

30 September. Sir John French was here yesterday; in great spirits I understand, but the 'footmen and clerks' are not allowed into the conference on these momentous occasions. We have the honour of calling his motor and opening the gate for it. The hangers on at the General Headquarters increase every day and they have nothing whatever to do from morning to night.

8 October. The General Headquarters are moving to Abbeville today . . . We start entraining at Compiègne as soon as we can . . . for Abbeville or somewhere in the neighbourhood . . .

We hear that F. E. Smith has been made a General Staff Officer 2nd Grade. Will you enquire about this, because if it is so, it is a scandalous job perpetrated by Winston! It means that F.E. is given rank of major and draws £600 a year army pay. If this is the case, I shall formally write and ask to be given the same rank. F.E. is a 2nd Lieutenant in the Yeomanry.

The plan to be carried out provided for the three army corps which had been on the Aisne to be deployed northwards between La Bassée and Ypres where they were to effect a junction with the Fourth Corps under General Rawlinson, which along with the Belgians completed the Ypres–Nieuport front to the sea. 'Our troops will be dispersed east of St Omer, 4th Division, 6th Division and 19th Brigade,' Castlereagh wrote to his wife from St Omer on 10 October, 'and if you draw a line from Dunkirk to Arras you have about the dividing line where we are and the enemy.' Pulteney and his Third Corps moved rapidly forward to Hazebrouck, and brushing aside all resistance captured the town of Bailleul where the General established his headquarters on 14 October, after which they crossed the river Lys to Armentières and held a line extending approximately 2,500 yards. For a few days Pulteney and his staff occupied the Mayor's magnificent house in Armentières as their headquarters but then moved back to Bailleul where they were to remain for many months.

The German objective was now the Channel ports. After occupying Antwerp the Germans tried to break through the Belgians between Dixmude and the sea, a manoeuvre eventually frustrated by the Belgian king who decided to flood the country in front of the German forces by letting in the sea by the Nieuport locks. Having failed north of Ypres, the Germans next attempted to break through south-east of the town, and a month's severe but indecisive fighting, known as the First Battle of Ypres, followed. 'We have had most desperate fighting every day lately,' Pulteney wrote to Edith Castlereagh on 24 October. 'The casualties have been very heavy but those of the Germans terrific.' And again, four days later: 'Have had a very anxious time since I last wrote hanging on by my eyelids to an enormous front, swept in all directions by terrific shell fire, men unnerved by the casualties, the continuous strain, etc. The losses break one's heart . . .' In fact the British casualties among all ranks, killed, wounded and missing, amounted to over 58,000 by the time the fighting petered out on 22 November due to bad weather and the state of the ground. With the end of the battle open warfare ceased, and trench warfare, which had begun on the Aisne in September, prevailed along the whole western front.

Here are some further extracts from Castlereagh's letters to his wife at this period:

Bailleul. 4 November 1914. Our losses are terrible and we are hardly holding our own. The Germans are losing thousands but still they press on and on: they are shelling places which have been quite safe . . . The shells were dropping into Neuve Eglise yesterday which is a point further than the Germans have hitherto reached. A few casualties and some houses were hit. These incursions are a great nuisance as the natives immediately begin trekking westwards. It is very sad seeing these wretched people with all their belongings they can carry on their backs, in wheelbarrows or in small carts trudging towards what they consider to be the nearest point of safety; that and the hospitals show what war is.

8 November. The Germans impress me more every day with their system. A staff officer walked down the Scots Guards lines the other day and said that orders were coming for them to retire; this was a German disguised; he however escaped undetected. There are several instances of the same sort of thing. It shows immense courage on their part. I do not know how you defeat a nation which has prepared in every detail for years.

7 December. Winston arrived here this morning looking very old and very flabby. I do not know what excuses he makes to come here, mere joyriding, and he has a destroyer to take him back again.

22 December. I only spent a few hours in the trenches 6.30 p.m. to 3.30 a.m. and got tight on rum. There was no shelling only sniping. I only flew for about ten minutes, a delightful sensation. I seldom enjoyed anything more. I was rewarded for going to the trenches, the Irish Fusiliers. I never saw people so pleased; they say the staff never go there and don't realise what they have to go through. There were 15 inches of water in the fire trenches.

27 December. There are going to be great changes and our status is going to be somewhat lowered. Haig and Smith-Dorrien are each going to command Armies consisting of three corps each and we are in S-Dorrien's Army. This means that we shall have no direct communication with G.H.Q. Very tiresome indeed and Putty is rather sad about it.

. . . I expect Cyril Hankey told you all about our visit to the trenches. These particular trenches are the most elaborate of their kind and there is no danger. The Germans opposite happened to be unfriendly, I expect they were Prussians. But in all other parts of our line, the two sides met and fraternised between the trenches.

9 January 1915. The rain is still going on and the trenches are flooded. I believe there was some fraternising yesterday and the day before between the two sides but the authorities are very down on this sort of thing.

During the first battle of Ypres, the Third Corps commander wrote to his aide's wife:

21 January . . . it really is a great shock to look at a map containing the whole line from Nieuport to Switzerland and see the very small length of it which the British Army is holding. It really is a revelation. The French are holding about twelve times as much as we are with a population five million less.

Charley wants to be off to his regiment. He is right in wanting to go because he is ambitious and wants to get on in his profession, so much that against my will I shall have to let him go after the present crisis is over. He has a rotten time now with me as he sees none of the fighting, with no chance either of making a name for himself, as a soldier. He is really only a flunkey so he feels, and comes round in the motor with me, but all the same I shall miss him. I have seen so much of his fretting lately I cannot stand in his way, but feel that he is doing the right thing now that his own regiment is short of officers.

Eventually Charley agreed to stay on for a time at Third Corps Head-quarters. Also his spirits improved after a spell of home leave and the fact that he received a mention in despatches and was promoted to the rank of Major. In February 1915 he was given compassionate leave twice, once to attend his father's funeral and the second time to deal with his father's affairs, although, as the General put it to the new Lady Londonderry, 'why he can't leave all the things to you to sign I can't imagine. You seem to have a splendid head for business.' Pulteney wrote to her in another letter at this time:

Charley seems a different man since he went away, but I will give him plenty of work and try to keep his mind interested. He is so nice about his mention in des-patches. Of course I should have liked to have got him a D.S.O. or a brevet but had to consider what others had been through in the trenches in comparison. However he will get his reward for his work in due course. The W.O. mark you up for a mention in despatches.

'Putty is a good carrier out of orders,' his aide wrote at this time. 'He has no ideas and what is tiresome no conversation. It is all 'oh, yes, top hole, what?' and filth: not that I blame him for a dirty mind, but there is nothing else and the A.D.C.'s job is to laugh and endeavour to tell him stories . . . All the others in the same post as myself are all babies; in fact I am too old.'

2

During the six months which elapsed between the first and second battles of Ypres, there was little in the way of news which Major Lord Londonderry, as he had now become, could impart in his letters home, unless he could send a letter by King's Messenger, which was eventually forbidden. He was not allowed to mention the location of the 3rd Corps Headquarters at Bailleul, near what the General called 'the immortal salient', and even a half-jocular allusion to Sir Douglas Haig as looking 'antediluvian' on one of his tours of inspection was rigorously deleted by the base censor. With the coming of the first fine spring days in March 1915, Londonderry's spirits rose, though he had to admit that, of all the foul climates he had ever encountered, Flanders was the worst.

However, the weather did not affect the vineries at Bailleul, which had some exceptionally fine specimens. Edith Londonderry was very anxious to obtain a cutting from one of these vines for Wynyard, and James de Rothschild, who was an interpreter with the Third Corps, brought one over with him when he came back on leave. This action eventually produced the wonderful grapes which are at Wynyard today. Unfortunately, when the Germans recaptured Bailleul in April 1918, they cut down all the vines, hacking every one to pieces; not a vestige was left, and the vineries were used as stables. Said Lady Londonderry afterwards, 'Our Bailleul grapes are a memory of their past glories.'

In the middle of April 1915 two prominent political figures turned up in the persons of Curzon and Balfour. They were each taken on a tour of the British front line trenches, Londonderry accompanying the latter but not the former. 'I should like to have gone with him this morning,' he wrote of Curzon, 'as I am sure his sonorous sentences would reverberate through the trenches.' Of Balfour he wrote on 19 April:

A.J.B. arrived to lunch yesterday. He looked tired I thought but it was very nice meeting him; I have been brought up in an atmosphere of adoration of A.J.B. as my poor father worshipped the ground he walked on and although an obstinate man he had not a will of his own in Mr Balfour's presence. We took him out to the same place as Lord Curzon and I think he enjoyed it. Putty came too, which was very wrong as it is too close to the Germans for a corps commander. You see only the soldiers and the soldiers in the higher commands count nowadays; late Prime Ministers may take any risks. As a matter of fact the danger is very small; there are a few stray bullets about . . . However A.J.B. took a special pleasure in standing in all the open places; it interested him far more because he *could see*, quite oblivious of the fact that the Germans could see him also.

Three days later, the Germans, in defiance of the Hague Convention, discharged clouds of poison gas against the French troops, causing a large gap in the Allied line and threatening to cut off the whole of the British troops in the Salient. In the fierce fighting which followed, the British were forced to withdraw to a line south-west of Hooge, thus reducing their line from 20,500 yards to 15,500, and the lost ground was not regained. 'Some of the victims of the gasses [*sic*] were brought in here last night,' Londonderry wrote from Bailleul on 3 May. 'I went to the hospital this morning and it was a heartbreaking sight. The men were like fishes lying on the bank gasping for breath, and nothing seems of any use. Oxygen is no relief. Pray heaven that medical science will discover what to do. The lungs I gather of those affected are filled with fluid. Of all forms of barbarism that seems the absolute worst.'

Six British infantry and three cavalry divisions were engaged in the battle between 22 April and 25 May 1915, and the casualties were even greater than in the previous autumn—over 2,000 officers and 58,000 other ranks. Fourteen Victoria Crosses were awarded. It was during the fighting, on 13 May, that Lady Desborough's eldest son the soldier-poet Julian Grenfell, who had been awarded the D.S.O. in the first Battle of Ypres and whom Londonderry had recently met, was wounded in the head by a piece of shell which penetrated his brain and from the effects of which he died in hospital a fortnight later. 'Poor Julian Grenfell,' Londonderry wrote to his wife at the time. 'The Desboroughs will be heartbroken. He was a fine creature and as brave as a lion. He was hit by a shell and I think the blow would have killed most people but apparently he walked into the hospital at Hazebrouck smoking a cigarette and at Boulogne wrote a long letter to his mother.'

After the fighting was over, Londonderry renewed his request to rejoin his regiment under the impression that at home he was thought to be sheltering behind the General in the latter's comfortable headquarters. Pulteney again did his best to dissuade him and wrote to Edith on 1 June:

> I cannot see Charley's point in wanting to go to the Cavalry now. To say that he is sheltering behind me is absolute nonsense. The crisis at Ypres is over and the Cavalry will do nothing for a long time to come. What Charley does not realise is the help he is to me in arranging things and saying the right things to the various people that come into touch with me . . . Don't let Charley think for one instant that he is not pulling his weight, because he is, he has and will continue to do so.

Meanwhile at home, under threat of a defeat in the House of Commons, Mr Asquith, the Prime Minister, had agreed to the formation of a Coalition Government, in which the Conservatives and Labour were represented besides the Liberals. A few days later Asquith visited the front, staying with French at G.H.Q. in St Omer. It was a very fine day, and the view from within a few miles of Ypres was 'wonderful, stretching as far as Ostend and the sea', as the Prime Minister wrote at the time:

> Ypres lay in the near distance smoking, but with 2 towers almost intact, and right up to it as far as one could see not a trace of war or devastation, trees uncut, crops growing, people working in the fields, just as in England. Through glasses one could

see Wytschaete [south of Ypres]—our weakest spot which we have never been able to retake—the English and German trenches running parallel, not more than 100 yards apart. Not a soldier was visible, and except for a little cloud of shrapnel in the sky pursuing an aeroplane, not a shot was fired.

I lunched at Bailleul with General 'Putty', whose 2 aide-de-camps are Pembroke and Castlereagh, and went over the Hospital. They have passed 47,000 wounded through it, and all the cases I saw were very bad ones, mostly head wounds, and one officer dying of the gas. I afterwards saw a farewell parade of the 16th Brigade who were going to Ypres—a fine lot of men, in the trenches since October. I made them a little speech, and they gave me three cheers.

Next day Londonderry gave his version of the visit in a letter to Edmund Gosse:

The Prime Minister was here on Monday but was not very impressive. He inspected one of the brigades belonging to the corps on the staff of which I occupy an insignificant post. He addressed a few sonorous phrases in characteristic style, 'If and when', 'Each of you and all of you', and although he was carefully primed with the actual counties borne by the battalions, he failed at the last moment and took refuge in 'Men drawn from great counties in the north and the south and the east and the west.'

I had to swallow the bitter pill of humiliation because, notwithstanding my feeble bleatings in the House of Commons and my stout fulminations from various platforms, all of which bear traces of bitter antagonism both personal and political against the P.M., I was consulted at the end of the proceedings by the brigadier as to whether three cheers would not be a fitting end of the proceedings and, would you believe it, I feebly said 'yes'; for heaven's sake don't tell my dear Mother or that the cheers compared very favourably with those accorded to Carson to the accompaniment of the Orange drum.

Londonderry was now determined to get back to his regiment and the General eventually had to let him go. On 25 June 1915 'Putty' wrote to his aide's wife:

Charley wont stay on any longer as A.D.C. He doesn't realise that he is learning more about the various arms of the service every day out here than he would learn in ten years of command of a cavalry regiment. It upsets me his going away at this time just as Reggie [the General's other A.D.C. the Earl of Pembroke] is doing the same thing, but there it is. He wants to command men and he does not get an opportunity; I am afraid I cannot give him one. I tried to introduce him to learning staff duties but he does not want to do that. Of course this infernal trench warfare is stagnation for both of them and they are bored to eternity.

I wish they only knew how I shall miss them. Then neither of them would leave me as there is extra stress on, just as the whole Corps is changing Divisions. It will mean a very different ménage because I can't have pals again as A.D.C.s but just 'beck and callers'. Charley I shall miss many more times than Reggie, but then I have known him since he was a lad. He keeps his tongue quiet which the other doesn't. Have always been able to tell and talk to him about things which I could not to Reggie. When they go, I feel I shall turn into a Smith-Dorrien and make them all frightened to come near me.

In the event Charley got his way and went back to the Blues, who were in the 8th Cavalry Brigade with the 10th Hussars and the Essex Yeomanry.

Half the regiment were with their horses at Aix-en-Issart, a few miles from Montreuil, while the other half were in the trenches. There was also a reserve unit at the London barracks in Regent's Park, and for several months in the latter part of 1915 Londonderry was in charge there, although he longed to get back to the regiment at the front, which he succeeded in doing in mid-January 1916. 'Of course,' his mother noted in her diary at the time, 'as I promised him I would not interfere with his plans, after the South African affair, I cannot do anything. He must please himself . . .'

'We have just done 6 days in the trenches, not a very pleasant bit of the line but nothing to complain of,' he wrote to Lady Desborough on 28 January 1916. 'The monotony and the discomfort was the worst part but all very salutary. I am glad to have got here and [my] position assured and all that is very gratifying . . . We were worried to death by trench mortars and rifle grenades; we have practically none to reply with and the war has been in progress for 18 months. We had a number of casualties, many more than the Cavalry can afford. I am now with people I have never seen before, and I am not sure that I want to see them again as in this dismounted work the Headquarters are all mixed up. I shall be glad when it is all over and I only hope that the system will not be continued as it is fatal to the efficiency of the cavalry and we shall be found wanting when we shall be called up to gallop across Belgium . . . I am going to see Putty one day and night soon.'

Meanwhile, at home, Londonderry had put two of his properties at the disposal of the authorities as hospitals, Londonderry House and Seaham Hall. 'The L. House hospital is expensive,' he told Lady Desborough, 'but I am helped there or else I could not run it—it costs me about £1,200 . . . The Seaham Hospital owing to the liberality of the allowance and the number of the patients or rather convalescents costs me nothing except sometimes the coals . . . I don't look sympathetic like a great many others do, so I must do something to show it.'

On his return to France Londonderry was appointed second-in-command of The Blues, and when the Colonel, Lord Tweedmouth, was away he would take over. Herbert Buckmaster, the actress Gladys Cooper's husband and founder of Buck's Club, who joined the regiment early in 1916, has put it on record that Londonderry was 'excellent to serve under and most helpful in every way'.

On 5 February 1916 Londonderry wrote:

> The Regiment comes out of the trenches about the middle of this month I am glad to say. Reliefs have been going on the whole time so I do not think that any one officer or man will have been in for the whole of the six weeks. I went back via the 3rd Corps. Dear old Putty sent a car for me and I spent one night there. It was delightful seeing him and he looked very well indeed. Very fat, and very cheerful.

I think he has put all his troubles behind him and is determined to do his best in whatever position he is. We had a very pleasant evening, our styles perhaps a little cramped by the presence of the Lord Primate of Ireland. He is a very old friend of mine and the right sort of cleric . . .[1] He had been down to see the Ulster Division and had also visited the Irish Guards.'

'So Charley has come out once more,' the 3rd Corps Commander, now Lieutenant-General Sir William Pulteney, wrote to Edith Londonderry after this visit. 'He will be glad to turn his hand once more to the wheel in the field, although some of them are taking their turn in the trenches. It does them a lot of good from the disciplinary point of view! They look so funny marching as infantry and how they get their kit up to the trenches without packs I don't know.'

However, 'Putty' had one grievance in that he had been passed over for promotion. 'When one is the senior Corps Commander out here and have had eleven Divisions through your hands, all of whom have done well, one is entitled to be heard,' he wrote at this time. 'Further than that the 3rd Corps got further East than any other Corps, has held the longest front of any Corps in the army for a whole year, has never lost an inch of ground, has got the best trenches and the best system of defences, although in the wetter piece of ground. It was bad enough being passed over as an Army Commander but to have five Lieut-Generals put over one's head is beyond the limit . . .'

Londonderry endorsed this view and loyally supported his former chief. 'All the new Army Commanders are all of them senior to Putty,' he wrote at this time, 'so that he really is in an inferior position to the one he held at the beginning of the war. He still commands a Corps but it is one of the Corps in the Army commanded by Smith-Dorrien who at the beginning was a corps commander . . . Some of the new army commanders may never come out and I suppose Putty would be the first to get a vacancy as the remainder senior to him on the list with few exceptions are of the fossil order . . . The 3rd Army Corps on any practical showing has been very well handled. It may not have figured so conspicuously as some other portions of the Army but after all this is to its credit. We have always been attacked and we have never had to retire and it was to the 10th and 11th Brigades on the Aisne that a large measure of the success of that prolonged battle was due'.

Nevertheless in the event the popular and much decorated 'Putty' was to remain a Corps Commander until the end of the war when he retired.[2]

[1] The Most Rev. J. B. Crozier, Protestant Archbishop of Armagh and Primate of All Ireland since 1911, had been a friend of the Londonderry family for many years. He was a keen horseman and cricketer and he also played rugby football.

[2] Following his retirement he was appointed to the comfortable post of Black Rod in the House of Lords which he held for twenty years. He died in 1941, aged eighty.

The Blues left Aix-en-Issart on 24 June 1916 to move into the war area of the Somme, where 'the big push' was due to begin four days later but in the event was postponed for forty-eight hours owing to the bad weather and the difficulty of the artillery getting any observation for their barrages. Since the offensive was initially carried out by the infantry, the cavalry were kept in the rear, so that on 1 July Londonderry was able to write to his wife, feeling that his regiment might join the fray at any moment. It is a touching letter.

> My most beloved wife,
> I will write you this note because I know you will like to have it, and it is just in case, but I have absolute faith in my 'étoile'. I am sure there is work for me after this war, and as I sit and write I am thinking very far beyond this week or ten days or whatever the time may be. But still if the Almighty wills otherwise, then I just want you to know that I love and adore you, that you have been everything that a wife or a loving friend should be or could possibly be to me and that I just leave you for a time and then we shall be together for eternity.
> From your loving and devoted husband.

The Battle of the Somme which began on 1 July 1916 was really a series of savage engagements with the enemy, which lasted intermittently for the next four and a half months and resulted in enormous losses on both sides. During the first thirty-six hours, for example, the famous 36th (Ulster) Division, in which many of Londonderry's friends were fighting, suffered 5,500 casualties in the neighbourhood of Thiepval, covering themselves with glory and gaining no less than five V.C.s for acts of conspicuous gallantry. Londonderry himself was to survive and see plenty of trench warfare during the battle, although commanding officers were forbidden to 'go over the top'; also the cavalry were not needed for some time. But he suffered a grievous loss when his great friend Harold Brassey, who had been his best man at his wedding, was killed in action later in July. 'I went to see where Harold was buried yesterday,' Londonderry wrote to his wife on 25 July. 'I found him at the side of a little cemetery for officers. There was nothing more to be done and I was told that a little white cross was being painted with his name on it. He is buried at a place called Bouzincourt. If the censor objects to this I cannot help it, but some of his friends may like to know.' One of them was Herbert Buckmaster, who took a photograph of the grave. 'He was my friend of 20 years,' Londonderry wrote to Lady Desborough, 'we went to Sandhurst together, we joined together and there was a link between us which I valued very much . . . The comfortable feeling of having his friendship was a rock that nothing could ever shake . . . and I shall miss him more than I can say . . . The real friends are so few and far between; but he was a real friend if ever there was one.'

Harold Brassey was only one of upwards of three-quarters of a million casualties on the allied side, while the Germans admitted to losing half a million men. The allied advance amounted to a mere dozen miles between Beaumont-Hamel, Fricourt and Combles before the front was again stabilised towards the end of November. Thus the British troops, in this part of the western front, were doomed to spend the ensuing winter in flooded trenches which the Germans had evacuated.

3

Life in the cavalry on the western front has been aptly described as thirty days of unutterable boredom and one day of indescribable fear. Londonderry lost his other close friend Charlie Helmsley, now Lord Feversham, who had been one of the 'triplets' with him in the House of Commons. 'I can't talk of my sorrows to you because they are so small compared to yours,' Londonderry wrote despondently to Lady Desborough, a few days after Feversham had been killed, in September 1916, 'but I have lost my other friend now and all the men I know are just acquaintances or confederates in pleasure. Charlie was a brother to me and his death is the extinguishing of many hopes and the destruction of many plans; but I honestly believe that those who fall in the war are the truly happy ones and that we are selfish to wish them back across the narrow line.'

Londonderry was none too happy about his own military prospects. On 30 October 1916, he wrote:

> I am getting very restless as I have been at anchor too long and I see no prospect of advancement. My wings are badly clipped here and I do not know how to get a move on. It is very worrying and the knowledge that after the war I shall have to start at the bottom again in politics, is very galling. I never anticipated being caught as a 2nd in command, which is just an understudy with no duties, for more than a short space of time . . .
>
> Everyone seems so contented with their little tasks and little responsibilities. Grown men doing children's work. The staffs are more ambitious and really I feel in sympathy with them. Then at home I see many no older, but probably wiser, controlling great undertakings. Altogether it is very tiresome and only shows the foolish way we are brought up: so that the moment there is a reality, we fall between two stools, and we cannot get on anywhere. There is my grumble and it is a relief to make it, because the only duty I have here is to laugh and be cheerful, and I believe I succeed.

In the following month he thought his chance had come when he was detailed to command a battalion of 800 men, but it was then discovered that a Lieutenant-Colonel at least was required to command such a large unit, so that Londonderry once more found himself as second-in-command, this time to Colonel Hardwicke. 'You know Philip Hardwicke and he is very nice,' Londonderry wrote to Lady Desborough, 'so I am quite happy but bored at not having my own show.' The battalion, a composite one drawn from the 8th Cavalry Brigade, was principally engaged in digging trenches and burying the dead on the Somme. Eventually Hardwicke departed and Londonderry took over the command with the temporary rank of Lt.-Colonel.

Londonderry had just arrived in England for a fortnight's leave at the beginning of December 1916 when Asquith resigned and the King sent for Lloyd George, who became Prime Minister of the second war-time Coalition Government. 'I saw my Mother at Springfield and also in London,' Londonderry wrote to Lady Desborough on his return to France. 'She was not in very good spirits and a bruised shoulder from a fall riding added to neuritis may have been the cause. She would like me to have been in the [new] Government, but there were difficulties as I pointed out if I had been asked which I was not.' He went on:

> Lord Curzon at dinner the other night said something about the war and asked me some question or other, so I told him that sitting next to him in a comfortable warm room, in complete security drinking old brandy, made me very warlike, but the other conditions sometimes made me wonder. I really do feel that a complete ignorance of war conditions is essential for our rulers and then they can maintain a stiff upper lip, which is important, or all the sacrifices will have been in vain.
> Will Germany collapse? One likes to feel that they are nearing that stage.

However, the German collapse was nearly two years away. Meanwhile Londonderry went back to his battalion and soldiered on through the battle of Arras in April 1917. On the 10th of that month as second-in-command of The Blues he took part in the attack on Monchy, a village held by the Germans on the road between Arras and Cambrai, galloping behind the infantry and helping to consolidate the village. But the going was very heavy over snow-covered ground. Buckmaster, who led one troop, later recalled how a bomb went off in front of them, probably struck by a horse's hoof. They then galloped into a terrible barrage, losing about 500 horses in the attack, although they captured 150 of the German garrison, while many dead lay among the ruins of the shattered buildings. Unfortunately General Bulkeley Johnson, the Blues commander, who was standing in a trench nearby, was killed by a machine gun bullet, and Londonderry once more took over the command of the regiment. But he was not to hold it for long.

On 8 May 1917, A. J. Balfour, who had become Foreign Secretary in the Lloyd George Coalition Government, wrote to Edith Londonderry who had been pulling strings on her husband's behalf:

> Sir Henry Wilson [Chief-Liaison Officer with French G.H.Q.] writes that he has been trying hard to find a job for Charley, so far without success, but he 'has his name down in his book' and he promises to be on the look out and help him if he possibly can.
> I am afraid this is all we can do at present . . . I wrote a strong letter to [General]

Kavanagh [the Cavalry Brigade Commander] suggesting that he should *send* Charley home on leave as I told him C [harley] does not realise how very necessary it is that he should come back and look after his own affairs. We shall see what happens.

Something did happen quite quickly, since Londonderry arrived home on indefinite leave a few days after his wife received Balfour's letter. On 15 May, Colonel Repington, the *Times* military correspondent, recorded in his diary that he dined with Theresa Lady Londonderry, her son and daughter-in-law, Edmund Gosse, Lord Hugh Cecil and the Duchess of Marlborough. 'We discussed the cavalry at Monchy. Lord L and his mother argued about Ireland at the end, and I find him very keen to throw himself into Irish politics with a view to a settlement.'

On the very next day Lloyd George addressed letters to the leaders of the Irish parties, the Nationalists and the Unionists, putting forward two solutions for the Irish question, either of which the Government was prepared to adopt. The first was that Home Rule should immediately come into force with the six north-eastern counties excluded from its operation, the question of this exclusion to be reconsidered by Parliament after five years. There was to be a Council of Ireland, composed of delegations from each of the two areas responsible for certain common problems, its decisions to be approved by a majority of each delegation. (Broadly speaking this was the scheme followed in the Government of Ireland Act, 1920.) The alternative plan, apparently something of an afterthought, which the Prime Minister suggested as 'a last resort', was 'a convention of Irishmen of all parties for the purpose of producing a scheme of Irish self-government'.

The first plan was unacceptable to the Nationalists as involving partition and to the Unionists as involving only temporary exclusion. However they both agreed to the proposal for a convention, although John Redmond, the ageing and ailing Nationalist parliamentary leader, insisted that the membership should include the Roman Catholic hierarchy and chairmen of county councils and other public bodies. This was to have the effect of making the convention unwieldy as well as unrepresentative, since the increasingly powerful Sinn Fein element in Ireland, which would have controlled the majority of county councils in the south in the event of fresh local government elections taking place, intended to boycott the proceedings, and duly did so. Meanwhile Carson went over to Belfast in the company of Londonderry, who like his father had been appointed Lord Lieutenant of County Down, and was invited to act as secretary of the Ulster Unionist delegation. ('Is it true your Charley is a private secretary?' General Pulteney wrote to Lady Londonderry in his usual bawdy style. 'I trust he has learnt to file the French letters properly.')

Carson had suggested to Lloyd George that the respective delegations should number altogether about fifty or sixty. ('I should think that anything else will be unworkable.') But in fact about a hundred delegates attended the opening meeting of the Irish Convention in Trinity College, Dublin, on 25 July 1917. The Ulster group was led by H. T. Barrie, Unionist M.P. for North Derry, and included H. M. Pollock, Chairman of the Belfast Chamber of Commerce, and other leading business and professional men, as well as the heads of the Protestant religious denominations in the north. The southern Unionists were led by Lord Midleton, formerly St John Brodrick, M.P. But apart from Londonderry, who was under forty, and one or two others, the convention as a whole was composed of elderly men. Nor were any women included. As chairman, after Redmond had declined the position, the delegates elected Sir Horace Plunkett, son of Lord Dunsany and a well-intentioned idealist who had formerly sat as Unionist M.P. for South Dublin but had devoted most of his sixty-three years to experiments in co-operative agriculture in Ireland.

It is noteworthy that Londonderry made a good impression on the chairman when the latter heard him speak for the first time. 'He had all the charm of his father and a good share of his mother's brains,' Plunkett wrote afterwards. 'He seemed to belong a little more to the later nineteenth and earlier twentieth century than either of his parents.'

4

While Lord Londonderry was serving in France, first with Sir William Pulteney and then as second-in-command of The Blues, his wife was busy with her own particular form of war work. Besides establishing a hospital behind the lines, she also kept an eye on the hospital in Londonderry House and would also visit the hospital at Seaham Hall with her mother-in-law. However, her principal achievement, for which she gained a well-earned honour, was the founding of the Women's Legion, a quasi-military organisation designed to free men, who had hitherto been engaged in home duties, for military service; but while well disciplined, it was not subject to army regulations. 'They will be taught to shoot with a service rifle and revolver,' Edith wrote to her mother-in-law, 'but they are *not* to be armed until possibly later on, if the movement grows and is any good, and they get recognised as a body like the Boy Scouts.' First, in the agricultural section, women were employed on the land, in the management of horses and livestock, in milking, dairying, thatching, threshing, fruit picking and similar work. They also ploughed both with horses and tractors. The training centre was in Rutlandshire, where the Cottesmore Hunt Committee put the hunt kennels at the Legion's disposal as a training centre. Next the Legion started a cooking centre which eventually produced 40,000 trained cooks, many of whom were sent to army camps, where the cuisine initially left much to be desired. Other Legionaires became motor and ambulance drivers, mechanics, despatch riders, and technicians, from which the Motor Transport Section was formed. They also drove for the Royal Flying Corps, and the Australian, New Zealand and Canadian forces.

'The women and girls of this section did yeoman service,' Lady Londonderry recalled afterwards. 'They drove through all the air raids wherever their duties called them. They drove ambulances at night, meeting the trains at all hours bringing home the wounded. I was in London doing a tour of inspection when the H.M.S. *Leinster* was sunk by a German submarine in the Irish sea. The Legion drivers were sent to Kingstown to bring back some of the survivors. This was no pleasant task, as they were hooted and jeered by the hostile crowds, and mud and stones were thrown at them. But they carried on quite unperturbed and cheerful, although most of them were strangers to the habits and mentality of this section of the Irish population. As a large proportion of the survivors were Americans, this incident was a great eye-opener to many of them.'

One application from a twenty-two-year-old French girl in March 1915 to join the Women's Legion amused Lady Londonderry by its literary style. 'Here I contribute to the physical, practical breeding of the future soldiers with a gendarme,' she wrote from her home on the Côte d'Or. 'I fire on the target in all positions. By preparing the young men of this country for this great hide and seek that is the present war, I teach myself to hide behind an obstacle, to leap over a ditch or to a tree. I am a good walker and I go easily on a bicycle. I know to do a dressing and to tend a patient. In short, I desire to know if it is indispensable to be English-woman in order to have the great honour to get in your women volunteer reserve.' One likes to think that a suitable job was found for this remarkable young Frenchwoman.

For her outstanding contribution to the war effort, Edith Lady Londonderry was created a Dame of the British Empire in 1917. Not yet forty, she was one of the most strikingly beautiful women of her generation. Less flamboyant than her mother-in-law, she had a better proportioned figure, with an equally strong personality which she exerted with a rather greater degree of subtlety than Theresa. Throughout her career, she never lost an opportunity of advancing her husband's political and personal interests in any way she could, employing her great charm to achieve her ends. Her husband was always inclined to be rather diffident, and she was continually pushing him forward and suggesting fresh outlets for his talents and skills which she persuaded him to develop. Her likes and dislikes of people, things, and places were not as strongly expressed as Theresa's—at least they were more cleverly concealed. She was also better dressed than Theresa, who usually wore either black or white. 'It takes so much less trouble,' Theresa used to say. Edith also had more taste in the matter of house furnishing and interior decoration as well as in dress, as befitted the changing times. For one thing she got rid of all the Victorian clutter, antimacassars and other bric-à-brac at Mount Stewart.

The first time that Lady Fingall visited Mount Stewart under the new dispensation, she asked her hostess in the drawing room: 'Did Nellie see this?'

'Oh,' said Edith, 'she did. She arrived unexpectedly after we had altered it.'

'What did she say?'

'She looked round the room,' was the reply. 'Then she said, "Some people like to live in a barrack. *I* don't." '

By way of relaxation during the war Lady Londonderry started a kind of club or society in Londonderry House which she called 'The Ark' and at the same time created a fictitious order which she called the Order of the Rainbow as being the sign of hope. The members were given the name of a beast or bird or magical creature, the member's name either rhyming or beginning with the first letter of the member's Christian or surname. Lady Londonderry herself was 'Circe the Sorceress', her husband, whenever he could attend, was 'Charley the Cheetah', Princess Helena Victoria, a most active member, 'Victoria the Vivandière', Carson was 'Edward the Eagle', Churchill was 'Winston the Warlock', Edmund Gosse was 'Gosse the Gosshawk' and Sir John Simon was 'Simon the Silkworm'. These were some of the original members, all of whom had to be engaged in some kind of war work. They originally met for dinner to exchange the news of the day and to talk politics, in spite of the fact that membership was non-party political. Later, when the membership was considerably increased, numbering fifty or so between the wars, the dinners were given up and suppers took their place in the large picture gallery on the first floor. When the present writer was admitted to the Ark he was named 'Montgomery the Mole', because he had the reputation of burrowing away and discovering other people's secrets.

Lord Londonderry was away from London so much during the war that he could seldom appear at the Ark parties. Throughout the summer and autumn and winter of 1917–18 he was kept busy at the Irish Convention, which met in Belfast and Cork as well as in Dublin. On 11 September he wrote to Lady Desborough from Mount Stewart:

> The Convention so far has passed a normal course, there are local touches of interest to me, but not worth writing, and of the main issue I really do not know where we are. A peace time job does not appeal to me, also it is an old man's work and I do not feel old, but my ambitions in another sphere having failed this does

WAR AND IRISH POLITICS

satisfy a desire to be someone and to be really filling a place somewhere which carries responsibility with it.

We meet in Belfast next week and I have some members of the Convention here, Archbishop of Dublin, Mahaffy, Midletons, Abercorns and one or two others. Last night I had a private confabulation with Labour, which was very interesting. The working man here does not look with such suspicion on a lord as his confrère in England does.

I am enjoying being in Ireland very much. I really like it infinitely better than England, and I get on better with the people.

I entered the Royal circle at the Viceregal Lodge and met rank and beauty in dazzling profusion. Another night I dined with the Lord Chief Justice (Sir James Campbell) and met old Mahaffy and Tim Healy which was most interesting and we sat talking for a very long time, Tim being in his best form; the softer side was represented by the amusing daughter of my host, a wild-eyed Celt and an acquaintance (no more than that) of Countess Markievicz.[1] I played bridge too, so beauty, politics and cards passed a delightful evening for me.

'The Sinn Fein movement is on the wane so long as the British Government do nothing foolish,' he wrote to his mother on 23 November, 'but you can never trust them. The Convention is hardly nearer a solution of the problem and I doubt if it will go over Christmas, but strange things happen in Ireland.' In the same month Londonderry proposed a federal scheme, which favourably impressed Plunkett and others in the Convention who hoped to convince the whole Ulster delegation of its wisdom. 'I think you will find,' Plunkett wrote to Barrie, 'that when the federal as well as the dominion way of looking at the controversy has been put into the minds of the contestants, the atmosphere will be immensely improved.' But some of the other Ulster delegates became alarmed. One of them, a Belfast linen merchant named Adam Duffin, argued that this was scarcely the time to be working on a new Irish constitution when everyone's energies should be absorbed by the war, and it might be better to wait and see whether, as the Redmondite Nationalists contended, Sinn Fein was merely a passing phase.

Among those with whom Londonderry discussed his scheme in Dublin was his father's old Nationalist friend Lady Fingall, whom he met one night at dinner. 'I am absolutely convinced of one thing,' he told her, 'and that is, so long as the British Empire exists, Ireland must remain politically within the circle of the United Kingdom; and whatever path is chosen, long or short, or through whatever intermediary stages man in his wisdom or his folly may ordain she shall pass, that Ireland will be governed in exactly the same manner as England or Scotland or Wales. My plan is a Federation . . .'

[1] Countess Constance Markiewicz, née Gore-Booth, a member of an old Unionst family, joined the rebels during the Easter Rebellion in 1916 and later supported the Republican side in the Irish Civil War. She was the first woman to be elected a Member of the British House of Commons (in 1918), but she never took her seat.

'What you said to me at dinner as to your ideas on Federalism immensely interested me,' she wrote to him at this time, 'for I believe, too, *that* to be the final solution of all our problems. Did you ever bring forward a scheme? Can it be advocated now? Dunraven, we know, is a keen Federalist; so was Lord Grey and many others I have met. Mr Bernard Shaw told me he would willingly stump the country preaching Federalism if he could get any one to help him.'

Since the Convention's proceedings were conducted in secret, Lady Fingall was unaware that Barrie, speaking for the whole Ulster delegation, had already announced that Londonderry's proposals should not be presented, 'as they did not think that such a course would ease the situation.' Meanwhile Lord Midleton, the leader of the southern Unionists, indicated that he was agreeable to an Irish Parliament with considerably more powers than under the 1914 Act, virtually dominion status. This attracted Redmond but not Londonderry and the Ulstermen, who saw the commercial prosperity of the province being placed in jeopardy. Redmond now appealed to Lloyd George. 'I am glad that you have sent for Barrie and his friends,' he wrote on 26 November, 'and I can only repeat that I feel convinced that it rests with you and Carson to make or mar the Convention.' Eventually Lloyd George agreed that, if Midleton's scheme was generally acceptable to the Convention, he would use his influence with the Cabinet and in Parliament to bring the scheme into law. Thus it looked to Carson and Londonderry as if the Prime Minister was going back on his pledge that Ulster should not be coerced. But in the event Midleton's scheme, to which Redmond assented, was to prove the undoing of both these politicians, since each in turn was to be disowned by his own party. On 14 January 1918, Redmond came into the conference hall and announced that he would not move his amendment accepting the Midleton scheme, since he felt that he could not carry the rest of the Nationalists as well as the Catholic hierarchy with him. 'The others will give their advice,' he said in tragic tones. 'I feel that I can be of no further use to the Convention.' He accordingly withdrew from the hall and was seen no more at the Convention. To one of the Ulster delegates who asked him to put his cards on the table, he replied sadly: 'I have no cards. I am a leader without a party.' Less than two months later he was dead.

'The Irish Convention is doomed and the sooner it is wound up the better,' Londonderry wrote to Lady Desborough on 16 March 1918. He went on:

> The smile of immoral glee which has sat on St John [Lord Midleton]'s face, since he was seduced, is gradually fading. His followers are not sure whether there is anything to be gained from his immoralities, and he is now feeling like a Japanese lady who for the good of her family has sacrificed herself, but is then denied admittance to her former home when returning shorn of virtue it is true, but with a

goodly pittance to maintain the family in ease and comfort. He oscillates now between bearding the R.C. bishops and shaking his fist at my colleagues; but he is still
good enough to retain his regard for me although the fact that I have maintained
my virtue has diminished his respect . . .

I meant to come over for this week end but I am lame with water on the knee, the
result of a kick out hunting in Limerick, the only day I have had over here. I then
processed behind Redmond's remains for 2¼ hours and this did the mischief. The
stout Protestants of the north with whom I am associated look on this as a direct
visitation for associating myself with Papistry. Perhaps there is something in it . . .

Ireland has always been a tragedy and I am at a loss to know what to do now. It
is such a pity that Ireland cannot be pushed a little further out into the Atlantic . . .
I am planless now. I do not know what place to drop into.

A month later the Convention adjourned indefinitely. A series of reports
was produced; Plunkett, the Nationalists, the Ulster Unionists, the southern Unionists and Labour all had their say. But there was no general
agreement. The Convention had failed, as Londonderry realised was
inevitable, because the fate of Ireland had passed largely into other and
younger hands—those of Sinn Fein. 'It is clear to my mind,' Carson
warned Lloyd George, 'that no settlement consistent with the interests of
Great Britain can be devised which will satisfy the Sinn Fein or the extreme Nationalist Party who sympathise with Sinn Fein. If therefore
attempt is made to bring Ulster into an Irish Parliament, to which they
are averse, you will have both Sinn Fein and Ulster in opposition to the
new Government, and I do not believe that any Government started under
such circumstances would have the least chance of success.' As for Midleton, Carson told Theresa Lady Londonderry, 'his scheme is the most
illusory and ridiculous I have ever heard of and I am sure Ulster would
have none of it.' Following the breakdown of the Convention, Lloyd George
tried to persuade Midleton to accept the Irish viceroyalty, but Midleton
declined when he found that he would have to support a double policy of
'autonomy and conscription' which he profoundly disliked. Conscription
was dictated by the acute manpower shortage on the western front, but
when Sir John (now Lord) French became Lord Lieutenant, he realised
that it would be hopeless to attempt to enforce conscription, so he relied
instead on volunteers.

After the Armistice and the General Election in December 1918,
French carried on in effect as military governor of Ireland, although the
country was fast drifting into civil war. One of the seven political advisers
whom the Lord Lieutenant appointed was Londonderry. This pleased his
mother. 'I am very glad he is such an Ulsterman and Irishman,' she wrote
at this time. 'I earnestly hope he gets a post in the new Government as I
think at 40 he ought to be in harness and he has brains for any post. So
far both in soldiering and politics, in racing parlance, he has never had
"the luck of the race".'

In Lloyd George's new Coalition Government Winston Churchill became Secretary of State for War and Air, the two portfolios being combined, with Colonel Seely as Under-Secretary for Air and Vice-President of the Air Council, which involved Seely usually taking the chair at meetings of the Council. At the same time Londonderry, on Churchill's initiative, was appointed unpaid Finance Member of the Air Council, with particular responsibility for demobilisation and disposals of surplus equipment and also generally answering for Air Ministry matters in the House of Lords. 'I had a charming letter from Curzon [Leader of the House of Lords] who welcomed me to the Front Bench,' he told his mother. 'Our Party deal in kind words and nothing else and friend Winston has come to the rescue just when I was going to turn into a "Local Magnate".'

His mother was disappointed that he had not received a paid post, the more so since, when Parliament was not sitting, he had to work at the Air Ministry from ten to five and also to put in a half-day on Sundays besides attending meetings which prevented him seeing her. He wrote to her on 24 January 1919 after he had been in the job for about a week:

> I am infinitely more disappointed than you are and I know that will be a great deal. My superiors, both paid by a grateful country, have gone away ostensibly on business connected with their public duties, so I (unpaid) have to carry on . . . I feel very sad, but these are the penalties of the life which you assert are so infinitely preferable to one of glorious independence. It means I shall never get home until inefficiency drives me out . . .

'Charley came in last night full of affairs,' noted his mother in her diary on 27 February. 'I hope he does not get under his Chief's thumb. I do not trust him [Churchill] for a second. Things seem very interesting just now. I have had an attack of bronchitis and a flabby heart. It is very annoying as I had to miss the Evening Party at St James's Palace last night. W[alter] L[ong] wrote me that Birdie and Edith looked two beautiful English ladies properly dressed, among an undressed throng.'

Theresa recovered, so that she was able to go to a dinner party at Lady Herbert's on 10 March. 'A good talk with Lady Londonderry about people and politics,' noted Colonel Repington who was also there. 'She told me that she had a temperature of 101 degrees the last time I dined with her, but refused to stay in bed. Her heart is troubling her and she ought to lie up, but it is the last thing she will ever do.' On the 11th she listened to a debate in the House of Commons and on the same day she wrote Edmund Gosse a note inviting him to dinner for the following Monday. But the dinner never took place. She was taken ill with influenza the same night and died four days later in 5 Carlton House Terrace.

'A great figure gone, and a real true friend,' wrote Colonel Repington when he heard the news. 'A *grande dame* of a period which is passing; one of the most striking and dominating feminine personalities of our time, terrifying to some, but endeared to many friends by her notable and excellent qualities. She was unsurpassed as a hostess, clear-headed, witty, and large-hearted, with unrivalled experience of men and things social and political, and with a most retentive memory and immense vivacity and *joie de vivre*. A heavy blow to her relatives and friends. In the last fortnight I have met her several times, and each time she seemed to be at her best. It seems scarcely credible that she is gone.' She was sixty-two, the same age as her husband when he died, and she was buried beside him in the Londonderry family vault at Long Newton in County Durham.

A memorial service was held at St Peter's, Eaton Square. 'A very large gathering,' noted Repington, 'with all the best known people now in town, and several Ambassadors and Ministers. Dignified and impressive and very sad.' Her son wrote to Edmund Gosse: 'I feel there is a blank in my life which nothing can fill and I shall forever miss my dear Mother's warm affection in every single thing I did.'

5

Londonderry could not have come to the Air Ministry at a more interesting and important time. A completely new air force was about to be created following a blueprint designed by the Chief of the Air Staff, Sir Hugh Trenchard. Besides acting as the ministry spokesman in the Lords, the Finance Member of the Air Council was responsible for the routine of demobilisation by age groups. When he took up his new post early in 1919, the Air Ministry had recently moved from the Hotel Cecil into a new building at the south-east corner of Kingsway, aptly named Adastral House. Both demobilisation and dispersal of surplus equipment each had its problems which caused Londonderry concern. For instance, there were attempts to use influence to procure the release of an officer or airman out of the regular order. One old friend of Londonderry's who attempted to do this was the Foreign Secretary Lord Curzon, who rang him up at Londonderry House. 'I have been trying to get hold of you at the Air Ministry, but no one seems to know who you are or where you are,' he fumed. 'I want my footman demobilised. He's a very useful man and does a lot for me.'

Londonderry explained that he had nothing to do with the release of men still serving with the colours, and in any event demobilisation was taking place in accordance with well-defined age rules and also with the needs of skilled technicians for industry. However, Curzon persisted that his footman was a most useful man and he must have him back forthwith, and as Foreign Secretary he would take full responsibility. 'I don't suppose,' he added, 'you would like to see me coming down to the House of Lords in my pyjamas!'

But Londonderry remained adamant, with the result that Curzon bore him a grudge for some time afterwards. This was to have unfortunate repercussions.

Londonderry's first meeting with the Chief of the Air Staff took place a few days after he had arrived at the Air Ministry. Some difficulty had cropped up over the liquidation of a war-time contract, and the Finance Member told his two private secretaries that he must go and see Trenchard. The secretaries looked at their chief in amazement and remarked that this suggestion was most improper. If the Finance Member wished to talk to the Chief of the Air Staff, he must send for him. 'That was not my idea of making a contact,' Londonderry subsequently recalled, 'for the establishment of immediate and friendly relationships with those working with me has been a fixed rule during all my public life.' He went on:

> In the outer office of the Chief of the Air Staff, a rather tremulous Maurice Baring, who was acting as Trenchard's private secretary at the time, beckoned to me not to make too much noise as the great man was at work at his desk. Eventually I was ushered in and, after a formal greeting, the C.A.S. began to tell me what he intended to do with this and that. He delved among piles of papers and found the one he wanted immediately.
>
> Then he went on with his short, decisive phrases with so much energy that I was a little taken aback. After listening for a while I ventured to remark, 'But what if I don't agree with you?' He looked up in doubt: there was a moment of silence: then he laughed as energetically as he had been talking. From that moment there was a complete understanding between us.

When the war ended, there was a vast number of firms and individuals engaged in one form or another of aircraft production on a cost plus basis, many of the firms lacking sufficient capital to carry on their work without Government assistance and subject to contract. Sir James (later Lord) Stevenson, head of a well-known Scottish firm of distillers and an additional Member of the Air Council, gave Londonderry a useful piece of advice at this time. 'I should get down to these contracts as soon as possible,' he said. 'The sooner most of them are cleared away the less likelihood there is of anything bordering on a public scandal. You won't sleep comfortably in your bed until these difficulties have been settled.' Londonderry and his civil servants took Stevenson's advice and the complicated contracts were gradually terminated, a process which took upwards of two years to complete. 'Happily there was no public scandal,' Londonderry later recalled, 'but it was a grim experience.'

Then there was the equipment question, since there were approximately 30,000 aircraft and engines for disposal, not to mention airfields, stores and so forth. In the event R.A.F. equipment to the value of

£5,700,000 was sold to the Aircraft Disposal Co., a concern which was jointly organised by the pioneer aircraft manufacturer Mr (later Sir) Frederick Handley Page, and Mr Godfrey Isaacs, Lord Reading's younger brother, who had been embarrassingly involved in the Marconi scandal a decade before. Shortly afterwards the company took over the remainder of the Air Ministry's surplus stock (roughly valued at £100 millions) in return for £1 million to be paid in cash instalments, plus half the profits from the sales. At the time these transactions were much criticised, but in the end they turned out well since the taxpayers got back several millions of pounds from what, but for the skilful handling of sales, would have been scrap metal and timber.

Although Seely did much to boost flying during the year that he served as Under-Secretary, and he took the chair regularly at Air Council meetings in Churchill's absence, he was never really happy in his post. After all, he had been War Minister himself and also a member of the Cabinet, and he could not disguise the feeling that he had been demoted. Also he felt very strongly that there should be a separate air service with a separate minister in charge. Lloyd George told Seely he was sorry, but at the moment it was essential to curtail expenditure and there was no alternative to the joint arrangement. Seely thereupon resigned.

Churchill considered that Londonderry had done well as Finance Member and that his handling of air questions in the Upper House had been good, so that it was natural that he should suggest him as Seely's successor. To the surprise of both the Secretary of State and the Finance Member, opposition came from an unexpected quarter—not from the Liberals or even Labour but from the Tories, Londonderry's own party. Particularly opposed to it was Lord Curzon, who still bore him a grudge over his footman. Curzon would also complain from time to time that Londonderry was not in his place on the Government Front Bench in the Lords when he should have known that the Finance Member was attending a meeting of the Air Council. 'What can I do?' said Churchill. 'Your own people are against you.' In the event Londonderry was passed over in favour of Major G. C. (later Lord) Tryon, an ardent Tory imperialist who lacked Seely's adventurous spirit. Londonderry protested to his chief that the selection of Tryon as Seely's successor was a deliberate slight upon himself, although he must have derived some solace from the fact that, like his father, great-grandfather and great-great-uncle Castlereagh, he was created a Knight of the Garter at this time.

In reply to his protest, Churchill wrote Londonderry a private letter which contained some sage advice:

War Office. 25.xii.19. There can certainly be no 'deliberate slight' in the action of a Government which has just conferred on you the highest honour in the gift of the Crown. I do not think their choice of Tryon was a wise one, but it arose entirely out of the Tory Whips' room view of what their men in the House of Commons expected. I am sure that an effort will be made to provide satisfactorily for you at the first opportunity. Bonar [Law] even suggested that in a few months Tryon might be moved to another post, and anyhow he authorised me to tell you that you stood first whenever a vacancy occurred which could be given to the Lords.

At this moment the only course for you to take is to be entirely good tempered and apparently indifferent and above all avoid anything which has the appearance of chagrin. You should continue to act as Finance Member on the Air Council and represent the department in the Lords. The substitution of Tryon for Seely will in fact give you a better and not a worse position. I am having his duties worked out by Robinson on this basis.[1]

I hope my dear you will be guided by me and will do as I wish; and then I am sure that your public career will open out satisfactorily; whereas quarrelling with the present regime will only strand you on the mud flats. I am very hopeful that we may find it possible to work together in the years that lie before us. It will indeed be a pleasure to me if that were so.

I am looking forward to coming to Wynyard on Monday next . . . We can then talk over the whole position. Do not on any account take any step contrary to what I advise till then. I am sure Edie will reinforce what I say. Yours affectionately, W.

So Londonderry carried on as Finance Member for the time being. Eventually, on 2 April 1920, in accordance with Bonar Law's suggestion, Tryon was moved to another post in the course of a Government shuffle, and since the opposition to Londonderry's appointment had by this time subsided, the Finance Member was appointed Under-Secretary in Tryon's place.

One of Londonderry's first official duties as Parliamentary Under-Secretary of State for Air was to introduce in Parliament the Air Navigation Bill, which when it reached the statute book was to become the basis for the international law of the air. Londonderry also proved useful with his wife on the social side, not only entertaining Air Force personnel generously in Londonderry House, but also giving formal receptions for the Coalition Government on the eve of the opening of Parliament and other official occasions. Thus, easily and effortlessly, did Edith Londonderry slip into Theresa's place as the leading Conservative hostess of her time. There was a tendency on the part of the personnel of the two other services, at least in these early days, to look down on the R.A.F., so that the aristocratic Londonderry's association with the force proved a useful corrective, the effect of which was greatly appreciated by Trenchard and the Air Staff. Also, Londonderry was to develop into an enthusiastic airman, learning to fly, getting his 'wings', and later often piloting his own aircraft.

On taking up his new appointment as Under-Secretary for Air, Londonderry was immediately conscious of the existence of an element of friction

[1] Sir Arthur Robinson, Secretary to the Air Council and Secretary of the Air Ministry.

with the Admiralty, whose 'dining out power' was considerably greater than that of the Air Ministry, an advantage which Londonderry was personally able in some measure to redress. He took an early opportunity of mentioning this friction to Trenchard.

'I am a little anxious as to what you say of the growing discontent the Navy with the Air,' the Chief of the Air Staff wrote to him at this time. 'I also am exercised with this discontent, though I feel it is not so much growing, but that it is at present there and permanent, and has been for some time. I feel that this may be to a certain extent due to personal dislike of myself, combined with my opposition to breaking up the Air Service—why it should become personal I cannot say.'

Londonderry, who happened to be on leave, sought to reassure him on the personal point, adding: 'I feel that I am outstaying my leave, but on the other hand I believe you are better on your own and pay too much attention to the Secretary of State. However, my only ambition is to help you to achieve your plan and I think success is already assured.'

Trenchard had already drafted a letter of complaint to Churchill, but Londonderry persuaded him not to send it. 'There is nothing personal in this,' the Under-Secretary repeated, 'and if there is it is the one thing to ignore even to Winston who always handles personal things badly. We are not going to get much help from either Service because the heads are terrified that the C-in-C of the next war is going to be an airman. We must capture the new generation and soft soap the old for the time being.'

'I must say you always write me letters that make me *purr* with pleasure,' Trenchard wrote back. Thereafter a strong bond of friendship developed between the two men. Eventually, when Trenchard retired, Londonderry told him: 'I shall never see a finer spectacle really than the way in which you grappled with the whole situation, liquidated the war situation and set to work a new Air Service . . . so I was glad when Winston decided to install you as head of the Force, and how wise was his selection.'

Towards the end of 1920, when Londonderry had been Under-Secretary for about nine months, the question of the viceroyalty of India came up. Lord Chelmsford, the incumbent Viceroy, was due to retire shortly and Londonderry, who had fancied the post from the time he had visited India before the war, evidently considered he was in the running. After all Curzon had only been thirty-nine when he was appointed, and Londonderry was now forty-two. But Lloyd George had other ideas in mind and in the event the Prime Minister's friend Lord Reading, the Lord Chief Justice, got the job, much to Londonderry's disappointment. But, even if he had secured it, there would have been difficulties, since Lady Londonderry was pregnant at this time, and she would certainly have insisted on the baby being born in England or Ireland; the baby was expected at the same time as the new Viceroy was due in Bombay, so that it would not have been possible for his wife to have accompanied him as vicereine.

At this period the Air Ministry was responsible for civil flying. In the summer of 1919 commercial companies began to operate services to the Continent, but they received no government subsidy and their services proved uneconomical so that they went out of business during the next eighteen months. This caused an outcry in the press with the result that Churchill announced a grant of £600,000 for the financial year 1921–22 for British companies operating on approved aerial routes, and he appointed a Cross-Channel Subsidies Committee under Londonderry's chairmanship to work out the details of how the money should be apportioned. This was put into effect in March 1921 and, although it had been announced too late to avoid interruption in the services, it was nevertheless in time to revive them. With their resumption it was possible to reduce passenger fares on the London to Paris route to £6 6s single and £12 return, which was the same as by railway.

By this time Lloyd George, concerned by the outcry over the alleged neglect of civil aviation by the Government, had decided that the portfolios of war and air should no longer be held by a single minister. Consequently, in the ministerial reshuffle which followed in April 1921, Churchill was shifted to the Colonial Office. Before he left Adastral House, he pressed the Prime Minister to appoint Londonderry Air Minister, but without success. In the reshuffle the Air Ministry was earmarked for a Liberal, and as it happened another kinsman of Churchill's, Captain F. E. ('Freddie') Guest, was appointed. However, the measure of importance which was attached to the post may be gauged from the fact that it did not carry a seat in the Cabinet.

Although not a statesman of the first rank and lacking Churchill's quickness of intellect, the new Air Minister was one of the most popular men at Westminster, where his reputation as a sportsman and big game hunter stood him in good stead. He was the first Secretary of State to hold a pilot's licence. He and Londonderry had been friends for many years and had served together in the war, which may have made Londonderry's disappointment rather easier to bear. Certainly Guest appreciated his loyalty. 'I know all the time how you must have felt and was deeply grateful to you for taking the whole incident in such a splendidly loyal spirit,' Guest wrote to him afterwards. 'In every way you set a great example; but for it my difficulties would have nearly swamped me. If it is ever in my power to thank you, I shall try and do so.'

The year 1921 proved to be a crucial one in both Londonderry's political and private fortunes. The Government of Ireland Act, passed at Westminster in the previous year, was a compromise which provided for the setting up of a separate Government and Parliament of Northern

Ireland with a limited measure of self-government, while major services such as foreign affairs, defence and the major proportion of finance were retained by Whitehall. The new subordinate Parliament was to consist of two chambers, a House of Commons with fifty-two members and a Senate with thirty-four members indirectly chosen in proportion to the party representation in the Lower House. On grounds of age Carson yielded the Unionist leadership to his lieutenant Sir James Craig, who became Prime Minister after the Unionists had won forty out of the fifty-two seats in the Commons. Meanwhile Craig invited Londonderry to become Leader of the Senate and at the same time to accept the portfolio of education in the new Ulster Cabinet.

'There was a real call of the blood in this invitation,' Londonderry wrote afterwards, 'for my family had been so long associated with Ulster. My father always sought to persuade me to make the Irish Question the main theme of my political activities . . . and if I had turned my back on the offer which James Craig had made to me, I should never have forgiven myself . . .' Winston Churchill, however, took a different view, under the impression that his cousin was leaving the Westminster political scene because he was disgruntled and disappointed that he had not been appointed Air Minister in Churchill's place. But this was not so, although Churchill could not convince himself or be convinced otherwise.

'Naturally I am sorry to learn of the step you contemplate,' Churchill wrote to Londonderry on 20 May 1921, 'and my advice, as a sincere well-wisher, with a certain amount of knowledge of the conditions now prevailing, would be adverse. However, every man must make his own career and, if you feel your duty calls you to the Ulster Senate, I cannot reproach you in any way; on personal grounds I am sorry that we shall not be working together.'

Lloyd George accepted his resignation from the Air Ministry with regret and also wrote wishing him well. However, although a new and important chapter in his political life was about to begin, Londonderry had every intention of continuing to keep in touch with air matters.

6

The Parliament of Northern Ireland, which had been created by the Act of 1920, assembled for the first time, for the transaction of formal business, in the Council Chamber of the Belfast City Hall on 7 June 1921. The Lord Lieutenant, Viscount Fitzalan, the last to hold the office of Viceroy and the only Catholic ever to do so, made the journey from Dublin to swear in the new Prime Minister, James Craig, and the members of his Cabinet.

Personally, Craig was a man of outstanding courage and inflexible determination, great integrity, trusted alike by friends and opponents. In the words of his successor, J. M. Andrews, who served as Minister of Labour in his government, his fundamental patriotism led him to fight tenaciously for the principles in which he profoundly believed. In him Unionist Ulster saw an epitome of itself. 'He was the symbol and embodiment of its ideals.' His besetting fault was a characteristic obstinacy—unlike the average English politician, he did not know the meaning of the word compromise. He was also to cling to office long after he had outlived his usefulness as a leader—indeed Ulster was to enjoy nineteen years of his monolithic rule. The Parliament which he was to introduce in Belfast's City Hall he was later aptly to describe as 'a Protestant Parliament for a Protestant people'. Thus under it Catholics, whom Carson had hoped as members of the minority faith would be seen to have nothing to fear from their Protestant neighbours, gradually came to assume the position of second-class citizens in the Ulster community. Besides Londonderry and Andrews, a County Down linen manufacturer, the other members of Craig's Cabinet were H. M. Pollock, a Belfast businessman who had been an Ulster delegate at the ill-fated Irish Convention, and now took over finance; Dawson Bates, a Belfast lawyer, who became responsible for home affairs; and Edward Archdale, an ex-naval officer and gentleman farmer from County Fermanagh who combined the portfolios of agriculture and commerce. Captain Hugh O'Neill was elected Speaker of the Commons, while Lord Dufferin became Speaker of the Senate. None of the Nationalist M.P.s turned up, and it was evident that they intended to boycott the assembly.

As soon as the formalities had been completed, both Houses adjourned pending the reply to the official invitation which Craig sent King George V to come over to Belfast and open the first session of the Northern Irish Parliament in person. Queen Mary was also invited, and to the great satisfaction of the new Government and the majority of the Ulster Parliament and the Ulster people both the King and Queen accepted, although their mail-bag at Buckingham Palace was full of letters beseeching them not to risk their lives, since Ireland was still in the throes of a civil war. The King specially asked Lord Londonderry to accompany him as Minister in attendance, and in view of this the British Cabinet decided that the presence of the Home Secretary would be unnecessary and that the Cabinet should be represented by the Chief Secretary to the Lord Lieutenant, Sir Hamar Greenwood. Nor did Lloyd George, who had been unwell, feel able to make the journey.

The Council Chamber of the City Hall had been converted for the occasion into a Senate; in place of the Lord Mayor's oak seat a three-tier dais had been erected covered with crimson cloth on which two gilded chairs rested so as to form temporary thrones. After the Sovereign and his consort had entered the chamber and taken their places on the dais, the Commons were summoned from an adjacent room by Black Rod exactly as at Westminster. Prayers were then read by the Protestant Primate of All Ireland, the Moderator of the Presbyterian General Assembly and the Senior Methodist Minister. Unfortunately the Cardinal Archbishop of Armagh declined to attend or to send any representative such as a Catholic bishop or even a chaplain.

The King's speech, in formally opening the Parliament of Northern Ireland, owed something of its emotional appeal to the South African General Smuts, who had come to London for the Imperial Conference held at this time and at a luncheon with George V at Buckingham Palace suggested that the speech might be redrafted as a plea for peace among his strife-torn Irish subjects. This was agreed to by the Cabinet and the King, the task of redrafting being given by Lloyd George to one of his private secretaries, Sir Edward Grigg, later Lord Altrincham, who was an expert on imperial affairs. The result was the most remarkable speech uttered by King George V in the whole twenty-six years of his reign.

'For all who love Ireland, as I do with all my heart,' the speech began, 'this is a profoundly moving occasion in Irish history.' The King went on to recall the happy days he had spent as a midshipman in Ireland and of how his affection for the Irish people had been deepened by successive visits since that time. He had therefore come in person, as head of the Empire, to inaugurate this Parliament on Irish soil. 'I inaugurate it with a deep felt hope,' he declared. The fact that within the Empire many races had come together in spite of ancient feuds, he said, encouraged him to look beyond the current sorrow and anxiety which of late had clouded his vision of Irish affairs. He went on:

> I speak from a full heart when I pray that my coming to Ireland today may prove to be the first step towards an end of strife among her people, whatever their race and creed. In that hope I appeal to all Irishmen to pause, to stretch out the hand of forbearance and conciliation, to forgive and forget, and to join in making for the land they love a new era of peace, contentment and good will . . .
>
> The future lies in the hands of the Irish people themselves. May this historic gathering be the prelude of a day in which the Irish people, North and South, under one Parliament or two, as those Parliaments may decide, shall work in common love for Ireland upon the sure foundation of mutual justice and respect.

There is no doubt that the King and Queen were greatly impressed by their reception everywhere. That evening, after they had embarked on the royal yacht, the King wrote in his diary:

> I think my speech was appreciated . . . Our visit has been a great success and everything has gone off beautifully. We really got a wonderful welcome and I never heard anything like the cheering.

In his speech the King had said he was confident that what he called 'the important matters entrusted to the control and guidance of the Northern Parliament' would be 'managed with wisdom and moderation, with fairness and due regard for every faith and interest'. Regrettably this confidence was not destined to be justified, although half a century was to elapse before the experiment in devolutionary government broke down and direct rule by Westminster was restored. Nor could it be said that the rival sections of the community to whom the King addressed his appeal were able to forgive or forget, let alone stretch out the hand of forbearance and conciliation. Indeed in the very week of the royal visit fifty-two attacks on the British forces were mounted by the I.R.A. including the mining and derailing of a troop train carrying men and horses who had formed part of the King's escort and were returning to Dublin, three soldiers and a guard being killed, and a large number of horses killed or mutilated.

In spite of this, King George V was generally acclaimed, at least in the north, for his courage and statesmanship in coming to Belfast with the Queen, and his courageous action had an immediate effect. At the next meeting of the British Cabinet in Downing Street, the Prime Minister proposed that the King's appeal, which 'had been very well received', should be followed up by an invitation to Sir James Craig and the Irish Republican leader Mr De Valera to meet with British government representatives in London 'to discuss the situation and if possible reach agreement'. In the event both Craig and De Valera accepted, but De Valera made his acceptance conditional upon a truce. The truce after some delay and argument came into effect on 11 July 1921. It did not include, as Lloyd George hoped it would, the surrender of arms by the I.R.A. As subsequent events were to show, such a demand would have been impossible to enforce. However, for the time being, the shooting and other terrorist acts stopped, although there were to be numerous violations of the truce before the Anglo-Irish 'Treaty' was concluded in December. After the British forces had been withdrawn from the south, the I.R.A. transferred their attentions to Ulster, much to the embarrassment of Craig and Londonderry and the rest of the northern Government.

Speaking in the Northern Irish Senate on 20 September 1921, Londonderry defended the action of the Ulster Cabinet in accepting Lloyd George's invitation to confer with him and his colleagues in Downing Street, so as to ascertain what had passed between him and De Valera. To refuse the invitation, he said, would have put them in the wrong before the British people and would have involved a risk of settlement behind their backs which might have been damaging to their interests.

After considerable comings and goings on the part of De Valera and his henchmen, the negotiations proper began in Downing Street on 10 October. The Sinn Fein delegation was led by Arthur Griffith, veteran pioneer of the movement, whom Mr Churchill described as 'that unique figure, a silent Irishman'. His principal lieutenant was Michael Collins, the romantic and handsome young gunman—he was only thirty-one— whom Lloyd George was to call 'one of the most courageous leaders ever produced by a valiant race', but whom Carson, Hamar Greenwood and Sit Henry Wilson regarded as 'the head of the murder gang' in Ireland. The southern group, included two lawyers, Eamon Duggan and Charles Gavan Duffy, and an economic expert Robert Barton, who was the only Protestant. The secretary was an Englishman who had become more Irish than many of the Irish, Erskine Childers, better known as the author of the thrilling adventure story *The Riddle of the Sands*. De Valera remained in Dublin, considering it beneath his dignity to attend as head of an independent state. The British negotiators consisted of three representatives from each of the two major political parties—the Prime Minister, Churchill and Greenwood for the Liberals, and Lord Birkenhead, the Lord Chancellor, Sir Austen Chamberlain, Leader of the House of Commons, and Sir Laming Worthington-Evans, the War Minister, for the Conservatives and Unionists. Lionel Curtis and Lloyd George's particular friend Tom Jones acted as secretaries on the British side. Craig was content to let the southern Irish get the best bargain they could from the British provided the political and territorial status of the six northeastern counties was not jeopardised.

Londonderry, who came over to London as often as he could manage at this time, learned much of what was going on from Churchill and Birkenhead and also from the painter Sir John Lavery, whose studio-house in Kensington was a convenient social meeting place for members of both sides.

Both the painter and his beautiful Irish-American wife Hazel had been friends of the Londonderrys for some years and both belonged to Lady Londonderry's Ark circle. Although he was a Belfast-born Catholic and his political sympathies naturally lay with the great majority of his Irish co-religionists, Lavery was friendly with the Ulster Unionists and Protestants, and his sitters included such politically diverse personalities as Carson, De Valera, both the Catholic and Protestant Primates, as well as Londonderry himself. It was while Lavery was painting the portrait of the Protestant Primate Archbishop D'Arcy at Mount Stewart that he wrote to Churchill a characteristic letter about the state of Ireland.

> You asked me the other day what I thought of my country's state, and I had not the courage to tell you.
> But if one artist may speak to another I will give you my beliefs.
> The Prime Minister has said that he is prepared for a million casualties and a five years' war. I believe that ten million and a fifty years' war would not bring about the result he desires.

I believe that Ireland will never be governed by Westminster, the Vatican, or Ulster without continuous bloodshed.

I also believe that the removal of the 'Castle' and all its works, leaving Irishmen to settle their own affairs, is the only solution left.

I am convinced with the knowledge I possess of my countrymen that such a situation would make her one of your staunchest allies instead of an avowed enemy for all time. Love is stronger than hate.

When he was about half-way through painting the Archbishop's portrait, Lavery received an anonymous letter addressed to him at Mount Stewart and headed in large block capitals 'THE LONDONDERRY AIR'. Underneath appeared the well-known lines written about Londonderry's ancestor by the poet Shelley in *The Mask of Anarchy*:

> I met Murder in the way—
> He had a mask like Castlereagh,
> Very smooth he looked and grim,
> Seven bloodhounds followed him.

The writer went on to ask whether the artist had no sense of shame, stating that 'sycophants and parasites' like him 'should be exterminated like vermin', and more of the same sort. Lavery showed it to his wife, saying, 'That's what comes of doing something for Ireland.' She said, 'Never mind, carry on,' and so he did.

'I could not help thinking what Lord Londonderry must have put up with on my account,' wrote Lavery afterwards, 'since it was entirely owing to his support that the Freedom of Belfast and the Honorary Degree at Queen's University came to me. I felt much in his debt, saying that I would remember him in my prayers, a form of repayment which I have always found economic and sometimes impressive.'

During the prolonged Anglo-Irish negotiations in London which lasted for nearly two months, due to so much having necessarily to be referred by the Irish delegation to De Valera in Dublin, Lloyd George succeeded in securing from Arthur Griffith a personal pledge of participation in the Commonwealth and allegiance to the Crown in return for the recognition of 'the essential unity of Ireland'. Northern Ireland, which was not consulted on this point, was to be given the choice of coming in to an all-Ireland Parliament, with certain safeguards, or of opting out within one month and retaining her present subordinate Parliament in Belfast, while sharing all imperial burdens and submitting to a Boundary Commission designed to redraw her border with the south as far as possible on sectarian lines. Southern Ireland was henceforth to be known as the Irish Free State and to enjoy the status and rights of a self-governing dominion like Canada. The members of the southern Irish legislature, Dail Eireann, were to swear to be 'faithful' to King George V 'in virtue of the common citizenship of Ireland with Great Britain and her adherence to and membership of the group of nations forming the British Commonwealth of Nations'. The oath, which was a compromise drafted by Birkenhead to meet Griffith's objections to an explicit oath of loyalty to the Crown, could of course be abrogated, as indeed it subsequently was, whenever the 'Free State' exercised the right, which she claimed by virtue of her dominion status, to secede from the Commonwealth.

The 'Treaty', actually 'Articles of Agreement for a Treaty between Great Britain and Ireland', was signed in the early hours of the morning of 6 December 1921. Its terms were immediately published to the world. 'I never thought,' remarked Carson when he read them, 'that I should live to see the day of such abject humiliation for Great Britain.' That it was a humiliation for the English Unionist leaders such as Chamberlain and Birkenhead, and the majority of English Unionist M.P.s who endorsed it, Londonderry for one could not deny. But then, as he wrote when reflecting on the 'Treaty' some years later, 'perhaps I have never been very sympathetic to the manner in which England has attempted to govern Ireland for the last eight hundred years, as I know that no Englishman can understand the Irish character . . . The main traditional and overwhelming difficulty is that Ulster and Ireland have never been united and that whatever form of government develops, which is to carry with it the happiness and contentment of a wonderful people, must recognise that over-riding factor'.

7

Christmas was spent at Wynyard, where the party included the Chief of the Imperial General Staff, Field Marshal Sir Henry Wilson. A few weeks previously, in the absence of Carson and Craig through illness, Wilson, accompanied by the Londonderrys, had opened the memorial tower to the Ulster Division at Thiepval on the Somme where the Ulster troops had suffered so heavily in 1916; the memorial had been dedicated by Archbishop D'Arcy and the other Ulster Protestant church leaders. The ceremony was also attended by Lord Dufferin, Speaker of the Ulster Senate, and his wife, and afterwards they and the Londonderrys and the Archbishop did a tour of the battlefields, which included Arras where Londonderry showed them what was left of Monchy, the scene of so much destruction when he was serving with his regiment in April 1917. The tour ended at Ypres where the Archbishop's son had been left for dead during the first battle of Ypres and was subsequently saved by Lord Dufferin, who spotted him while riding past and sent out a stretcher party which brought him to a field hospital.

Wilson confided in the Londonderrys at this time that he expected soon to be unemployed as he had had profound differences with Lloyd George over the Prime Minister's handling of the Irish question and the 'Treaty', and he was sure that his four-year term as C.I.G.S. which was due to end in February 1922 would not be renewed. At heart Wilson was a politician rather than a soldier and, when a vacancy arose for North Down in the Westminster House of Commons, largely due to Londonderry's influence Wilson was selected for the constituency and had an unopposed return, being the only Field Marshal who had ever become an M.P. 'We discussed the possibility, necessity and probability of forming a real Conservative Party,' Wilson wrote in his diary after lunching with the Londonderrys at this time. 'Lady Londonderry is working hard to this end with Salisbury, Northumberland, Carson, Ronald McNeill, and I am sure this is the right thing to aim for. And I believe if they would get a fine leader it is a real possibility.' Unfortunately Wilson was not to live to see the break-up of the Lloyd George Coalition, since almost exactly four months to the day after his election to the House of Commons he was gunned down by two I.R.A. terrorists and died on the doorstep of his London house in Eaton Place.

In Dublin De Valera, who had repudiated the 'Treaty', resigned as President of the Dail, and in the ensuing contest with Arthur Griffith was defeated by 60 to 58 votes. The 'Treaty' was thereupon ratified by a similarly narrow majority, 64 to 57, and the country was split as between the 'treatyites' or 'Free Staters' and the 'anti-treatyites' or 'Republicans'. A Provisional Government was set up with Michael Collins as chairman and finance minister, charged with taking over the machinery of government from the British departments, framing a constitution for the new Free State, and working out a viable administrative relationship with the north on such matters as police and other services which had previously been shared. This involved Collins and his colleagues in visiting London and meeting their British and Ulster opposite numbers there.

When Collins first came to London for the 'Treaty' negotiations, there was what Londonderry called 'a very unhealthy curiosity to meet this celebrity, and surreptitious parties were arranged to which people of varying importance were invited'. These were mostly given by Sir John Lavery to whom Collins was sitting for his portrait. 'I received my invitation and more than one,' Londonderry afterwards recalled, 'but I refused deliberately to meet Michael Collins in a social atmosphere and I gave as my reason that, whereas I would certainly meet him in the conference chamber, I was not willing to meet anyone who, whatever his motives and reasons may have been, had been a party to the murder, sometimes in cold blood, of brother officers of my own and many friends who lived in Ireland.'

The conference eventually took place in Churchill's room in the Colonial Office on 30 March 1922. Besides Churchill, Worthington-Evans and Sir Ernest Pollock, the Attorney General, were on the British side;

Collins, Griffith, Duggan, Kevin O'Higgins, and Hugh Kennedy as legal adviser represented the south, while Craig, Londonderry, and Edward Archdale constituted the Ulster delegation. The first two from each of the three sides together hammered out a draft agreement. The conference of the 'Six' continued until five in the afternoon, when agreement was reached. Collins and his colleagues promised to co-operate 'in every way in their power' to restore peaceful conditions throughout Ireland. For their part, Craig and Londonderry agreed to reorganise the Ulster police so that the 'specials' keeping law and order would consist of equal numbers of Catholics and Protestants. Collins agreed that all border attacks by the I.R.A. would cease and that the southern boycott of Ulster goods should be called off. Churchill promised a British Government contribution of £500,000 for relief work in Northern Ireland, one third for the benefit of Catholics and two thirds for Protestants. The draft was then sent to the basement of the Foreign Office to be printed, after which it was examined by the full conference and eventually signed at eight o'clock. The document, which Churchill read to the House of Commons later that night, began with the words, which were Churchill's own: 'Peace is today declared.'

Defending the agreement in the House next day, Churchill went out of his way to praise the Ulster delegates for having 'lent a helping hand to the Irish Free State and to the cause of peace in Ireland'. The agreement, he said, was intended to bring to an end 'the religious and partisan warfare in Belfast itself and to the acts of repeated injury and counter-injury which have been done by Catholics and Protestants one against the other'. At the same time he uttered some words of ominous warning, that there would be forces in Ireland 'anxious to wreck these arrangements by violent action, by treacherous action, and, if possible, to throw suspicion upon the good faith of those with whom we have entered into a covenant . . . We must be prepared for attempts to mar all this fair prospect'. Events were soon to prove how right Churchill was.

Prompted it appears by Lady Londonderry, Churchill thought it might help matters further if Collins and Londonderry could meet for an informal talk. At first Collins jibbed at this but eventually agreed and the meeting took place at the Colonial Office next morning. 'I can say at once that I spent three of the most delightful hours that I ever spent in my life,' Londonderry recalled afterwards, 'and I formed a conclusion of the character of Michael Collins which was quite different from the one which I would have formed if I had only known him as I had read of him before this particular interview. His enthusiasm was delightful as he unfolded his plans for the future in stirring phraseology. Perhaps I knew history a little better than he did and perhaps also I knew the power which he had over his followers and also the power which I had over mine when he entreated me to join with him in a really big conception. We parted and, as a matter of fact, we never met again . . .'

Before returning to Dublin, Collins scribbled a note in pencil to Lady Londonderry from the Laverys' house in Kensington:

> 5 Cromwell Place,
> S.W.
>
> Forgive me. I bitterly regret my outburst about L. You were very kind to arrange the meeting, and I am well aware that I was very miserably minded to listen to W[inston Churchill].
>
> It is all very well to tell me as you do that he has no 'interest' in you. But how can you expect me to believe that, feeling as you know well how I feel? So you must forgive my bitterness, and try to imagine what it means to be a man like myself, entirely self-made, self-educated, without background and trying to cope with a man like Lord L., a man who has every advantage I lack.
>
> This is not self-disparagement, a mean quality that I think I do not possess; but I cannot help recognising the fact that you and he speak the same language, an alien one to me, and he understands to perfection all the little superficial things that matter in your particular world—unimportant things maybe—but oh! my God, not to be underestimated with a woman like you. I know that instinctively.
>
> I feel savage and unhappy, and so I blame you for a situation for which I alone am to blame, but I contrast myself with him, my uncouthness with his distinction, my rough speech with his unconscious breeding and the worst of it is I *like* and admire him, and feel that he is brave and honest.
>
> On one point alone I believe myself his superior.

Of the precise nature of that point the note affords no clue and one can only speculate. Love of Ireland? Possibly. More likely, Collins considered his hold over his followers greater than Londonderry's over his. 'Whatever happens to me,' said Collins to a friend, 'my own fellow countrymen won't kill me.' Yet they did, on 22 August 1922, in an ambush a few miles from his birthplace in County Cork. And when the boundary issue came up a little later, Thomas Jones, the Assistant Secretary of the British Cabinet, noted in a reference to Ulster Unionist intransigence that Londonderry was 'the only reasonable negotiator, and he is too weak to bring along the rest of his party'.

Afterwards Londonderry recalled that Churchill considered the Craig-Collins pact was 'an epoch-making document but which I took much more philosophically'. In fact, it lasted barely a fortnight, since civil war broke out in the south on 14 April when the Republican 'Irregulars' led by Rory O'Connor seized the Four Courts in Dublin. Six weeks later the Irregulars were dislodged from the building with the help of British arms and surrendered to the Provisional Government forces, but not before they had mined and fired the building which was blown up, incidentally destroying besides the law courts building the Irish official records going back to the Middle Ages, an irreparable loss to historians. The civil war, which continued for the greater part of the next twelve months until it was called off by De Valera in May 1923, resulted in great loss of life and property on both sides of the border, since the 'Irregulars' carried the war into the north. Although Stormont Castle, Craig's official residence on the outskirts of Belfast, was attacked, as was Mount Stewart, the attackers were repulsed, since both buildings were well guarded, but other fine houses were destroyed, while many citizens including one prominent Unionist M.P., were gunned down by the I.R.A. in the streets of Belfast and elsewhere in the province.

Meanwhile in England the Lloyd George Coalition finally disintegrated following a Conservative Party meeting at the Carlton Club in October, and Bonar Law formed a purely Conservative Government. The new Prime Minister offered Londonderry the post of Air Minister. Londonderry asked for forty-eight hours to think it over, and having seen Craig in the meantime refused Bonar Law's offer. Why he did so he explained in a letter to Lady Desborough:

Mount Stewart. 25 October 1922 . . . I have made a sacrifice this time. I have never made one before that was fairly disinterested. This may destroy my prospects, and although if I am really good enough it cannot do that, and if I am not good enough it doesn't matter. But judging dispassionately at this moment, as I have done, I have followed the right course. I came here to help deal with a crisis; that crisis is not over and it amounts to running away if I follow the path of my personal ambition . . .

I knew I was of a certain value here, that I filled a place which no one at the moment could fill, but I did not realise that my suggested departure would really create consternation. Craig had a reception at Stormont last night and I had expressions from colleagues, friends, officials, which I never anticipated; it was a revelation to me: and James Craig himself too. I really felt like leaving the front line for a soft billet at G.H.Q.

You must judge me as your knowledge and wisdom dictate; but I want you to realise what I have given up; the summit of many ambitions, a post in the Cabinet, a partnership with a real true friend like Jim,[1] and a renewed association with Trenchard. Nothing but conviction could have impelled me to make that sacrifice.

Londonderry remained at his post in the Education Ministry in Ulster. On 19 January 1923, he wrote despondently to Churchill from Mount Stewart:

I have tried to get a place in the train 'bleu' [to Cannes] but I understand every place is booked up for days and weeks ahead. I am doubtful also of being able to get away. There is a heritage of difficulty here and as one question is disposed of another crops up immediately. I have always loved your optimism and your encouragement

---

[1] James, 4th Marquess of Salisbury, was the first to state publicly, in the *Morning Post* in June 1921, that the Coalition Government no longer possessed the confidence of the Conservative and Unionist Party. In the Bonar Law Government he became Lord President of the Council and Leader of the House of Lords.

and also your assistance when you were responsible for us, but I feel very gloomy now and I really do not see a break of any kind in the clouds.

The Free State is an impossible proposition and no one can make a success of the idea embodied in that title, and it is merely a question of whether at some stage of the descent of Ireland to anarchy and chaos the British Government will step in, and tan Ireland like a large nanny which has mutinied against a long suffering nurse. If Ireland is to be left to its own devices, it is an ugly sore and in the end may poison the whole body of the Empire.

All the analogies of a dominion are faulty. There is really no inbetwixts and betweens. I see that so clearly here. You must be independent or dependent, you can't be one day one thing and the next day another. Either your government governs or it does not govern. I won't weary you in your well-earned holiday with grumbles, but I feel very depressed from a source of impotence and inability to do anything to save the disaster.

So Londonderry carried on in Belfast in a temporary office pending the building of the new Parliament and government offices at Stormont. On 14 March 1923, he introduced an excellent measure which laid the basis of education in the province and which became known as the Londonderry Act, establishing a non-sectarian basis for schools and teachers' training colleges but at the same time providing ample facilities for religious instruction. 'The State is non-sectarian,' he said, 'but not secular in the sense that it takes no interest in the moral upbringing of the children.' He continued:

The State, as does the individual, looks to the Churches to give the lead in Christian idealism, and I feel we need not look in vain. Do not let it be said that these same Churches, all possessing a proud history of good deeds, responsible as they have been for almost all the education in past years, are now, with all the opportunities that the community can possibly give, the stumbling-block in the way of an ideal system by a determination to segregate their flocks and create from birth a division when union is so essential to the well-being of the province. There are schools in existence where children of different denominations work together and play together, and who will assert that this association is anything but beneficial for all concerned?

The State itself can do but little in this direction. It can afford, and under this Bill it does afford, opportunities, and I look with confidence to the future believing that in the new spirit of the new era dawning before our eyes, tolerance and a mutual respect will replace prejudice and jealous mistrust. But beyond giving opportunities for denominational instruction the State cannot go.

Under the old system inherited from Dublin Castle, all the schools, apart from some technical colleges, were voluntary bodies run for the most part by the churches, and public policy was administered by three departments in Dublin which dealt direct with the numerous committees of management. The 1923 Act made each county or county borough in Northern Ireland the responsible authority for each area, acting through one or more education committees; initially there were eighteen committees. Parents were required to ensure that children between six and fourteen years received elementary education, which was defined as 'both literary and moral, based upon instruction in the reading and writing of the English language and in arithmetic'. Each committee had a duty to prepare schemes for the provision of elementary and secondary education, and they were empowered to accept the transfer of existing schools from voluntary managers—in practice from any of the Churches. However, religious instruction was not to be given in elementary schools within the hours of compulsory attendance. Neither were local education authorities permitted to provide such instruction in schools under their control, nor were they entitled to take into account a teacher's religious denomination when making an appointment.

'All the quarrels between Roman Catholics and Protestants arose out of the teaching of the Bible,' Londonderry argued; and, as he 'wished the children of all denominations to meet in the same schools and grow up in a friendly atmosphere', he thought that 'this could only be achieved if there was no Bible instruction and if Roman Catholic and Protestant children mixed in the same schools'. Unfortunately this proved impossible.

The transfer was not easy, since all the major Churches opposed the Act. Eventually the Stormont government bowed to the combined pressure of the Protestant Church and the Orange Order and passed an amending Act which met their objections by providing that education authorities could adopt a programme of 'simple Bible instruction' which teachers could be required to give as part of the ordinary school course. But the Catholic hierarchy never became reconciled to the 1923 Act notwithstanding that the able and enlightened Secretary of the Education Ministry, Bonaparte Wyse, was himself a Catholic, and the Catholic authorities faced the financial consequences which their refusal to co-operate entailed. Naturally they claimed that as taxpayers they were entitled to as much support for their schools as was given to the State schools, to which the Government retorted that the Catholics could always send their children to the State schools like members of other denominations and thus receive their due as taxpayers. Eventually, after Londonderry had ceased to be minister, the State agreed to pay sixty-five per cent of the cost of putting up new buildings and extending or improving old ones, a more generous arrangement than that adopted in England or for that matter in the United States, where the Ulster Government's alleged oppression of the Catholic population has been so often denounced.

It was only in the field of higher education, that is the Queen's University, Belfast, that Protestants and Catholics met together in the lecture room and tutorial classes as well as in sporting and other extra-curricular activities. In the spring of 1923, the Chancellor, Lord Shaftesbury, whose family had been connected with Belfast since its foundation, resigned his

office. Londonderry was the unopposed selection of the university con-
vocation to succeed him.

One of the new Chancellor's first official acts was to confer honorary
degrees on the Duke and Duchess of York, the future King George VI
and Queen Elizabeth, who spent two nights at Mount Stewart during their
visit in July 1924. It was the first occasion since the Duke's father had
opened the Parliament of Northern Ireland in 1921 that a member of the
royal family had visited the province, and its success showed that for the
time being at least sectarian strife had died down and peace had been
largely restored. 'Our reception has been astounding,' wrote the Duke to
his father. 'There is no other word to describe the wonderful enthusiasm of
the people of Belfast. They turned out in the streets at any time of the day
and night, and the noise they made cheering was quite deafening.'
Londonderry did not disillusion the royal couple by telling them that the
cheering all came from Protestant and 'loyalist' throats, and that care was
taken to avoid the Catholic and Nationalist parts of the city during the
royal tour.[1]

---

[1] On 4 November 1920 the Londonderrys' eldest daughter Maureen, who had grown
up to be an extraordinarily beautiful girl with the makings of a brilliant public speaker
(which she later became), was married in Durham Cathedral to the Hon. Oliver Stanley,
younger son of Lord Derby. Then, on Good Friday 1921, which happened to be Lady
Day (25 March), since Easter was early that year, the Londonderrys' youngest daughter
was born and appropriately christened Mairi. Five months later their first grandchild
Michael was born to the Stanleys, so that the Londonderrys had the unusual experience
of becoming parents and grandparents in the same year. Both babies were born at
Mount Stewart, which had recently been modernised with central heating and a new
electric light system.

Londonderry, who was a member of the Jockey Club, continued to keep up his
father's stud at Wynyard, breeding and racing in the family colours of lilac and yellow
with black cap. After the war he had several successes, notably with Polemarch, who
won the Gimcrack Stakes at York as a two-year-old; after winning the Rous Plate at
Doncaster with the same colt, he succeeded in carrying off the coveted St Leger on the
same course in 1921, winning comfortably by 1½ lengths at odds of 50 to 1 against. He
pulled off a nice double at the same meeting when his horse Glanmerin won the
Portland Handicap Stakes, a five furlong sprint, by three lengths. Later he was to
repeat his initial successes with Columcille, who won the Newbury Summer Cup, the
Bibury Cup and the Great Yorkshire Handicap, although he never won another classic
race.

CHAPTER V

THE RAMSAY MACDONALD SYNDROME

I

BONAR LAW'S PREMIERSHIP lasted barely seven months, since he was suffering from throat cancer. He resigned on 20 May 1923 and died in the following October. Many people thought that he would be succeeded by Curzon, the Foreign Secretary, who had been presiding at Cabinet meetings during Law's final illness. But in the event the King sent for the Chancellor of the Exchequer, Stanley Baldwin, whom Curzon described as 'a man of no experience, and of the utmost insignificance— not even a public figure'. However, when it came to the crunch, Curzon swallowed his pride and agreed to continue as Foreign Secretary under a leader whom he had just described so contemptuously. As things turned out, Baldwin only stayed in Downing Street for very little longer than Bonar Law, his departure being precipitated by his decision to call a General Election on the tariff issue in November. In the result the Conservatives were defeated and found themselves in a minority of 97 in the face of the combined Labour (191) and Liberal (158) figures. Churchill, who had returned from his working holiday in France, stood as a Liberal and Free Trader and had a three-cornered fight in West Leicester, in which he came second to Labour. The Lloyd George Coalition Tories like Birkenhead and Austen Chamberlain, who had not been asked by Baldwin to join his government when he took over from Bonar Law, now openly backed the official Conservative line, although some of them were unhappy both about the timing of the election and the main question on which it was fought. Thus Birkenhead found himself speaking for the official Conservative candidate in Newcastle-upon-Tyne.

'One line to wish you well,' Londonderry wrote to Churchill from Wynyard on the eve of the poll:

> The topsyturveydom of politics bewilders me and I wonder when we shall fight under the same banner instead of maintaining a delightful friendship while being in opposing camps.
>
> F. E. [Birkenhead] came here last night and I was particularly pleased because we have always clung to you, but been so far apart at intervals as the poles. However when the opportunity came I naturally jumped at it and sent him a wire to come

here after his Newcastle speech and he replied in exactly the same spirit. Very
characteristic.
Again the best of health. I wish I could do something for you.

The King thought that Baldwin should not resign until he and his
followers had been defeated in the House of Commons. This duly happened on 21 January 1924 at the end of the Debate on the Address when
a Labour amendment was carried by seventy-two votes, all but eleven of
the Liberals combining with Labour to defeat the Government. Baldwin
resigned next day, and the King invited Ramsay MacDonald as the leader
of the next largest party in the Commons to form an administration,
having just sworn him a Privy Councillor. MacDonald agreed and so
became the first Labour Prime Minister in English history.

James Ramsay MacDonald, a Highland Scot of illegitimate birth and
a widower with two sons and three daughters, was fifty-seven when he
moved into No 10 Downing Street. His appearance was striking with his
sensitive face and delicate features, his wavy dark hair showing signs of
grey, while his voice was soft-spoken and persuasive, his range of knowledge extensive for a largely self-educated man, and his characteristic
outlook that of the artist and romantic rather than the pragmatical politician. He had no difficulty in forming a government, although he had to
seek help from the Liberals in some posts such as that of Lord Chancellor,
which was filled by Lord Haldane. He himself took the office of Foreign
Secretary as well as Prime Minister and Leader of the House of Commons,
which many considered a mistake since his inevitable preoccupation with
foreign affairs made it difficult for him to do himself justice as parliamentary leader and no doubt diminished his interest in his Cabinet's domestic
programme. Nevertheless the King liked him from the moment of their
first meeting. 'He impressed me very much,' noted George V. 'He wishes
to do the right thing.' In this he was unlike the extremist Labour M.P.
George Lansbury who, much to the King's annoyance, had gone out of his
way to express a threat and a reminder of the fate which had befallen the
Stuart monarch who had 'stood against the common people'. As he took
leave of MacDonald, and his principal colleagues (J. R. Clynes, Arthur
Henderson and J. H. Thomas), the King made an appeal to them which
they could never forget: 'The immediate future of my people, and their
whole happiness, is in your hands, gentlemen. They depend upon your
prudence and sagacity.'

Shortly afterwards the King and Queen gave a dinner for MacDonald
and the principal members of his government and their wives, to which
others were invited from the Opposition including the Londonderrys.
The Prime Minister was asked to take Lady Londonderry in to dinner.
At the table he was placed between Queen Mary and Lady Londonderry,
the Prime Minister being on the Queen's left and Lord Haldane on her

right. Ramsay MacDonald and Lady Londonderry took to each other at once, finding a common bond in the Scottish Highlands and Gaelic folklore to which they were both devoted. Before they parted the Prime Minister invited Lady Londonderry and her husband to visit him at Chequers, and this they lost no time in doing. Indeed the first names to appear in the Chequers Visitors' Book under the new dispensation, in February 1924, were those of the Londonderrys.

The Prime Minister and Lady Londonderry now began to exchange letters. At first the correspondence was quite formal and confined to purely political subjects, of which the most important was the trouble which arose over the border between Northern Ireland and the Irish Free State. Article 12 of the Anglo-Irish 'Treaty' of 1921 provided for the setting up of a Boundary Commission, consisting of one representative of Northern Ireland and one of the Irish Free State, with an impartial arbitrator. As the latter, Mr Justice Richard Feetham, an English-born and Oxford-educated South African judge, agreed to serve at the British Government's invitation. Unfortunately both sides in Ireland held differing views as to how the article should be interpreted, the north considering that its application should be confined to minor boundary rectifications, and the south envisaging substantial transfers of territory, such as south Armagh and the adjacent town of Newry. Furthermore, Craig and his Cabinet refused to nominate any representative. Meanwhile the Labour Cabinet in Downing Street referred the matter to the Judicial Committee of the Privy Council, which reported at the end of July that additional legislation would be required to appoint a third commissioner, in the absence of whom the Boundary Commission would be invalid. MacDonald prevailed upon a reluctant Baldwin not to oppose the necessary legislation, which he intended to introduce in a brief autumn session of Parliament. At the same time he sent two of his ministers, Arthur Henderson (Home Secretary) and J. H. Thomas (Colonial Secretary), to Dublin to see the Irish Free State Prime Minister William Cosgrave and to discuss the problem with him and let him know about the proposed legislation.

On 5 August 1924, Ramsay MacDonald wrote privately to Lady Londonderry from the Foreign Office:

> This new Irish trouble is most worrying. I am rigidly opposed to hasty legislation, but I must make it clear that the Government means to keep faith. I know that you will do your best to get your friends to meet us reasonably within the period between now and the end of September.
>
> Do not let us revive these evil passions of hate and strife. We were not meant to be torn by such things, and I shall not countenance in any way the too evident intention of Mr Lloyd George and his miserable minded following to make party capital out of a grave tragedy. This is a thing to settle between friends who wish to be happy rather than squabble over by dishonest politicians and hard mouthed bigots.

The difficulty about our expressing a view that clause 12 was meant to be a rectification of the boundary is that apparently the south people had a different pledge from Lloyd George. In my view, the wording of the clause shows that it contemplated a rectification only, and I cannot believe that any arbitrator would undertake a different view. I understand that is Feetham's view, but may be mere gossip. If the Government here began to interpret this, it would only be jumping out of the frying pan into the fire.

Craig was suffering from a recurrence of an old complaint diagnosed as spotted fever. During his illness, which confined him to bed, Londonderry presided at the Ulster Cabinet meetings and also went to London with a Cabinet brief when necessary. He was there on 8 August when he had a talk at 10 Downing Street with Dr Thomas Jones, the influential Assistant Secretary of the Cabinet. Asked by Jones what the Ulster Cabinet would do, Londonderry replied: 'Everything depends on Craig's health.' His own view, Londonderry went on, was that having put up a fight they ought not to refuse the appointment of the necessary third commissioner now, but he was 'not sure if he could carry that because of Craig's pledges'. He thought the House of Lords would reject the measure, egged on by Birkenhead.

A few days later, Lady Londonderry, who was in Ireland, replied at length to Ramsay MacDonald's letter:

Mount Stewart. 12 August 1924 . . . The Southern Irish can be very charming but they certainly are an inconsequent race—in fact, very like children and when given too much latitude, they get out of hand. It does not really signify what government they have, they must always be 'agin it'. Hence the present attitude of the self-styled Republicans who really represent the anti-government party. The mere fact of two British Cabinet Ministers going over to negotiate with the Free State will give them an entirely wrong idea of their power for doing good or evil. Too much attention is bad for the young and causes them to show off.

You ask me to do my poor best to help towards peace and get my friends to meet you reasonably. But to enable us to do this, you must be reasonable too and keep the faith with Ulster. So far Sir James Craig has always kept his people under control, (the South never), but there is a point beyond which men of Scottish blood will not be led and that point will be reached when they think that the British Government has not kept its word to them, pledged in the 1920 Act . . . Ulster never asked for this form of self-government and when it was reluctantly accepted, it was accepted for a certain clearly defined territory. It is most important to my mind that the British Government should say what Ulster's territory is under the 1920 Act, seeing that it is an accomplished fact and was forced on her by Great Britain on the understanding that it was absolutely final . . .

The original North-East Ulster (Uladh) was won by a MacDonald who was the first to touch these shores, by cutting off his left hand and throwing it from the boat on to the land which he claimed. Hence the bloody hand of Ulster. Won't you, another MacDonald, extend to us the other hand, the right hand of fellowship and maintenance and throw us the olive branch? This is my request to you. I am on the other side of the water, but not of the world, as you suggest, nor do I think, though we certainly are in opposite camps, that our ideas are necessarily so wide apart or that we may not have the same goal in view. I certainly did not receive this impression at Chequers, and I shall be surprised if the future makes me think otherwise ...

You may rely on my helping you all I can to keep the peace, only you must help us too.

The Prime Minister's next letter reached Lady Londonderry a month later from his Scottish Highland retreat at Lossiemouth. 'It is now no use pursuing the subject further,' he wrote on 13 September, 'as apparently the decision has been taken that Ulster is not to appoint its representative, and so, much to my regret, we must legislate.' He went on:

I have done my best to keep passion in chains and I shall continue to do so, though I wait events with some disquiet of mind. Sometimes I think that the war has struck the British Empire a deadly blow and I am indeed no pessimist. When the finer sentiments and acquiescences that hold us all together become the subject of wild propaganda, they retire like a shy girl and without them the house falls to pieces. The next stage will be when the Commission reports. Anything may happen then.

As you perhaps saw at the time, I got away from London before you arrived on the 19th [August]. And now the summer is past and I must return. What a fool! The moors and sky and sea were never more beautiful or more alluring, porridge and milk never tasted better nor a meal of pulse more satisfying; and I have to bid them all farewell and return to decorum and high feasts and the grey skies of a frowning world.

'You gave me a terrible dressing down, however,' he concluded. 'Ah, that red hand of Ulster. Why will you always think we are your enemies? Especially when we are giving you such good advice.'

Craig returned to duty after a three-week convalescent cruise in the Baltic, and the Ulster Cabinet met at Cleve Court, Carson's country house in Kent, to ratify its decision not to appoint a member of the Boundary Commission. This upset the King when he heard about it, and he asked his private secretary Lord Stamfordham to write to Craig to say that, while His Majesty sympathised with the Ulster Premier in his difficulties, at the same time he felt that the solution to the problem was only to be found by agreement between him and Cosgrave on the border question. Baldwin, with whose party the Ulster Unionists were affiliated, now saw Craig and afterwards summarised his attitude and that of his Cabinet:

Craig is willing to accept, 'under duress', as he puts it ... If the Commission should give away counties, then of course Ulster couldn't accept it and we should back her. But the Government will nominate a proper representative and we hope that he and Feetham will do what is right ...

The Lords are the curse. They will never let the Bill through except on the definite assurance that Ulster will accept it. Craig's first idea was to fight the Bill all along the line: the Lords to let it through at the last. But I showed him the snag and told him that he would have to consider at his leisure whether some pronouncement should be made by the 30th [September] so that the Bill could be let through. If the Lords once reject it, we may be in grave difficulties.

The Boundary Commission Bill duly passed the Commons on 30 September, without opposition from the leading Conservatives. An additional measure was necessary to enable the Government to nominate a member of the Commission to represent Northern Ireland, and this caused some perturbation in the Ulster Cabinet, whose members were still in London awaiting the parliamentary outcome.

Londonderry wrote to his wife in Ireland:

Londonderry House. 2 October 1924 . . . We nearly had an Ulster crisis and a revolt against James Craig which I hope events have settled for us but I fear with a certain amount of damage to his position. The position of P.M. of Ulster is not an enviable one.

You will have seen the rumour of Carson being put on the Commission by the Labour Government. Craig jumped at it and as near as possible split the Cabinet However it is all settled now. Carson does not accept, though I believe he has not shut the door to being approached should the Bill pass. The different moves and counter-moves, the whisperings and rumblings amongst the Cabinet and the Ulster members of the Constitutional Club are all too many to describe in a letter, Craig sitting all the time at his water logged residence at Goring. Carson stayed here last night.

Whether we have done right or wrong remains to be seen, but I feel we have taken a logical and honest course, and when faced with difficulties as we are it is not only wrong but also folly to do otherwise. Now we fight the Bill in the Lords with the results which I can't foretell. You will have seen also that the Conservative leaders ran away in the Division which will not please the rank and file.

Here in the atmosphere it looks like a political crisis and a General Election. I doubt if it matters very much what the issue is on which the Government fall: it would never be an election solely on the H[ouse] of L[ords]. Salisbury lunches here today.

'We have had a desperate time here,' Londonderry wrote again to his wife next day. 'Everything changing from minute to minute and James I fear rattled. I am doing everything I can to maintain his position, but it has had a shake in the Cabinet and the party. It would be most tiresome if I was called to succeed him by his giving up the P[rime] M[inister]ship and would not suit me at all, although I feel I am tied for life to Northern Ireland unless I was lifted out [to a post] like Paris or India, but neither of these appeals to you nor to me very much.'

In the event the Labour Government was defeated on a relatively minor issue, the charge that in withdrawing the prosecution of Mr J. R. Campbell, the acting editor of the Communist *Worker's Weekly*, for sedition, the Government had 'interfered with the course of justice'. MacDonald refused the Liberal offer of a Select Committee of the House with the result that the Conservatives combined with the Liberals on 8 October to defeat the Government by 364 votes to 198. The Irish boundary legislation had already passed through the Lords without any trouble in the face of Craig's modified attack. It reached the statute book on the day following the Government's defeat, when the King reluctantly granted MacDonald's request for a dissolution.

In the General Election which followed, Winston Churchill, who had been received into the Conservative fold by Baldwin after coming within an ace, as an 'Independent and Constitutionalist', of beating the official Conservative at a by-election earlier in the year, stood as a 'Constitutionalist' for Epping which was regarded as a safe Tory seat. Londonderry wrote to him during the campaign to say how delighted he was that 'we shall have the full value of your powerful support'.

> As you know it is what I have always hoped and yet the bridge seemed impossible to build. I have always felt in complete sympathy with all your ideas and yet I never could see how in normal times we could be on the same side.

Polling took place on 29 October and resulted in a sweeping victory for the Conservatives, who were returned with a majority of 215 over the other two parties; the Liberals were virtually wiped out, and Labour's voting strength in the Commons was reduced from 191 to 151. The Conservatives were helped, particularly in marginal seats, by the publication of the 'Zinoviev letter' on the eve of the poll, a document which subsequently turned out to be a forgery but was widely believed at the time as evidence of Soviet Communist infiltration of the British working class.

On 4 November 1924 MacDonald formally tendered his resignation to the King, who thereupon entrusted Mr Baldwin with the formation of a new Government. In this Baldwin included the leading Conservatives in the Lloyd George Coalition, Austen Chamberlain as Foreign Secretary and Birkenhead at the India Office. Also, as much to Churchill's surprise as everyone else's, he appointed him Chancellor of the Exchequer.

Londonderry had been a member of the Irish Privy Council since 1918. In the next New Year's honours, to his gratification, he was made an English Privy Councillor and for this he had the Ulster Premier to thank. 'I was very pleased and proud when Baldwin told me he was going to recommend me for P.C., and doubly so when I found it was the only one,' Londonderry wrote to Craig as soon as the honour had been announced.

> This was entirely due to your friendly efforts on behalf of my unworthy self, and makes one more of those debts of gratitude to you which I can never repay. I feel it reflects honour on Ulster and our Government, and that relieves a little my feeling of unworthiness. Characteristically you commend our small efforts, but we were all powerless without your wonderful vision and your amazing courage in situations of almost hopeless complexity, and it has been a pride and pleasure to serve you.

Unfortunately it was not to remain so for very much longer.

2

On 1 December 1925, the Treaty of Locarno was signed in the Golden Room of the Foreign Office in London by the Foreign Ministers of Britain, France, Belgium, Italy and Germany. Thus the five signatories guaranteed the inviolability of the German–Belgian and German–French frontiers and so, it was hoped, the establishment of peace in western Europe. 'I pray this may mean peace for many years,' the King noted in his diary at the time. 'Why not for ever?' On the night before the ceremony the British Foreign Secretary, looking round the Golden Room, noticed a blank space on the wall. He was told it was normally occupied by a portrait of King James II which had been removed for cleaning. As Chamberlain felt that the image of the Stuart monarch was not perhaps the most appropriate for the occasion, he got in touch with Londonderry and asked if he could borrow a portrait of his celebrated ancestor Castlereagh. Londonderry was fortunately in London at the time and immediately obliged with the best known portrait by Sir Thomas Lawrence which was then at Londonderry House; and so it came about that the picture of the moving spirit of the Treaty of Vienna looked down upon the later treaty which like its predecessor was designed to preserve the peace of Europe.

Two days later another document of historical importance was signed, this time in Stanley Baldwin's room in the House of Commons. It supplemented and amended the Anglo-Irish 'Treaty' of 1921 and settled the thorny question of the border between Northern Ireland and the Irish Free State on which the Boundary Commission had sat for a year and completed its Report. As will be recalled, James Craig, the Ulster Premier, had refused to appoint a commissioner, and Ramsay MacDonald had consequently been obliged to introduce legislation empowering the British Government to appoint one and the legislation had only just reached the statute book before the Labour Government fell and MacDonald resigned. The Commission was finally constituted with Mr Justice Feetham as chairman, Professor Eoin MacNeill, the Minister of Education in Dublin, as the Irish Free State representative, and J. R. Fisher representing Northern Ireland. Fisher was an elderly Ulster Unionist and as a local newspaper editor had been in the confidence of Carson and Craig; he was not noted for his discretion. The first meeting of the Commission was held on 6 November 1924, and it worked steadily if somewhat intermittently through 1925 until the early autumn.

With his great Education Act on the statute book, although he had reluctantly agreed to the erosion of its underlying secular concept by an amending Act, Londonderry's thoughts increasingly turned towards the other side of the Irish Sea and he began to consider moving, particularly since he had been able to devote very little time to his business interests, and the coal industry was presenting more and more problems. 'I understand the Boundary Commission is likely to report soon,' he wrote to Churchill from Mount Stewart on 2 November, 'and then the situation becomes much easier for me, as the process of loosening roots here should reach its maximum point when I am free.'

He was still interested in the Indian viceroyalty. Edward Wood, Minister of Agriculture in the Baldwin Government, had been offered the appointment by Birkenhead, the Secretary for India, and had turned it down. 'I thought it was all settled,' Londonderry wrote to Churchill, 'and though I was not in agreement with you that the selection was the best, still it was not altogether bad.' He went on:

> It is vitally important that someone should go who could command the respect of all the Indian community. Reading has not been a success and I always regretted his selection not solely because I wanted the appointment myself, but because I knew for every reason he was entirely unsuitable. You always have great influence wherever you are and I am sure you have now, so please let me impress upon you with all diffidence the necessity of sending a gentleman in the first place and next someone with a record of achievement of his own or his forbears.
>
> The names I see canvassed really carry no weight, and so much depends on the next five years. Of course I would give anything to go myself and it is a post I know would suit me (this bombast is only for your private ear), but that is out of the question. I should be powerless without Edie and she is determined not to think of it because of the family growing up and perhaps she is right: so as you know I have made no move on my own behalf. I know a vacancy in the Ministry affords me a chance which as you realise means a great deal to me at this moment, but that is of no importance in my mind compared to the vital importance of the right man to go to India.
>
> Years ago I set my heart on India, so I have watched it ever since even to this time when for me it is out of the question. Ronaldshay is much better than all the named selections but he has a tiresome wife but this could be got over. Then there is Northumberland who has many valuable qualities for a post of this description.
>
> Forgive me for writing but I feel we have so many dangers and difficulties to face in the next few years that a great deal depends on wise appointments now.

In the end Wood accepted the appointment and went out to India as Lord Irwin after Baldwin had sent for him at Chequers, asking him to go and telling him that the suggestion that he should had originally come from the King. 'He certainly has many of the qualifications,' Churchill wrote to his cousin at the time. 'It is a pity that your domestic affairs prevented you from being a candidate.'

The first draft of the Boundary Commission report was agreed by the Commissioners on 5 November 1925, exactly a year after its first sitting. Unfortunately, two days later, the Conservative *Morning Post* published a map giving a partially accurate picture of the proposed boundary changes. It is virtually certain that this was deliberately 'leaked' by

Fisher, who had recently visited the border area with his two fellow Commissioners and forecast the result in a number of private letters to the wife of an Ulster Unionist M.P., with whom he was particularly friendly. Public confidence was badly shaken by this premature publication, although Craig and his Cabinet were relieved by the relatively small transfers proposed and seemed disposed to accept them. In the South, however, there was marked disappointment, amounting to a sense of betrayal, notwithstanding that the Free State stood to gain on balance both in territory and population if the proposed transfers were implemented. In fact, Eoin MacNeill had assented to the award, but pressure mounted for him to resign because it was felt he had not got enough; he did so a fortnight later, ostensibly to avoid having publicly to endorse findings which were unacceptable to the majority of his fellow countrymen.

Baldwin thereupon invited the Free State Premier William Cosgrave and his principal colleagues to come to England for a conference with the interested English ministers. Craig was also warned to make himself available if called. From the first day's discussion which took place in London, two possibilities emerged. One was to accept the existing boundary. That, in the opinion of the Free State representatives, would only be possible for them in the event of their getting concessions from the North. The alternative was to impose the line of rectification prescribed by the Boundary Commission. 'If that is agreed to,' Baldwin told the southern Irishmen, 'then we shall have to consider how to put it through with the least possible disturbance.' The conference was then adjourned to Chequers, where it reconvened during the weekend of 28 November. Meanwhile Baldwin undertook to consult Craig, which he did, warning him to be ready to come down to Chequers that weekend and to bring anyone he wished to have with him. Instead of suggesting one or more of his ministerial colleagues, Craig asked if he could bring Charles Blackmore, the Secretary of the Northern Irish Cabinet, who was a civil servant. Baldwin offered no objection, although he must have thought it strange that Craig did not at least suggest bringing Londonderry too, since the latter was thoroughly familiar with the question at issue, he had been a member of the Irish Convention in 1917 and had been a party to the negotiations resulting in the Craig–Collins Pact in 1922.

'You know,' wrote Lord Birkenhead in his usual caustic style, while the details of the amending agreement were being worked out during the next few days, 'I always contended and advised my colleagues that Article 12 of the Treaty meant and could only mean, a rectification of frontier and not a reallocation of great areas and towns.' He continued:

Sumner and Cave, then briskly competing for the Woolsack which they rightly thought would soon be vacant, took, or purposed to take, the opposite opinion; and so advised the House of Lords. It is satisfactory to me that the Commission's finding has so completely confirmed my own view and discharged me of the responsibility which individually I incurred in relation to my colleagues . . .

The discussions were conducted by Churchill, Salisbury and myself on behalf of the British Government with three Irish Ministers. Incidentally they have resulted in the establishment of a greater degree of cordiality between Southern and Northern Ireland than has ever existed. They have both developed a competitive enthusiasm in the task of plundering us.

Churchill saw Craig in the Treasury Board Room on the morning of 3 December and officially informed him that agreement had been reached on the previous night. 'You have done the right thing in a big way,' said Craig.

In the result, the 'Amending Agreement supplementing the Articles of the Treaty' revoked Article 12 and thus preserved for Northern Ireland the entire six counties as defined by the Government of Ireland Act, 1920. It also waived the Free State share of the British National debt amounting to £155 millions which it had agreed to pay under the 'Treaty'. Thus Craig's slogan that 'not an inch' of Ulster territory would be surrendered was implemented, while the Free State was given a present of a substantial sum which it would otherwise have had to pay the British Treasury. The signing took place quite informally in the Prime Minister's room in the House of Commons the same afternoon, in the presence of the three Commissioners, whose report on which they had toiled for a year was consequently scrapped and was never officially published. For some reason Salisbury, who was supposed to sign, had second thoughts, since he looked at his watch, got up and said: 'Excuse me, I have an appointment.' Noting this, Craig whispered to Ernest Blythe, one of the Free State signatories who was sitting beside him: 'This fellow can't take his fences!' Baldwin looked somewhat taken aback at Salisbury's withdrawal, but Birkenhead pushed the document in front of the Prime Minister saying: 'Go ahead!' Baldwin thereupon inscribed his signature, followed by Churchill, Joynson-Hicks, Birkenhead and Amery for the British Government; Cosgrave, Kevin O'Higgins and Blythe for the Irish Free State; and Craig and Blackmore for Northern Ireland. Immediately afterwards Baldwin gave a dinner at which Cosgrave and Craig were the principal guests.

Londonderry was deeply offended at his exclusion from all these negotiations, which he considered a deliberate slight, and this confirmed him in his determination to leave the Ulster Government at the earliest opportunity. Craig afterwards admitted that he should have included him, excusing himself on the rather feeble ground that Londonderry might have held up the proceedings and that it was essential for him to have Blackmore, who was thoroughly *au fait* with the business. But he agreed that he had been at fault and he deeply regretted his mistake, particularly when Londonderry, who had preserved a dignified silence in public, resigned from Craig's Government a few weeks later, pleading that it was necessary for him to devote more time to his coal mining interests. The public exchange of letters between Craig and his Education Minister was outwardly cordial, but Londonderry's resignation, the first of a Cabinet Minister in the Ulster Government, was a severe blow to Craig's administration. His departure removed not only the Government's most aristocratic member but also its most tolerant and moderating influence. During the remaining fifteen years of Craig's Premiership the trend in government was to become increasingly reactionary and monolithic.

Londonderry was succeeded as Education Minister and Leader of the Senate by Viscount Charlemont, a colourless nonentity, who is chiefly remembered in Ulster for the fact that his wife eloped with his chauffeur. Six months later she was killed in an air raid, which the Puritan Ulster folk regarded as a fitting punishment for her adulterous conduct.

3

For the next three years Londonderry was out of political office though not out of politics, since his wife following the family tradition entertained on a magnificent scale for the Conservatives. The most splendid gathering was the reception in Londonderry House on the eve of the opening of each new Parliament and parliamentary session—'catering his way to the Cabinet,' as Birkenhead rather snidely called it, though he himself frequently enjoyed the Londonderry parties, at which the generous amount of brandy which he consumed no doubt contributed to the undermining of his health and hastened his relatively early death. Ironically, it was Birkenhead's decision in October 1928 to leave the Baldwin government for the City to make money from lucrative company directorships which created the Cabinet vacancy which Baldwin invited Londonderry to fill.

Two years previously there had been a rumour that Londonderry was to become British ambassador to France, which Lady Desborough gleaned and relayed to him, but in the event there was nothing in it. 'I have heard nothing about Paris and cannot see why the P.M. should send me,' he wrote to her from Wynyard. 'I don't think it is my job at all.' Nor at that time was he seeking any government post, as he was enjoying his newfound freedom after his stint in Ulster.

I am rather liking the free lance complex and expect to continue in that state altogether. I really do like the freedom of it and I have time now to do all sorts of things I have always wanted to do without trammels and collective responsibility which is in one scale, whilst the honour and prestige and importance of being a member of the Government are in the other.

I don't care about the Government either and I am sure I should not agree. They have all served together for years and are a sort of executive of a Trade Union speaking a language which I don't understand and should never learn. No, I regret India very much. It would have just been the climax and after it I could have come home and adopted the sort of life I am leading now. I apologise for egotism.

That life consisted of looking after his estates and his collieries, indulging his interest in horse breeding and racing, hunting, shooting, sailing, playing bridge, and entertaining with his wife in their various country houses, as well as in London, besides seeing his children grow up and encouraging their interests. Although he was no longer in the Ulster Government, he continued to come to Mount Stewart regularly, since he was Lord Lieutenant of County Down as well as Chancellor of the Queen's University.

Much of 1926 was spent by Londonderry, along with the other colliery owners, in trying to settle the economic difficulties which beset the coal mining industry, then still in private hands. While the French occupied the Ruhr after the war, the German miners were idle and the British industry did well in comparison with its European competitors so that the miners' wages rose. But with the French withdrawal from the Ruhr in the middle of 1925 and the return of German production to full capacity, coupled with the over-valuing of the pound, exports of coal from Britain declined almost to nothing. The mine owners consequently demanded longer working hours in the pits and lower wages, which the miners' leaders bluntly turned down. On the owners then threatening a lock-out, the General Council of the T.U.C. intervened to support the miners' case with the Government. Fearing a coal strike, which the T.U.C.'s answering threat of an embargo on the movement of coal might well turn into a General Strike, the Government proposed the payment of a subsidy to be spread over nine months while a Royal Commission was investigating the industry; the Cabinet agreed on the sum of £10 millions—actually it worked out at £23 millions—thus affording a breathing space before the inevitable test of strength between the miners and the owners. 'My Father has now come out as the coal King and at the moment is the central figure in the picture,' Londonderry's son Robin Castlereagh wrote to a friend at this time. 'His one object, naturally, is to stop the strike and I am thinking there may be a chance of success unless the Commission issues a poor report. The time is very short, but the signs in Durham County are more than hopeful.'

The Royal Commission had been set up under the chairmanship of the ex-Liberal Minister Sir Herbert Samuel and it reported on 11 March 1926. It recommended a drastic reorganisation of the industry including the nationalisation of royalties and the amalgamation of smaller pits, also an immediate reduction of wages. In the knowledge that the subsidy was due to end on 30 April, the Government accepted the report and left owners and miners to settle the details between them. The owners now demanded not only lower wages but increased productivity which meant longer hours of working; they also rejected nationalisation and preferred to operate wage agreements on a district rather than a national basis. The miners' reaction was summed up by A. J. Cook, the left-wing Secretary of the Miners' Federation: 'Not a penny off the pay, not a minute on the day,' while Herbert Smith, the Federation President, when asked what the miners could do to help the industry answered: 'Nowt. We've nowt to offer.' In vain both Baldwin and the T.U.C. General Council tried to persuade the miners to accept some wage reduction, hoping that in the event the owners would make some concessions, but the miners' leaders would not budge.

Londonderry was not a participant in these negotiations, although he was a prominent owner. However, he wrote to the Prime Minister when time was fast running out:

Mount Stewart. 13 April 1926. I am very sorry to see that notwithstanding all the efforts which have been put forward by so many in different capacities the whole weight of the controversy has been thrown on your shoulders. As you know, I am, and have purposely remained, on the outside, but I am pleased to see that the owners have done everything they could in these later stages to come to an agreement with the miners. Cook and Smith dare not take up any other attitude, because neither has any real personality, and they are simply trying to obtain a continuance of the subsidy, and so discharge what they consider to be the duties of their positions. They know there are many others ready and willing to take their places should they falter.

The situation is undoubtedly a very difficult one and one which must be in some very important respects considered as a whole.

I can only take in many of these respects a very local point of view. I can sell every ton of coal I can produce, but this is not the universal case and many miners' leaders and people qualified to hold valuable opinions take the view that we shall never be able to dispose of more than 250 million tons of coal per annum . . .

The ending of the subsidy was immediately followed by a lock-out, which began on 1 May. The miners thereupon delegated their authority as a negotiating authority to the T.U.C. General Council, which called a General Strike; this began two days later. The strike, which the Prime Minister denounced as 'a challenge to Parliament' and 'the road to anarchy and ruin', collapsed after ten days when the T.U.C. General Council called it off unconditionally and Baldwin promised that the Government would do all it could to bring miners and owners together for a lasting settlement. Everyone went back to work except the miners, who maintained their own desperate strike. Attempts at a negotiated settlement, in which Churchill played a leading part, met with no success, and the stoppage dragged on unhappily for the remainder of the year.

On 4 September Churchill invited two of the more moderate owners,

Sir David Llewellyn and his cousin Londonderry, to dine and sleep at Chartwell. Tom Jones, the Deputy Secretary of the Cabinet, who sympathised with the miners, was also included in the party. Afterwards Jones remarked in his diary that Winston was 'humming' with coal all the time—'discussing it from every conceivable angle' and at that moment was 'walking in the grounds with "Charley" Londonderry and owing to the echo his voice can be heard a quarter of a mile away . . . W. is a most brilliant and incessant talker—his sentences full of colour and alliteration and frequently military metaphor. He is always deploying guns or barrages on the owners or the men'.

Londonderry wrote to Churchill on his return to the north-east after he had met the other Durham owners:

Wynyard Park. 6 September 1926 . . . Cook and Smith can do what they want in the name of the Federation when it suits them, but [Evan] Williams [President of the Mining Association] cannot do this by the character and constitution of the Mining Association. So far he has refused to meet the Federation on National lines, as he is bound to oppose a National agreement, but I am hopeful that you will have been able to overcome his quite legitimate attitude by interposing your support of District variations within the ambit of a National agreement.

I attended our meeting today and with difficulty I was able to carry the meeting with me on these lines. I accepted the Federation as a body which in some form was bound to be in existence, and we agreed that our district arrangements should be subject to the acceptance or rejection of the Federation, but not if we could help it to variation by the Federation. That means that wages, hours and conditions of working should be district arrangements and that other matters should be for the Federation to discuss and arrange with the Association . . .

We all have our different points of view. You approach it as a Minister, a statesman and as one who naturally wants a settlement for every reason. I approach it as one who is in politics, has a certain experience of conferences and administration etc etc, and also as an owner. Cook and Smith want nationalisation and to save their faces; the owners want to get back to work and to make money but are obsessed with the idea that they cannot make money on National lines. They trace all the troubles to the growth of the National idea and the case is a very strong one indeed. The railway arrangement is a failure because the porter at a wayside station gets the same wage as the porter at a big and profitable station. To illustrate what I mean further, when I pressed my friends as to how far they would go on National lines, the answer was they could accept a national agreement which allowed for the working at a profit of the poorest district.

I do feel however that if you will consider the owners' point of view as sympathetically as you consider the point of view of Cook and Smith, not more and not less, and bring your great powers of exposition of the pros and the cons, the merits and the demerits, I feel you can manage it.

The great point for district settlements which is being lost sight of is that a trivial local dispute would not have the effect of holding the country to ransom, which is what Cook and Smith want, by the power of the Federation to be able to do. My idea is that if the Federation (Cook and Smith) are judiciously handled Cook and Smith will be only too glad to climb down on the bare recognition of the Miners' Federation, but if you give them the smallest inkling that your mind is moving from the equilibrium away from the owners' side of the table even by a hair's breadth then they will fight like tigers for the National agreement and nothing but the National agreement. If I were in their place I would probably do the same.

It is interesting to compare this letter with one written a few days later by Londonderry's son Robin Castlereagh, who had been staying with his father at Wynyard:

> My Father has temporarily left the coal dispute and is taking a well earned holiday. I am very afraid that some of the owners, now they have the upper hand, may become offensive and ruin all chance of a lasting peace. I should not be at all sorry to see the end of the Miners' Federation and the industry run entirely by districts, as a central authority in such an industry must mean the subordination of economics to politics. It is surprising how the men stick to Cook, but I believe that their loyalty is due to the fact that Cook cannot be bribed or tempted to become like Thomas or Hodges who have left their class. Then too he is a good speaker and an attractive personality.
>
> I do feel that it is time that the status of Trade Unions was looked into, as the intimidation is bad and a great deal more than one reads about in the papers. I think a properly conducted secret ballot before any strike is essential, but it is very dangerous to interfere and already the Government are so alarmed about the next election.

In a subsequent letter prompted by some criticism of the owners which Churchill had made in his constituency, although he had criticised the miners just as strongly, Londonderry somewhat unwisely remarked that the owners were 'fighting Socialism' and that the Miners' Federation was 'one of the most powerful army corps in the field against us'. This drew a sharp rebuke from Churchill. 'You say that the owners are fighting Socialism,' he replied on 3 November. 'It is not the business of Coal Owners as Coal Owners to fight Socialism. If they declare it their duty, how can they blame the Miners' Federation for pursuing political ends? The business of the Coal Owners is to manage their industry successfully, to insist upon sound economic conditions as regards hours and wages, and to fight Socialism as citizens and not as owners of a particular class of property.'

Londonderry was inclined to be touchy and occasionally something in the nature of a love–hate relationship developed between him and his kinsman. For instance, when Londonderry complained as he did at this time that company taxation was more onerous and exacting than ever before, Churchill pointed out that this was not so in a detailed letter which no doubt had been drafted by one of the Treasury officials. This prompted Londonderry to retort that Churchill was 'unfriendly', to which the Chancellor replied in a letter in his own hand. 'You make the great mistake in supposing that I am "unfriendly"', he wrote from Chartwell, 'because I reply in businesslike terms to a lecture on my public misdeeds and shortcomings which you set out to give me.'

What answer do you expect me to send? You address me on public matters. You complain and criticise. I take the trouble to defend myself; and to set out certain relevant facts which I do not gather you challenge. Then you say in effect 'Aren't we friends after all?' Of course we are: but it is no part of friendship to neglect to reply to criticism. I take criticism in good part, but not if I am to be gagged.

Even in the House of Commons I am allowed to reply: and if any member had used your tone and arguments I should have tried to answer them suitably. But that would have nothing to do with friendship.

The miners gave in just over a fortnight later, forced to return to an eight-hour day, instead of the previous seven hours in the pits, and to such local wage scales as they could best obtain at district level. Their surrender to the owners was brought about by 'the only other lever . . . we all dislike', in Londonderry's words, 'the lever which has ended most of the previous strikes—the lever of want'. As L. S. Amery put it, they were 'a beaten and resentful army'. The miners were never to forget the tragic conflict and the cold and hunger in the pitmen's homes which marked it.

4

Lady Londonderry's correspondence with Ramsay MacDonald languished after the Irish Boundary Commission had been set up but revived in April 1926 when she drove out by invitation to his Hampstead home, Upper Frognal Lodge, where he gave her a copy of his book of essays *Wanderings and Excursions*, which she had seen lying on his table and fancied because some of the essays recorded his impressions of the Scottish Highlands. 'You know how much I like reading about that dear part of the land,' she wrote in thanking him for the gift. 'Sometimes I feel that love of the Highlands, which is bred in the bone, is almost a disease!!! Wherever one is, there is always the almost unreasonable wish to get back there. I find it a perfect nuisance!!!' She reciprocated by giving him a copy of the life of her father Henry Chaplin, which she had written. She had previously given him her mother-in-law's short life of her husband's ancestor the Foreign Secretary Castlereagh.

A little later, while looking through some of the family papers at Wynyard, she came on a bundle of letters from Disraeli to Frances Anne Lady Londonderry, the colliery heiress who had befriended and patronised him as a young politician. 'They are really most entertaining,—about all the events of the day,' she wrote. 'I know they will interest you as much as they have me. I think they should be published when edited and notes put to them—and a short introduction. You must advise me.'[1]

[1] The correspondence was published in 1938 under the title *Letters from Benjamin Disraeli to Frances Anne Marchioness of Londonderry* with an Introduction by Lady Londonderry.

The Prime Minister did not share her feeling for the Tory leader. 'Dizzy I do not love; I am a Scotsman,' was his comment.

> I do not admire yellow waistcoats, glass jewellery, a curled lock, and I suspect a hooked nose and bad breath. His letters to Lady Bradford were awful—neither those of a good downright lover nor of a sincerely affectionate friend, but of a mawkish idiot . . . One of these days I shall 'burst out terrible' and shall lose your regard for ever and ever. We shall look at each other across space with dull eyes; if you do anything at all, you will just tilt your nose on high and I shall cock my bonnet at a proud angle. So I must subdue the east winds and try and pacify you as Dizzy did to Queen Victoria.

In 1927, he wrote her a bantering letter when he heard that Robin Castlereagh was going to take part along with his son Malcolm in an international conference in Hawaii on Pacific relations which had been organised by Lionel Curtis on behalf of the Royal Institute of International Affairs:

> *The Hillocks, Lossiemouth. 11 June.* I am writing this just to tell you that I am so glad that your son and mine are to be thrown together in a Honolulu trip. Mine is acting as a kind of Honorary Secretary to the deputation.
>
> If your son makes mine a Tory I shall never look with any favour on the name Londonderry, and when I come in [to power] I shall forfeit all your heirlooms without a halfpenny of compensation, and if my Left is too strong I shall allow you to be guillotined, though, as I could not bear to see it, I shall turn my back upon the scene. On the other hand, if yours becomes a decent Labour man, I expect to receive from you, and your husband, your warmest congratulations!

After a somewhat chequered career at Eton and Oxford, followed by a year in the British Embassy in Rome as an Honorary Attaché, Robin, now rising twenty-five, had more or less settled down and, encouraged by his parents, begun to take an interest in politics as well as the family collieries. 'They want me to stand up here,' he had written from Wynyard to his friend Adrian Holman in December 1926: 'I think I shall do so, as there is no chance of getting in.'

> After all I feel that I must take on a political career of some sort because it is the only job that gives one a chance of taking an intelligent interest in the various properties my Father owns. We have mines at Seaham, agricultural interests here and in Ireland and an estate in Wales. If one has property like this, one has no real claim to it unless one takes a proper interest in it and I feel that an attempt in a political direction is the only way to do this and at the same time pretend one is doing something. I must admit I have contempt for the average M.P. but I think that if I got into the House it would give me the backing I need to run our family business.

Unfortunately the same sympathetic *rapport* which had existed between Londonderry and his father was missing with Robin, whose father considered him 'a very difficult boy, never friendly or playing up in any way'. There may well have been faults on both sides, but the fact remains that

Londonderry never succeeded in winning his son's confidence let alone affection. At his private school, where he was coached by the best Yorkshire professional, Robin showed every sign of becoming a first class cricketer. But when he went to Eton, he gave up the game 'for lack of enterprise', according to his father. He was also nearly expelled for stealing cigarettes at the instigation of another boy, Lord Kinnoull, who was later to marry a daughter of the celebrated London night club queen Mrs Kate Meyrick. However, the contention that the incident was no more than a boyish prank, which indeed it was, prevailed with the school authorities and Robin was reprieved. From Eton he went up to Christ Church, Oxford, where his father thought he should have done better at work, although he got a pass degree. It used to be said that proficiency at billiards was a sign of a mis-spent youth. However that may be, Robin excelled in this pastime, getting a half-Blue and making a break of 94 in the University match against Cambridge. His father complained that he showed no interest in field sports with the exception of shooting, although Robin used to say of the Wynyard shoots that whenever he went out he could never hit anything. Riding and hunting he disliked, and during his coming of age celebrations at Machynlleth, where his father hunted the local hounds, he disappointed him by appearing 'bored to tears' and going home. 'I fear he hasn't an element of sport in his whole composition,' his father remarked. On the other hand Londonderry did give him credit where he felt it was due. 'One can't have everything,' he told Lady Desborough, 'and his sense of duty and real talent for speaking is an invaluable asset in these days. Public duties are for me against the grain but luckily he likes them and does them well.' Indeed Robin was to develop into a brilliant public speaker, particularly at political meetings and proposing and replying to after-dinner toasts at which he excelled. He also had a delightful if rather whimsical sense of humour and fun, although he was naturally shy on first acquaintance.

His father hoped that he would take to politics seriously and find a seat in the House of Commons, preferably as one of the members for County Down where he obtained what amounted more or less to a promise of the next reversion, since Down was still a two-member constituency. Meanwhile Londonderry packed him off to Rome where he had arranged with the British Ambassador, Sir Ronald Graham, that he should be appointed as Honorary Attaché. Here he made a particular friend of Adrian Holman, a career diplomat some years older than himself, who was Second Secretary, and with whom he was to carry on an amusing correspondence for some years. His duties at the Rome Embassy, where he arrived in November 1924, do not seem to have been unduly onerous; they largely consisted in helping to transcribe and decipher or encipher telegrams in the Chancery in addition to the social round.

A somewhat embarrassing incident occurred shortly after his arrival. Several boys had recently been expelled from Eton for a serious case of stealing. The subject came up during a discussion at an embassy lunch, at which the artist Lord Berners, who had formerly been a member of the Embassy staff, was present. The Counsellor, Howard Kennard, who knew nothing of Robin's relatively harmless escapade, leaned across the table to Berners who was sitting opposite and remarked in an audible tone of voice which Robin must have heard: 'Morals have evidently changed at Eton since our time. *We* didn't mind a bit of buggery but we did draw the line at stealing!'

A more serious embarrassment for the unfortunate Robin occurred a year later following Edward Wood's appointment as Viceroy of India. This resulted in a by-election for the safe Conservative seat of Ripon which Wood had represented in the House of Commons for the past fifteen years. Londonderry immediately got in touch with Sir Stanley Jackson, the then Conservative Party Chairman, with a view to Robin being selected. Jackson agreed to use his influence to this end and sent a telegram to Robin suggesting he should accept the nomination if invited by the local association. According to Robin, Jackson accepted for him before Robin's wire of 'emphatic denial' arrived. Robin, who was immediately sent home by the ambassador at his father's request, was naturally upset and wrote on 6 November 1925 to his friend Holman, then on leave:

> The whole affair is a farce as this election is a big one and with an experienced candidate should show how the land lies for the Government. Under any circumstances I should wisely have said 'No', but in addition I cannot very well bolt from N. Ireland, where I am more or less pledged.
> I meet my father on Monday when a savage row will take place and I shall probably have to go immediately to Ripon, thank the Conservative party managers for the honour etc and retire gracefully before some terrific swell, who knows the job. I shall then return to London and pursue my furious relatives over to Ireland, finally returning here to collect my things.

While one can appreciate the logic of the argument, it seems a pity that he did not seize the opportunity. It is true that he was only a few weeks off his twenty-second birthday, and no doubt if he had been elected he would have been the 'baby' of the House. But others, for example Lord Winterton, had been only twenty-one when they became members and soon got to learn the ropes at Westminster. Ripon was just over an hour's drive from Wynyard and with Robin's remarkable gifts of speech there would have been no difficulty over his return for this constituency. Also there seemed no chance of a vacancy in Down for some time, and in fact it was not to occur until 1931. As things turned out, Robin was to be adopted for Darlington early in 1927, and although it had once been held by the Tories the result was now bound to be uncertain, particularly if a Liberal candidate intervened to split the Conservative vote. 'I understand the poor boobs want to get me because they hope to shove all the expenditure on to my father's shoulders,' Robin wrote at the time of his adoption. 'The whole prospect fills me with intense gloom.' The seat had been won by William Pease, a local businessman and Mayor of Darlington, for the Conservatives at the 1918 election; but in the by-election which followed Pease's death in 1926 it switched to Labour in the person of a school teacher from the south named Arthur Shepherd, by whom Robin was now opposed.

Later that year came the trip to Honolulu, of which Robin wrote a characteristic account on his way home from the Ambassador Hotel in New York:

> It happened that Lady Astor was stopping with my parents in Ireland for, I regret to say, a temperance meeting, and she mentioned that her son was leaving for Honolulu on a Conference. She suggested I went too and the long and short of it was that I hastily packed my grips, fixed my passport and headed hard for the Hawaian Islands.
>
> At the conference a fearful lot of balls was uttered, but the discussions on China were extremely interesting. The Chinese delegates stuffed us up with a lot of prophecies as to the future, every one of which has since proved to be singularly incorrect, and my faith in Chinese Nationalism has been severely shaken . . .
>
> I had a comic trip over to San Francisco, as I sat at table with a bunch of missionaries and their wives and really behaved superbly. I may be a fearful humbug, but I certainly enjoyed it. I quite got into their holy atmosphere and there was one occasion when the head missionary and myself complained to the Captain about the drunken behaviour of one of the guests. This I think was the greatest moment of my life. Every morning I played those mad deck games with my pious associates, but never once did I say . . . any . . . rude word . . .
>
> I intend to see the international polo games on Long Island . . . then a week's shooting in Minnesota, winding up with the Dempsey–Tunney fight in Chicago. I shall then be utterly broke and shall return sadly home.

In another undated letter, written a little earlier, Robin described how he nearly ran down the British Foreign Secretary, Austen Chamberlain, while driving a new American car:

> I very nearly presented you F.O. people with the chance of a new chief a fortnight ago. I was heading for Arlington Street to rescue my mother from a luncheon party of Lord Salisbury, to which, needless to add, I had refused to go. I was driving with the maximum of conceit and corresponding minimum of skill, when to my dismay I discerned a familiar figure—top hat, frock coat, eye glass, apparently scanning horse shit in the road and incidentally directly in my path.
>
> Luckily the excellence of my four-wheel brakes saved the life of Austen C., but the excellence of my apology was drowned by the yells of hilarious laughter from my 4 year old sister [Mairi]. Austen lunched at home [Londonderry House] next day, but I did not dare attend, having burst into unrestrained mirth at my juvenile sister's mirth.

By the way if your opinion of your chief—you a future Ambassador[1]—is adverse, I will take pains to get into a similar situation and forget my four wheelers; if favourable I will desist.

It is tempting to quote from these witty and informative letters. Here is one which begins with a reference to the visit of King Amanullah of Afghanistan:

Wynyard Park. 4 April 1928. Many thanks for your letter. I laughed a lot at your stories of the genial ruler of Afghanistan, affectionately known to the crowd as King 'Have Another'. I have seen nothing of them except the procession to the Mansion House and I never saw a bigger gang of cutthroats. One of the staff must have been very tight as he waved his arms about and made fearful grimaces. This needless to say was very popular and he was cheered to the echo. I am told that the King had to bring all his biggest toughs, as had he left them behind they would have usurped his throne. The incident that amused me most was when he rang a fire alarm by mistake and scores of engines dashed out to his glee and their not unnatural annoyance . . .

I am afraid I shall not be able to manage Paris. I am so incredibly broke that when I am through up here at the end of May, I shall shut myself in Ireland for two months and economise.

Holman had recently been transferred from Rome to the Paris embassy and was always asking Robin to come for a weekend or longer, although Robin usually pleaded poverty. On one occasion, however, when he did go over, the visit had a curious sequel. Robin met a French lady whose morals were not exactly irreproachable and they spent such an enjoyable few days together that when the time came to say good-bye she asked for his London address as she said she sometimes came to London and would like to see him again. She had not caught his name though, having very likely been introduced by Holman, thought he was connected with the embassy and might even be an English *milord*. Robin's response to her request was to take out his wallet, fish around inside and produce a visiting card which he solemnly handed to the lady, telling her that he would be delighted to see her any time she came to London at the address on the card which also bore his name. The lady accepted it with thanks and looking at it read: 'The Rt. Honourable Stanley Baldwin, M.P., 10 Downing Street, S.W.1.' History does not relate the nature of the lady's reception when she presented herself at No 10—if indeed she ever did.

In October 1928, Birkenhead resigned as Secretary for India and left the Government. Baldwin thereupon moved Lord Peel from the Office of Works to the India Office and offered Londonderry the resulting vacancy, which carried a seat in the Cabinet. Instead of summoning him to Downing Street for this purpose, the Prime Minister paid Londonderry the compliment of calling on him at Londonderry House. 'You must get into

---

[1] Robin's prophecy came true. Sir Adrian Holman, as he then was, became Ambassador to Cuba in 1950, where he remained until 1954 when he retired from the service.

harness at once,' he told him. 'I want you in the Cabinet for the Office of Works.' Londonderry was flattered by Baldwin's gesture and immediately accepted the offer. He moved into his new office building between White-hall and Storey's Gate towards the end of October. He thought that he owed the promotion to Craig and wrote to thank him ('S.B.'s good opinion of me is based, I know, on the far too flattering things you have said about me'). In fact he owed it to Churchill, who urged it on Baldwin.

Although he was only to hold the office for eight months, Londonderry thoroughly enjoyed the work of a department with such a wide range of responsibilities ranging from the upkeep of the royal palaces and the furnishing of Government offices and embassies abroad to the protection of ancient monuments, the control of art galleries and the care of the pelicans and waterfowl in the lake in St James's Park. He also, by a quirk of irony, found himself responsible for the construction of the new Nor-thern Ireland Parliament buildings and offices at Stormont. Furthermore he liked and got on well with the able and cultured Permanent Secretary of the Office of Works, Sir Lionel Earle, whose experience in the field of fine arts he found invaluable. The only matter of any difficulty with which he had to deal during his brief term of office was that of the controversial equestrian statue of Field Marshal Earl Haig, since the department was responsible for any statue in the metropolitan area for which money had been granted by Parliament, and Parliament had voted £5,000 in this particular case. Unfortunately Lady Haig objected to the design of the horse, which had been approved by experts on equestrian art as well as sculpture. In the event Londonderry supported the opinion of the experts, which he reinforced by securing the approval of Lord d'Abernon, a note-worthy authority on horse breeding and an art connoisseur, who 'agreed that the statue was a fine piece of work'.

Meanwhile Robin Castlereagh's accounts of political feeling in the country held out little encouragement for the Conservatives during the run up to the General Election. He also disapproved of his father's political involvement with the Baldwin Government.

> I have been very busy lately and have had a moderate time. I live up here entirely alone in an immense house which is practically shut up and is not very cheerful. I have had to do a lot of work for my Father who is away—Colliery Company meet-ings, political meetings and bazaars etc, which added to my own show in Darlington and the [Conservative] Junior organisation of the County have kept me on the move the whole time.

> *Wynyard Park. 16 December 1928* . . . I need not point out that things are very bad and that the Conservatives will get it in the neck at the Election. The average voter in the North has a simple mind. He sees that unemployment and distress are as bad as ever and that dear old Baldwin with his record majority has not cleared things up. This is the basic fact and no amount of argument will get round it . . . I cannot help feeling that if Labour does come in, they will not be so very pernicious. I take it

that Ramsay is a more capable Foreign Secretary than Austen, whom I regard as a buffoon. They may do a lot of harm internally, but I do now think they have the wild men in check, and I have confidence in men like Snowden and Thomas.

I cannot help feeling too that private enterprise is not doing too well in industry. It needs some form of control, merely to effect amalgamations and induce more up to date methods. As for coal, half the owners don't know a colliery from a cowpat and there is no personal connection at all . . . I am not a very good Conservative at heart and therefore I do not view the advent of Labour with much alarm . . .

Winston may be coming here to speak at Darlington. His speeches are of course very good, but they are so well prepared with the jokes carefully worked out, that to me they are unreal and insincere. I like to hear F.E. who always appears to speak very genuinely and I expect he does as he is always tight.

I shall spend Xmas in London. Economy has forced us to close this place and I am afraid that it may remain closed indefinitely.

Wynyard Park. 23 March 1929 . . . It is very dreary living alone here, but there is lots to do and the chief benefit is the economy. Very necessary in my case.

Politically things are getting very lively and I have heard the 'Red Flag' recently. What a tune and what words! On form we should make a good show, but there is now a Liberal up against me as well and his intervention will be very harmful. The Conservatives are for it this time. Lloyd George will hold the balance and there will be another Election very soon.

Like you F.O. people I deplore the existence of politicians and regard it all as a rare waste of time. There is too much politics and it will ruin the country. People like myself—of little intelligence and no knowledge—are alright in politics, but the good brains should be employed in business and industry. Look at America . . . If our big employers are right out of touch with the men, you can hardly blame the latter for preferring state ownership. All this must be altered, but I am afraid the Socialists may go too far. Still if they can be kept out for a bit, they will then come in and form a good and go-ahead Government.

I am now off fishing for pike. This is illegal, I understand, after the middle of March but I don't care.

On 9 March 1929, two days before Parliament was dissolved and electioneering began in earnest, Sir Philip Sassoon, then Parliamentary Under-Secretary for Air, gave a lunch at his house a few doors from Londonderry House in Park Lane. The guests included Churchill, Austen Chamberlain, Lord Hailsham, Londonderry and other Cabinet ministers as well as Thomas Jones, the Deputy Secretary of the Cabinet. 'Winston had travelled through the night from two meetings in Scotland,' noted Jones in his diary for that day, 'and was very proud to have heard his son address an audience of about 2,000 for 20 minutes without a note, just over 17 years of age. So we all stood up and drank the health of Randolph II, and passed compliments to Londonderry's young son who is likely to win a seat at Darlington, and Quintin Hogg who is not in the Cabinet yet as he has his Greats to do. Londonderry told me that Blumenfeld in the *Daily Express* prophesies a clear majority of 30 for the Government.'

Baldwin also thought the Conservatives would carry the day. But in the event it was 1923 all over again, the Liberals holding the balance with 59 seats as between Labour's 287 and the Conservatives' 261, although owing to the eccentricities of the British electoral system slightly more people in the aggregate voted Tory than Socialist. Among the Conservative casualties was Lord Castlereagh at Darlington, who was defeated by 1,105 votes. On this occasion the Liberal secured over 6,000 votes, many of which would have gone to Robin if the Liberal had not intervened as he did, and in all probability Robin would have regained the seat for the Conservatives if he had had a straight fight with Labour.

Ramsay MacDonald, the new Prime Minister, wrote to Lady Londonderry, who had been in Darlington for the final days of Robin's campaign, sympathising with her over his defeat. 'I wish you had come to the hotel in Darlington,' she replied. 'A photograph of us together "in the porch" for the Darlington Liberal paper would have been perfect. I should very much like to go down and see you at Chequers one day and bring my son who is so fond of your boy. I don't think you have met mine.' She added in a postscript, referring to the choice of Margaret Bondfield as Minister of Labour: 'I am *so* pleased at a woman becoming a Cabinet Minister.'

Meanwhile her husband left the Office of Works solaced by a charming letter from the Permanent Secretary. 'I can assure you that there is not a man in the office who has come into contact with you who does not regret your departure,' wrote Sir Lionel Earle. 'Out of the eleven or twelve Ministers I have served at the Office of Works, none has so appealed to me and I feel this to be the feeling of everyone who knew you. We shall miss you greatly.'

5

In his second government, a minority one like the first, Ramsay Mac-Donald was wise not to combine the Premiership with the Foreign Office as he had done in 1924; instead he appointed as Foreign Secretary the veteran Labour leader Arthur Henderson, who had served in Asquith's wartime coalition government and had played a signal part in the founding of the League of Nations. It was well for MacDonald that he did so, since there were two international meetings in London during his first eighteen months in Downing Street, the Naval Conference and an Imperial Conference. Nevertheless, although he worked prodigiously hard, indeed over-worked, he was always glad to get away to Chequers and constantly pressed Lady Londonderry to come down there for a walk and a gossip and he would switch his engagements whenever he could to suit her convenience. He also took to accepting invitations to lunches, dinners and suppers at Londonderry House, particularly supper on Sunday nights when Parliament was sitting. After he had joined Lady Londonderry's Ark Society and she asked him to call her by her Ark name of Circe, their correspondence became more familiar. 'The invitation to enter your Ark delights me,' he wrote to her from 10 Downing Street on 8 July 1929. 'What ponderings it awakens! Am I to escape the flood which is sure to come upon this ungodly nation? What am I to be?—a bear? a serpent? a wolf (in sheep's clothing or not)? a lamb? What? I am sure that the doves are already chosen . . . I am in the midst of a despatch to a friendly Power so I cannot pursue this speculation . . . Life is really *hard* and I am trying to stave off the day when you and yours will enter the prison house where I am, and you will put your thumbs down and your stiletto in, and Chequers and Downing Street will see me no more.'

In fact he became Hamish the Hart in the Ark, but he jibbed at calling his friend the Tory hostess Circe, explaining why in a characteristic letter:

Nay, nay, surely not Circe. Was she not a *wicked* witch? Witches I love. But they should be good and romantic, and of the family of that delightful creature Diana. The golden plains of Heaven have no attractions for me, nor have the sedate angels who spend eternity like the chorus at Oberammergau. I want green fields, I want walks with someone who can smile and blush—to wit, Diana. But Circe! Circe is uncanny. Circe's mother was met by Macbeth. Circe cannot dance, Circe cannot sing, Circe has no quaint humours. Circe belongs to the Deils who were never in Heaven.

I like the sad Deils who fell and in whose personality of reminiscence are the scents and the loveliness of the spring flowers which, in idea, still bloom amidst the ashes. No! it must not be Circe. Circe is on the films, in the night clubs. She is a vulgar jade, a bad egg, a snare *and* a delusion. Circe is not a lassie of the hills and the heather, of our sunsets and our east winds. Only drunken men write verse to Circe. She is, in short, a hussie. I love snares but not hussies. So let us postpone the christening.

However, the formal 'Dear Lady Londonderry' now gave way to 'My dear Ladye', when he wrote, which he did seldom less than once a week. Gradually this style became more intimate—'My dear', 'My dear one', 'My dearest Ladye', and finally 'My dearest Friend of All', while he usually ended with 'Ever devotedly Hamish', the name by which she invariably addressed him. All his letters were written in his own hand, and he seems to have found relief in writing to her as a kind of therapy similar to that which his Liberal predecessor in Downing Street, Henry Asquith, experienced when he wrote to Venetia Montagu. 'How I miss you, dearest of all friends, and most desired of all companions,' he wrote on one occasion, when he was feeling particularly lonely. And again: 'I just blush to tell you that I love you more and more and long and long to talk with you.' They were almost certainly not lovers, at least in the generally accepted physical sense, and their relations in this regard probably did not go beyond occasionally holding hands under the rug while out driving in her Rolls (she was incidentally one of the first motorists to have seat belts fitted). The style of his letters to her—and there are more than four hundred preserved in the Londonderry archive—were often romantic and whimsical, and being at heart a lonely man—his wife, to whose memory he was devoted, had died in 1911—he needed a 'pen pal' to whom he could unburden himself without reserve, and sometimes too without discretion, on political and social matters. Certainly he acquired the habit of opening his heart to her both by letter and in conversation, just as her husband did with Lady Desborough.

Another reason which brought the Prime Minister into closer contact than hitherto with both the Londonderrys was that shortly before the General Election he had been adopted as Labour candidate for the Seaham Harbour division of Durham, where the Londonderry mines were situated. Thus he exchanged the Welsh mining constituency of Aberavon where the Labour organisation was weak, and there were excessive demands upon his time and pocket, for another mining constituency which he was assured he need not visit more than once a year and where no subscriptions would be asked for and the whole organisation maintained from local sources. The vacancy was caused by the decision of the sitting member and well-known social reformer and Labour historian Sidney Webb not to stand again.

The Labour Prime Minister's friendship and association with the Conservative hostess, which neither attempted to disguise, became a topic for the news and gossip columns of the press and began to worry Mac-Donald after he had been in office for a little over a year. 'Promise to let me judge whether accepting invitations from you damages me or not,' he wrote to her from Chequers on 12 September 1930. 'My fear is that you may be injured amongst your folks by asking me to sit at your table. And for harbouring these hesitations as to what people will say, are we not fools?'

Of course, he also enjoyed the royal occasions, particularly when Lady Londonderry was a guest and he had an opportunity of showing off his uniform as an Elder Brother of Trinity House. 'Yes, we had such a nice time,' he wrote after one of these gatherings. 'Never have I been such a happy courtier, nor have I lived so completely up to my gold lace and scarlet as I did that evening at Buckingham Palace. The King smiled, the ladies were graceful, the scene glowed, the final procession to the supper room was regal and I walked on air. You started it in that simple and becoming black frock.'

The unexpected deaths of mutual friends and acquaintances always produced a letter from the Prime Minister. 'Verily, F.E. was a tragedy,' he wrote when he heard that Birkenhead had died of pneumonia aggravated by his drinking habits that autumn. 'But doesn't one feel life and death equally?' When Lord Dufferin, chairman of the Senate of the Parliament of Northern Ireland, Lady Ednam and others were killed in an air crash when their plane broke up in the air while returning from a weekend in Le Touquet earlier in the summer, he wrote:

> I thought of you when I read of that terrible accident and saw who were in it. These things seem so cruelly useless apart from one's personal grief, that one revolts and at the same time feels so impotent: and when one thinks of that crushing 'no more', the whole world seems to come tumbling down under an earthquake of despair. We must just go on with the curiosity in our hearts which beats with a little catch in its breath when the old Scottish pagan paraphrase of Ecclesiastes hums through our minds: 'The living know that they must die too.'

He was touched personally when the Air Minister, Lord Thomson, was killed in the crash of the airship R 101 in northern France while on a proving flight to India in October. 'I am lonely and broken and just want to be alone and try to forget what has happened,' he wrote to Lady Londonderry when he heard the news.

> My devoted friend and companion has gone and, I fear, suffered. I do not know if you knew that Thomson and I were Jonathan and David. He was so gay when he bade me farewell on Friday. 'I shall never let you down' were almost his last words and they hum in my ears night and day.

Although Lady Londonderry had no more than a nodding acquaintance with Thomson, she knew and admired his talented friend the author Princess Marthe Bibesco, who later wrote Thomson's biography and became a frequent visitor to Mount Stewart.

Princess Bibesco also made a pilgrimage to Lossiemouth since she was aware that Thomson went there often. The Prime Minister wrote to Lady Londonderry of this visit:

> I have just taken Her Serenity round some of the places which one she cared for loved. I like her. She has a heart and feels. She talks of things that matter and holds her peace when the best of language would be but chatter. What else matters?
> I too, according to many of my friends, was a traitor and spy during the war, but you know I was not; whilst you, according to many of my friends, are a horrid and bad woman, and I know you are a dear good creature. So there. There is a little churchyard near this where he used to go when here because it is beautifully quiet and solemn, and because I shall be taken there in due time. He used to write her about it, and I am taking her there tomorrow. I take no one there whom I do not trust. So there!

Besides paying a duty visit to the King at Balmoral that autumn, the Prime Minister was also the guest of the Duke and Duchess of Sutherland at Dunrobin Castle, and he stayed with the Londonderrys themselves at Loch Choire, a shooting lodge near Kinbrace which belonged to the Duke. The pseudo-democrat Beatrice Webb, who had refused to adopt her husband Sidney's title—he had rejoined the Government and been created Lord Passfield to strengthen the Labour representation in the

Upper House—made the following caustic comment when she read of the
Prime Minister's peregrinations in the social columns of *The Times*:

> Alas! Alas! Balmoral is inevitable; but why the castles of the wealthiest, most
> aristocratic, most reactionary and by no means the most intellectual of the Con-
> servative Party? 'Because', J.R.M. would answer if he laid bare his soul, 'I am more
> at home with them than I should be with you or any other member of the Labour
> Party.' Considering that he represents Seaham his friendship with the London-
> derrys amounts to a public scandal. This silly little episode will do the P.M. untold
> damage with the non-commissioned officers of the Labour movement. He *ought*
> not to be more at home in the castles of the great than in the homes of his followers.
> It argues a perverted taste and a vanished faith.

Londonderry, who had been attending the meetings of the Conservative
Shadow Cabinet, received a telegram from Baldwin, now the Leader of
the Opposition, asking whether he and his wife would give the customary
reception at Londonderry House on the eve of the next session of Parliament. He replied in a letter from Loch Choire Lodge on 11 October:

> I am always glad to give the party, as you know, if it is necessary, and this was my
> understanding with Neville [Chamberlain].[1] He very kindly tried others but I
> expect they all declined. My difficulty is that I have to plead poverty for so many
> urgent calls, when the newspapers write us up as the perpetrators of Bacchanalian
> orgies. I hope Neville is right when he thinks these parties do a great deal of good.
> We get the smug-faced citizens of London with their wives and daughters who
> vote Conservative anyway. I always wish that we could touch the other strata
> where the bulk of the votes lie: but please rest assured that we are always delighted
> to do anything that gives *you* the smallest assistance . . .
>
> We are having a small reception for the Imperial Conference on the 20th [October].
> I set great store by this because I want to do the best I can for the Dominion
> Ministers, and I do hope that you and Mrs Baldwin will be good enough to come.
>
> Ramsay MacDonald was here for a couple of days. I liked him very much but he
> is not the man for his job, and he is obviously pressed along in directions in which he
> has no desire to go.

The reception for the Dominion and Commonwealth Prime Ministers
was a great success. 'I must write before I turn in,' MacDonald wrote to
Lady Londonderry the same night, 'and say how grateful I am, in my
various capacities as head of this Government, Chairman of the Imperial
Conference, and Hamish, for the trouble you took to receive us tonight.
You were splendid, our overseas visitors enjoyed themselves, and I know
it has all been most helpful. Good night, my Dear Ladye.'

Among the overseas visitors was the Canadian Prime Minister Richard
Bennett who had recently scored an easy election victory over the Liberal
party leader Mackenzie King. Bennett took an immediate liking to his
host and hostess and on his return to Ottawa he wrote to George V
pointing out that the term of office of the present Governor-General was
shortly coming to an end and suggesting that Lord Londonderry would

[1] Then Chairman of the Conservative Party.

be a most acceptable successor. Although the appointment of Governor-General of Canada was made by the King, the convention had come to be recognised that it was on the nomination of the Canadian Prime Minister. Hence the offer was formally conveyed to Londonderry on 21 January 1931 by Lord Stamfordham, the King's Private Secretary. 'If you are able to give this proposal your favourable consideration,' he wrote, 'I must point out that Mr Bennett, the Prime Minister, is very anxious that whoever succeeds Lord Willingdon should take up the duties as soon as possible. I further venture to add that I have every reason to think that if your acceptance were even for only two years you and Lady Londonderry would be warmly welcomed.'

When he received this letter, Londonderry and his family were staying at Ranksborough, an attractive small house at Langham near Oakham, which he used as a hunting lodge for himself and his family when he gave up Springfield. After talking over the proposition with his wife, they decided against it, and Londonderry went up to London and saw Stamfordham at the Palace and handed him a formal letter respectfully declining the offer, which if accepted he felt would entail 'a complete severance for a certain length of time at all events of those ties political and industrial' with which he had been 'very closely associated for a number of years' and which he felt it his duty to continue. Before they parted, Stamfordham suggested that Londonderry might write privately to the King who was at Sandringham, giving the reasons which had influenced his decision. This Londonderry did as soon as he had returned to Ranksborough.

After expressing his 'deep appreciation' of the 'great honour' which the King had proposed to confer upon him, he went on:

I fear it is becoming more obvious every day that the positions in which we are invited to represent Your Majesty are rapidly becoming sinecures and apart from entertaining and visiting different parts of the area, there are no responsible duties to perform. When I was in Canada some years ago I realised the purely figurehead position of the Governor-General, and moreover since the developments in the direction of independence and the name of the British Empire being superseded by the meaningless phrase the British Commonwealth of Nations, the King's representatives are very clearly shown that they have no responsible executive duties to perform. The loyalty to Your Majesty I am glad to think remains the same, in fact I believe it increases in strength, but the position of Your Majesty's representatives and their capacity for active participation in Government is for good or evil a thing of the past.

Baldwin did ask me five years ago if he should send my name forward then, but I particularly asked him not to do so for the reasons which I have ventured to give Your Majesty. I should like to have gone to India with all its difficulties and responsibilities, because there are great problems to be solved, but that is not to be.

The Governor-Generalship of Canada means for me an end to my activities here. I have tried to take a part in politics and also in industrial matters. I have been a member of Your Majesty's Government here and I think very probably if Your Majesty had a Conservative administration that I might be called upon as a member of the Cabinet. These are the reasons which make me unwilling to give up for good, because I feel it would be almost impossible for me to pick them up again, these interests and duties which I have made the object of my life.

'Your Majesty has invariably shown me so much consideration,' Londonderry concluded his letter, 'that I have thought it right to explain why I have found a difficulty in accepting the honourable position of representing Your Majesty in Canada. I do hope my reasons will commend themselves to Your Majesty.'

Londonderry need have had no apprehensions. The King quite understood the reasons. 'Under the circumstances I think you were quite right,' he wrote from Sandringham. 'Mr Bennett was anxious to have you, so I had to make you the offer. India of course would have been quite different. You have so much work and so many interests at home, that G.G. of Canada, with practically all the powers gone which he used to have, I am sure would not appeal to you. It is not easy to find someone, who would suit and be ready to go, but I must try again.'[1]

6

By this time there is no doubt that the friendship between Ramsay MacDonald and the Londonderrys, as indicated in the Prime Minister's known enjoyment of the Londonderrys' hospitality and particularly his visits to Londonderry House, had begun to do him harm. It found expression in an anonymous letter sent to MacDonald from a Seaham Harbour elector, complaining about a reference in a local paper to his being 'in the company of Lord Londonderry, looking round his house in London and the people here are up against it. He is not our friend'. The *Sunderland Echo* had also reported a speech made by Robin Castlereagh in Washington, Co. Durham, in which he had castigated the Prime Minister for refusing an invitation to go down one of the Londonderry colliery pits. The invitation, he said, had been extended when he met the Prime Minister at his father's house in London, and he added that he considered it an 'impertinence' for a man who represented a mining constituency 'to abuse the coal industry on the ground of inefficiency when he has not been down a single pit in his own area'. Ramsay MacDonald sent Lady Londonderry the anonymous letter in which the writer warned the Prime Minister that 'when the next election comes you will get a great surprise. . .' In his covering note the Prime Minister declared that he had been misquoted. 'I should not notice it but for Castlereagh's

[1] The Earl of Bessborough, art patron and former M.P., who had a French wife and himself spoke French fluently, was eventually selected.

intervention,' he assured Robin's mother. 'I never said what he quoted. It is not the management that is inefficient but the whole organisation of the trade. Moreover, conversation in a private house is immune from quotation in public. Don't trouble or worry about it, however. I shall take no notice.' Nevertheless the Seaham Harbour voters were to remember it when the time came.

The next election did not turn out to be quite the shock for the Prime Minister that his anonymous correspondent envisaged. It followed on the economic crisis of three months earlier with the possibility foreseen by Neville Chamberlain of 'a panic in the City, a hundred million deficit in the Budget, a flight from the pound, and industry going smash'. The crisis, which split the Labour Party and led to the formation of a 'National' Government under MacDonald's Premiership, has been frequently described by historians and need only be noticed here mainly in the context of the Prime Minister's letters to Lady Londonderry. The crucial date in the political calendar was 24 August 1931 when the leaders of the three political parties met the King and, in Baldwin's words, 'Ramsay, with real courage, deserted by some of his leading colleagues and his Party, offered to form an *ad hoc* Government to put through the financial legislation necessary and then dissolve for a general election which will probably come in October'. The offer, endorsed by Baldwin, and Samuel for the Liberals, was warmly welcomed by the King. Later the same day MacDonald returned to the Palace, resigned as Prime Minister of the Labour Government and kissed hands on his appointment as Prime Minister of the new 'National' Government. 'The general opinion among my friends here is that I have committed suicide,' he wrote to Lady Londonderry the same night. 'I shall soon awaken in the shades. In any event my programme of bowing myself out has begun with a rogue's march. I shall welcome a sight of you again, and put on a collar and shirt which will hide the hangman's rope now round my neck.'

MacDonald limited his Cabinet to ten members; and, although as Prime Minister he could not count on the support of more than a handful of his own Party, he insisted on Labour having four places, the same number as he allotted to the Conservatives, leaving the balance of two to the Liberals. He also insisted that the financially orthodox Philip Snowden should continue at the Treasury, while Baldwin became Lord President of the Council. All the other places were outside the Cabinet, including the Office of Works to which Londonderry returned.

The House of Commons passed the emergency Budget and Economy Bill with little opposition, and under pressure from the Bank of England the Government rushed through Parliament in a single day a Bill suspending the Gold Standard, with the result that the pound fell by a quarter of its previous value in terms of dollar and other foreign currencies.

Londonderry wrote to his wife from the Office of Works shortly after
he had taken over and been to see his cousin at Chartwell:

> I stayed with Winston for the week end and I played tennis in the morning and
> golf in the afternoon . . .
> I think the whole situation is very difficult. Of course the villain of the piece is
> Snowden and I am very sorry that he is being extolled as a patriotic citizen: he
> must have known the situation or ought to have known: he has been in charge of
> our finance, he has gone on spending and has frightened people and foreign countries
> and now gets out of his just punishment by hanging on to all of us who will have to
> bear the burden of his misdeeds. I think the P.M. is a bit to blame too, but certainly
> has the excuse of trusting Snowden.
> This arrangement now of course will save the Socialists a lot of the condemnation
> they so richly deserve. I am not happy about the National Government at all . . .

Churchill's son Randolph was also spending the weekend at Chartwell,
and Londonderry's opinion of him was far from flattering:

> I formed the opinion that Randolph though clever and intelligent is the most
> boring unattractive boy I have ever come across. I do not think he can help being
> conspicuous all his life, but his boringness and conceit will militate against his
> success. Of course he is very young and may change, but he has none of the charm
> of Winston.

Here are a few extracts from the letters which the Prime Minister found
time to write to Lady Londonderry at this critical period in the country's
fortunes:

> *Lossiemouth. Saturday* [*29 August 1931*] . . . I was so glad to have your good
> wishes and your encouragement in doing what you can easily understand may have
> been the right thing but was assuredly an unpleasant one. And the choirs of the
> earth praise me. Mayhap those of Heaven condescend to join in the chorus. I am a
> little weary but not a *little* buoyant.
> I am so grateful to your better half—or is it quarter? In any event as I have
> always stood for the equality of women in all things with husbands, pray observe
> that we now enter upon new relations, and that you too must obey my orders . . .
> You will go down in Mammie D[illon]'s eyes,[1] as I go down in those of my Seaham
> friends who will not now nominate me as their candidate. Thus I gain you as a
> colleague but shall lose you as a constituent. Life is all a balancing of good and bad.
> Of course I get many congratulations. That is the joy of all newly married people.
> But as Ecclesiastes warns us, time goes, and the wonderful, like a child's toy, loses
> its wonder . . .
> I hope that what I have done may help the country and perhaps stir the hearts
> of the people outside. We need a pool of Siloam in these days. My own fisher folks
> are walking on air. This is one thing said by an old fisher who can but pace up and
> down the harbour waiting for his final voyage: 'Man, hae ye ever seen the like. The
> Tories are doon, curse them, an' Jamie is on top o' them. Baldwin is like a doggie wi'
> a string roon his neck. They're comin' here, the day, in their motors just tae look
> at back o' his hoose'—and so on. I love them. They also tell me that the glass has

---

[1] Mrs Malcolm Dillon, wife of Londonderry's chief colliery agent at Seaham
Harbour and a staunch Conservative who hated MacDonald.

gone up and the fishing has improved since the change of Government. They will always be proud and certainly remain faithful whilst this weather and luck lasts.

10 Downing Street. 8 September . . . The political situation is full of currents and counter currents, reasonable and unreasonable, so how long we shall last I know not . . . Oh for a stroll in the sun. In an hour I leave for the House of Commons.

Work has been so heavy that I have not been able to see Charley, but I'll do so soon.

I wonder if I'll make a mess of it today. I am unhappy, and wish it were over. My love has not been dried up by my worries . . .

10 Downing Street. 16 September . . . The road here is not smooth, nor is it open or straight. The world and the mind of man do not bow down to us and meekly and graciously decide that because we are, they will do what we should like. Winston changes from day to day as to his hopes, his fears and his advice; your Tory flock bleats in varying volume for office and power—and that bleat is mingled with one more hesitating and fearing, lest they be defeated at the election; the mischief maker is about and gives trouble, and finds that that is the easiest job to which he has ever put his hand; I, a busy little ant, run hither and thither, occupied all the time, and kept within the narrow bounds which a flattering Fate has imposed upon me. Work elbows out friends, closes doors upon them, holds me, orders me about like a mistress and demands the same homage from me.

10 Downing Street. 17 September . . . We splash along here. We have thoroughly discredited the Front Opposition Bench and have made it share with us the street corner curses of its Back Bench followers. They are not happy and behave like demoralised men . . . The election—when is it to be? how is it to be fought?—worries me a little . . .

Sandwich Bay. 23 September. The pitcher has gone to the well once too often and I am in a nunnery by the sea getting patched up. On Monday night I came to grief with a pain in my old useless head and on Tuesday morning life became intolerable, so I sent for Horder[1] and I was immediately doomed to exile . . . so here I am for a couple of days by the sea, allowed to do what I like, when I like and how I like. One of the things I like to do is to write to you and begin whilst waiting for a telephone message from your jo [Baldwin] who is doing my work in my absence . . .

I am in some doubt as to whether an election is inevitable. Your folks are not behaving too well. The chances they now have as a party are too tempting for them. But what am I to do? What is to be my part? 'Confound your politics,' say I. I am an unregenerate Socialist. How can I kick against the pricks? What trouble you give me. Go, plunge into the sea. Spout, splash and be happy. I look on from the shore clad decently in Rogart tweeds.

Chequers. 3 October . . . The trumpets will soon be blowing. I have not decided whether I shall fight Seaham or not. I want to be free to go about during the election and Seaham would tie me up more than is desirable, and yet a victory at Seaham would be worth much and I feel I ought to take what risk there is . . .

When the election is over your friends will demand a good many new places in the Cabinet and they will not allow me to choose their men, I am afraid. How would Charley stand with your jo? Couldn't you buy a new and enticing feather for Betty [Baldwin]'s hat? Oh, you women! What could we do without you? You make us kick against the pricks. You make us dream mad dreams and see impossible visions —and pursue them. Eve is still the applewoman; Adam longs for a bed of wild

---

[1] Sir Thomas (later Lord) Horder, the well-known physician.

thyme, the scent of meadows, the coral shore of Jamaica. Poor Adam! And he goes on cultivating, cultivating by the sweat of his brow. Bless you, though the plough blisters his hand and his feet . . .

On the same day as he wrote this letter, the Prime Minister had an audience with the King, who had cut short his holiday at Balmoral and come back to London to see MacDonald, whom he heard had no heart for a General Election and was thinking of throwing in his hand. When MacDonald intimated during the audience that he was beginning to feel that he had failed and that he had better leave his post, the King told him bluntly that in this event he would not accept his resignation, that it was his positive duty to find a solution, and that he was 'the only person to tackle the present chaotic state of affairs'.

MacDonald thereupon went back to the Cabinet, and two days later, shortly before midnight, a formula was devised to which all the members agreed. The National Government would go to the country and ask for a 'doctor's mandate' to apply every remedy they could agree on to cure the country's ills, each Party issuing its own manifesto with a general pronouncement from the Prime Minister in his name alone. This was to lay emphasis on party co-operation as long as the crisis lasted. Parliament was immediately dissolved, and polling in the General Election was fixed for 27 October. The King declared himself to be 'very pleased' and congratulated the Prime Minister when he came to the Palace to ask for a dissolution.

In the event the Prime Minister decided to contest Seaham as a 'National Labour' candidate, although he was far from confident of the result since by this time he had been formally expelled from the official Labour Party. 'My Dear Ladye,' he wrote a few days before the poll, 'do see that your following vote. This is looking an ominous thing at the moment. They must do it quickly, however.' He need not have worried as he was returned with a majority of nearly 6,000 over his official Labour opponent. A bare dozen other 'National' Labour candidates were returned, but they included the Prime Minister's son Malcolm. Elsewhere in the country the Conservatives virtually swept the board, winning 473 seats which together with their 'National' Labour and 'National' Liberal allies enabled them to count on a total strength of 521 in the new House of Commons. Official Labour came back with a mere 52 members, the whole of their Front Bench having been defeated with the exception of George Lansbury. Incidentally Robin Castlereagh, who had eventually been adopted for County Down, was returned unopposed, one of the very few to have no contest in this election.

The Prime Minister retired to Chequers for the following weekend and invited Lady Londonderry to come down for a walk and a meal. She did so on the Sunday, and they had a long walk in what the Prime Minister recalled to her afterwards as 'woods of gorgeous raiment and in a land of serene dignity and graciousness, and you made me forget everything which did not belong to that order of things. I was your attendant gillie'.

'I am having a job over this Cabinet making,' he wrote to her next day while she was on her way back to Mount Stewart.

> I do not understand some people, and why should I? Simpletons have given good service to the world. It is the gee-gaws of life, its robes and its ribbons which lead us astray and make us ashamed of ourselves. But we two shall continue to understand each other—and esteem each other—won't we? I never sought these things out: I just walked into them and rubbed my eyes wondering at my surroundings, and always hoping to get out of them. But Fate walks behind me with a prod.
>
> I hope you are having a good crossing and perhaps dreaming of the woods and hill sides of Sunday. When you send me fondest love mine flows in to fill the vacant space so that you are robbed of nothing.

Edith Londonderry's day at Chequers had not been in vain. During the evening of 5 November 1931, it was announced from No 10 Downing Street that Lord Londonderry had been appointed Secretary of State for Air in the new National Government with a seat in the Cabinet. The choice of this ministry was certainly not Baldwin's. Had it been left to him, he would in all probability have appointed Sir Samuel Hoare, who had been Air Minister in Baldwin's previous government. Anyhow it was unnecessary for Lady Londonderry to send Baldwin's daughter a new feather for her hat, as Ramsay MacDonald had suggested. What she did do was to send the Prime Minister's daughter Ishbel a jar of the sweet-smelling pot-pourri she used to make at Mount Stewart. 'Congratulations on your husband's new office,' Ishbel replied in her letter of thanks for the gift. 'I am afraid my first thought was "Lucky man he will be able to make use of that note paper with the address in blue".'

Londonderry's new appointment aroused intense interest in Northern Ireland. When he and his wife arrived at Aldergrove, then an R.A.F. airport, they were besieged by the press, as the plane was ahead of time and they had a quarter of an hour's wait. 'There were camera men and reporters everywhere, so we fled to the mess room,' Lady Londonderry wrote to the Prime Minister when they reached Mount Stewart. 'It is really too bad. One climbed over the wall last night, but the intrepid Mrs Hoyland [the housekeeper] dealt with him and called him some fearful names, according to her own account! As she comes from a mining district in Yorkshire, I can believe it.'

'I got the Air Ministry through Ramsay and I am eternally grateful,' Londonderry told his wife looking back some years later: 'that was part of the assistance you gave Ramsay at a very critical time when your help and support and mine too in a much smaller way was vital to him. But I think we built up a lot of jealousy and animosity . . .' Or, as he put it in his autobiographical *Wings of Destiny*, 'now, indeed, I was "Ramsay's man".'

7

The new Cabinet, which now reverted to its normal size, hardly reflected the strength of the parties in the House of Commons. However, the Conservatives were in the majority, since after considerable wrangling between MacDonald and Baldwin they were allotted eleven out of the twenty places available, while the Simonite and the Samuelite Liberals together got five places and National Labour (MacDonald and his small personal following) four. Baldwin was content to continue as Lord President and, as compensation for the relatively small salary (£2,000) attached to the office, to have the use of the Chancellor of the Exchequer's official residence at 11 Downing Street, an arrangement to which the Chancellor, Neville Chamberlain, was agreeable. 'It was very comfortable,' Baldwin remarked of the house afterwards, 'and I could always keep my eye on my Prime Minister.' Simon and Samuel got the Foreign Office and the Home Office respectively. Otherwise the Tories had most of the plum jobs, such as the service ministries which, besides Londonderry at Air, went to Hailsham (War) and Eyres-Monsell (Admiralty). Two of the junior posts, Under-Secretary for Home Affairs and Under-Secretary for the Dominions, were filled respectively by Londonderry's son-in-law Oliver Stanley and the Prime Minister's son Malcolm.

After these appointments had been approved by the King and the constitution of the National Government completed, the Prime Minister broadcast to the country on what he and his colleagues hoped to achieve. He spoke from a prepared script. This so impressed Lady Londonderry that she sent him her congratulations when she heard it at Mount Stewart:

> Your delivery was excellent and voice perfect. Over here they heard every word, as if you were in the next room. Sitting listening to you, no one would have dreamt that you had a written speech. I feel quite certain that you should do this always, as it gives you confidence, whether you use notes or not. When you are addressing the world at large, it seems to me so much better, and will save you so much work and thought, and the result could not be better. So please turn the idea over in your mind once more.

On the eve of the opening of Parliament, Lady Londonderry gave the traditional after-dinner reception in Londonderry House, on this occasion for the National Government. She stood at the top of the grand staircase wearing a tiara and displaying the family jewels to perfection. The Prime Minister was beside her, while Londonderry took up his position just behind them. It was a glittering scene which Ramsay MacDonald enjoyed to the full, although he afterwards had second thoughts when he was attacked by some of his erstwhile Labour colleagues: 'If I stick to this job and be your supporter at the top of the stairs,' he told her shortly afterwards, 'I shall be a more solitary figure than ever—a mule, in short, with a hybrid ancestry and no possible posterity.' He also passed on a remark he had overheard an Opposition Labour member make in the House of Commons lobby about his new role as Prime Minister: 'A few months ago he sang the Red Flag. Now he whistles the Londonderry Air!'

MacDonald was now sixty-seven and he showed his age and the strain of his previous premiership of a minority government culminating in mass unemployment and economic crisis. In February 1932, the international Disarmament Conference opened in Geneva under Arthur Henderson's chairmanship. MacDonald should have led the British delegation, but he was unable to do so since he was in a nursing home recovering from an operation after glaucoma in the left eye had been diagnosed. The nursing home was only two doors away from Londonderry House in Park Lane, so that Lady Londonderry was able to look in and see him during the fortnight he was there. Afterwards he spent three weeks convalescing at an hotel in Newquay. He returned to London in the middle of March and was advised by his doctors to spare his sight and rest as much as possible. Easter fell early that year and he spent it quietly with the Londonderrys at Ranksborough, going back to Downing Street by train in the afternoon of Easter Sunday (27 March). 'As for yourself,' he wrote to her the same evening, 'I loved the talk last night, I loved your going to Church today, I loved the companionship into Peterborough. When I got on to the platform, your place was taken by the engine driver who came up and greeted me genially and said encouraging things to me. I ought to be happy and indeed I am.'

Tommy [Horder] came at 6.30. He travelled up [from Petersfield] just to dine with me, and returned by the 9.30. He heard that I was dining alone here and said he could not bear to think of it. That a P.M., he said, made as I am and standing in the world as I do (that is his folly, not mine) should sit alone in a room in shadow, with no one to speak to and no companion but his own thoughts (little did he know what these thoughts might be) simply horrified him. So he came up to dine with me, and we walked in dashing rain to the Athenaeum, had a cigar afterwards in the Smoking Room, walked back here in pouring rain, and parted.

We gossiped on everything from Thomas Hardy to Fleet commanders, from strange individualities to rules of life, from what it is which sustains a man to Mr Baldwin and Bonar Law, from what he thought when I was at Newquay to marriages which fail and marriages which succeed. A pair of old women, were we not? He said he was very disappointed that you had not stolen some essential part of my clothing so that I could not return to London, and ended by sending his love so as to save me the labour of sending mine.

So here I am in a silent house, save for the rattling of a door, the falling of ashes from the grate, the ticking of a clock and the rain falling outside—and a silent presence of some who are dead and one who is living. The clock now strikes a late hour and I shall try and sleep.

André Tardieu, the French Premier, was due in London for discussions on Germany and the European situation generally. Lady Londonderry had recently met him at a luncheon in Paris where she praised MacDonald warmly, and Tardieu promised to write to her in the role of intermediary. For her part Lady Londonderry wrote to MacDonald on the eve of Tardieu's arrival. She hoped she might get him to supper on the day before the Conference was due to begin, but Fleuriau, the French Ambassador, had arranged an all-male dinner at the embassy.

Ranksborough. 31st March . . . When I telephoned to you this evening, I had just found Tardieu's letter, sent on from London, about meeting 'Hamish the Hart' before the great conference at 11 a.m. (he said) on Monday—wishing to meet your august presence for one small ½ hour before the official meeting.

I tremble when I consider how many precious ½ hours of yours I have wasted— yet not wasted, because I derived untold good from them, and I yet hope you may not have wasted your time and feel better for a mutual talk. For however eminent you may be—and you are—yet you are the most human, loveable human being I have chanced to meet on this glorious earth. As things are I shall not come up until Monday, yet if there is any chance of seeing you on Sunday after 5 p.m. I will come up with Charley . . .

I am so very glad all has come off right. I know you hold the ace of trumps in your hands, therefore all is well. Don't let France play the part of 'a pound of flesh' etc . . . between ourselves I dislike France! but I am all for using her. Much love and 1,000 blessings.

Ranksborough. 1st April. Just got yours of the 31st. I am *so* sorry about our supper, but there it is. Charley still suggests I should come up Sunday with him, but this seems rather pointless if I can't see you . . . You might not be as late as you think at the Embassy, especially as you and Tardieu will have met first.

I feel somehow that all is going very well. The tone of both Tardieu's letters to me was so hopeful—if only he was able to see you! I feel sure he asked Fleuriau to include Charley at the Embassy on Sunday as he likes him so much and I feel he does not get on with someone else!![1] C. can manage foreigners very well and speaks their language which flatters them!!

. . . If I come up on Sunday, I will ring you up. Once before, if you remember, from Hungary I rang you up in the midst of a grave conference with 'our joe', ours, I now say, not mine—so if I should interrupt an international conference, what matter!! But better still, you might ring me up here, Sunday morning, and tell me your news.

The upshot was that Lady Londonderry returned to London with her husband on the Sunday, 4 April, and after the dinner at the French Embassy Tardieu left the embassy alone. The other members of the French delegation were unaware where he was going—they supposed he had gone for a breath of fresh air. The delegation were accommodated in the Hyde Park Hotel next door to the embassy and after waiting until midnight the others went to bed. Tardieu did not get back until 1.30 a.m. having in the meantime gone to Londonderry House for an intimate talk

[1] The reference is to Simon, the Foreign Secretary.

with MacDonald over whisky and sandwiches which Lady Londonderry discreetly organised.

But, alas for Lady Londonderry's endeavours, the French remained as obdurate as ever on the question of their disarming—they were the strongest military power in Europe—in the absence of a watertight security arrangement, while the British Cabinet felt it could not give new guarantees to France under which British forces might conceivably be engaged in a war on the European Continent. 'I do my best to have confidence in the French,' MacDonald noted in his diary on 7 April, 'but am always defeated . . . The diplomacy of France is an ever active influence for evil in Europe.'

'I am *so* sorry your news was ill tonight after all your hard work,' Lady Londonderry wrote to him the same night. 'Personally I should *go* for the Germans, they can't pay and you and France between you can coerce them. I hate seeing you worried by these Dagos.'

MacDonald felt sufficiently recovered to go to Geneva after the Easter adjournment later in the month. Londonderry went on ahead as acting head of the British delegation, which was accommodated in the Beau Rivage Hotel, but he first met the Prime Minister briefly in the Paris embassy, when it was arranged that Lady Londonderry should travel down to Geneva on the same train. But Londonderry cautioned his wife in a letter he sent her as soon as he reached the Beau Rivage:

> *British Delegation to the League of Nations. Geneva. 14 April.* I arrived all right this morning after having dined at the Embassy with Mrs Holman[1] and Charles Mendl[2]; the Ambassador [Lord Tyrrell] was away but I believe returns this morning. I arranged for you to stay there on Tuesday night so all you have to do is to write to Mrs Holman or the Ambassador. Then you can come on with the P.M.
>
> You had best stay in the train until after he has been met and photographed, and I will be there and bring you here. I really am rather frightened of the gossip and I believe there has been some talk in the papers about 'petticoat influence'; the P.M. said something about this at lunch. However I am not really worried about it. You will find out if he is thinking anything about it when you see him before he leaves for Geneva; but you must remember that everyone is ready to gossip and say unkind things.

The Prime Minister had a recurrence of his eye trouble and had to return to London and go into the nursing home for a second operation at the beginning of May. 'I feel so worried about you,' wrote Lady Londonderry on 2 May. 'What is it? Shall I come and see you tomorrow morning, or what would you like me to do? You wrote me such a very charming and dear letter, I cannot bear to think of you worried and wretched. This letter carried all my love and the flowers.' On 11 May she visited him on her way to a Court Ball, looking particularly radiant in a

[1] Wife of Robin Castlereagh's friend Adrian Holman.
[2] Press Secretary.

new evening dress. After she had left, MacDonald scribbled a note in pencil from his bed:

My Dear,
  You were very beautiful, and I loved you. The dress dazzling in brilliance and glorious in colour and line, was you, and my dear, you were the dress. I just touch its hem, and pray for your eternal happiness wondering at the same time what generous archangel ever patted me on the back and arranged that amongst the many great rewards that this poor unwelcome stranger to this world was to receive was that he would be permitted, before he returned to his dust, to feel devotion to *you*.

The Prime Minister was fit enough to attend the opening of the conference on German reparations which met in Lausanne in June and lasted for three weeks. Lady Londonderry saw him just before he left London:

Londonderry House. 12th June. That glimpse of you yesterday was very nice—but rather disturbing as I could see you were distraught, and small wonder. But things are often at their worst before they begin to clear. If only Lausanne can keep up appearances, or close with appearances, all would be well. But at the moment, with Germany as she is, no Government and no one with any real authority to represent her, it seems pretty hopeless. Still, if anyone can do anything, it will be yourself.
  I am not looking forward to my visit next week [to Windsor Castle]. It is a horrible waste of time. If only one could have a whole week like that with nothing to do—somewhere in Scotland—that would be grand, wouldn't it?

The Prime Minister, who was accompanied by the Foreign Secretary, broke his journey in Paris for talks with their opposite numbers, which MacDonald found exhausting. He wrote to Lady Londonderry:

British Embassy,
Paris
[13 June 1932]

My Dear,
  I have come in after a tiring day and am lying down to prepare for a tiring night on the train to Lausanne so I ring you up for a talk. Are you at Windsor in the flesh? Are you in good form? We have had a long talk in the morning, a long lunch, a long drive to Versailles, a long stay in the Little Trianon, a long tea there in Marie Antoinette's room with the same strawberries and cream. I shall never see these places, however, unless I am alone or with one other person who is not likely to come—though as a matter of fact she once came to Chillon.
  We have had quite good talks and at the end of them were cordially friendly. I am amused at the obeisance of the silkworm [Simon]. He tells me every minute or two how amazed he is with the lessons in diplomacy which he is getting, the development of cases, the leading of 'those who are with young' etc etc. Amongst other things he is now convinced that the promising infant which he was to produce in public at Geneva with all men looking on in rapt wonder and with ecstatic feeling was a false expectation and a futile effort in maternity, and he now admits that the Air Force must continue to fly and even drop bombs which may even fall upon Londonderry House by mistake and destroy the beautiful and Puritanical Lady of whom he is so eloquent and enthusiastic. So Charley can tell H.M. that it is all right and he need

not worry. Now that's that. (By the way C. had better say nothing about this to our colleagues until we report ourselves.)[1]

There's a lot of things I could report to you, but you don't want to hear about them. So I shall just tell you that I am well, naughty, and so terribly fond of you that I ought not to tell you how much. I only wish that there were lady Cabinet Ministers and that they (e.g. she) were on the Lausanne delegation.

H.

Lady Londonderry's visit to Windsor, which included the customary banquet on the anniversary of the battle of Waterloo, seems to have passed agreeably enough, judging by her letters.

Windsor Castle. 14th June. My dearest H, I was so delighted to get your letter. The tone of it seemed more hopeful, French and everything. I am writing in the sitting room of Victoria Tower in pyjamas, as I did at Geneva and picturing you back there in those nice rooms. I should like to be with you so much. This I hope will find you all right at Lausanne.

H.M. is in tremendous form. Obviously he wanted to say something about you to me. Stopped with great difficulty, and said it was a dirty story he could not remember!! Isn't it a pity for all of you? I can guess what is going to be said before the words are spoken!!

I do hope your headaches are better. When you write, just tell me this, as it is what I want to know most . . .

'There is altogether too much dressing up here for my taste,' she wrote four days later. 'Tonight tiara and all, Waterloo night in the gallery, but a lovely sight. It is not difficult to look and feel young in this crowd of aged hags!!'

By the way, don't you want a female Minister or Mistress of Education? I should make such a good 'Maîtresse du Cabinet'. I think it an excellent idea. Poor old Sir Donald—but he wasn't much use to you which is all that I think about—but it is an extra worry for you now.[2]

Much much love. I do want to hear how you are . . . Their silly joke here is that I am 'coming out' next year!!

Macdonald replied from Lausanne three days later:

British Delegation,
Hotel Beau Rivage Palace,
Lausanne.
Friday [17 June 1932]

My Dear One,

Yours from Windsor just received is so nice that I have read it twice. Why was I not in the monarch's pocket when those lively conversations were going on! Would it not have been a great occasion when my protests or assents broke into the

[1] This was the draft Convention for the Abolition of Military Aircraft which had been drawn up by Simon with Hankey's help in May during Londonderry's absence in Geneva and approved by the Cabinet provided the French and Italians agreed it. But nothing came of it.

[2] Sir Donald Maclean, President of the Board of Education and a Liberal, died on 15 June 1932. He was succeeded by the Conservative Lord Irwin, former Viceroy of India and later Earl of Halifax.

flow! I gather that he neither admonished nor warned you, but took a fatherly and friendly interest. Interesting man. I imagine the talk and the scene. I knew you would love Windsor. It is a place after your own heart.

I was out for an hour this afternoon and went over part of our way. It was so beautiful in a bright afternoon sun, and Lake and hills were in full glory and majesty. I leant over the arm rest of the car to touch your shoulder. Why were you not there? But I came back to hear your voice and was happy. We are silly, aren't we, and yet I confess I love to be silly—with *you*. I wish I could write what I feel, but in the first place I am tired and dull, and in the next it would be indiscreet, and we are both clad in the armour of discretion.

I warmly second your proposal for a 'Maîtresse de Cabinet', but you sit in neither House, so I am not so much interested as I would be otherwise.

I keep well. The work is heavy and keeping business going in an orderly and methodical way is a pretty arduous job. I have to study every move in the game so as to shepherd my flock on to the green meadow. The Silk Worm works hard even if his hand is not steady. He will always be a great lawyer but never a good diploma-tist, and though he provokes me sometimes he will not upset me. I hope to finish the job before my quickness of mind and steadiness of hand fail me by overwork. My hand occasionally kicks but I spare it as much as I can.

The only thing I lack is you to come blowing in to lift me away from everything but serenity and the things which pertain to beauty and happiness. You dear thing, how do you do it? What is your secret? Why do I write these letters, and why love to have yours? It is too bad of you to keep me in the dark. What potion did you put in my wine that night at Buck[ingham] Pal[ace]? But if it be a secret which when told ceases to be effective, I do not want to know it.

The moon is full and its path on the Lake and light on the hills make the world heaven. It *is* beautiful. Would we were together looking upon it.

Your fondly and devotedly,
Hamish

The Lausanne conference was a personal triumph for the Prime Minister, although unfortunately its benefit turned out to be short-lived. Reparations, which MacDonald had denounced at the time of the peace settlement after the war, were ended in exchange for Germany agreeing to pay three milliards of francs into a fund for European reconstruction. Nothing was said about war guilt or disarmament, which annoyed the Germans at home, while the Anglo-French understanding for periodic consultation remained. MacDonald was satisfied and heartened by the crowd which assembled at Victoria Station to greet him on his return. 'It was a full-flying end,' he noted in his diary on 10 July. 'The King and Queen in the garden at the palace, C[irce] in her mansion, and the curtain falls.' Later he sent her a bunch of press cuttings about the conference praising him, which she gratefully acknowledged from Mount Stewart. 'They thrill me,' she wrote. 'You never talk enough about yourself and that is what I long to hear.' Again she yearned to be with him in the Scottish Highlands:

The Highlands are to me rather in the nature of someone we are much in love with, unlawfully almost. They are ever present in my thoughts—deep down in my nature is incessant longing to be there. This longing never leaves me, and haunts one's thoughts. Altogether it can be quite a nuisance. I believe this is always so, to anyone who has the call of the blood in their veins, and explains why all the Highlanders always return whenever they can to their native place—even when like myself of mixed blood, it will not be gainsaid. This anyhow you and I know and understand and share together.

8

Meanwhile Baldwin had proposed that all naval and military aviation should be scrapped, so appalled was he by the Japanese bombing of women and children in Shanghai and other Chinese towns. Although opposed by Londonderry and the Air Staff, the Cabinet agreed that the Prime Minister and Simon should sound out the French and Italians in Paris and Geneva. As Sir Maurice Hankey, the Secretary of the Cabinet, put it, this was only done 'very tentatively and ineffectively', owing to Londonderry's attitude and MacDonald's consequent lack of enthusiasm. Neither were the French in favour of the proposal. Had anything come of it, the abolition of the bombing aeroplane would have meant the end of the French and British air forces.

Afterwards Hankey wrote in his diary:

> The fact is that Ramsay MacDonald has a very soft place for the Air Force. He loves flying. Lord Thomson was his best friend. Lord Londonderry, the present Air Minister, and Lady Londonderry are now the best friends of that rather lonely man, and have shown him innumerable kindnesses. There is no doubt that he 'blanketed' the proposal and Simon was not the man to thwart him, though he believed in the plan.
>
> After June [1932] the matter remained in abeyance. I mentioned it once or twice to Ramsay MacDonald as the one direction in which progress in disarmament could be made, but found him unenthusiastic. Baldwin, though very disappointed—for he wanted to make a speech at Geneva on the subject—lay low.

MacDonald would have liked his Egeria to come to Balmoral, particularly as Lady Londonderry was in process of forming the Personal Service League with Lady Reading, Lady Peel and other 'society stars', which as Thomas Jones later put it, 'stirs up the leisured class to give or make garments for the distressed areas and does this with much success. Most of them have suddenly discovered after ten years that there are workless men and women short of food and clothing, and they want to cover the land with depots for free distribution'. But women, even the wives of ministers, were seldom invited to Their Majesties' Scottish retreat. However, on this occasion, the Queen promised to be the League's patroness. 'Do you know the P.M.'s den here?' MacDonald wrote from Balmoral on 31 August. 'It is quaintly Victorian and I like it though it is a bit cold for a Highlander so I have brought some scent of the Oriental kind, and I hear Queen Victoria's ghost sniffing and aerial voices whispering: "Albert, what is this? It was not in our time." '

MacDonald thought that the Personal Service League, as then constituted, was 'over classy', and when it had been strengthened it would be a good idea if it could co-operate with the National Council for Social Service, so he deputed Tom Jones, the Assistant Secretary of the Cabinet, to try to co-ordinate the two bodies. The matter came to a head as the result of a broadcast by the journalist S. P. B. Mais early in 1933. Jones thereupon wrote, none too kindly, of his meetings with Lady Londonderry:

> Some weeks ago Mais, broadcasting accounts of his visits to the poorer areas, referred to Seaham Harbour and to weary men pushing bicycles along the sea-wall weighed down with sacks of coal got from the coast face at great risk. This was interpreted as an attack on the P.M. who is the Member for Seaham and on the Londonderrys who are the local coalowners. She [Lady Londonderry] 'went off the deep end', went North to find out the facts in three days, came back with a Memorandum, saw S.B. who rang me up . . .
> Next day I saw her Ladyship in Park Lane. The butler took me up in a narrow lift to a study or boudoir in the roof of the house and I had half an hour or 40 minutes with her Ladyship, who talked at me about starving and dying children, ordered cocktails, 'phoned to a servant to take the dogs out for their exercise, demanded to know what Ellis and his Council were doing about it, flattered the Pilgrim Trust for its activities, all with a ceaseless volubility and an attempt to charm and hypnotise which entirely failed in its object. She is 54 and still handsome and a few years ago must have been extremely so. She is perfectly dressed and I am sure means well.

Jones suggested that Lady Londonderry and her colleagues should meet the women on the committee of the National Council of Social Service, such as Joan Fry and Lady Denman, women of long experience of work with the unemployed. But the meeting was not a success. 'Lady L. came with a Dame Florence Simpson,' according to Jones. 'She was agitated and overwrought, kept "scrambling eggs" with a pair of gloves, hiding and revealing fingers blazing with diamonds. It was the oddest situation.' Co-operation seemed impossible. However, to quote Jones, 'we lowered the temperature of Lady L's hostility a good deal but [Sir Alan] Barlow at the Athenaeum on Friday—he is the P.M.'s new Private Secretary—said she had described me as a "hard-hearted Bolshevik Quaker" '.

Eventually Lady Londonderry gave up the struggle, as she told the Prime Minister, after Hitler had become German Chancellor:

> The [Personal Service] League is too important to go cadging about for money, especially with the Queen as Patron. It should be done as I hoped and intended. I do not propose to try any more. Everything I do is short circuited. The really vexatious thing is that the rich people like the Marks's won't give to anything that is not 'top dog' and they are all trying to curry favour with H.R.H. [the Prince of Wales] but don't quote me as saying this, but it is the fact.

As long as the two societies are running against each other, the P[ersonal] S[ervice] L[eague] can never be run on a national basis . . . I believe if I gave up being President, the N[ational] C[ouncil of] S[ocial] S[ervice] would be far less antagonistic. My name is objectionable to them! ! Anyhow nothing is worth bothering about. I have made my effort, and that's that . . .

We live in horrible times, but I would not change them since you are you. But what a strange fate has thrown you up against the World [to] be the bulwark which you are. You are the most human and understanding of men, and yet by force of evil Junkers the upholder of Britain's might. Sometimes I wonder if the Powers aloft are not laughing at all our efforts.

Ramsay MacDonald appeared from time to time at Geneva while the Disarmament Conference was sitting, and he would send Lady Londonderry reports on the progress or rather lack of progress of the proceedings. 'I hope you will ring me up from London,' he wrote on one occasion from the Beau Rivage, 'though I do not hear very well on the 'phone, and the lines are tapped both here and in Paris. I just long to see you, my dear.' In the result she went to Geneva, where she heard him deliver his moving speech to the assembly on 16 March 1933, in which he proposed specific limitation of armaments, mentioning figures for the first time. This was henceforth known as the MacDonald Plan.

Another representative of his country at the Geneva Conference was the Secretary of the Hungarian Legation in London, the Marquis Alphonse Pallavicini, familiarly known as 'Fono' to his friends, who included both MacDonald and Lady Londonderry. He had the misfortune to be involved in a motor accident at this time when he was driving with Lady Londonderry and they were returning one night from dinner at Sutton Place, near Guildford, then owned by the Duke of Sutherland, in which they collided with a bus on the Portsmouth road, both receiving injuries, Lady Londonderry sustaining a broken thumb and multiple cuts and bruises to her head. 'My thumb being broken does not help me very much in dressing,' she told the Prime Minister in one of her letters, 'but it is my left one and I am doing nothing to it. It is not in a splint, only a guard. I have three stitches in my scalp and they shaved a bit off, like a monk! ! It looks rather like the remains of an old rook's nest! ! Altogether with bloody eyes and bruises I look most interesting. Wasn't I clever to keep it out of the papers! !'

Unfortunately it did get into the press as the result of Pallavicini suing the London Passenger Transport Board for negligence, an action which he lost, in spite of the gallant support he received from his companion in the witness box. There was plainly a conflict of evidence, and in finding for the Board the jury seemed to have been influenced by the impression they gained that Lady Londonderry was having a night out with someone who was not her husband, who was moreover a foreigner, and furthermore a particularly dangerous type of foreigner, namely a Hungarian, besides which the couple had probably dined at the ducal table not wisely but too

well and were in a hurry to get home. Nor was Lord Londonderry particularly pleased at having, in addition to his wife's medical expenses as
the result of the accident, to pay all the unsuccessful plaintiff's legal costs,
since the Marquis was an impoverished member of the old Hungarian
nobility and received a mere pittance for his job at the Legation.

On 7 June, the MacDonald Plan was accepted by the Conference as the
basis of the future convention, and two days later a four-power pact was
initialled by France, Germany, Italy and the United Kingdom. Mac-
Donald telephoned the news to Lady Londonderry, and the same night
she wrote to him:

> *Londonderry House. 9th June.* My dearest H, Your telephone message gave me
> *such* joy, not only as the greatest event, but on account of the success of your very
> dear self. I only hope it has not been at the expense of your health. My whole heart
> goes out to you in joy and admiration at the manner in which you have pulled it off.
> Bless you, and all my love is yours. Now, do take things easy . . .
>
> Please don't say 'No' to anything until I have seen you. So much depends on
> you, and at this moment you really are the 'Sovereign people' and no honour is too
> great. This achievement is no ordinary one, and no one can love you more than our
> Sovereign Lord the King and he can do no more than confer the highest gift that
> he has to give on you. So *please* think quietly over what I say with all humility to
> 'Hamish the Proud' but I say it with all sincerity and because I know that the British
> people at heart will think it right and good.
>
> Thank you, again and again, for having let me know. To hear it, in your own dear
> words, was wonderful. I still feel breathless. I always knew you were a great man, so
> I cannot be surprised, but I am doubly proud and pleased.
>
> All my love, dearest H, from Circe.

This probably represents the high-water mark in Ramsay MacDonald's
public reputation and also in Lady Londonderry's affection and esteem
for him, although they were to remain close friends until his death. She
was naturally disappointed that he was not given the Garter or at least the
Thistle for his achievements at Geneva. But, to his credit, he refused all
honours, and he could have had virtually anything he wished at the
Sovereign's hands. He was content to be a Fellow of the Royal Society,
to which he had been elected in 1930, and he wanted nothing more. In
spite of his constant craving for Lady Londonderry's company he
remained a solitary and lonely figure, as many of his letters to her testify.
'No one is with me here today and by the fire in the Long Gallery I sit
alone,' he wrote to her from Chequers on 6 October 1933. 'The Cromwell
portraits look down through the shadowy light and are the only company
I have.'

CHAPTER VI

FINALE

I

OF THE EIGHT ministers who held the office of Secretary of State for Air between the two world wars, Londonderry has probably received the most criticism. Unfortunately his term of office coincided first with the Disarmament Conference at Geneva and later with Germany's rearmament in the air. His appointment of Sir Edward Ellington as Chief of the Air Staff after Sir Geoffrey Salmond's premature and unexpected death in April 1933 was unfortunate, certainly in the light of hindsight. Ellington, although he had a good brain, was a rigid and orthodox militarist who held steadfastly to the view that there could be no war with Germany before 1942, although Liddell Hart and other experts did their best to convince him to the contrary. At the same time, as we have seen, Londonderry strove hard and successfully to preserve the nucleus of Britain's air force when all military aviation was under attack at Geneva, impeded as he was by the Foreign Secretary, Sir John Simon. Later he was to set up the departmental committee under the eminent scientist Sir Henry Tizard which developed the discovery of radar, and he was also to promote the designs of the Hurricane and Spitfire fighters which were to play such a vital role in the Battle of Britain in 1940. Thus, having pleaded unsuccessfully for more money for the R.A.F. when all development of larger types of military aircraft stopped during the disarmament discussions, Londonderry was afterwards blamed for not having done enough when Hitler eventually announced, as he did in the spring of 1935, that Germany had an air force in defiance of the terms of the Versailles Treaty.

In 1932 and 1933 not a single new squadron was added to the uncompleted Home Air Force, which had aimed at the formation of fifty-two squadrons between 1923 and 1928. Indeed by 1933 only forty squadrons had been formed, and of these no less than thirteen were 'non-regular' squadrons which could not be regarded as part of the first line. With the final breakdown of the Disarmament Conference in 1934 and the knowledge obtained from reliable intelligence sources that Germany was secretly rearming in the air, the British Government in July of that year announced the first of a number of alphabetically numbered expansion schemes, which were to succeed one another at irregular intervals until

November 1938, the last (Scheme M) being precipitated by the Munich crisis. When the second of these expansion schemes was under discussion in the Cabinet in March 1935, Londonderry still being minister, the Air Staff underlined the problem in terms which the minister endorsed:

> It may be said that the roots of our difficulties lie in the slowing down and then the stopping of the 52-squadron scheme. Under normal conditions it is impracticable to lay down a carefully thought out programme of development, slow it up, stop it for a year or two, and then resume not only at a rate calculated to overtake the delay but also to deal with a further expansion superimposed upon the original scheme.

Arguments with the Treasury and the Foreign Office during this period were so protracted that, as one of Londonderry's successors as minister, Sir Kingsley Wood, put it, it was not surprising 'if the belief had been engendered in certain parts of the Air Ministry that no Government really meant business in the matter of Air Force expansion and that they were prepared to accept permanent inferiority in the air as compared with at least one continental power, France'. Also, with the discontinuance of all development of the larger types of aircraft during the Disarmament Conference in deference to the views of the Treasury and the Foreign Office, experimental orders were concentrated on small types of aircraft which would be suitable for use overseas where the primary responsibility of the Royal Air Force lay. Furthermore, it was unfortunate that during the same period civil aviation was concentrated, for reasons of economy, on the development of large flying boats. 'Germany, on the other hand, was developing large civil landplanes and the work done on these aircraft was most valuable when she came to build up her own Air Force.'

During the Christmas recess in 1933–34, Londonderry made a morale-boosting flight to the various R.A.F. stations in the Middle East and India. At the same time Lady Londonderry, accompanied by three of her daughters, Margaret, Helen and Mairi, flew privately on a sightseeing tour of Palestine and Egypt. Her letters to the Prime Minister describe her impressions at the time:

> *King David Hotel, Jerusalem. 27 December 1933.* How are you? Not having heard since leaving, I am wondering how all goes. You are often in my thoughts. The three girls and I are here; our pilot is Mr Muntz in his Dragon.[1]
> We have had a wonderful time, flying over the Desert to Petra and then to Jericho. It is very cold, but bright sun, but it looks like stormy weather, so we may be marooned here. We hope to join Charley for one night at Amman. He takes off for India from there on the 1st. He is now at Khartoum or on the way there . . . We are by way of going to Damascus from here and flying over Galilee.

[1] Alan Muntz founded Heston airport with Sir Nigel Norman and was also concerned with similar undertakings including Indian National Airways, besides being an engineer consultant who later developed the Pescara free piston engine system and other inventions. In 1934 he married Lady Margaret Stewart, much against her parents' wishes; they were divorced in 1939.

This place is very bewildering, so much so familiar, and the reality so different. Such a mixture of warring races and creeds, yet each so pious in their various devotions, but ready to slit each other's throats at any moment. We were at Hebron today and saw all the tombs of the Patriarchs. What a country for flying, as most of it is impossible without. It was very thrilling coming over the stupendous Wadi and flying up the Dead Sea.

Mena House, Cairo. 3rd January 1934 . . . I thought of your account of the Holy Land [in *Wanderings and Excursions*] when we were there. I wish you had been our guide. The weather, although divine compared to England, has not been too good but lots of sun on the whole, and we are all very fit and well except for mosquito bites. It is only when you come abroad that you really appreciate the comforts of home . . . I hate being away for so long, and missing seeing you, much more than you imagine . . .

Charley had a great time here, everyone very pleased with him. He is very fit and well. He had a great flight from Amman to Baghdad. I have had letters from all the foreigners loud in praise of his speeches on the Air, including even a German friend!!

One item of expenditure, fortunately earmarked by the Government, was for the construction of the new R.A.F. buildings at Cranwell which were completed during Londonderry's term as Secretary of State and which, as will be seen, he was able to persuade the Prince of Wales to declare open. He also encouraged the Prince to take an interest not only in the air but also in non-party political, industrial and social questions, including coal. In fact, it was the latter which had caused Londonderry's first difference with Baldwin, and was to rankle for some time. Early in 1929, at the height of the economic depression, when Baldwin was still enjoying his second term as Prime Minister and Londonderry was at the Office of Works, the Prince had accepted an invitation to pay a three-day visit to the coalfields in the north-east. Londonderry, who seems to have been unaware of the visit until he read about it in the papers, although the Prince went with Baldwin's blessing, complained that he had not been properly consulted and furthermore that the visit had been 'thoroughly stage-managed' in the most unfortunate and damaging manner for himself and his fellow coal owners in the area, quoting some of the Prince's comments upon what he saw like 'appalling conditions', 'perfectly damnable', 'ghastly', and so on.

'I am bound to say that I resent the whole of this tour and I think it has been carried out under the most unfortunate auspices,' Londonderry wrote to Baldwin on the Prince's return to London.

The Public seems to be quite unaware that most of the miners in Durham live rent free or receive a rent allowance; that they also receive free coal and, if they are off work three days a week, they receive the dole!

There was one typical instance which was brought to my notice of how the Prince of Wales was shown a pay bill of nine shillings which, of course, was supplemented by the dole. This latter information was not given to him and his remark was 'Is that due to bad management?' to which he received the reply from the miner, 'No, to hard management.'

However, there was nothing which Baldwin could do about it except sympathise. The fact was that Londonderry was not generally considered to be a bad owner, as Baldwin's friend John Davidson, the Conservative Party Chairman, admitted in an otherwise unsympathetic opinion. 'As a mine owner in Durham he had quite a good reputation,' wrote Davidson of Londonderry in his memoirs, 'but the people who were his agents were regarded as a pretty hard lot.' Even Sean O'Casey conceded a point in Londonderry's favour. A few weeks before the Prince's visit, he wrote to Lady Londonderry: 'I read that Lord Londonderry has kept an unprofitable mine open to save the miners the hardship of unemployment, and this, even to my jagged Communistic outlook, was a very good deed, indeed.'

Besides learning something about coal and similar topics, Londonderry felt that the Prince of Wales should be allowed to see some of the confidential state papers, notably the Cabinet papers. He mentioned this to the King's Keeper of the Privy Purse, Sir Frederick ('Fritz') Ponsonby, a most experienced courtier who had begun his official career as Queen Victoria's Assistant Private Secretary. Hitherto the Prince and his brother the Duke of York had only been shown a selection of Foreign Office telegrams, a concession which the King had granted with considerable reluctance, since he held that it was no part of the duties of his elder sons to have access to such confidential information. However in this instance, when Fritz Ponsonby raised the matter with the King, the latter promised to look into it and to consult the Prince's private secretary Godfrey Thomas. The result was not encouraging as Ponsonby informed Londonderry from Buckingham Palace in November 1933:

> The King told me that in reply to his inquiries, Godfrey Thomas explained that the Prince of Wales rarely reads the Blue print from the Foreign Office. Apparently H.R.H. is always in such a hurry that he is quite incapable of reading anything. He finds difficulty in reading the newspapers and only glances at the Head lines in the cheaper newspapers. Under the circumstances the King thought it a sheer waste of time to let him have more to read.
>
> I argued that if H.R.H. was given more interesting papers to read he might overcome his reluctance to read anything and by degrees get interested in the questions of the day.
>
> The King replied that if H.R.H. really wished to understand the problems that the Government had to deal with, it would be a different matter, but as he had never expressed a wish to have more papers sent him, it would be better to drop the whole idea.

And that in fact was what was done, although the King made a point of thanking Londonderry through Ponsonby for putting forward the suggestion.

In announcing the modest Air Force expansion Scheme A in the House
of Lords in July 1934—Baldwin made a similar announcement in the
Commons—Londonderry, as he subsequently recalled, took the line that,
'although we still ought not to abandon all hope of something materialising
at Geneva, the idea of parity in the air with any Power within striking
distance must be a cardinal principle of policy. If this new policy was
effectively carried out it would strengthen our influence for peace, and,
far from inaugurating a new race in armaments, might effectively stop
one'.

> From now on there was a new spirit in the Government and the country. At least I
> had persuaded my colleagues to think in terms of air parity, and I was now much
> easier in my mind. What we aimed at was security against possible attack. Winston
> and Rothermere were far from satisfied, and at the same time the Socialists were
> infuriated that we were even adding one squadron, or proposing to add one, to our
> attenuated Air Force, although they were remarkably bellicose in every other
> direction.

Throughout the summer and autumn of 1934 the Air Ministry's
estimates of present and future German air strength increased steadily.
When the Cabinet met on 28 November on the eve of the autumn session
of Parliament, it was agreed that Baldwin should intervene during the
opening debate on the Address in the House of Commons later that day
when the question of the relative British and German air strengths was
expected to be raised by Churchill. At this Cabinet several alternative
estimates of Germany's current air strength were before the ministers,
varying from a Foreign Office calculation of 600 to a French one of 1,100.
The Air Ministry estimate, according to Londonderry, was 1,000 military
aircraft, including first line, reserve and training, while production of
machines was estimated at between 160 and 180 a month. At the same
time Londonderry suggested that it would be most unwise to mention
specific figures in the House of Commons which might be challenged by
Germany, a view shared by the Permanent Secretary of the Air Ministry,
Sir Christopher Bullock.

Since Britain's first-line strength at this time was 500 machines com-
prised in forty-three squadrons, while Germany did not possess more than
300 first-line aircraft, what Baldwin stated in the House was substantially
accurate. His statement was designed, as he had earlier told his Cabinet
colleagues, to let Germany know in 'clear but friendly terms that Britain
was aware of and not indifferent to what was taking place there in the
matter of air rearmament', or, as Londonderry put it in a private letter to
the War Minister, Lord Hailsham, 'either to bring the Germans back to
Geneva' or to make sure that 'they will stand arraigned in their true
colours before the world'.

'It is not the case that Germany is rapidly approaching equality with us . . . even if we confine the comparison to the German air strength and the strength of the Royal Air Force immediately available in Europe,' said Baldwin. He continued:

> Germany is actively engaged in the production of service aircraft, but her real strength is not 50 per cent of our strength in Europe today. As for the position this time next year, *if she continues to execute her air programme without acceleration* [author's italics] and if we continue to carry out at the present approved rate of expansion announced in Parliament in July . . . so far from the German military air force being at least as strong and probably stronger than our own, we estimate that we shall have in Europe a margin—in Europe alone—of nearly 50 per cent.

Churchill, who had his own intelligence sources, claimed that the Germans would attain parity with the R.A.F. within the next twelve months and would have double Britain's air strength by the end of 1936. Baldwin challenged these figures as being 'considerably exaggerated', but he did not predict, as was later suggested by his opponents, that Britain would have a safe margin of superiority by the latter date. What he actually said in the debate, to quote his own words, was that 'it is impossible to give any accurate estimate for longer than two years, but that we were able to maintain a position not inferior, whatever happened'.

Meanwhile Londonderry had made an accurate prediction in a private letter to the Prime Minister:

> As a result of this debate, it will go out to the country that we have known all about the rearmament of Germany, that we have been helpless in the face of it, and that we are unable to propound any policy except that of preparing for another war. Limitation is the first step, and the sole hope of escape from the lunacy of the race in armaments to which the continued uncertainty as to the extent of German preparations is certain to give rise.

Several personal experiences which Londonderry and his wife had in 1934 may be briefly noted. On 7 June, while piloting his own plane, an Avro Cadet, the Air Minister narrowly escaped being killed when coming in to land at Heston aerodrome. While turning to avoid a tree, his engine stalled and he crashed, overshooting the aerodrome. The present author happened to be working in the library at Londonderry House when he came in, his face streaming with blood from a badly cut lip. Fortunately his injuries were minor, and he had recovered sufficiently to attend the twenty-fifth anniversary celebrations of Louis Blériot's pioneer flight of the English Channel in July 1909, which were held a few weeks later at Buc aerodrome in France and during which the veteran flyer who was present was so overcome with emotion that he fainted.

Later in July, Ramsay MacDonald spent a few days at Mount Stewart on his way to Canada for a part-holiday and part-fact-finding mission. Lady Londonderry had put several books in his room which she considered suitable for bed-side reading. One of them was a novel by Elinor Glyn entitled *Did She?* At breakfast next morning his hostess asked him if he had looked at the novel and how much he had read of it. 'Oh, about fifteen pages,' he replied, with a characteristic twinkle in his eye. 'In fact, until she did!'

On 31 August the first civil airport in Northern Ireland was opened by the Governor, the Duke of Abercorn, on Londonderry's land at Newtownards which he presented to the Government for the purpose. The Governor, who was not a flying enthusiast, remarked at the official luncheon that the only flying he intended to do he 'hoped would be in the next world'. Thus he was not a passenger on the inaugural flight in the party which included the Air Minister and the present writer in a DH89. This aircraft was a twin-engined de Havilland biplane, later known as the Dragon Rapide, and was put into service on the Belfast route, being the latest British aircraft in production for commercial air transport, carrying eight passengers with a crusing speed of 130 m.p.h. and a range of 560 miles. Hitherto commercial and privately-owned aircraft had been obliged to use the R.A.F. station at Aldergrove as the Ulster terminus for their flights. In a broadcast account of the opening ceremony, attended among other aviators by the Duchess of Bedford and Dr Oliver St John Gogarty, who arrived piloting their own machines, the present writer remarked:

> The inhabitants of Ulster must be grateful that the land which has been made available for the airport is owned by the present Air Minister. For it is largely owing to the active interest taken in the project by Lord Londonderry, whose family has been closely associated with the province for generations, that Ulster can now boast one of the best equipped aerodromes in the British Isles.

Finally, in September, the Prince of Wales flew to Cranwell to open the new buildings of the Royal Air Force College. In introducing him, Londonderry referred to the College as 'the very heart and centre from which the R.A.F. derived its vitality. It was there that it continually renewed its strength and year after year received its inspiration'.

Since Sir Philip Sassoon, the Under Secretary for Air in the Commons, was not a member of the Cabinet, and Londonderry sat in the Lords, Baldwin, who was Lord President of the Council, had come more and more to answer for air policy in the Lower House. The arrangement would have worked well, if Londonderry's relations with Baldwin had been easy and intimate. They were neither and the consequent failure in communication led to some unfortunate misunderstandings. There was no bond of sympathy between them. As Baldwin afterwards told Robin Castlereagh, 'I always tried to be friendly with your father, but he was aloof and standoffish,' although Baldwin was careful to add that he could always count on his complete loyalty as a colleague. ('Loyalty is the rarest virtue in politics.') For his part Londonderry regretted that he was never able to gain Baldwin's confidence. 'I often tried to get closer to you but I did not succeed,' he told him after he had ceased to be a minister. 'I think, as a matter of fact, that I was a little too outspoken and that you resented once or twice the opinions which I expressed, while others, who may be said to be more far-seeing in their own interests, have taken good care not to cross you in any way.' Londonderry also complained to Baldwin, looking back some years later: 'Although you were responsible for the more important Air matters in the House of Commons, you never consulted me once, but were in the habit of sending for little Bullock, who always informed me, of course, but who never seemed to convey to you the real points we wished to be emphasised, as there were always misunderstandings after all your speeches relating to Air matters in the House of Commons.'

At the beginning of March 1935 a Government White Paper on defence, which had been mainly drafted by Sir Maurice Hankey, who was Secretary of the Committee of Imperial Defence as well as Secretary of the Cabinet, was published over the Prime Minister's initials, after it had been approved by the Cabinet. It underlined the extent of Germany's illegal rearmament and indicated that, if unchecked, this would lead to war. It was described, when it was debated in the Commons, as being a declaration that British defence should be strong enough 'to repel an aggressor or to fulfil obligations', a proposition which failed to find favour with the Labour Opposition. Nevertheless the danger was reinforced from Germany itself by Goering, who announced on the eve of the debate that the Reich possessed an air force in defiance of the Versailles Treaty and by Hitler, a few days later that the German army was to be raised to thirty-six divisions (half a million men) and compulsory military service introduced. This was followed by an elaborate review by Hitler of the veterans of the Great War, and two days later Berlin had a trial blackout. The world of diplomacy was taken completely by surprise, and many, who ought to have known better, were convinced that Germany was already completely rearmed. Some time previously it had been announced that Simon and Eden, the Parliamentary Under-Secretary at the Foreign Office, would pay an official visit to Berlin on 5 March to meet Hitler, but the Fuehrer cried off at the last moment on the pretext that he had a cold. Eventually, after the dust had begun to settle, he agreed to see the British ministers on 25 March.

On 17 March, Lady Londonderry, who had just flown over from London to Mount Stewart, wrote to the Prime Minister:

How I feel for you in all this worry. I had a most unpleasant feeling all the while I was flying over in the plane yesterday as I read *The Times* but particularly the

D[aily] T[elegraph] that all was not well, and made a note on paper to ask you as soon as I saw you if you could not go to Berlin yourself and take C[harley] (about the air). Of course S.S. [Simon] too, but then you would have been two to one. I felt so uneasy all the time—strange, wasn't it?—as all the business was going on at the time. Even now I must fain believe we are blundering and this move must be pure bluff. And yet all along I have thought they are far more prepared than they are generally given credit for. All this on top of your other worries is too much . . .

I should like half an hour every day to teach all these people opposing the White Paper exactly what to expect from Germany should trouble come. It would open their eyes.

When Simon and Eden met Hitler at the Reich Chancellery in Berlin, the Fuehrer repeated that the Luftwaffe had already reached equality in numbers with the R.A.F. This statement was palpably untrue, and neither minister apparently made any attempt to contradict it. The fact was that at this date the Germans had only one operational squadron in being, although they were hoping soon to form from fifteen to twenty squadrons from their training establishments, which would include a number of gliders, while Britain's first-line strength was between 800 and 850 aircraft, a fact which was known to the Germans at this time.

Hitler's claim, which received extensive publicity in the English press, caused considerable alarm, and Londonderry was singled out as a scapegoat particularly in the Rothermere and Beaverbrook papers. In April Churchill told his kinsman that there were 'definite intrigues' afoot to get him out of the Air Ministry. Londonderry himself sensed this since he wrote to his wife on 27 April:

He [MacDonald] is very sensitive about my appointment I think, and flinches whenever some criticism is made. It does not matter if the attack comes from an enemy or a visionary, he becomes terribly scared and warns me for my own good . . . I have several enemies and now the election approaches there are one or two who would like to have my place. If I survive I think it will be on your merits. I am sure the P.M. would never sponsor me again and S[tanley] B[aldwin] has always resented (I think) our support of the P.M.

Anyway I see myself being squeezed out. I do not know that I mind very much as I am sure my present post is already allotted, but I should be sorry to leave the Air. Anyway in the 4 years we have sown a good crop at the Air Ministry and my would be successors want to reap the harvest. However I am not taking all this lying down and I am preparing to counter attack strongly when I can get the charge formulated.

A few days later he saw his friend Lady Desborough, to whom he communicated his fears about his position. 'I can't bear you to have the least worry or preoccupation,' she wrote to him on 4 May. 'But alas alas that is so unrealisable in this troublesome world. The most unfair thing however that *could* happen—even in this world—would be any denial of credit to you for what you have done in this office. Jack Salmond was here on Thursday and I wish that you could have heard all that he said of the love and trust you have inspired all through the Air Force.'[1]

When they met again at a State Banquet given at Buckingham Palace on 9 May to mark the Silver Jubilee of King George and Queen Mary, Churchill repeated his warning in a most emphatic and decisive manner. Londonderry replied that he was quite aware of the opposition to his continuing as Air Minister but that, at long last, he had succeeded in establishing a policy of expansion.

But Churchill was not impressed. 'Look out, they are going to kick you out,' he said. 'I should resign if I were you.'

Although he felt that Churchill did not realise the struggle he had had to maintain the Air Force at all, Londonderry instinctively knew that Churchill was right. However, Londonderry told him that, whereas he might have given up the unequal struggle before, now that the Government had agreed to his proposals this was surely the time for him to stay on. But Churchill did not agree and continued to urge resignation as the right course. 'You ought to have a great campaign all over the country on the subject of rearmament,' he added. 'It has got to come to that.'

2

By this date the Cabinet was under considerable outside pressure for a more rapid expansion of the R.A.F. than Londonderry and the Air Staff considered practicable in the circumstances. Consequently on 30 April 1935 a small Cabinet Sub-Committee, known as the Air Parity Committee and consisting of Sir Philip Cunliffe-Lister, later Lord Swinton, Walter Runciman, later Lord Runciman, and William Ormsby-Gore, later Lord Harlech, was appointed to recommend, in consultation with the Air Ministry, what should be done to implement the Government pledge, which Baldwin had given, of 'air parity with our nearest neighbour within striking distance', as rapidly as possible.

Cunliffe-Lister and his two colleagues got to work straight away and produced a report in under ten days. Their report came before the Prime Minister on 10 May, the day after the State Banquet at which Churchill had warned Londonderry of the danger of his position. In its expressed view, Hitler's claim of parity with Great Britain in first-line aircraft must be taken to be true.

MacDonald found the whole report 'very unsettling', noting in his

[1] Marshal of the R.A.F. Sir John Salmond was married to Lady Desborough's daughter Monica. He succeeded Trenchard as Chief of the Air Staff in 1930 and held the post until 1933 when he was briefly followed by his brother Geoffrey.

diary on the same day that he was 'taking the matter in hand' personally.
He went on:

> The Air Ministry has been caught napping. It is likely, as always happens on such
> occasions, it will be condemned for sins which were not sins, but it has not been
> looking far enough ahead. It is not only short in numbers but in planes. I was taken
> aback when I was told the position. It was undoubtedly much hampered by our
> efforts to pull something out of the Disarmament Conference and the German start
> was greater than its informers told it.

At a ministerial meeting two days later, at which Londonderry and
Cunliffe-Lister were both present, the Air Minister calculated the number
of German pilots as 4,000, whereas Cunliffe-Lister put it at twice that
amount, and went on to advise that the Air Ministry figure was unacceptable. This cast a serious reflection upon the quality of the Air Staff's
intelligence, which was believed in political circles to be inferior to the
intelligence branches of the other two service departments.

After Londonderry had told his wife about the further trouble that was
brewing, she wrote to the Prime Minister more in sorrow than in anger
that he had been kept in ignorance of the intrigue which had been going
on against her husband. Since there is no trace of her letter in the Mac-
Donald Papers, it is likely that the Prime Minister destroyed it, as he
seems to have done with other letters of hers, which he considered too
intimate or confidential to be preserved. However his reply has survived,
and although it is undated it was almost certainly written about the middle
of May 1935.

> *10 Downing Street.* I have been uneasy for some time on the subject you have
> written to me. Its origin was friction between departments[1] which I have done
> everything I could to suppress, but the new German trouble has made an awkward
> situation. Frequently I have told you about party developments, but never could get
> a private word so matters have drifted, as I really could not write of them. Now my
> health compels me to ease myself of the weight of my burdens. That is inevitable,
> and when it comes I shall be pretty well out of it and decisions will be more in
> Conservative hands than ever. For weeks I have been struggling against heavy odds
> and great depression, and the limit is passed.

According to MacDonald's diary, his physician Tommy Horder, who
had seen him at this time, told him that, although his resignation was not
essential on health grounds alone, he undoubtedly needed a rest. At the
same time the Prime Minister also noted in his diary:

> Press full of jubilee ceremonies with indications that the stage is being cleared and
> the real play is the bailing and trial of the Government. That Baldwin is coming in
> is being taken for granted as is also the strengthening of the Tory element.

While she appreciated the reasons for MacDonald's impending retire-

---

[1] The friction between departments, to which MacDonald referred in his letter to
Lady Londonderry was, of course, between the Foreign Office and the Air Ministry.

ment, Lady Londonderry was concerned about the removal of his influence at the Foreign Office which must result, rightly concluding that if and when Baldwin took over as Prime Minister he would move Simon from this post and install a Tory.

> *Londonderry House. 18 May.* Your letter has just come. I am so glad I wrote. I should never write to you in anger. I might say things to your face. I was only speaking to you as a friend and demanding justice not from you but the Government. Far from anger, I have been feeling deeply for you. It hurts me to think of you after all you have done being treated like this.
>
> You keep saying you have tried to talk with me, but dearest H, you have avoided me. I have tried all I can to see you. I have been at home a lot, but nothing seemed to suit you—not even today. You say you warned me about all this. I can not call it to mind—only the very vaguest references to intrigue which I thought referred to yourself, and I have had a few encounters on this score. I longed to know more so as to lend any weight I had to counter-attack. As soon as we meet, we can compare notes.
>
> Your decision is perhaps the best, but it disquiets me—but the F.O. is the most frightening without you, as Anthony Eden is not man enough for the job now.
>
> I heard fearful accounts from Herr Melchior[1] last night [about Germany]. I so wanted you to meet him. He supped here with me after the Opera. We sat up till 2 a.m. The situation is dreadful.
>
> Do, dearest, let us try and meet soon. I so want to see your dear self, and hold your hand and thank you for all [you have done].

The Prime Minister was unable to see Lady Londonderry immediately, as he had to go off to Edinburgh for a royal jubilee function. However he found time between engagements to send her a few lines from Holyrood Palace: 'Tell Charley to be firm without being violent, quiet without yielding on points of importance or of right.'

MacDonald knew that Charley's days at the Air Ministry were numbered. He had already discussed some of the changes which Baldwin intended making when he moved across from No 11 to No 10 Downing Street, and he gathered that Londonderry would be replaced by Sir Philip Cunliffe-Lister, on the ostensible pretext that in view of the accelerated air expansion scheme which had been agreed by the Cabinet it was necessary to have the Air Minister in the House of Commons, although he was given to understand that Londonderry would not be dropped altogether but transferred to another post. Cunliffe-Lister's Air Parity Committee findings meanwhile resulted in the new Scheme C being adopted, thus superseding the less ambitious Scheme B favoured by Londonderry and the Air Staff. The Cabinet agreed that this should first be announced by Baldwin in the House of Commons on 22 May.

Replying to a defence debate on the previous day in the House of Lords, in what was to be his swan song, Londonderry made a dignified speech, surveying his ministerial record and justifying what he had been

[1] Lauritz Melchior, the well-known tenor, was having a Wagnerian season in London.

able to achieve in the circumstances. He concluded with the words of Milton's *Areopagitica*, in which he looked to the future of the force which he had striven so hard in the face of great difficulties to save from extinction during the past four and a half years:

> Methinks I see in my mind a noble and puissant nation rousing herself like a strong man after sleep and shaking her invincible locks. Methinks I see her as an eagle mewing her mighty youth and kindling her undazzled eyes in the midday beam.

Unfortunately Londonderry on the spur of the moment inserted a remark earlier in his speech which was not in his brief, and which was to do him untold damage. Speaking of the period of the Disarmament Conference when he 'kept impressing on his colleagues and the country generally the vital nature and the place of the Royal Air Force in the scheme of our defence', he added:

> I had the utmost difficulty at that time, amid the public outcry, in preserving the use of the bombing aeroplane, even on the frontier of the Middle East and India, where it was only owing to the presence of the Air Force that we have controlled these territories, without the old and heavy cost of blood and treasure.

Curiously enough this identical statement had been made by Londonderry in the House of Lords some months previously, but it had passed unnoticed. Now it raised a howl from Labour and was immediately seized upon as a stick with which to beat the Government. 'My name became forthwith associated with air bombing and all its attendant horrors,' Londonderry afterwards admitted wryly.

> It was soon made clear to me that my statement of fact had been unfortunate, however much it was justified. It was not calculated to catch votes, and after all a General Election was in the offing. From a purely political point of view my statement of fact had made me an embarrassment. My personal position was not made easier by certain intrigues against me in the Government, intrigues which became so apparent that they were the subject of comment in the Public Press.

'It was all very unfortunate,' Baldwin subsequently told Londonderry's son. 'I feel now that your father should have offered his resignation at once. As you know, there was an outcry. The Opposition seized the opportunity and made it the spearhead of their election and pre-election campaign, but a far bigger outcry came from the Conservative Party. Members were beginning to look to their seats and here was a Cabinet Minister giving the enemy ammunition free and for nothing'. Hence the demand, which Baldwin had to face at the time: 'The Air Minister must go.'

Londonderry did go. He was unlucky as the advocate of air rearmament in the Cabinet and in the country. His unfortunate reference to the bombing aeroplane was to dog him for the rest of his life. Shortly before the outbreak of the Second World War, he was to remind Baldwin of the case he had tried to put forward with such unfortunate results for himself:

> I think looking back that you, Ramsay and Neville, lost confidence in me because you were frightened by the propaganda of Winston and Rothermere in 1935, which asserted that the Germans were overwhelmingly strong in the air and were ready almost at a moment's notice to bomb all the great cities in this country. You had refused to listen to our advice on rearmament and I am sure you became anxious lest the propaganda might be correct and you might be confronted with the charge of having failed in your duty of establishing the security of this country. I think that is why you threw me to the wolves . . .
>
> Of course, I was perfectly right all through. It was vitally necessary to rearm, as Monsell, Hailsham and myself continually told you, but the Germans instead of having at that time an overwhelming air force had nothing but a few formed squadrons. Of course, training and organisation were proceeding very rapidly. My information had to be right, as I had all the ordinary opportunities of gauging the strength of Germany in the air, and if I wanted to get to know anything more, I was able to get it through the Secret Service; but you, Ramsay and Neville brushed all this on one side and immediately assumed I was wrong and did not know my job.

On 22 May 1935, Baldwin outlined the substance of Scheme C to a packed House of Commons. During the debate Churchill claimed that 'there is no doubt that the Germans are superior to us in the air at the present time, and it is my belief that by the end of the year, unless their rate of construction is arrested by some agreement, they will be possibly three or even four times our strength'. Although this claim was questionable, Baldwin did not contradict it. In fact, he seemed to concede the justice of Churchill's statement, since he admitted that he had been misled as to the rate at which German rearmament in the air had been proceeding during the previous six months. With regard to the figure of fifty per cent numerical superiority of the R.A.F. over the Luftwaffe he had given them, nothing had since come to his knowledge, he said, to make him think that the figure was wrong. He went on:

> I believed I was right. Where I was wrong was in my estimate of the future. There I was completely wrong. I tell the House so, frankly, because neither I nor my advisers, from whom we could get accurate information, had any idea of the exact rate at which production could be, and actually was being, speeded up in Germany in the six months between November and now. *We were completely misled on that subject.* [Author's italics.] I will not say we had no rumours. There was a great deal of hearsay, but we could get no facts, and the only facts at this moment that I could put before the House are those which I have from Herr Hitler himself, and until I have reason to doubt them, which I have not at present, I put those figures before the house.

Baldwin was loudly cheered by the Conservative majority as he sat down at the end of his speech. The House of Commons usually warms to a man who confesses that he has been at fault, and in this instance, as Churchill observed, 'there was even a strange wave of enthusiasm' for him. 'Indeed,' Churchill added in the account of the debate which he subsequently wrote in *The Gathering Storm*, 'many Conservative Members seemed angry with me for having brought their trusted leader to a plight from which only his native manliness and honesty had extricated him; but not, alas, his country.'

So far as the unfortunate Londonderry and his advisers were concerned, Churchill wrote in the same work:

> The Air Ministry now led its chief into an elaborate vindication of their own past conduct, and in consequence was entirely out of harmony with the new mood of a genuinely alarmed Government and public. The experts and officials at the Air Ministry had given Mr Baldwin the figures and forecasts with which he had answered me in November. They wished him to go into action in defence of these statements; but this was no longer practical politics. There seems no doubt that these experts and officials of the Air Ministry at this time were themselves misled and misled their chief. A great power, at least the equal of our own, long pent-up, had at last sprung into daylight in Germany.

According to Baldwin's biographer, G. M. Young, one of these officials thought it right to offer his resignation for having misled the Lord President. Young does not state who he was, but he does give Baldwin's comment: 'I misled myself.' That may well be. Londonderry himself subsequently denied that Baldwin had been misled. 'He was continually being informed by me, not only of German rearmament in the air but of *the approximate rate of that rearmament*' (author's italics).[1]

Whatever the merits of the matter, Londonderry was 'a man of unquestionable loyalty and patriotism', to quote Churchill again, and he did try hard during a period of severe financial retrenchment to keep a nucleus of an air force in being and get as much as he could from 'a severe and arbitrary Chancellor of the Exchequer'. It was therefore 'an odd and painful experience' for him, 'after having gone through several years of asking for more to be suddenly turned out for not asking enough. But apart from all this his political standing was not sufficient to enable him to head a Department, now at the very centre and almost at the summit of our affairs. Besides, everyone could see that in such a time the Air Minister must be in the House of Commons'.

Towards the end of May 1935 it became generally known that Ramsay MacDonald was to retire before the Whitsun recess and that he would be succeeded by Baldwin, who intended to reconstruct the Government as soon as he had moved into No 10 Downing Street. Among the changes it was rumoured in the press that Londonderry would not only hand over

---

[1] MacDonald noted in his diary (28 June 1936): 'Londonderry's reply to the P.M. [Baldwin] is causing some disturbance and is damaging the P.M. The trouble lies between L.'s credulity and the P.M.'s supreme laziness. L. misunderstands facts and the P.M. Londonderry.'

the Air Ministry to Cunliffe-Lister but would be dropped altogether from the Government. This rumour led Lord Hailsham, the War Minister, who was a particular friend of Londonderry's, to intercede for him with Baldwin, pointing out that 'he has worked very hard and loyally for four years, and under him the Air Ministry was able to produce a vast scheme for expansion which most of the Cabinet professes to believe a reasonable one at short notice'. As a result, Baldwin decided not to drop Londonderry altogether but to ask him to continue in the Cabinet as Lord Privy Seal and at the same time to take on the Leadership of the House of Lords, which involved responsibility for arranging government business there. A few days later Baldwin saw Londonderry and made the offer which Londonderry asked if he could think over for twenty-four hours. In conveying it Baldwin laid stress on the need for having the responsible minister in the House of Commons, adding that he proposed to appoint Cunliffe-Lister, who had the necessary qualification for 'hustling' in the department, and who with his wider experience of business and industry in general, demonstrated by his handling of the Air Parity Committee, would be better qualified to deal with the expansion of the R.A.F.

Next day Londonderry wrote to Baldwin privately in what was to be his last letter from the Air Minister's office in Gwydyr House, accepting his offer, albeit with some misgivings. 'You will understand it is a bitter disappointment to me to give up at this point the work of development which after a long struggle is now decided upon, to say nothing of leaving those in the Ministry who have never spared themselves all the years to help me in what at times in these three and a half years has been a desperate work.' While agreeing with the Prime Minister-designate upon the necessity of having the Air Minister in the House of Commons, Londonderry emphatically denied that he was incapable of 'hustling', as Baldwin seemed to imply. 'I think I can claim to be as capable of that as any one,' he declared, 'and the record of my work here, especially when as recently the occasion has demanded it, will prove what I say.'

'I am greatly relieved to get your letter,' Baldwin replied the same day somewhat disingenuously. 'I have learnt in the course of many years to have a sincere regard and affection for you and those feelings were intensified by our conversation yesterday. Of course, you continue in the Cabinet: it was, as I told you, my desire and that of our colleagues that you should remain with us.' This was not altogether true, since Neville Chamberlain for one wished Londonderry to be dropped altogether and, as we have seen, it was only as the result of Hailsham's pleading that Londonderry was reprieved.

Baldwin's real view was reflected in what he subsequently told Robin Castlereagh about his father and also in what Baldwin's close friend and political confidant John Davidson, who was a member of the Government though not in the Cabinet, was to write about Londonderry in his memoirs:

Although it was clear that the Air Ministry was absolutely right in refusing to equip the R.A.F. with obsolescent aircraft, there seemed to be a certain lack of drive in their programme. I know that S.B. attributed the responsibility to Londonderry personally . . .
He owed his preferment really to the fact that Ramsay MacDonald greatly enjoyed standing at the top of the staircase in Londonderry House as the first Minister of the Crown in full evening dress . . .

Against this unsympathetic assessment must be set the tribute the departing minister received from Sir Christopher Bullock, the Permanent Secretary of the Air Ministry, expressing on behalf of the staff 'our regret at losing a Secretary of State who has so whole-heartedly identified himself with the well-being of the Ministry and the Force'.

The years during which you have been Secretary of State have seen remarkable activity and progress under your guidance—and this in the teeth of many difficulties. The two successive programmes for the far-reaching expansion of the Royal Air Force were sponsored by you and promulgated by the Government during your tenure of office.
Equally it fell to you to initiate and pilot through the great new scheme for the further development of our Imperial air communications, the announcement of which, last December, marked an epoch in the history of British civil aviation. We have all known that we could always rely on you for support and we feel your departure the more because of the consideration and courtesy which you invariably showed all of us.
It is some compensation that we know we can rely on your continuing, in your new Office, the friendship and help you have given us ever since you were first associated with the Ministry as Finance Member, and subsequently as Under-Secretary of State, 15 years ago.

Among the hundreds or so letters Londonderry received at this time, probably none gave him greater pleasure than one from the pioneer aviator and holder of the first pilot's certificate issued by the Royal Aero Club, Colonel J. T. C. Moore-Brabazon, M.P. (later Lord Brabazon of Tara). 'I cannot allow you to leave the Air Ministry without a word of appreciation and regret from myself,' wrote 'Brab' as he was affectionately known to his many friends inside the House of Commons, where he sat on the Parliamentary Air Committee.

You had an almost impossible task, your inclinations being very often, I feel sure, opposed to the Government.
But you brought an enthusiasm and an atmosphere to the R.A.F. that was badly wanted and which you with your great position alone could give.
Everyone is in your debt, and you will never be forgotten. All your flights, getting a pilot's certificate, your 'at homes' were all good shows.
The R.A.F. still wants a lot of bringing out. They have still an inferiority complex relative to the other services, but you did a great deal to put them where they should be, a sort of swagger guards division.

I hope I was not too much of a thorn in your side. I hope with any criticism I made I did you no harm personally. I should hate to think I ever did that, as if I was P.M. tomorrow, my first appointment would be to ask you to go back.

Perhaps the fairest judgment on Londonderry's record at Gwydyr House has come from his successor Philip Cunliffe-Lister. He always thought that Londonderry had had 'a thankless and impossible task'. Owing to the fact that no designs of new bombers were undertaken until well into 1934 and no new squadrons had been added to the R.A.F. since 1931, Londonderry had no opportunity to give the aircraft industry either orders or encouragement. However, as Cunliffe-Lister put it in his autobiography, 'he and his professional colleagues deserve credit for having maintained the spirit, the tradition and the training of our small Air Force in those disappointing days'. Churchill added in *The Gathering Storm*: 'The great achievement of his period of office was the designing and promotion of the ever-famous Hurricane and Spitfire Fighters . . . Londonderry does not mention this in his defence, but he might well have done so, since he took the blame of so much he had not done.'

3

The change-over in Downing Street, which took place just before the Whitsun recess, was one of the most rapid in English politics. After getting a farewell cheer in the House of Commons when he answered a question on protection against air attack raised by Churchill, Ramsay MacDonald rushed off to Buckingham Palace, where he had an audience with the King lasting fifty minutes, at the end of which he surrendered his seals of office. 'You have been the Prime Minister I have liked best,' the King told him; 'you have so many qualities, you have kept up the dignity of the office without using it to give you dignity . . . I wonder how you have stood it—especially the loss of your friends and their beastly behaviour.' King George had already assured him that he understood his desire to take no titles, which as a retiring Prime Minister he could easily have done. Baldwin, who had been kept waiting for a quarter of an hour, was received as soon as MacDonald had left the audience chamber and kissed hands on his appointment as Prime Minister for the third time. At five o'clock the new Prime Minister was back in Downing Street and asking his colleagues, who had been specially summoned to meet him in the Cabinet Room, to place their offices at his disposal so that the Government might be reconstructed. This disposition was done by word of mouth, and an hour later the ministers handed over their seals of office at a Privy Council at which MacDonald presided for the first time in the Palace—the King had made it a condition with Baldwin that MacDonald should have the office of Lord President which Baldwin had previously held—when the new ministers received their seals and took the oath. By 7.30 MacDonald was on the train bound for Lossiemouth, while Baldwin and his wife were in possession of No. 10.

The new Lord President's first duty had been to swear in his son Malcolm, the youngest newcomer to the Cabinet, who at the age of thirty-four became Colonial Secretary in place of Cunliffe-Lister; the latter now took Londonderry's place at the Air Ministry, while London-derry, as already noted, became Lord Privy Seal and Leader of the House of Lords. Lady Londonderry was against his accepting this office, feeling (as Londonderry later recalled), that 'it was merely another stage in the plot of squeezing me out altogether. She said I ought to refuse office under the new P.M. and begged me to retire. However, I was unfortu-nately persuaded to the contrary by several of my intimate political friends'. Londonderry does not mention who these friends were, but there can be little doubt that they included Hailsham and Lady Desborough. This is how they saw it, in Londonderry's words:

> They regretted that such a situation had ever arisen but, even so, there was no reason why I should refuse to carry on in the Government. If I refused to serve it would show I was obviously disgruntled, and that I had left in a fit of pique because I was no longer to be Secretary of State for Air. After all, if I remained in the Cabinet I could take an official interest in the Ministry which I knew so well, and which I realised was of such importance in the future of the country.

Nevertheless, as Londonderry also put it: 'It was a great grief to me to leave the Air Ministry, for I had fought for years what seemed to be a losing battle, and when the ideas for which I stood were at last coming to be accepted, I was removed to a sinecure position.'

The other changes which Baldwin made were kept to a minimum, although the new Cabinet consisted of twenty-two instead of the previous twenty, this being due to the admission of the two youngest members, Malcolm MacDonald as Colonial Secretary and Anthony Eden, who at the age of thirty-eight entered it as Minister for League of Nations Affairs. Among the other changes, Londonderry's son-in-law Oliver Stanley became Minister of Education, taking over from Lord Halifax, who went to the War Office in place of Hailsham who became Lord Chancellor; Sir Samuel Hoare replaced Simon as Foreign Secretary, while Lord Zetland went to the India Office in Hoare's place, and Simon became Home Secretary as well as Deputy Leader of the House of Commons, partly as a solace to his wounded pride at losing the Foreign Office and partly in an endeavour by Baldwin to preserve the Govern-ment's 'National' facade, although it was becoming more and more Conservative in complexion. Finally, as had been previously agreed, Ramsay MacDonald moved into the agreeable office of Lord President of the Council formerly occupied by Baldwin, although of course he had to give up Chequers.

'Our last visit,' wrote MacDonald in his diary on 7 July. 'Went round the house and bade it farewell. Walked up Beacon Hill and bade it farewell and bowed my adieux to the wide landscape which had taught me peace so long. Everything has changed. Shall I be able to settle down in harmony with my life or shall I be unable to forget? What divine days I have spent here and in an hour or two the curtain falls.'

At first all went well for the new Lord Privy Seal. Lord Lucan and the other Government Whips soon introduced him to his duties, while Lord Ponsonby of Shulbrede, the Leader of the Labour Opposition, proved unexpectedly friendly and cooperative. The first test came over the Second Reading of the India Bill, when it was thought that Churchill's opposition in the Commons to its modicum of self-government for India might encourage a revolt of some of the more reactionary Conservative peers. However, the Second Reading was duly moved by Lord Zetland and carried by a comfortable majority, thanks largely to Londonderry's skilful handling, which brought him a warm note of congratulation from the new Prime Minister. 'It was splendid,' wrote Baldwin, 'and it was delightful coming as a first fruits of your term as Leader.'

Nevertheless Londonderry, who had been accustomed to the work of a large department, felt that he did not have enough to do and he asked to be put on several Cabinet committees. But the Prime Minister, who was busy with other things, ignored or overlooked his request. By the time Parliament reassembled after the summer recess, Italy had invaded Abyssinia, and economic and financial sanctions were immediately applied by all members of the League of Nations except Italy's satellites. Thus the doctrine of collective security, which had recently been reinforced by a stirring speech by Britain's new Foreign Secretary at Geneva, seemed to be in operation at last, though France seemed less than wholehearted and her Premier Pierre Laval was suspected of coming to a secret understanding with Mussolini.

On 16 October the Cabinet met in the disquieting shadow of Laval's backsliding and intrigues, and Baldwin began to question whether Britain could rely on the French at all. He reminded his Cabinet colleagues that 'we must be careful not to be drawn into a quarrel with France as well as Italy', following the activities of the sanctions committee at Geneva. This latest development seems finally to have determined him upon an autumn election, since at this same meeting a Cabinet committee was set up to draft an election programme in the light of the worsening international situation.

Londonderry saw this as the writing on the wall so far as his own future political prospects were concerned, and he immediately addressed an urgent note to the Prime Minister asking to see him 'as we are now committed to an election and a new Parliament'. They met later that afternoon.

Their interview was far from reassuring for Londonderry, who wrote to Baldwin next day:

> *Londonderry House. 17 October 1935.* Thank you for yesterday. I always regret that I see you so seldom and perhaps I am now diffident in these matters. I am writing in case I did not put before you my exact point of view and the reason after long cogitation that I asked to see you.
>
> Since I left the Air Ministry I told you that I had done no work which is literally true. You will remember my asking you if I could be on Committees and you asked me to let you know which Committees I wanted to serve on. I wrote to you and named the Committees but received no answer to my letter.
>
> As Leader of the House of Lords I feel that my position is an impossible one unless I am able to be closely in touch with yourself and those who control policy. Rightly or wrongly I have felt that there is an influence which has the effect of excluding me from participating in those matters which even as a member of the Cabinet and certainly as Leader of the House of Lords I ought to be fully aware of . . .
>
> You asked me if I should be happy in a different kind of life. Happy is a relative term. I am happy in all work, the more strenuous the better: but I am uneasy in the position in which I stand now because I bear full responsibility and have neither power nor knowledge.

On 18 October Baldwin asked the King for a dissolution, with effect from the following week, 'to obviate uncertainty and particularly interference with Christmas trading', polling to take place on 14 November and the new Parliament to assemble on 3 December. This was agreed to and Parliament was duly dissolved on 25 October.

In the past Londonderry's position as a peer had enabled him to play an active part in election campaigns, but Conservative Central Office made no use of his services on this occasion. He must have noticed the lack of invitations to speak or otherwise take part in the election campaign, during which he remained at Mount Stewart. The fact was that he had become an electoral liability for his party, who were aware that his now notorious 'bombing' speech was being widely used against the Tories by Labour, although in the circumstances of its context this was decidedly unfair.

Conservative Central Office estimated the Tory majority at 100, perhaps somewhat higher. In the event the Conservatives won 432 seats, which gave them a majority of 247 over the combined Opposition. Both the MacDonalds lost their seats to official Labour, which increased its representation to 154.

'I am not biased by friendship when I say that the triumph is a personal one for S.B.,' wrote Tom Jones on learning the results.

He has made no mistakes. He timed the election correctly in his Party's interest. Six months hence and it is certain the results would be less favourable to him. He has only very slowly and with obvious reluctance proclaimed the need for more armaments; he has avoided all trace of the *Daily Mail*'s lust to arm the nation to the teeth and has also kept clear of Winston's enthusiasm for ships and guns. He has strictly confined the extent to which he was prepared to move against Italy and distinguished Mussolini from the Italian people . . . Over all he has thrown that halo of faith and hope, free from meretricious ornament, which inspires confidence. The effect is to gather to the Tories a large voting strength of Liberals and un-attached folk who like his sober and sincere accents, and who are afraid of the menace to small owners and investors associated with Socialism.

Baldwin's first task on the morrow of electoral victory was to review the composition of his ministerial team. He had previously hoped to make considerable changes, but this had been ruled out by the size of his majority, since each member of the Cabinet tended to regard the result as a vote of confidence in himself as well as in the Cabinet as a whole. There was also the consideration of whether it would not be preferable in a time of international crisis to keep the Cabinet substantially intact with the balance of parties unaltered. The changes, which in the event he did make, Baldwin reduced to a minimum. He even retained the two MacDonalds, though well aware that the problem of finding them seats in the new Parliament would not be easy. In the Government, however, Malcolm MacDonald changed places with J. H. Thomas, whose removal from the Dominions Office was necessitated largely by the general dissatisfaction with his handling of Anglo-Irish relations.

The only one of his former colleagues whose services Baldwin dispensed with was Lord Londonderry. Since Halifax now needed little or no pressing to stay on rather than retire to hunt the fox in his native York-shire, and Baldwin set considerable store by the moral weight which his presence lent to the Government, Halifax agreed to take Londonderry's place as Lord Privy Seal and Leader of the House of Lords, thus enabling Duff Cooper, the Financial Secretary to the Treasury, whom Baldwin wished to promote, to become War Minister with a seat in the Cabinet. There was some talk of bringing in Churchill; but due to the opposition of the Government Whips, and also probably of Neville Chamberlain, Baldwin decided to exclude him. 'As for Winston,' Baldwin told Davidson in a strangely prophetic letter at this time, 'I feel we should not give him a post at this stage. Anything he undertakes he puts his heart and soul into. If there is going to be a war—and no one can say that there is not—we must keep him fresh to be our war Prime Minister.'

'Internally S.B.'s main troubles are over the defeat of the MacDonalds,' wrote Tom Jones at this time. 'S.B. has "dropped" Londonderry and kept out Winston, but it is not quite easy to preserve the 'National' facade and get rid of Ramsay.' In the event, MacDonald remained Lord

President of the Council, though he was by now politically of little account as well as being pathetically senile.

Londonderry was given his quietus in a letter which it must have caused Baldwin some pangs to write:

> *10 Downing Street,*
> *Whitehall.*
> *21 November 1935*

My dear Charley,

I have been working for three days on one of the most difficult problems with which I have ever had to contend, and I am profoundly distressed that I find myself unable to offer you a place in the new Government. The refusal of Ramsay to serve unless accompanied by Malcolm and Thomas and the desire of Halifax to continue have upset my calculations and I have more men than places.

You remember our talk in the House: you know what I feel. You have ever been a loyal and trusted friend: I think I know what you will feel. Yet I have faith to believe that our friendship is too firmly based to be broken by a cruel political necessity that obliges a PM—and none have escaped it—to inflict pain on those they hold not only in regard but in affection.

> Always yours,
> S.B.

At the same time he addressed a consolatory letter to Londonderry's wife:

My dear Lady,

I have written Charley a letter which I fear will distress him. I have never before written on such matters to the wife of a colleague. But you have always been so kind and understanding to me that I cannot refrain from sending a line to you. It is on such occasions that I understand in the depths all that Lord Salisbury meant and felt when he said, 'Politics is a cursed profession.'

And he did not use words lightly.

Next morning, Londonderry's son Castlereagh, who had heard the news the evening before from Oliver Stanley, went round to Londonderry House with his sister to see their father. 'He was a tragic sight,' Castlereagh later recalled. 'I never really knew before the meaning of the phrase: "A broken man". He was sitting sideways in his chair with his legs dangling over the arm. Holding a letter in his hand and with the tears running down hie cheeks, he kept muttering: "I've been sacked—kicked out." The letter was from Baldwin giving a number of reasons for not including him in the Cabinet.'

Later the same day Londonderry pulled himself together and replied to Baldwin, but with less than his usual warmth:

> *Londonderry House,*
> *Park Lane, W.*
> *22 November 1935*

My dear S.B.,

I have received your letter and I need not say that I acquiesce in your decision, but I have received it with some surprise because I recollect that you very expressly said that if I joined your Government in June I might retain the leadership of the House of Lords as long as I wished to do so. This hardly corresponds with your present decisions: nevertheless I quite recognise that you must only look at public considerations in determining the composition of your Government.

As to personal friendships I can warmly assure you that nothing will be changed in that respect.

I am,
Yours very sincerely,
LONDONDERRY

Baldwin subsequently denied that he had given Londonderry any such assurance with regard to the leadership of the House of Lords. 'No PM is in a position to make such a promise,' he told Castlereagh in answer to the complaint that his father had been badly treated by Baldwin. 'No Minister could ever take such a promise as valid. It does not make sense. He must have misunderstood something I said. I know that I never wittingly said anything of the sort and that in his disappointment he must have got hold of the wrong end of the stick.'

Whatever may be the truth of the matter, there is no doubt that Londonderry was under the impression that he could continue to lead the Lords if he wished and if it was within Baldwin's power to enable him to do so; his letter quoted above certainly lends some confirmation of this. At all events his sense of injury did rankle with Londonderry for long afterwards, and it was the increasing bitterness he felt towards Baldwin that eventually prompted his son, who was one of the Prime Minister's supporters at that time in the House of Commons, to complain about the manner in which his father had been treated. Londonderry's feelings suffered further hurt when it was announced that Cunliffe-Lister, his successor as Air Minister, had accepted a peerage with the title of Lord Swinton, particularly when one of the reasons which Baldwin gave Londonderry for shifting him from the Air Ministry was the need for the Minister to be in the Commons. 'But no one can foretell the results of an election and the ensuing complications,' Baldwin explained to Castlereagh. 'I found it more convenient to make Cunliffe-Lister a peer. But the reason he was chosen to replace your father was that with his wider experience of business and industry in general he would be better qualified to deal with expansion.' Apparently the reason he went to the Lords was that this would leave him freer to get on with the job in hand. However, in his case, history was to repeat itself, since in May 1938 Swinton was obliged to resign because Neville Chamberlain, who by this time had succeeded Baldwin as Prime Minister, 'felt he must have a Secretary of State in the House of Commons who could pacify the House'. Swinton was offered another Cabinet post but, not wishing to make the same mistake as Londonderry, he wisely declined. 'I think I was right,' he wrote afterwards.

It was not a happy time for Londonderry and his wife. The only one of his former colleagues who wrote him a sympathetic letter that Christmas was Hailsham, the Lord Chancellor, his closest friend in the Cabinet. In it Hailsham referred to the Hoare–Laval agreement for the partition of Abyssinia, whose premature disclosure caused an acute crisis in the Cabinet and the country, from which Londonderry had escaped.

Carters Corner Place,
Xmas 1935

Dear Charley,

This is just to thank you for your card, and to wish you luck for 1936. If you were a malicious person, the last three weeks would give you great satisfaction to see what a mess we got into as soon as you left us! As it is, you'll only be doing your best to serve the State in some other capacity and I hope gaining a little more appreciation this time. I feel lonelier than ever on the Woolsack without my leader on the Front Bench.

Mildred and I are both so grateful to you and Circe for your constant loyal friendship. I hope the misfortunes you have so little deserved are over, and that 1936 has only happiness in store for you both.

Yours ever,
Douglas

4

While he was Air Minister Londonderry had always hoped to be able to visit Germany and see for himself something of the country and its leaders, but for one reason or another this had not proved possible; he had been disappointed when MacDonald sent Simon and Eden to Berlin in March 1935 and he had not been included in the party. But now that the situation had changed and, as he put it, he had 'gained a position of great freedom and less responsibility', he determined to make the visit, taking with him his wife and youngest daughter Mairi, who was particularly interested in flying. He planned to go early in January, but the King's illness and death which occurred later that month obliged him to postpone the trip. He eventually took off from Croydon with Lady Londonderry and Mairi on 29 January 1936, the day after the King's funeral, in a Junker machine which Goering, the Reich Air Minister, had placed at his disposal, although it was understood that the visit was to be purely private and unofficial.

During the next seven weeks which they spent in Germany, Londonderry was welcomed and entertained with lavish hospitality not only by Goering but also by Hitler himself and the other top Nazi leaders besides the Luftwaffe chiefs. He was flown all over the country and shown everything he wished to see from training establishments to aircraft factories. Goering, who did not dissent from Londonderry's assessment of Germany's current air strength, although he did not himself quote any precise figures, explained that his primary object was to train instructors and consequently he and his ministry were passing fewer trained pilots into the squadrons than the British were. He laid much more emphasis on the construction of aircraft, and Londonderry was shown how the wings and fuselages were being manufactured and assembled in three distinct operations, the manufacturers working three shifts of 500 men. Goering also remarked that by using a different classification the number of British squadrons in existence represented double the number of German squadrons. 'I did not press any particular question,' Londonderry noted in his diary, 'because I was more desirous of getting a general idea of the German policy of expansion, but I did express the hope that Germany would take a leading part in the policy of limitation.' Goering, Ribbentrop and Von Neurath gave dinners or receptions, and in addition Goering and his wife laid on a Wagner concert after dinner in their house in Berlin. Hitler also gave a dinner in Londonderry's honour in the Chancellery after they had talked together for two hours.

When he was introduced to the Fuehrer by Ribbentrop, the only other person besides the interpreter, Herr Schmidt, who was present at the interview, Londonderry noted that Hitler appeared extremely embarrassed and awkward. 'I even had to take the lead in sitting down,' Londonderry added, 'a lead which he followed with gratitude.' As might be expected, Hitler did practically all the talking, while Londonderry listened. Much of what he said consisted of a tirade against the Soviet Union and the dangers of Bolshevism. The admission of Russia to the League of Nations, he said, reminded him of the story of Reynard the Fox, who overcame the suspicion of the other animals towards him by his humble demeanour, and after he had been admitted to their Animals' League killed one beast after another, because their former united common defence against him had ceased. 'It is exactly the same with Russia and the real League of Nations,' he went on. 'Russia would make use of the League of Nations solely to strengthen her position and through the channels of the League to deliver moral attacks on other countries with greater ease.' Finally she would give the death-blow to the League itself, which would become what he called 'a paper illusion' and would be represented by a few typewriters. 'Russia would then, at the conclusion of this process of change, stand forth as a mighty Power, let fall her mask, and live only for World Revolution.'

Londonderry broke in at this point to remark that in England 'we did not attribute so much importance to the Bolshevist menace as conditions were actually different', and Bolshevism presented no danger as far as England was concerned. Hitler did not seem particularly impressed by this argument, but he conceded that Germany and Britain must try to understand each other's mentality. He made it clear that he was determined to remove the remaining injustices of the Versailles Treaty, including the question of the former German colonies which he asserted had been unjustly taken away from her and whose return he considered necessary for a people of sixty-eight millions. 'Germany wants to live in close friendly alliance with England,' he concluded, 'and for England perhaps the time will come when she will have to consider the question whether an active friendship with Germany, or whether the possession of a couple of colonies which for the British Empire are not of very great value, is the more important.'

The visit ended with a week at Garmisch-Partenkirchen where the Londonderry party were the German Government's guests for the Olympic games. 'Here again we met both the Fuehrer and General Goering,' Londonderry noted, 'and we were again struck by the enthusiastic welcome which each received on every occasion when they appeared. I was particularly interested in seeing General Udet, one of Germany's most famous flying "aces", navigating a glider over the Games themselves and performing the most remarkable evolutions in the air.'[1] There was no doubt in Londonderry's mind from what he had seen, from bomber stations to schools for blind flying, that Goering had turned the Luftwaffe into a real *corps d'élite*.

Before leaving Germany Londonderry passed on everything he had learned during his visit to Group Captain E. P. Don, the British Air Attaché in Berlin, who had been very helpful to him during his visit. But, when Londonderry got home, he found that none of his former Cabinet colleagues with the exception of his son-in-law Oliver Stanley, who listened politely to what he had to say, showed any interest in his experiences. Baldwin was too busy to see him, but he did succeed in talking to Ellington, who was still Chief of the Air Staff, and also to Maurice Hankey, who was Secretary of the Committee of Imperial Defence as well as of the Cabinet. 'I had hoped Sir Maurice Hankey would pass on my opinions to the Cabinet,' Londonderry noted later, 'but I am not sure that he did so.'

The author and critic Harold Nicolson, who had been returned as National Labour Member for West Leicester at the General Election and was an ardent Francophile, wrote to his wife at this time in characteristic vein:

> My new pal Maureen Stanley asked me to come round and meet her father who is just back from hob-nobbing with Hitler. Now I admire Londonderry in a way, since it is fine to remain 1760 in 1936; besides he is a real gent. But I do deeply disapprove of ex-Cabinet Ministers trotting across Germany at this moment. It gives the impression of secret negotiations and upsets the French. But we are incorrigibly irresponsible in such things.

Nicolson was not the only one to take this line. Shortly afterwards Ramsay

[1] Udet was Member for Research and Development on the German Air Staff. He committed suicide in Berlin in 1941.

MacDonald went to a lunch party given by a somewhat eccentric American hostess named Mrs Corey. 'Rather spiteful talk on the Londonderrys' visit to Hitler,' he noted in his diary at the time, 'but they have certainly laid themselves out for it.' The fact was that few of those with whom Londonderry was in contact wished to hear about Germany. Among those to whom he looked in vain was Halifax, who had taken his place in the Cabinet as Lord Privy Seal and had been his contemporary at Eton. Looking back afterwards Londonderry wrote to a friend:

> I never really got on with Baldwin or Chamberlain and I thought my old school-fellow was the best channel I could use to get across to the Cabinet what I wanted. I do not hold the same opinion of Halifax as you do. I may be a little jealous of his *savoir faire* as a super yes-man although his technique does not appeal to me. But he failed me absolutely . . .

'The stark tragedy of it all,' Londonderry wrote some years later during the Second World War, 'was that, even at that dangerous moment, early in 1936, there were many in responsible quarters who did not seem to care and who went on still thinking in terms of Versailles and Locarno and the League and all the rest, when it was obvious that Hitler, like Gallio, cared for none of these things.' Since there was nothing further that Londonderry considered he could usefully do, he went off to Sutherland for a few weeks' fishing, where he would have a chance to think things over quietly in the light of his changed position.

While Londonderry was fishing the waters of the Brora, Hitler's troops marched into the demilitarised zone of the Rhineland, an action for which the conclusion of the recent Franco–Soviet pact was made the excuse by Germany. On the other hand, Hitler put forward a number of offers, including twenty-five-year non-aggression pacts with France and Belgium to be guaranteed by Britain and Italy, an international air pact, and Germany's return to the League. 'The offers which he has made are of a definite character,' Londonderry pleaded in a letter to *The Times* on 12 March, 'and I sincerely hope our rulers will meet them in their move towards peace in the same manner as they accepted the German naval offer, which met with determined opposition from France, as a real example of the policy of limitation of armaments, a policy which I have always supported and which I believe is the first and most important step towards disarmament'.[1]

Lady Londonderry, who had also gone to Sutherland, had to leave before her husband's tenancy of the house was up. He stayed on alone, and before he left he unburdened himself to her on the subject of his

---

[1] In June 1935, an Anglo-German Naval Agreement was concluded in which Germany undertook to confine her tonnage to 35 per cent of Britain's (45 per cent for submarines), to come into operation on 1 January 1937.

personal political position in a long and very frank and revealing letter from which the most significant extracts follow:

> *Uppat House. Brora, Sutherland. 30 March 1936* . . . I am afraid my seeming dis- satisfaction and set back has worried you a great deal and probably we mind it more for each other's sakes than our own. I feel I have let you down. I have not justified the faith you have had in me and it is for these feelings really that I feel irritated with Baldwin and those who brought about my downfall.
>
> On reflection I do not believe I ever was a good Cabinet Minister or colleague because I like to lead and control and I detest supporting and playing a minor fiddle in the band. That is the reason I was quite happy at Education in Ireland, at the Office of Works and above all at the Air Ministry: where I could not get on was with Craigavon as my chief, or with Baldwin and Neville Chamberlain because they were my Chiefs and I resent domination and overlordship. Apart from my not having a good counsellor's intelligence and guile perhaps, I never seemed to get on with most of the important colleagues, so I must close that chapter and my only regret would be if you were disappointed and was hoping that I would return to the fray and try and win some public position or other. You must tell me what you want and I would not spare myself in trying to get it.
>
> I have noticed your scathing criticisms and condemnation of those who have bested me lately, but I think you are doing them injustice owing to your intense loyalty to me. They are easily criticised as I do not look on any of them as supermen. They have very difficult tasks and it can be said that they are doing their best according to their lights. But I do not think they are worth worrying about or bearing them a grudge.
>
> I want such an impossible thing: I want influence but I do not want to join the team. I believe if the offer was made to me of some post in the Cabinet I should refuse it. So with those sentiments we must take stock of the position.
>
> I have not yet got into my stride: I have been put out of it and I am just a bit unbalanced. I know politics interest me and I am only playing at coal (which Robin adores) and the business men do not enthuse me very much. I can enjoy myself and I have loved this month but that was because you were here and Mairi too, so I feel with your approval and advice I shall play for a bit and not force myself with prominence. My stock is not very high as was shown by the reception of my letter [to *The Times*].
>
> I am glad I can see much more of you now as I didn't bring you into my work: it is a failing of mine which I have become conscious of, that I am a bad cooperator and must have my own show. And I do want to make you happy and contented . . . I can't think how I have been so thoughtless because you have always been on the pinnacle no matter where everybody else was and I have always thought you understood that: I know everybody else has. But I hate the thought of ever having made you unhappy and I shall devote everything to make you happy . . .
>
> We shall have to accept a lot of boring things I know: we shall be left out of everything and it will be a trifle galling, but if you understand it and are ready for it, and I have got you, I feel I don't mind.

Edith Londonderry considered that her husband, though more far-seeing than his erstwhile colleagues, was less of a politician or place-hunter and consequently impatient of their procrastinating habits, since they were all waiting, though some might not be conscious of it, 'to see which way the cat jumped'. 'With all your perspicuity,' she told her husband, 'you suffer from too much diffidence and are liable to consult too many people instead of relying on your own judgment. Your first impressions are nearly always right and it is failure to act on them with more vigour that has enabled your colleagues to push you on one side.'

Meanwhile Londonderry continued to complain to Baldwin that he had been shabbily treated by him, being 'kicked out' of two Cabinet posts inside five months without the Prime Minister publicly indicating any reason. Although the reasons were widely enough known, it would in all probability have been better if he had taken Churchill's advice and resigned when Churchill advised him to do so. As it was, Londonderry nursed a grievance against Baldwin for the rest of his life, although he went through a form of reconciliation when, at his son Robin's suggestion, he proposed himself as one of Baldwin's sponsors when the latter took his seat in the House of Lords in 1937 as Earl Baldwin of Bewdley, an offer which was gratefully accepted.[1] However, Londonderry had already epitomised his case in a formal letter which he addressed to Baldwin when he was still Prime Minister on 18 May 1936 and which concluded with these words:

> Nobody realised more than I did the difficulties of a Prime Minister but I felt that I could quite safely leave myself in your hands. But as I naturally took no steps to safeguard my public position, all the damage that could be done to it has been done. I have felt it necessary, therefore, to write to you on these matters because I consider it imperative that my position in the form of this letter should be placed on record amongst my papers, not only for my own satisfaction but for those of my family who will follow me and will be wholly ignorant, as most people are, as to why I was practically removed from public life without any reason whatsoever being given by the Prime Minister of the day.

Baldwin returned a brief acknowledgement, asking for a little time to digest and reply to this letter. 'I am more than usually busy,' he wrote, 'and with more accumulated and accumulating difficulties than usual.' But he never sent any further response, and, although he saw Londonderry during the Abdication crisis, he did not mention the letter. Londonderry wrote again several times but his letters remained unanswered. Meanwhile he had paid a further visit to Germany and afterwards produced a short book, *Ourselves and Germany*, in which he described his meetings with Hitler and Goering and other leaders in the light of Britain's failure to come to an understanding with Germany and the deterioration in Anglo-German relations which had begun when Germany had been denied a place at the Disarmament Conference at Geneva. The book, which appeared in the spring of 1938, had a modest success; it was serialised in

[1] New peers are introduced in the House of Lords by fellow-peers of the same rank. Londonderry, although a titular Marquess, was able to act in this capacity, since his Marquessate was an Irish creation and he sat in the Upper House by virtue of his United Kingdom peerage of Earl Vane.

the *Evening Standard*, and Londonderry received numerous letters from a wide range of correspondents to whom he had sent copies, both in England and abroad. These included King George VI, Queen Mary and the Duke of Windsor, who had recently visited Germany with the Duchess, most of Londonderry's former Cabinet colleagues, experienced British diplomats who had served in Berlin like Sir Horace Rumbold, and leading Germans who had entertained Londonderry such as Goering, Von Papen and Hitler himself. This encouraged Londonderry to reissue the book as a paperback, an early one to appear under the imprint of Penguin Books, bringing the story down to Munich and also adding a selection from this interesting correspondence.

Londonderry was still feeling sore at Baldwin's failure to answer his letters. Shortly before Christmas 1938, he sent Baldwin a copy of the paperback, 'as you expressed so much interest in the original edition', together with a copy of his letter of 18 May 1936, and again reproaching Baldwin for his seeming neglect.

> I still repeat that if only I had a little more power, and could have induced the Government first, and the Press next, to take some notice of my activities, we should be in an entirely different position to that in which we find ourselves at the present moment . . .
> You will understand, therefore, that it has been most disappointing to me to have felt most completely impotent during this crisis, when I know I was right, owing to my weakened political position to get anything across.

Londonderry's gesture finally brought forth a characteristic reply in Baldwin's own hand:

> *Astley Hall,*
> *Stourport,*
> *Christmas Eve, 1938*
>
> Dear Charley,
>   You are a faithful friend. The little book arrived last night and I shall read it with care. It is tragic how the Germans seem to do everything to neutralise all the efforts of men like yourself who have done everything in your power and risking all kinds of misunderstandings to obtain understanding, and through understanding, Peace.
>   I am distressed if I ever failed to answer any letter of yours. I don't think I have a record of much of my own correspondence. It is large: I write all private letters myself and rarely keep a copy. It is perhaps not wise but I am too old to change now! I was never methodical and I must have been the despair of my secretaries. But you are the last man I would wittingly offend and I have always regarded you as a true friend in good times and bad, and I have had my share of both as you have.
>   Bless you and all good be with you in this dark world.
>   Yours ever,
>   S. B.

To this Londonderry rejoined with another long letter, of some fourteen typewritten pages, in which he went over the ground again. 'I could not refrain from smiling when you associated me with your ups and downs,' he concluded. 'I had never experienced any downs that I could complain of with any justification, until with one stroke you wiped me off the political map, whereas notwithstanding the downs which you may have experienced, you retired from an active part in public life in a blaze of glory.'

It had always been Londonderry's ambition to become Viceroy of India and he had been very disappointed when Baldwin chose Edward Wood in 1926. Then, as he reminded Baldwin when they met in London in May 1939, 'Ramsay was frightened of criticism and sent Willingdon, and you sent Linlithgow, the result, I am told, of the best bit of lobbying ever done. So my star was properly set.'

> What I mind is that you left me under a stigma which has done me personally and publicly untold harm: but I believe one only really minds things if one thinks they can be rectified. I have long since realised no one can rectify them now. I sometimes feel rather shamefaced *vis-à-vis* my ancestors. I feel that they are murmuring: 'Well, he might have done better than that,' and with the motto I have always had graven on my heart: 'Luck is the superstition of the incompetent', I find I have no answer to make.

At their meeting, Baldwin had cautiously observed that time would tell whether Londonderry was right in his attitude to the Germans. 'It will not take fifty years to discover whether I was right or wrong,' Londonderry wrote back next day. 'I was obviously right and the Government obviously wrong and I am enclosing two letters I wrote to a Committee to consider German rearmament in November 1934. You were on the Committee, but you all brushed me on one side.'

Londonderry's object in these letters, which were marked 'secret and personal' and were addressed to Lord Hailsham, then War Minister, was to persuade Germany to return to the League of Nations and to reach an accommodation with her which would restore her lost prestige and at the same time render her secure from attack by the French on the west and the Poles on the east. This should be done, he had argued, while the Germans were still 'not in a position to challenge the world'. Otherwise 'this situation will be entirely altered in a comparatively short space of time, and we shall find ourselves up against ultimatums from Germany and a power behind those ultimatums which will plunge the world once more into the catastrophe of war'. And this, as Londonderry was later to record, was exactly what happened on 3 September 1939, just short of five years after his warning to the Cabinet Disarmament Committee.

5

Londonderry's son Robin Castlereagh had also tackled Baldwin about his treatment of his father, telling him bluntly that he spoke not merely as a son but as a member of the Conservative Party and that in his opinion his father had had 'a raw deal'. Baldwin defended himself in the course of a long interview which took place in the Prime Minister's room in the House of Commons shortly after the General Election of 1935 at which Castlereagh had again been returned as M.P. for County Down, this time after a contest with an Irish Republican whom he defeated by the enormous majority of 45,593. (Yet even this majority did not satisfy Castlereagh: 'Fully ⅛ of the county did not vote, and I am sure the Papists voted to a man,' he wrote to the present author after the result. 'Big agricultural districts are bad voters, but whole villages in Down failed to vote. These are the people who loudly proclaim their loyalty and yet cannot bother to cast a vote against a Republican. They make me sick.')

During their talk Baldwin recalled how Neville Chamberlain had urged that Londonderry should be dismissed for his 'bombing' speech when Baldwin was reconstructing the Government on taking over from Ramsay MacDonald. 'My first duty when I became P.M. last June was to groom the Party for an election, and any Minister who had erred would be asked to go,' he said. 'I know my many weaknesses as a P.M., not the least of which is my inability to be a good butcher. It is not in my nature. An F.E. or a Winston would not hesitate: to them public service comes before sentiment and your Father would have been dismissed at once. I could not do that. To me it is all wrong. Your Father had given years of devoted service to his country, and you cannot summarily fire a man with such a record. We had already decided to make a change at the Air Ministry. With the increase in air strength we felt we required a man with more experience of business and industry in general; such a man too should be in the House of Commons . . . Instead of asking him to resign as I was advised to do, I actually promoted him to the leadership of the House of Lords, thinking this would be a very appropriate wind up to an honourable career.'

'I have been candid,' Baldwin went on. 'I shall be more so.'

I do not think your Mother has been a very happy influence on your Father in politics. She is a very remarkable person. She was a creative genius in the war. It was she who first set the women at work. There was a mass of feminine energy warped and wasted in the suffragette movement. She diverted it into the war effort. She has great charm, vitality and courage—priceless assets. But if allied to faulty judgment they become even greater liabilities . . .

I have Highland blood in me and I understand the bond which unites all Highlanders, but ninety per cent of people do not. To them your Mother's friendship with Ramsay is an act of political expediency to help your Father's political career. All his life Ramsay has fought against everything your Father stands for . . . Poor old Ramsay was a doughty fighter in his early days. It was tragic to see him in his closing days as P.M., losing the thread of his speech and turning to ask a colleague why people were laughing—detested by his old friends, despised by the Conservatives. Your Mother certainly provided a refuge for Ramsay for which your Father paid a high price.

1a Robert Stewart 1st Marquess of Londonderry by Anton Rafael Mengs painted in Rome in 1762. From the original at Mount Stewart.

b Lady Frances Pratt, daughter of Lord Chancellor Earl Camden and second wife of the 1st Marquess, at Mount Stewart. From a portrait by an unknown artist.

c The Temple of the Winds at Mount Stewart built by the first Marquess in 1782.
National Trust of Northern Ireland.

2a The Congress of Vienna. Castlereagh is sitting in the middle with his legs crossed, Metternich is standing on the left, faced by Wellington on the extreme left, while Castlereagh's brother Stewart is standing second from the left behind the table. Talleyrand is sitting on the right with his hand resting on the table. The chairs were subsequently presented to Castlereagh by Metternich and are now at Mount Stewart. From an engraving of the painting by J. P. Isabey, *National Trust of Northern Ireland*.

b Robert Stewart Viscount Castlereagh, later 2nd Marquess, from the portrait by Sir Thomas Lawrence in the possession of the present Lord Londonderry at Wynyard Park.

c The table on which the Treaty of Vienna was signed, flanked by the chairs used by Castlereagh and Stewart at the Congress. The table is now at Wynyard. The portrait by Lawrence above the table shows Castlereagh in his robes worn at the coronation of King George IV. *Ulster Museum*.

3a The 3rd Marquess as General Sir Charles Stewart in hussar uniform with the Talavera medal and star, from the original by Sir Thomas Lawrence.

b Lady Catherine Bligh, first wife of the 3rd Marquess, with their only son Frederick, later 4th Marquess, by Lawrence.

c Lady Frances Anne Vane-Tempest, second wife of the 3rd Marquess, from the original by A. J. D. Drahonet.

All three portraits are in the possession of the present Lord Londonderry at Wynyard Park.

4a and b The 3rd Marquess (then Lord Stewart) and his wife Frances Anne in their rooms in the British Embassy in Vienna when Stewart was ambassador, from the original drawings by Johann Ender in the possession of the present Lord Londonderry.

c The Tsar Alexander I with whom Frances Anne Lady Londonderry had a curious love affair, from the original by Sir Thomas Lawrence in the possession of the present Lord Londonderry at Wynyard Park.

d Hambletonian, Sir Henry Vane's unbeaten racehorse, being rubbed down after his match with Diamond at Newmarket in 1799. This famous painting by George Stubbs was formerly at Londonderry House and is now at Mount Stewart. *National Trust of Northern Ireland.*

5a Frank Encampment in the Desert of Mount Sinai 1842, from the original water colour by J. F. Lewis in the Paul Mellon Collection at the Yale Centre for British Art. The 4th Marquess (then Lord Castlereagh) is lying on the right and listening to a speech of welcome from a local sheikh.

b Elizabeth Lady Castlereagh, formerly Lady Powerscourt, wife of Frederick the 4th Marquess, in 1847, from the original portrait by Charles Adams at Mount Stewart. *National Trust of Northern Ireland.*

c Christmas at Mount Stewart 1856, from a drawing by an unknown artist at Mount Stewart. The 4th Marquess is on the right wearing riding boots. *National Trust of Northern Ireland.*

6a Garron Tower, built by Frances Anne Lady Londonderry on the County Antrim coast, near Carnlough, in 1848 and

b The entrance to Garron Tower. Left to right: Lord Herbert Vane-Tempest, Lord Castlereagh (later 6th Marquess), Lady Aline Vane-Tempest (later Lady Allendale), Mary Cornelia wife of 5th Marquess, George Henry 5th Marquess.

The brass plaque was subsequently removed when Garron Tower was sold and is now in the possession of Lord Antrim at Glenarm. From photographs in the possession of the present Marquess.

7a Mount Stewart, County Down, from a Victorian water colour by an unknown artist. *National Trust of Northern Ireland.*
and b Wynyard Park, County Durham, about 1840, from a water colour by James Carmichael Wilson in the possession of the present Lord Londonderry at Wynyard.

8a and b Charles 6th Marquess and his wife Theresa as Viceroy and Vicereine of Ireland, from photographs taken about 1886. *Author's collection.*

c Charley Castlereagh (later 7th Marquess), Helen (later Lady Ilchester), and Reginald, at Mount Stewart.

d Reginald Viscount Helmsley, Theresa Lady Londonderry's lover and reputed father of her son Reginald. From photographs in the possession of the present Lord Londonderry.

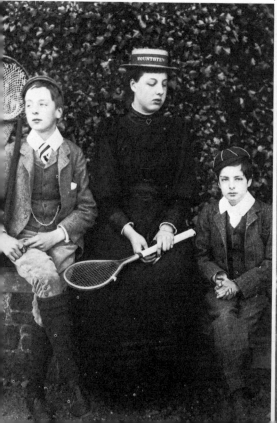

9a Shooting party for the Prince of Wales at Wynyard, October 1890.
Front row: 6th Marquess in the centre with Lord Randolph Churchill on his left.
Second row: The Prince of Wales in the centre, with the Duchess of Manchester on his
   right and the Duchess of Montrose and Lady Randolph Churchill on his left.
Back row: Theresa Lady Londonderry is second from left; the Princess of Wales is standing
   behind the Prince and on her left are Lord Herbert Vane-Tempest, Henry Chaplin and
   Count Herbert Bismarck.
9b Shooting party for King Edward VII at Wynyard, October 1903, when a meeting of
the Privy Council was held, the first in a private house since the reign of Charles I.
Front row: Hon. Mrs George Keppel on far left; Theresa Lady Londonderry third from
   right and Duchess of Devonshire second from right.
Back row: The King fifth from right with the Duke of Devonshire and the 6th Marquess
   on his immediate right. Lord Castlereagh (later 7th Marquess) on the extreme right.
From photographs in the possession of the present Marquess.

10a Lord Castlereagh election-eering at Maidstone in 1910. *Author's collection.*
and b Edith Lady Castlereagh, wife of 7th Marquess, in 1912. From the portrait by Philip de László in the possession of Lady Mairi Bury at Mount Stewart.

11a The 7th Marquess when he was A.D.C. to General Sir William Pulteney in the First World War. *Author's collection.*

b General Sir William Pulteney ("Putty"). *PRO Northern Ireland.*

c Edith Lady Londonderry, D.B.E., as Commandant of the Women's Legion, from the portrait by Philip de László in the Imperial War Museum.

12a Plâs Machynlleth, the Londonderrys' Welsh property. The figure in the foreground is Lord Herbert Vane-Tempest, the 6th Marquess's younger brother who was killed in a railway accident in Wales in 1921. *PRO Northern Ireland.*

b Royal Visit to Plâs Machynlleth, July 1911.
Front row sitting (l to r): Lord Stamfordham, Mrs Sneyd, Princess Mary, Queen Mary, Theresa Lady Londonderry, Lady Bertha Dawkins.
Back row standing (l to r): Mr N. W. Apperley, Lord Revelstoke, Prince of Wales, 6th Marquess, King George V, Lord Herbert Vane-Tempest, Col. the Hon. C. Legge, Major Clive Wigram, Mr Malcolm Dillon.
From a photograph at Plâs Machynlleth.

13a The Irish Convention, 1917. Sir Horace Plunkett is addressing the convention in Trinity College, Dublin. The Ulster Unionist delegation is seated at the front semi-circular table on the left, Lord Londonderry being at the right end of this row. *PRO Northern Ireland.*

b The 7th Marquess, Finance Member of the Air Council and later Parliamentary Under-Secretary for Air, leaving the War Office with Mr Winston Churchill, M.P., Secretary of State for War and Air, in 1919.

c The First Northern Ireland Cabinet, 1921. (l to r): E. M. Archdale (Agriculture and Commerce), R. Dawson Bates (Home Affairs), 7th Marquess (Education), Sir James Craig (Prime Minister), H. M. Pollock (Finance), J. M. Andrews (Labour). In the background is the Secretary of the Cabinet, Sir Wilfrid Spender. *Authors collection.*

14a Londonderry House, demolished in 1962 to make way for a hotel subsequently built on the site.

b The grand staircase at Londonderry House.

c Lady Londonderry receiving guests at an eve-of-Parliament reception in the 1930s. The blurred figure behind her on the right is that of the Prime Minister Ramsay MacDonald. *Author's collection.*

15a The 7th Marquess saying good-bye to his daughters Helen and Margaret before setting out on a flight in a service aircraft when he was Air Minister. *Authors collection.*
b Lady Maureen Stanley, the 7th Marquess's eldest daughter. She married the Hon. Oliver Stanley, son of Lord Derby, and died in 1942 aged 41. *Radio Times Hulton Picture Library.*
c House party at Mount Stewart for the christening of the 7th Marquess's younger grand-daughter Annabel now Lady Annabel Goldsmith by the Archbishop of Armagh, July 1934. Front row, l to r: Duchess of Sutherland, Archbishop of Armagh, Lady Castlereagh, Lady Londonderry (Jane, now Lady Rayne, on her lap), 7th Marquess.
Back row, l to r: The author, Lady Elizabeth Leveson-Gower, Lady Margaret Stewart, Lady Mairi Stewart, Lord Castlereagh (later 8th Marquess), Lady Helen Stewart. *Belfast News-Letter.*

16a Ramsay MacDonald at Mount Stewart with Lord Hailsham (left) and the 7th Marquess (right) when the latter was Air Minister, and b the 7th Marquess with Hitler and Ribbentrop in the Berlin Chancellery in 1937. *Author's collection.*

Certainly Lady Londonderry's affection for Ramsay waned little, if at all, and they continued to correspond and meet from time to time, although she cannot have been unaware of the gravamen of Baldwin's criticism. After some difficulty parliamentary seats were found for both Mac-Donalds, Ramsay for the Scottish Universities and Malcolm for Ross and Cromarty, where a vacancy occurred due to the death of the sitting National Liberal M.P., and Lady Londonderry, who had useful connections with the local Conservatives in the latter constituency, undoubtedly contributed to the son's return. However, despite being heartened by this success and glad to be back at Westminster again, Ramsay railed at Baldwin in his diary for his lack of consultation, considering him 'putty' in the hands of his party and soon likely to be elbowed out of the leadership by Neville Chamberlain. Although MacDonald was still in the Cabinet, his Tory colleagues grated on him more and more and he began to think, looking back, that the break in 1931 had not been 'good' for him. ('My kith and kin are the common folk.')

There was a rumour current at this time that Ramsay MacDonald's physical and mental decline arose, at any rate in part, from the fact that he was being blackmailed by a well-known cocotte with whom he had slept during one of his many visits to the capital cities of Europe in the 1920s. The blackmail money was said to have been paid from Secret Service funds, and MacDonald's indiscreet letters to her were bought from their recipient and destroyed. Whether or not he did have an affair of this kind in the 1920s is a matter of conjecture. But the suggestion that the blackmailer was paid from Secret Service sources is highly unlikely, to say the least, and has been discounted by MacDonald's official biographer David Marquand, who has been unable to find any reference to the alleged affair in MacDonald's diaries and other papers.

In 1936, Ramsay MacDonald brought out a book of his travel experiences—he had always been a keen walker—and he sent Lady Londonderry a copy which genuinely enraptured her. 'Don't you think it the best you have written?' she wrote to him on 20 September from Mount Stewart. 'Anyhow I like it the best. It has such a charming inviting style.' She went on:

> I often think of you and miss you, although I revel in freedom and escape from London. We are going to stay with Marthe Bibesco in Roumania, also we go to Hungary next month, then almost approaching from the sublime to the ridiculous, we become Mayor and Mayoress of Durham on 9th November. We have withstood this dignity for years—but no further excuse. Also it being coronation year seems available.
>
> And what of S.B. poor thing? I don't think he is physically ill at all. His nerve has gone. I doubt if he will run in the Coronation Stakes, even if Lucy [his wife] is ever so determined.

But Baldwin's nerve was far from gone, as became evident in his skilful handling of the Abdication crisis. In this, Lady Londonderry had a contingent interest since, a few days after Mrs Simpson's divorce decree *nisi* had been pronounced at Ipswich Assizes, the two happened to meet at some gathering in London when Lady Londonderry spoke to her frankly and freely, warning her that the English people would never tolerate her marriage to the King, which would be quite contrary to constitutional tradition, since she had two ex-husbands still living. At this date Mrs Simpson's friendship with the King was being openly gossiped about in English social circles, and it was a topic for comment in the American and foreign press, but as yet it had not been mentioned by an English newspaper.

Mrs Simpson was grateful for Lady Londonderry's advice and wrote telling her so from her house in Regent's Park next day, 6 November:

> I have been thinking over all you told me last night. I have come to the conclusion that perhaps no one has been *really* frank with a certain person in telling him how the country feels about his friendship with me, perhaps nothing has been said to him at all. I feel that he should know however and therefore I am going to tell him the things you told me.

Someone had told Lady Londonderry that Mrs Simpson was with the King when he opened Parliament three days previously. 'In fact,' Mrs Simpson remarked, 'I was doing some very interesting shopping in Harrods that morning.'

A month later, when the crisis was at its height and the King had not yet made his final decision, Londonderry wrote to Baldwin that he hoped that abdication would not be hurriedly forced upon the monarch. There was talk in the air of a King's Party being formed with Churchill as its leader, and since Londonderry was known to have discussed the crisis with his cousin on the Sunday before the King formally abdicated, Cyril Hankey, Sir Maurice's brother, who was a friend of Londonderrys, expressed the hope that 'Charley would not do anything foolish'. But he need not have worried. Londonderry felt as the Prime Minister and Cabinet did, and the majority of people in the country. When it was all over and Edward VIII had departed into exile as Duke of Windsor, Lady Londonderry wrote to Baldwin congratulating him on his brilliant management of the affair.

'You wrote me one of the kindest letters I have ever had,' the Prime Minister replied on 19 December 1936. 'It has been a strange time and the end of it was inevitable, but there were possibilities of real trouble in the situation, trouble beyond the comprehension of the silly people who fluttered round Mrs Simpson. However all is well, and some day we will talk about it for it is not a subject I care to write about.'

Next day Ramsay MacDonald wrote to her from Lossiemouth:

What horrid days the last three or four in London have been, and yet how much
worse they might have been.

   . . . Everybody up here seems to have known the two members of the cast in the
Royal drama all their lives and talk of them as life-long problems by their pet
Christian names . . . The farewell speech has touched many hearts but no heads up
here. The old remember their youth and the young dream of their opportunities.

'Touching and pathetic and yet not appealing,' so MacDonald found
the King's broadcast. 'I perhaps am prejudiced by the immediate harm
he has done, and when the future opens up I shall see, as indeed I believe,
that it was all for the good. Still, one does not respect so much as be
thankful for the tools of Providence.' That, too, was Lady Londonderry's
view.

The year 1937, Coronation year, was to be a busy one for the Londonderrys. Londonderry was Mayor of Durham, as his father before him had
been for the Coronation year of King George V, he was also Chancellor
of Durham University, which celebrated its centenary that year, and he
was Honorary Air Commodore of an auxiliary fighter squadron, No 607,
stationed at Usworth; he likewise filled a similar position in an Ulster
auxiliary bomber squadron, No 502 at Aldergrove. In the same year he was
elected Grand Master of the Guild of Air Pilots. Then, as Lord Lieutenant
of County Down and Chancellor of the Queen's University, he had to play
his part in organising the state visit of the newly crowned King George VI
and Queen Elizabeth to Northern Ireland, which took place at the end of
July. Before that the King and his consort had dined at Londonderry
House, so that socially as distinct from politically the Londonderrys
remained as secure as ever, and few if any people refused an invitation to
Londonderry House.

Because of the hospitality he and his wife and daughter had received in
Germany during their visit the previous year, the least Londonderry felt
he could do was to invite Goering and his wife to stay at Londonderry
House for the Coronation, and he sent them a formal invitation in this
sense. This invitation was politely but firmly declined. 'We are not
coming to the Coronation,' Goering wrote back. 'You will certainly
appreciate that after all the agitation against my coming to England, which
was carried to the extent of holding meetings at which I was called all
kinds of insulting names, it is quite impossible for me to attend the
Coronation. Moreover I feel that relations between Germany and England
have unfortunately grown very much cooler of late, so that such a visit
would serve little purpose.' However, the Ambassador Von Ribbentrop,
who represented his Government at the Coronation, with his wife stayed
both at Mount Stewart and Wynyard and they also put in an appearance
at the Londonderry House parties. Personally Londonderry never thought
highly of Ribbentrop, whom he regarded as an arrant snob; he also

disapproved of his attribution of 'Von' before his surname after he had married the champagne heiress Anneliese Von Haenkel, whose company he used to represent as a commercial traveller. 'You know,' Londonderry remarked to the present author during the Ribbentrop visit to Wynyard, 'a few years ago this man was touting champagne round Europe and getting more kicks than ha'pence. Now everyone is fawning on him—myself included!'

The deterioration in Anglo-German relations, due partly to further infractions by Germany of the Versailles Treaty and partly by her actions during the Spanish Civil War, was brought home to Londonderry when he revisited Germany in response to a stag-hunting invitation from Goering. This time he found the local atmosphere considerably changed. There was a warlike feeling in the air, accentuated by the military ma-noeuvres which were taking place in Mecklenburg, of which Londonderry was allowed to see something, including a new Heinkel bomber which he inspected at Prinzlau aerodrome. But Goering was too involved with the manoeuvres to go hunting, and in the result Londonderry was handed over to the ex-Chancellor Von Papen, who had narrowly escaped being shot at the time of the 'blood bath' in June 1934, although (as he told Londonderry) it was he who had advised President Hindenburg to invest Hitler with the supreme political office in the state. Londonderry left with a feeling of depression that Germany was hell-bent on rearming as rapidly as she could, a feeling reinforced by Hitler's expressed intention that his country would never go back to the League of Nations.

Shortly after his return home Londonderry heard the news that Ramsay MacDonald, who had set out on a health voyage to South America, had died suddenly at sea a few days after embarking at Liverpool. He had retired at the same time as Baldwin after the Coronation, but unlike the Conservative leader refused to take a peerage, although the offer was repeated twice. His last meeting with the Londonderrys was at a lunch in Londonderry House a few days before he sailed. 'The Government got no support during their talk,' was how he described the conversation at table that day. Lady Londonderry's friend Henry ('Chips') Channon noted in his diary on 9 November 1937: 'I feel few will regret him.'

> Yet he had a disarming smile and aristocratic appearance which lent colour to the legend of his birth—an illegitimate Dalhousie! How much happier he was after 1931, when he carted all his old followers and began to breathe freely in the more capacious Conservative air. We treated him with respect, but he inspired no affection and no liking. He could never say yes or no to any ordinary question, never. Evasive, subtle and eel-like, he trusted no one. I saw him sometimes in those early months of the first Labour Government when London society very wisely decided to take him up rather than ignore him. Defiant at first, he soon took to grandeur and high life and wallowed in it like a man who has been starving all his life . . .
>
> At the end of Questions [in the House of Commons] Neville Chamberlain gave a

perfect, if slightly perfunctory, tribute to MacDonald, although there was no feeling of loss in the House on any side. Nevertheless ex-Prime Ministers do not die every day, and the House adjourned as a mark of respect.

'Who will be the next to go,' mused Channon, 'Baldwin or L.G.?' Ironically enough, it was Chamberlain himself, almost exactly three years later.

As might be expected, Lady Londonderry wrote more kindly of Ramsay MacDonald after his death than Henry Channon, who had no particular knowledge of or interest in the Scottish Highlands. This she did in *Retrospect*, a book of reminiscences which she published in 1938.

> He loved beautiful things—books, pictures, beautiful women, and lovely jewels and colours. And why shouldn't he? He was, for these days, an old-fashioned Socialist. His aim was to improve, not to destroy. He fought against privilege and inequality of opportunity ... When equality of opportunity—witness his own career—had been achieved, and he had time and leisure to review the past, I know he was dissatisfied and greatly disappointed with most of the leaders of his party. Ramsay, being a Celt and an Highlander, was of different blood and outlook from most of them ... In some ways, as I often told him, he was almost feudal, with a deep love and respect for the past. He was proud of the old families, but disliked the new with a bitter hatred and the system in which money has made all things possible which the past excluded.

'All that you say about Ramsay is timely and true,' wrote Bernard Shaw, to whom she had sent a copy of her book. 'I knew him in his old Socialist days before you were born. He was not really a Socialist in the academic sense: he was a seventeenth century Highlander who was quite at home in feudal society and quite out of it among English trade unionists. As a leader of English labour he was, as Beatrice Webb put it, a facade: amid chieftains and ladies bright he was himself.'

6

This seems a convenient point in the narrative to mention Edith Lady Londonderry's main interests besides politics. First and foremost was gardening. When she and her husband first came to spend some considerable time at Mount Stewart in 1921 on his appointment as Minister of Education in the first Government of Northern Ireland, she considered the house and surroundings were 'the dampest, darkest and saddest place' she had ever stayed in. Large ilex trees almost touched the house in places and other large trees blocked out the light and air. Like the majority of Irish gardens in those days, the existing ones at Mount Stewart were about a mile away from the house, approached by a walk through the grounds called 'The Ladies Walk', which afforded the ladies of an earlier age almost their only form of outdoor exercise. Cypresses and rhododendrons were the principal trees or shrubs besides the ilexes, while the bare space between the south side of the house and the sea was broken only by large clumps of pampas grass. During the Great War, when the house was converted into a convalescent hospital for soldiers, sailors and airmen, the grounds and surroundings had got run down, so that there was much to be done in the way of cleaning up and improving the general appearance. Ulster landlords at that time were asked by the Government to employ as many demobilised men as possible, and twenty or more gardeners were immediately recruited for work in the grounds and the new gardens which Lady Londonderry planned.

Her first discovery, which she had never appreciated on her earlier brief visits, was the sub-tropical climate which enabled plants like mimosa to flourish in the open air instead of in heated greenhouses. The new gardens which she proceeded to lay out were where the pampas grass had been. Fortunately she had the benefit of the advice of two experts. One was Sir John Ross of Bladensburg, who had a remarkable collection of rare trees, shrubs and plants on his estate near Rostrevor in the south of the county; the other was Sir Herbert Maxwell of Monreith in Wigtownshire, who also owned a wonderful garden of rare species. Both these gardening maestros gave invaluable advice which helped to make the Mount Stewart gardens what they became thirty-six years later, in 1957, when Lady Londonderry handed them over to the National Trust.

It is impossible to describe these gardens in detail, but five features at least deserve brief mention. First, there is the Mairi Garden on the south side of the house with its agapanthus and arum lilies and a small fountain with a statue of a child marking the spot where Mairi used to be placed every day when she was a baby in her pram for her afternoon sleep. Secondly, beside the Mairi Garden, there is the Dodo Terrace with its loggia and animals carved in stone by local craftsmen together with a stone Ark, the animals representing different members of Lady Londonderry's 'Ark Club' under her spell as Circe. Then on the west side is the Shamrock Garden, a paved garden in the form of a shamrock, surrounded by a twelve-foot-high hedge of *cupressus macrocarpa*, in the centre of which is a left hand, the Red Hand of Ulster, picked out in flowers of red and white. In the centre leaf of the shamrock is a large topiary yew with a table-like top on which stands an Irish harp. Further away to the north near the lake is the Jubilee Avenue Walk, planted to commemorate the Silver Jubilee of King George V and Queen Mary in 1935: here rhododendrons proliferate with eucalyptus trees.

To the north of the house, above the lake, is 'Tir-N'an Oge' (Gaelic for 'The Land of the Ever Young'), a hill planted with a variety of shrubs including olive trees grown from seed sent from the Mount of Olives outside Jerusalem. On the summit is the private family burial ground, where both the seventh Marquess and his wife as well as their daughter

Margaret are now buried. The ground is surrounded by a high wall and guarded by statues of Irish saints. Japanese maples, southern beeches from Latin America, Chinese roses and Burmese silver holly also grow here.

'Gardens are meant to be lived in and enjoyed', wrote Lady Londonderry as she prepared to hand them over to the National Trust, 'and I hope they may long continue to be a source of pleasure to those who visit them as they have been in the past.'

Lady Londonderry's other abiding interest was her large and extremely varied number of artistic and literary friendships, and the correspondences she kept up with her friends in this field, notably John Lavery, Edmund Brock, who both painted a number of family portraits, the composer Rutland Boughton, Edmund Gosse, John Buchan, Harold and Vita Nicolson, Osbert Sitwell, Compton Mackenzie, Bernard Shaw and many other Irish writers, such as W. B. Yeats, George Russell ('A.E.'), James Stephens, Lady Gregory, Oliver St John Gogarty, Shane Leslie and above all Sean O'Casey. She also 'took up' a brilliant young Scottish pianist named Duncan Morison and greatly encouraged him in his professional career. It made not the slightest difference that some of these correspondents were poles apart from her politically as well as socially— Sean O'Casey, for instance, was a Communist and an atheist, while she was staunchly Tory and High Church, coming out strongly in favour of the Revised Prayer Book of the Church of England, eventually rejected by Parliament. Her action in this sphere incidentally made her unpopular in Northern Ireland, where the Revised Prayer Book was regarded by the majority of Protestants as sanctioning Papist practices. Rutland Boughton's politics too were decidedly Communist; nevertheless she invited him to stage an open-air performance of his opera *The Immortal Hour* in the gardens at Mount Stewart.

Not all her friends for one reason or another found it convenient to accept her invitations. 'I am sorry,' wrote George Russell, excusing himself from a 10.30 p.m. supper party at Londonderry House. 'I am too old for suppers at that hour. I would be half asleep by eleven o'clock. My favourite sage is Laotze who preached the gospel of being natural. It is not natural to have supper at 10.30, at least not in my interpretation of the universe.' W. B. Yeats occasionally came to Mount Stewart, and he would sometimes call at Londonderry House when he was passing through London. 'It was good of you to write that there is "always a cook and room" at my service in your London house,' he wrote in August 1935, shortly after his seventieth birthday, from his home outside Dublin. 'That is an honour and a kindness an old man of letters knows how to value. Perhaps in a few months I may avail myself of it. I shall be in Ireland all September but sometime in October go to Majorca to escape the Irish winter and try amid the quiet of a strange scene to begin writing verse again.'

The Irish Nationalist and Catholic Shane Leslie, on the other hand, who was a keen bibliophile as well as an engaging author, jumped at an invitation to visit Mount Stewart in 1933 to see the library. 'I have been very fortunate of late amongst libraries,' he wrote from his family home, Castle Leslie, in County Monaghan in the Irish Free State. 'Last week I found the long lost copy of Swift's Poems with his pen corrections and the week before I found a Third Folio of Shakespeare at Caledon. The Swift was at Lough Fea and I am at my most agreeable occupation of making the British Museum squirm with envy. By the way I have no evening clothes in Ireland as I wear a kilt which would probably be confiscated by the Ulster Customs. Will you excuse me in a travelling suit?' He came with his mother Leonie, Lady Leslie, who was still alive—she was one of the three beautiful Jerome sisters, another being Winston Churchill's mother. It was the only occasion I ever saw Shane Leslie wearing a lounge suit. In all his later visits he invariably wore a saffron kilt, when he had discovered that his fears about the Ulster Customs were groundless.

Lady Londonderry would sometimes receive invitations to come south of the border when she was at Mount Stewart. 'If at any time this summer you intend to tour the West Coast,' Oliver Gogarty wrote to her in 1931, 'very kindly let me know because I would like you to see the new beauty spot which Renvyle House Hotel opens in Connemara.'

> It was our country house on a lake by the Atlantic, and, as we own the hotel into which it has now been turned, we would be glad to offer you its hospitality. With Yeats's plays and Abbey [Theatre] dancers, the idea is to found an Irish Bayreuth; or at least to provide a refuge from jazz. The district west of Loughs Mask and Corrib is lovelier than Killarney; and, as we can show you water-lilies within 30 yards of golden seaweed and damson-coloured hills reflected in the lake, it would be a calamity if you went touring in Connemara 'and I not to know'.

The domestic demands of Mount Stewart during that hectic summer of 1931 which witnessed the formation of the National Government in London made such a visit impossible. But, though she never went to Connemara, she would often lunch with Gogarty when she was in Dublin at his fine Georgian house in Ely Place.

Gogarty was always a particularly welcome visitor at Mount Stewart, where his native wit set everyone laughing. He was a brilliant mimic and one of his best performances, which he was always pleased to give, depicted Yeats receiving the Nobel Prize. The poet was first shown receiving the award with an air of lordly disdain and even lack of interest. But as soon as he moved away from the audience the poet would be seen carefully examining the cheque to make sure that it had been made out for the right amount. Gogarty was instrumental in forming the Irish Aero

Club which in turn helped to give birth to the Irish commercial air line
Aer Lingus. He further endeared himself to Lord Londonderry by flying
a small plane with an open cockpit from Dublin to Newtownards for the
opening of the first civil airport in Northern Ireland in 1934, crossing the
Mourne mountains in a blinding rainstorm and landing safely in spite of
hitting a sheep which had strayed on to the runway.

With George Bernard Shaw, Lady Londonderry kept up a characteristic
correspondence over the years, each sending the other author presentation copies of their works. 'I think you may be allowed to read this novel,'
he wrote to her in 1931 on the flyleaf of *Immaturity*, the first volume of his
collected edition, 'but the Preface had better be reserved for the children:
it is hardly fit for your eyes. Children can stand anything. Besides, I value
your illusions about me.' When she gave him a copy of her autobiographical *Retrospect*, he uttered a word of warning after he had read it:

> That book will get you into trouble by one immortal sentence. 'Now,' sez you,
> 'you very rarely see anyone who looks like a lady.' You should be careful how you
> tell the truth so recklessly: the poor things can't help themselves; and they are
> really better than the upholstered fraud the Victorian lady, whom, by the way, you
> don't in the least resemble and happily don't remember. I, being 82½ do.

'We are now so damnably old that we have to regard ourselves as
morally dead,' he wrote to her in December 1938; 'but I still go on writing
from mere habit; and though we don't go out at night we indulge in a
luncheon party occasionally with anyone who will put up with us.' The
result was an invitation to lunch at Londonderry House a week or so later.
Shaw had had an inoculation the day before and evidently went out too
soon, as he fainted in the hall as soon as he arrived and eventually had to
be sent back to his flat in Whitehall Court accompanied by a footman and
a trained nurse as well as by Mrs Shaw. He made a rapid recovery and
next day was well enough to write a long letter to his hostess, part of
which follows:

> I was extraordinarily lucky in flopping where I did yesterday. Inconvenient for you
> but ideal for me. I had just given up my coat and hat and umbrella when I found that
> I could not stand, and put my hand against the wall to steady myself. Next thing I
> knew I was flat on my back with Charles, unaccountably looking 20 years younger
> than when I saw him last, kneeling by me and trying to rub some warmth into my
> cold hand which was very comforting. I was perfectly happy in spirit, though
> physically convinced that if I moved I should be sick. I felt quite willing to lie there
> for a month, but could not forget that this would hardly be a suitable arrangement
> for the household.
>
> I had presence of mind to say Howdye do to Charles, who presently transported
> me to the library, where I became completely conscious of you, looking so resplen-
> dent that I concluded I was delirious and never thought of saying Howdyedo. You
> are an amazing pair. You said that Mairi Mairi (quite contrary) was to have sat
> beside me at lunch; and I was on the point of saying 'Why doesn't she come and sit

beside me now?' when it occurred to me just in time that the still possible spectacle of her idealised celebrity being violently sick might make her a cynic for life . . .

Your footman was evidently a non-Aryan refugee doctor in disguise: he was immensely capable and did not leave me until he planted me safely in bed; and Sister Chigi was a jewel. Today I am quite well—exceptionally well in fact. It did me a lot of good seeing you both . . .

A wonderful box of flowers has just arrived and thrown Charlotte into transports. She said quite spontaneously, 'They are so well grown and healthy and beautiful, like herself.' That just hit it off.

'Never could I have imagined anything like your kindness—all of you!' wrote Charlotte Shaw when she had got her husband down to their house at Ayot St Lawrence.

There was an atmosphere of goodness, and help and strength in your house I have *never* felt before in trouble. I think it comes from you and your husband and radiated through all your people. I can only say *Thank you*!

The little Nursie was an angel to me that night. I cannot imagine how I could have got on without her.

The glorious flowers came down here with me, and are as fresh as when they were gathered. A joy.

Although it was written some years later, during the war, Shaw's letter to Lady Londonderry on the occasion of his wife's death may conveniently be quoted here. For some time Charlotte had been suffering from *osteitis deformans*, at first wrongly diagnosed as lumbago. It caused her much pain and was incurable: she died eventually from its effects.

4 Whitehall Court. 16 September 1943. Bless you, my dear, Circe, I am not a bit sorrowful. In our eighties we had nothing to hope or desire, but a happy ending to our pains and distresses; and they all lifted and fled miraculously at the end. The last thirty hours were blessedly happy; and she shed all her years and furrows and recovered all her good looks, babbling to me incessantly and unintelligibly, but like a pleased child learning to talk, until her breath failed. It was indescribably touching; but it made all grief and sorrow impossible.

At Golders Green yesterday I had nothing but music: the music of Handel which she loved best.

So all's well that ends well.

G.B.S.

Sean O'Casey was a friend and protégé of Bernard Shaw as well as Edith Londonderry, and both were kind to him in their respective ways. Shaw gave him literary advice and encouraged him to persevere with his writing when the Abbey Theatre in Dublin had rejected *The Silver Tassie* after his earlier successes with *The Shadow of a Gunman*, *Juno and the Paycock*, and *The Plough and the Stars*; Lady Londonderry always made him and his wife welcome at Londonderry House and spoke to the publishing house of Macmillan on his behalf with the result that, with the exception of a few early ephemera which came out in Ireland, Macmillan published all his plays and other writings in England. 'Playwriting is a desperate trade,' Shaw told him. '£300 a week for just long enough to get you a living at that rate, and then nothing for two years. Your wife must support you (what is she for?), and when she is out of work you must go into debt, and borrow and pawn, and so on—the usual routine.' Lady Londonderry's help took a more concrete form in the shape of a banker's guarantee of £200 towards the costs of the New York production of *Within the Gates* in the autumn of 1934.

They first met in 1926, when the O'Caseys were living in Chelsea, and Sean sent her a copy of *The Plough and the Stars* with the following note inscribed:

> A common humanity binds us all together. We cannot break its bonds asunder, nor cast away its bands from us.
>
> Differ as we may in degree or in circumstances we remain equally rich in the common human heritage of sorrow and pain.

'As for me,' he wrote to her in 1934, 'I really gathered you as a friend in spirit when, eight years ago, you quietly and cleverly placed a mantle of courtesy and kindness round the shoulders of a Dublin labourer, full of Shakespeare and full of ignorance, that came lumbering into Londonderry House with Mary Grey and J. B. Fagan.[1] I found gentleness and a grand quieting courtesy in the midst of purple and fine linen.'

Here are some typical extracts from other letters:

> *Hillcrest, Chalfont St Giles. 23 October 1931* . . . We are here now in Mid-Bucks, down among the Beeches, Larches and Pines, far from the rushing Bus and the swallowing Tube. We found London too dear to live in, and seek here an easier effort to supply the things that belong to our peace. After a long delay and many efforts we have—Eileen hunted it out—a pretty, simple, compact house with a garden and cherry orchard, on the crest of the Chiltern Hills. In the last few weeks I have, in a way, reverted to type and have been busy with hammer, saw, shovel and pick . . .

> *8 December 1931* . . . I think I remember you, in writing about the result of the recent election, mentioning the 'innate common sense of the English people.' Innate common sense! Poor bleating sheep that have never gone astray. What they heard from Ramsay MacDonald, Snowden, Lord Reading and Stanley Baldwin frightened them, and it was post and saddle and spur for the polling booth! Their security threatened and their imagination flamed for the first—and last, probably—time, and they saw England as a heap of ashes. And the simple sheep imagine that 500 men can work miracles, create the Kingdom of Heaven in their hearts . . . They haven't enough imagination even to lose a war! They have great qualities but they are not transcendental qualities. They have had centuries in which to build; the Irish have had but a decade, so we must be fair and judge in relativity. God knows I wish well to the English people but I try to look all things in the face.

---

[1] Fagan, the son of a well-known Belfast surgeon, was an actor-manager, playwright and producer, who was responsible for the first London production of O'Casey's *Juno and the Paycock* in 1925. The actress Mary Grey was his wife.

October 1933 . . . I have had a bad time for some months with heart and nerves . . .
It was found at last that my heart was sound; my nerves are better, and here I am
spending myself as before. Indeed I worked harder when I was sick than when I was
well.

My new play will be published shortly. It is a strange work, and different to all
that went before. Macmillan's think it the finest thing I have yet done. I'm busy
now talking about its possible production in London early in the New Year. It is
called *Within the Gates! a play in Four Scenes in a London Park*. Let me send you
one of the first copies, will you? [He did so, inscribing it, 'To the time when all shall
have life and have it more abundantly.']

I hope to have another volume called *Windfalls* out soon, too, consisting of things
written, past and present. Part of this, I hope will be a story called 'I Wanna
Woman,' which the printer of *Time and Tide* refused to set, calling it obscene and
indecent; though Lady Rhondda and others thought it contained a good wholesome
moral lesson! The poor little story caused quite a stir . . .

Now I hope you are well, and Lord Londonderry; your boy and his wife and their
baby; and all your fine girls.

Give them the blessing of an Atheist and a Communist, and, I hope, a poet.

7th November, 1933 . . . Life is flinging aside all the idolatry of the past and gone
style, and is beginning to express itself and for itself the pain, the joy, balance and
theme of its own life in its own way, and for its own need. You yourself have
banished the Sedan Chair for the Rolls Royce and glad indeed was I you had, when
I was ill, and wanted to get to London.

And I am a Gael—I wore the kilts even for years. 'A Gael I without shame to
myself or harm to others.'[1] A Gael, alas, England's brain, England's backbone,and
England's beauty. I see few failings in the Celt, and many qualities, and you have
almost all the qualities; may God preserve them and develop them in you forever!

I see life only that it can and must be better. The evil, or what we call, evil,
springs, not from sin, but from ignorance and stupidity, and there is more of these
here than in the countries that gave you birth and me birth. Nelson, they prate of
Nelson; but where would he have been were it not for the thousands of Irish gang-
pressed into the British Navy after the rebellion of '98'?

He spent a few days in August 1934 at Mount Stewart on his way to
New York for the American production of *Within the Gates*. Although the
play had only a modest success in America and was actually banned in
Boston, it was unnecessary for the author to touch the guarantee, which he
duly returned to Lady Londonderry. About the same time he was able to
sell the film rights in *The Plough and the Stars*, which he told Lady
Londonderry should secure him financially for a couple of years. Nevertheless he was constantly plagued by money troubles, and although she
offered to help him out he always refused her offers, thanking her 'for the
Gaelic grace and goodness of your kindness'.

Lady Londonderry had a great affection for Sean and Eileen O'Casey
which was warmly reciprocated on their side. Both the O'Caseys belonged
to the Ark, and Sean was the only member admitted who was not in the
conventional evening dress for the Ark suppers—he habitually wore a

[1] These words were written in Gaelic.

polo-necked black sweater and plum-coloured trousers. Indeed he was once refused admission by a new doorkeeper at Londonderry House to a party being specially given in his honour and he had to be summoned back from his Chelsea flat with profuse apologies from his hostess.

O'Casey was entranced by 'beautiful Mount Stewart', and after his first visit he penned a fitting benediction to its owners: 'Brigid and Columcille, with all the other Irish saints beside them, be with you both, and with your charming household, now and forever.'

7

On his return to England after his third German visit, Londonderry was still hopeful for an Anglo–German understanding, even with the Nazi regime. But Churchill, to whom he wrote at the time on the subject, was not so sanguine. 'You must surely be aware that when the German Government speaks of friendship with England,' Churchill observed to his cousin on 23 October 1937, 'what they mean is that we shall give them back their former colonies, and also agree to their having a free hand so far as we are concerned in Central and Southern Europe. This means that they would devour Austria and Czecho-Slovakia as a preliminary to making a gigantic mid-Europe block. It would certainly not be in our interests to connive at such policies of aggression.'

This proved a remarkably accurate prediction. Indeed, even as Ribbentrop, who had been appointed German Foreign Minister, was giving his farewell reception as ambassador on 11 March 1938 in the German Embassy in Carlton House Terrace, Hitler's troops were marching into Austria to consolidate the *Anschluss*. Mass arrests followed indiscriminately of Austrian anti-Nazis or suspected anti-Nazis. Among them were two Tyrolese guides who were well known to Lady Londonderry and were making preparations for the international ski race for which she had presented a silver cup. This caused her to write to Ribbentrop with a sense of anger which she barely concealed after sending him an irate message through the German Chargé d'Affaires in the London embassy.

Mount Stewart. 19 March 1938. I had to fly over here for the week end, but before I left I saw Herr Wiedmann, your Counsellor, in London, and asked him to let you know how very strongly we all felt about the arrest of the guides in the Tyrol. I had also written to Goering, as he is not only a friend but a great sportsman.

I am particularly concerned with Hans Falconer and Hans Schneider. Both are friends of mine. Hans Falconer has stayed with us here and in London. We know him very well. He was arranging the big international race at Obergurgl, for which I had given the challenge cup. The race was called the Londonderry Snow Eagle race, and it should have taken place on April 24th. I intend naturally to withdraw the cup, even if someone else takes Falconer's place. Believe me when I say that the arrest of these two guides has raised a storm of indignation in London throughout the sporting world.

German mentality and ours must be poles apart. With what object must you antagonise all your erstwhile friends over here? What good do you hope to do by imprisoning honest men like these guides? How can you suppose that anyone with anything at all could be disloyal to their own country Austria? Is not everyone entitled to be loyal as long as their cause lasts? Now that that cause is over, as in the present case, you should at least give them the chance to serve the country under German rule. To imprison them for not having wished to do so before is neither just nor right . . .

I feel so very strongly about it all that I might even go to Vienna myself to find out what is going on. At least I hope your friends have not seized on and impounded my Cup and that you will give orders for it to be returned from Obergurgl to the British Embassy in Berlin.

I cannot express in sufficiently strong words the chagrin I feel at what is happening, and the utter impossibility of finding any common ground to work on between English and Germans when these sort of outrages are permitted. If the German Government is going to continue to treat these splendid Tyrolese mountaineers in the same manner as the Italians are doing on the southern side of the mountains, it will indeed be ironical . . .

In addition Lady Londonderry asked about the fate of Baron Louis Rothschild, who had been arrested, and she also inquired of Goering about Baron Franckenstein, the Austrian ambassador in London who had anticipated his recall by resigning. 'I hope you will take this letter in the spirit in which it is meant,' she concluded. 'I have been very frank with you, I know, but the situation requires it.'

While this letter reflects Lady Londonderry's feelings, there is some doubt as to whether it was actually sent to Ribbentrop, as no acknowledgement has been found among Lady Londonderry's papers. However, there is no doubt that she wrote in similar terms to Goering, as his answer is extant. The following is a translation of the relevant portion:

Karinhalle, Schorfeide. 22 March 1938 . . . I have instructed the Police to ascertain whether Falconer and Schneider have been arrested. If they have been rightly arrested, they will remain so; if they have been wrongfully arrested, or arrested through a misunderstanding, then they will be liberated at once. I am treating your letter as confidential, as it is only thus I can receive it. When a request is accompanied by a threat it is impossible for me to grant it, for I have never in my life done anything under pressure, and never will. In addition, I can assure you that no man, either in Germany or in Austria, will be persecuted on account of his Catholic faith.

Every Austrian who has been against us in the past, but is now ready to work with us, is heartily welcome. Only those who have behaved as criminals will be refused a pardon, and that simply because otherwise it would be misunderstood by the people . . .

With regard to the former ambassador, Baron Franckenstein, I think I am able to assure you that no one here intends to take any action against him. It was to be expected that he would be recalled, as he, like the Paris and Prague Ambassadors, all occupied very exposed posts. I am, however, convinced that Baron Franckenstein,[1] if he will work, unreservedly for the German Fatherland, will be very welcome

---

[1] He promptly became a British subject, and was killed in an air crash in 1953.

to us. I personally have never heard anything to his disadvantage. I hope that he
will shortly be in Berlin where one can talk with him. I also believe that you have
no need to worry about your friend.

Meanwhile Londonderry continued to correspond with Goering, with
whom he got on best among the Nazi leaders. He would send on Goering's
lengthy replies to the Foreign Office where they were promptly pigeon-
holed. On the night before Chamberlain's visit to Munich in September,
he happened to run into Ward Price, the *Daily Mail* special correspondent, who told him that he was proposing to fly to Munich by the ordinary
commercial service for the signing of the settlement. Londonderry
offered to take him in his own private machine next morning. In Munich
Londonderry had brief talks with Ribbentrop and Goering, also with
the press, and people he met casually in the street, who were all obviously
relieved that the crisis had been averted and cheered Chamberlain
rapturously, although Londonderry had previously told the British
Prime Minister when he set out on the first of his air journeys to see
Hitler, 'You are two years too late!'

'In my conversation with Ribbentrop,' Londonderry noted afterwards,
'I took occasion to mention how the high hopes which had existed in my
mind some time before, when he first came to England, had more or less
disappeared.' Londonderry attributed this, so he told Ribbentrop, to
Germany's inability ever to carry out to the full any undertaking which she
gave.

> I told him that I was full of forebodings because of this invariable feature which
> appeared in any international negotiations as far as Germany was concerned.
>
> Ribbentrop was very impatient and took exception to my criticisms which he
> asserted were quite unfounded.

Their interview came to an abrupt end and Londonderry never saw
Ribbentrop again. Goering, on the other hand, was 'very jubilant, and
said that he was quite sure that this was the way to establish peace for all
time'. But, he added, significantly, '*Der Chamberlain macht immer
Schwerigkeiten*' (Chamberlain is always making difficulties.) Londonderry
did his best to defend Chamberlain, although he did not think much of
the notorious paper that he and Hitler had signed as 'symbolic of the
desire of our two peoples never to go to war with one another again'.

Londonderry was attacked, particularly in Socialist quarters, for this
visit, and he was accused of being pro-Nazi and a supporter of dictator-
ships. He replied in a speech at Sunderland on 10 October 1938 that he
had gone to Germany with one object in mind—'to see the reaction of the
German people to a meeting which I believed to be historic, and for which
I had been working for some years.' He added that he went as an onlooker,
avoiding the leaders, though he could not escape having a word with

Ribbentrop and Goering, and talking to the people he picked out at random in the streets, his great hope being that the four-power settlement would put an end to war, provided the powers decided to act in concert.

'Your policy is certainly being tried,' Churchill wrote to his kinsman on 5 November, 'and I see nothing for it at the moment but await the results of Chamberlain's hopes and experiment.' He went on:

> I view the immediate future with the deepest anxiety, but I am comforted to feel I have no responsibility for the neglect of our defences or for other aspects of the Government's policy. It is incredible that we should have been brought so low in five short years. There is plenty more to come.

'You say my policy is certainly being tried,' Londonderry replied:

> I feel you will agree that there is a great difference between trying it at a time when the Germans were weak and defenceless, and when they were very strong and arrogant . . .
>
> The only difference that I can see between us is that I wanted to get hold of the Germans when they were weak and defenceless and try to make them good members of the comity of nations as Castlereagh did with France, and you on the other hand never believed that policy could succeed. I do not know who was right, but my policy was never tried until it was, I regret to say it, too late. Now I expect our thoughts follow the same line.

On 10 November 1938, the day Londonderry wrote this letter, the civilised world was shocked by the barbarous onslaught on the Jews which took place in Germany in revenge for the assassination of a member of the German Embassy in Paris by a half-demented Jewish youth whose father had been deported to the East by the Gestapo chief Heydrich. In the result 20,000 Jews were arrested in the Reich, 191 synagogues and 171 apartment houses were burnt down, and 7,500 shops smashed and looted, the whole operation being a police action disguised as a popular riot. Londonderry wrote a long letter of expostulation to Goering in which he remarked:

> I have always been sympathetic to your demand for justice after the war, but I have never been in sympathy with the National Socialist form of Government. In fact I find it to be opposed to all those doctrines of Government which, I am quite convinced, in the end make for the progress and well-being of the nations.

To be fair to Goering, he had been in favour of the policy of controlled Jewish emigration but during the previous few days had been compelled by Hitler to hand over Jewish matters for which he had been responsible to Heydrich. Hence the pogrom. Nevertheless Goering did not reply to Londonderry and that was the end of their correspondence. 'This was the last letter I wrote to Goering,' Londonderry afterwards recalled. 'I had realised for some time that the situation was intolerable and that we were inevitably drifting into war.'

One important unpaid job which Londonderry took on at this period was the running of the Civil Air Guard, formed to utilise the facilities afforded by the light aeroplane and other flying clubs, as distinct from the civil flying schools which were fully occupied in giving instruction to short service entrants to the Volunteer Reserve. Its object was to provide a body of men and women with knowledge of flying to assist the R.A.F. in the event of an emergency. By March 1939, as the then Air Minister Sir Kingsley Wood told the House of Commons, the Civil Air Guard had already enrolled 1,400 members in possession of a pilot's 'A' Licence, and 3,800 were undergoing training as fighter and bomber pilots, instructors, observers, wireless operators, air gunners, ferry and ambulance pilots and generally in communication duties. Consequently it provided a useful additional reserve, particularly for the training of pilots and air crews, 'thus lightening the task of the flying schools', in the Minister's words, 'and providing a valuable addition to our training resources'. As the presiding Commissioner of the Civil Air Guard, Londonderry earned considerable credit for himself in his quiet way, although he never claimed it; nor indeed was it recognised by the authorities in any tangible manner.

Throughout the spring and summer of 1939, as the shadow of war loomed nearer, there was a mounting public demand that Chamberlain should include Churchill in the Government. But the Prime Minister remained deaf to all such appeals until the outbreak of war involved a reconstruction of the Government which brought Churchill back to the Admiralty in the same post he had occupied at the outbreak of the First World War. From the moment of Hitler's denunciation of the German–Polish non-Aggression Pact of 1934, Churchill regarded war with Germany as inevitable. Londonderry thought the same, though he persuaded himself until the last moment that it might be averted and he even offered himself as an intermediary to this end.

About this time, the society hostess Emerald Cunard gave a dinner at her house in Grosvenor Square to which the Londonderrys and Churchills among others were invited. The occasion turned out to be particularly unfortunate for Londonderry as he got involved in a violent altercation with his cousin when, as he later recalled to 'Chips' Channon, 'he argued with Winston, and said that France was unreliable and rotten and could not be depended upon. Winston lost his temper, being a fanatical Francophile; and could not forgive Londonderry then, and certainly not later, for being proved right'.

Early in August Londonderry was approached by Lord Winterton and some other Members of Parliament, suggesting that he should go to Berlin and see Hitler in the hope that he might have some influence upon him to moderate his aggressive designs. Londonderry at first demurred on the ground that it was too late but eventually was persuaded to agree to make the attempt, and he informed Lord Halifax, the Foreign

Secretary, accordingly. Halifax was dubious and after talking it over with
Londonderry told him he would not oppose his visit but that he had misgivings. Londonderry then went to see Dr Dircksen, who had succeeded
Ribbentrop as ambassador and told him of his plan. 'You have been making
some very strong speeches lately,' the ambassador replied, 'and I am not
sure that your visit would be welcome.'

Londonderry replied that it was because he had made 'strong speeches'
that he wished to have an interview with the Fuehrer 'to tell him exactly
what I thought and explain the general attitude of the British people'.
Thereupon, the German ambassador agreed to make arrangements for
the visit, for which Londonderry proposed to fly over in his own private
aircraft. However, immediately afterwards Londonderry received a note
from Halifax to the effect that it had come to the Foreign Secretary's
knowledge that Londonderry was engaged in a plan 'to keep the ball
rolling', and asked him particularly to give up the idea of going to Berlin.
Londonderry agreed, informing the ambassador he had cancelled the
proposed visit. Londonderry could never understand the reason for
Halifax's sudden change of mind. It may well have been due to the fact
that there was another intermediary in the field in the person of Birger
Dahlerus, a Swedish businessman and friend of Goering, who had
proposed that Goering should make a secret visit to England, landing at a
deserted airfield on 23 August and being taken direct by car to Chequers.
To this plan Goering, Chamberlain and Halifax were agreeable. But the
idea was knocked on the head by Hitler, who was now determined on war.
He sent the Prime Minister a message to the effect that he did not think
that Goering's visit would be 'immediately helpful'. The reason became
clear next day when the stunning news of the Ribbentrop–Molotov pact
was announced. Thus Germany's eastern flank was secured, at least for
the time being, and Poland's fate was sealed, since a secret protocol was
attached to the pact providing for the partition between the Reich and
the Soviet Union of that unfortunate state, whose integrity Chamberlain
had guaranteed to no purpose.

'On September 3rd 1939 we were once more at war with Germany,'
noted Londonderry. 'It was the end of a chapter.'

8

Londonderry was in London when war was declared. The two women who
played the most important parts in his life reacted differently to the news
in their letters to him. 'All sorts of rot are going on here,' Lady Londonderry wrote from Mount Stewart. 'Air raid warning and black outs!! As
if anyone cared or wished to bomb Belfast—but there it is, and we are
under orders. Well, here I stay, as no one wants me and I can work here

. . . I think Hitler is going out like the Götterdämmerung!! I hope so anyhow.'

Ethel Desborough had immediately handed over both her country houses for war purposes. On 10 September she wrote to Londonderry:

> You have been more than ever in my thoughts, but somehow I have hardly put pen to paper. First there was the rush of completely 'evacuating' Taplow—one's whole life for 52 years packed up in 3 days . . .
>
> Our 240 occupants (190 London babies and 47 attendants) seem happy at Taplow. Panshanger is to be a Maternity Hospital—we are keeping the West wing for ourselves. Five London families evacuated to the village at Panshanger returned to their homes the next day. They were at the different farms, and were given beautiful new milk—but the women said that they and their children preferred beer, which they drank at every meal in London . . .
>
> You do not know the consolation you are in my life. I have thought so much of the years.

The years of the Second World War were not happy ones for the Londonderrys, although they did not show it outwardly. Nevertheless they threw themselves wholeheartedly into various kinds of war work. Much of Lord Londonderry's time was spent at Mount Stewart, carrying on his normal civic duties, in addition to which he became Northern Ireland Regional Commandant of the Air Training Corps. He enjoyed being airborne with the cadets. 'It is quite amusing, as it gives me an opportunity for flying,' he told Lady Desborough, 'and the boys seem to like it very much.'

'I congratulate the Marquess on escaping all responsibility for this monstrous aggression on European peace by a Government of Dunderheads,' Bernard Shaw wrote to Lady Londonderry on 1 January 1940.

> I can understand an English Cabinet being unable to bear leaving Hitler and the Reich victorious in the Polish war, and therefore for the moment first fiddle in the European concert. But when Stalin knocked him out, he was only second trombone. And anyhow we could have found a better excuse than 'No case: abuse the plaintiff's attorney.'
>
> And after Poland, Finland! We shall presently be attacked from the west, through Ireland, the British Finland, and shall have to re-occupy it and swallow all our virtuous indignation.
>
> Forgive me: I should not have dragged in the tiresome subject. But who can refrain from spluttering? One folly after another!

If things did not turn out as Bernard Shaw anticipated, it was because De Valera, the Irish Prime Minister, was determined to preserve his country's neutrality at all costs, which he succeeded in doing while denying the use of the 'treaty' ports to the Allies, which resulted in great loss of life to British merchant seamen. (The ports had been handed back to southern Ireland by the Chamberlain Government, an action which Londonderry had always deplored.) As Honorary Air Commodore of No 502 Auxiliary Squadron stationed at Aldergrove, Lord Londonderry would invite many of the R.A.F. officers who had been posted to Northern Ireland to Mount Stewart. As a result Flight-Lieutenant Viscount Bury, who had been seconded from the army for flying duties, met Mairi Stewart, the youngest Londonderry daughter. They were married in the private chapel at Mount Stewart on 10 December 1940.

There was some talk that Londonderry would be invited to rejoin the Northern Ireland Government, but Lord Craigavon, still Prime Minister, made no move in this direction. Neither did his successor John Andrews, who took over on Craigavon's sudden death in November 1940. Nor did Churchill, who was four years older than his cousin, offer him any post, as he might have done when he moved into Downing Street. The Air Ministry, which Londonderry would have particularly liked, went to a Liberal, Sir Archibald Sinclair. So Londonderry carried on with his civic and flying duties in Northern Ireland, encouraging both the Ulster university graduates and flying cadets by words and example. 'France, our ally, has been forced to make terms, so our course is plain and clear,' he declared at the Queen's University graduation in July 1940 at which as Chancellor he conferred degrees. 'We shall not lay down our arms until Nazism is destroyed and the countries of the world can enjoy the blessings of peace based on freedom and independence.'

Londonderry's daughter, Maureen Stanley, died tragically in 1942 at the early age of forty-one and, in an endeavour to distract his mind from this blow, he set about writing an account of British air policy in the context of his two terms of office at the Air Ministry and his later attempts in a private capacity to promote an understanding with Germany. His work, which was published by Macmillan in 1943 under the title *Wings of Destiny*, was dedicated to Lord Trenchard, so-called Father of the R.A.F., to whom Londonderry gave the chief credit for the successful outcome of the Battle of Britain.

> Not only will the Battle of Britain [he wrote] be referred to as one of the great events when these island shores were saved from invasion as in Elizabethan and Napoleonic times, but it will also stand out as the occasion on which the Air Arm destroyed 2,375 German machines in three months in successive day and night raids. The policy of the Independent Air Force, which Trenchard and his devoted band spent their lives to establish, was the policy which won the most signal victory of modern times. History will record that the Battle of Britain in the late summer of 1940 was the first time the great German Luftwaffe met its match and for the first time was decisively defeated.

Although she was sixty when the war broke out, Lady Londonderry proved a most active and energetic President of the County Down Branch of the British Red Cross and also of the Durham Branch, particularly in training men and women in first aid, ambulance work, nursing and the like, as well as providing parcels for prisoners of war and furnishing help for air raid victims and other war sufferers, such as bombed-out refugees. Outside Belfast and the counties of Antrim and Down, the Red Cross was virtually non-existent in Northern Ireland. This prompted Lord Londonderry to take the initiative in forming branches in the other four counties (Tyrone, Londonderry, Fermanagh and Armagh) with the help of the Primate D'Arcy, Archbishop of Armagh. In order to co-ordinate all these activities, Londonderry, at the suggestion of the Red Cross authorities in London, now formed a Central Committee of which he became first President and in 1941 purchased a house in Belfast (63 Donegall Pass) as the Committee's headquarters.

Lady Londonderry also resuscitated the Women's Legion, of which she was President, and formed a special flying section consisting of qualified pilots for such duties as ferrying machines, besides ground personnel for cleaning and greasing them as well as wireless and parachute maintenance work. Writing to Herbert Morrison, the Minister of Home Security, on 19 August 1944, Lady Londonderry described the work of the Legion's mobile canteens in London during the period of intensive bombing:

Night after night they went to the East End where they fed the Auxiliary Fire Service and the Air Raid Precautions rescue parties, as well as the bombed and homeless victims of the raids. They were one of the very first organisations to realise the value of shelter feeding, which did so much to keep up morale. Three of our women were killed in the fearful Blitz on Bermondsey. They were then driving cars for the W.V.S. and as the expected personnel did not turn up, the then Commandant and her two officers took the mobile themselves, thus meeting their deaths.

It was during this time of the bad Blitz that the Ministry of Food asked the Women's Legion to help them. With the bombing came the destruction of the docks area, leaving acres of wrecked homes and a wholesale evacuation to outside areas. This meant that the dockers had either to live in shelters, or leave home at 5 a.m. In both cases the feeding problem became acute; many of the men had not had a hot meal for three weeks. This was in the depth of that very cold winter [1940–41]. The Ministry of Food will tell you how pleased they were with the hot meals provided in those days.

Later the work was continued for the dockers before and after D day to facilitate the special loading programme of vessels used in the invasion of Europe, and at the height of these operations the Legion provided a million meals a month. General Eisenhower, the Supreme Commander of the Allied Expeditionary Force, was greatly impressed by the consequent saving in man-hours, and on 15 July 1944, a few weeks after D day, he wrote to Lady Londonderry: 'I should like to take this opportunity to say how grateful I am for the help your organisation has given to the Allied forces under my command. It has been much appreciated.'

Lord Londonderry now had to make provision for the future. 'I am toying with the idea of pulling down Wynyard and making a smaller house for Robin to live in,' he had told Lady Desborough in December

1940. 'It is no use labouring sentiment. Wynyard is 98 years old and no more. It is only an idea at the moment, but in view of the tremendous changes this insane war will bring about, we must think of everything.' However, nothing came of this, since Wynyard Hall was taken over by Durham County Council as a teachers' training college, although a wing was retained for Robin, who had joined up with the Royal Artillery at the beginning of the war and was given leave from his parliamentary duties to serve overseas. 'I have been immersed in settlements, wills etc. etc,' Londonderry wrote to Lady Desborough at one stage of the war, 'and I have realised that when the will is read out there will be the usual long faces. However I must hang on to keep the Government out of Death Duties as long as possible. To add to the complications my lawyer's premises have been totally destroyed by fire.' Unfortunately, as things turned out, Londonderry did not make over Wynyard to his son until 1945; and, although he himself was to die a millionaire in 1949, the estate could not escape death duties, which it would have done had he lived for another year. Also, as Robin was to die in 1955, the estate had to bear two levies of death duties within the comparatively short space of six years.

Another projected disposal which failed to materialise was that of Londonderry House, which had been requisitioned by the army for the duration of the war but which the National Trust seriously considered accepting after the war. The present author remembers being in London on leave during the war when he learned that Lord Londonderry was paying one of his comparatively rare visits to the house. So he called one Sunday morning and rang the bell at the Hertford Street entrance. A few moments later, the door was opened by Londonderry himself, and as he did so he shouted down to the solitary 'odd man' in the basement. 'It's all right, I'm answering the door!' When Lord Esher, the chairman of the National Trust, asked how many indoor servants the Londonderrys employed before the war, the answer was, 'Twenty-eight in the kitchen and sixteen in the steward's room.'

James Lees-Milne, who was then working for the National Trust, has recalled an evening in July 1944 when he was invited by Lady Cunard to dine in her suite at the Dorchester. 'The party consisted of Freya Stark, the heroine of the party,' he noted in his diary at the time, 'Nancy Mitford, Lord and Lady Londonderry, Oliver Stanley and the Duke of Devonshire. I sat next to Emerald and Lady Londonderry . . . She told me that this evening's flying bomb made for Londonderry House, but on seeing it swerved to the left over the Park, and exploded near the Serpentine. Lord Londonderry . . . is very handsome and patrician . . .'

In the course of conversation at this dinner, according to Lees-Milne, the Duke of Devonshire related that he had received an indignant letter of remonstrance from the Duke of Wellington complaining that Devon-shire's daughter-in-law Lady Deborah Cavendish, who was a sister of Nancy Mitford, had given her son at his christening the name Morny, a diminutive of one of the Wellington titles, Earl of Mornington. 'How would you like it,' wrote Wellington, 'if I christened my grandson Harty or Burlington?' (Marquess of Hartington and Earl of Burlington were two of the Devonshire titles.) Nancy said, 'But Debo christened him after her favourite jockey. She had never even heard of the Duke of Welling-ton!'

'You should have put this duke of a hundred years creation in his proper place,' said Lady Cunard, turning to Devonshire, whose family had acquired two dukedoms in the seventeenth century. 'You must have courage, Eddie.' Whereupon Londonderry interpolated, 'I too am only a peer of mushroom growth!'

One thing which annoyed Londonderry greatly during the war was the censorship of his mail, and he was convinced that the letters he wrote, as well as those addressed to him, were subjected to a special scrutiny on account of his alleged pro-German sympathies before the war. In one instance, however, the censors had a case. In May 1943 a 'great Te Deum' was held in St Paul's Cathedral to celebrate the allied victory in North Africa. The King and Queen, as well as the sovereigns of Norway and Yugoslavia and other royalty and leaders including General De Gaulle, and members of both Houses of Parliament, received invitations to attend. The service was originally fixed for noon. Londonderry happened to be in London at the time and the butler at Mount Street opened the invita-tion which had been sent there informing him of the time of the service, and sent off a telegram with this information to Londonderry House. The censors stopped the telegram and informed the security authorities, who 'at once decided', in Henry Channon's words, 'that the great church, crowded with all the notabilities of England, might prove too tempting a target for the Luftwaffe; so it was decided to alter the time [to 6.0 p.m.]. Even so there was some uneasiness all day that the Germans might get to know and bomb us. But nothing of the sort happened. Instead, though it had been hurriedly organised, we had an impressive effortless English service'.

In an undated letter to Ethel Desborough, probably in 1943, London-derry opened his heart to her as he had never done before, 'because,' as he put it, 'that is the cross I feel I have to bear and it is a tremendous effort to be self-controlled, pleasant to those I continually meet and as helpful as I can be in these terrible days'. He went on:

When Baldwin removed me I instinctively knew that I had finished, that my active life was over and that I had to fall back on resources which it is difficult to cultivate when you have been in the middle of politics as I had been since the end of the [last] war. In your letter you say so kindly, 'The swing of the pendulum will come.' But of course I know it won't be for me and I confess that knowing this, as I have known it, I have touched almost the lowest depths of despair, and it has been the example of courage like yours and others which have kept me going.

I was so fortunate in so many ways. Whatever I touched seemed to turn to gold. I seemed to succeed in everything, not brilliantly or exceptionally, but still everything went well, everyone helped me, and I seemed to have so many friends and well wishers, and then suddenly it all came to an end. I tried loyally to carry on outside, then I dabbled in diplomacy with an idea which I know was correct but I could not somehow work it with anyone who counted. Then I did a lot of flying. I made speeches which people seemed to want to hear; we went on entertaining and everyone seemed to want to come.

Then I had some bitter exchanges with Baldwin and Chamberlain whom I knew were wrong although I commended Chamberlain for Munich but regretted everything he subsequently did. Then I fell out with Winston because I wanted to achieve by what I thought was statesmanship what he wanted to achieve by war. That quarrel I think originated some time before because I was never really fond of F.E. who completely absorbed Winston to the exclusion of W's allies like myself, and I disagreed with both and rightly disagreed over their Irish policy which has had such fatal results. So I really planned a bad crash and was not strong enough or clever enough to strike out on my own.

So the war, the crisis of our lives, finds me completely isolated and under a sort of shadow which I cannot get away from. Politicians burn their boats and of course there are many who have come to greatness but have kept it to themselves, unlike me in this letter, and this will be the only letter of the kind which you will get from me. You are so clever and observant that you probably have known all I have told you but have wanted to keep up my spirits. However I want you to know that I have no illusions about it and that I am bitterly disappointed. I had great chances and I missed them by not being good enough and that really sums up the whole thing.

I am intensely lucky. But for this cussed war I am quite happy at home and I pray that will go on. A politician who has missed is really terribly out of a job. You are not wanted for the big things and there is really no place in the smaller things. All the many figure head duties were very good accompaniments to the central and dominating duty, but they are uninteresting by themselves and it is so difficult to keep oneself up to the mark. I have always been physically fit because I have made that a business: exercises etc. etc, but I find it very difficult to keep mentally fit with the only exercises I can employ and I get the nightmare of running to seed. I was always so sorry for Hailsham, because the moment he took off his harness he became an old man.

I get so impatient about the attitude towards me in books and articles with reference to my German activities and I hate special pleading, and if I do write retorts and I have written 2 or 3 in public, no one seems to read them or notice them. Winston has been distinctly unfriendly and I often wonder why he never would take the trouble to find out what I was at. We had an altercation at Lady Cunard's once when I told him the French were no use and our slavish adherence to the French and their world policy was a mistake. That was the summer before the war. W. did suggest to me to resign when Chamberlain at last consented to re-arm and I wish I had done so because my loyalty to my old colleagues afterwards precluded me from joining Winston which I would like to have done. Then the way Baldwin treated me entailed a certain dignity on my part which I think was completely misunderstood.

Edward Halifax a short time ago said he thought I made a mistake in going on after I was Secretary of State for Air, but you and I talked that over and at the finish I certainly took your view. It all has worked out badly and I know it is some inherent fault in myself. However I know I have got to carry on and I am doing my best.

You may wonder why I have written this to you. The reason is that I feel you are omniscient and that I do not want you to think that I am so conceited as not to realise that with all the advantages I had and with your constant and affectionate help I have been a miserable failure. I think poor Edie realises this and I know Robin does too, but E is constant in her support and her care for me and I never would believe from anything she says that I have failed to give her the position she should have had.

Londonderry continued to feel aggrieved by the result of his differences with Churchill, who did not include him in the Conservative Caretaker Government which he formed in May 1945. 'Winston's determined attitude towards me is all the more incomprehensible,' Londonderry told Lady Desborough shortly afterwards, 'and I doubt if I shall ever know why he went out of his way to destroy me which he certainly did.' However, Robin Castlereagh seems to have sensed the reason accurately enough when he told Stanley Baldwin's son in a letter he wrote to him after his father's death that it was his pre-war attitude to Nazi Germany. 'This cost him the friendship of his friend, relative and colleague Winston Churchill.' Another post which he might have filled was Governor of Northern Ireland, but on Churchill's advice the King appointed a retired Vice-Admiral, Earl Granville, who was married to Queen Elizabeth's elder sister Lady Rose Bowes-Lyon. 'As you know we did not want it,' Londonderry wrote to Lady Desborough at the time, 'but from the letters I am getting some people seem disappointed. However, the fact of the Queen's sister coming has given a lot of satisfaction.'

After the war he made a number of charitable dispositions of his property. In 1945 he presented his Welsh mansion and grounds, Plâs Machynlleth, to the people of the town, after the girls' school which had been evacuated there for the 'duration' returned to London. He also converted Dene House, which he owned at Seaham Harbour and which had been the chief colliery agent's house, into a sanatorium for sick miners. Meanwhile Seaham Hall continued to be used as a general hospital, while the Royal Aero Club occupied most of Londonderry House rent free as a national aviation centre.

During the war Londonderry had taken up gliding and he went on with this, showing enthusiasm and courage. Towards the end of 1945 he met with an unfortunate mishap while practising at the Ards airport. He wrote to the present author at the time:

Mount Stewart. 11 January 1946 . . . I did not have a flying accident. I was unfortunate in the cable which launches the glider into the air breaking at exactly the wrong moment. In fact in this elementary gliding it is the only danger which can be said to exist and this should be eliminated by good staff work. As I have been head of the A.T.C. in Northern Ireland for some three years and have been working hard to get winches and cables put on a high level, it can be said that the responsibility falls on me. I would only add that we have been clamouring to the Air Ministry for a new cable for something like six months. However, I am not complaining—it was the fortune of war—but I am afraid I shall be immobilised for some weeks yet.

His accident was followed by a series of strokes, which impeded his power of speech. He wrote what was to be his final letter to Lady Desborough, since he had a further stroke shortly afterwards which prevented him from writing in his own hand.[1]

Mount Stewart. 21 September 1947 . . . I have been ill but am all right now in the sense that I have had a light warning and that I have got to go slow and realise that my active life is really over. I have only just realised that I have never stayed in the same place for 10 days and in the forties, 1940–1947, the war years and after I have had endless worries and sorrows with you and Edie my only real friends and supports. That is the whole story really.

I was trying to do every little job because I have had to realise that I do not come into the bigger ones, here, London, Durham, and I went over for the meeting of the House of Lords in August and several little duties. I left London in the morning perfectly well. The sun seemed to be hitting the front of the aeroplane and making it all very bright and hot. I wasn't flying it; but to cut a long story short I arrived here not feeling at all well and got straight into bed where I remained for a fortnight. I then felt quite well, did a little more than a wise person would have done, got another warning in the form of my speech not being clear and my right hand not being as efficient as it should be, and was told by the doctor to rest completely for 3 weeks and I should be perfectly well. I am nearing the end of a fortnight and feel perfectly well but I have got to remember that as regards activities and rushing about I am 70 . . .

I am doing nothing and have cancelled endless small jobs so as to concentrate on Princess Elizabeth who comes to Wynyard on the 22 October to lay a University foundation stone. After that I am proposing to lead a much easier life and a more pleasant one. One's regrets have just got to be forgotten . . .

I really am not bothering about politics. I think all the politicians are quite useless. I have been reading the histories of the last century and all the politicians were actually the most terrible liars, foreign affairs was a game, and no one ever wrote a letter or a despatch without his tongue in his cheek. I now see why I failed to understand the very second-class people I had to deal with and how glad they must have been to get me out of the way. I am sorry I failed to handle Winston because he really could have saved the war instead of gaining the credit which he fully deserves for winning it, and we are now paying the price. However he and Chamberlain were on different lines.

I am getting much interest from letters I am getting from a few people, who think I was right and everyone else wrong, who come across my books at libraries,

[1] Lady Desborough died at Panshanger, aged eighty-four, in 1952. An obituary letter in *The Times* described her as 'a lady of great age, lying half paralysed in a huge empty house, and saying with the heart-rending ghost of a gay smile "We did have fun, didn't we?" '

but that the historian will deal with in years to come I think . . . If only someone had been powerful enough to combine Chamberlain with his passion for peace with Winston even as late as 1937, we need never have had the war with its ghastly results as the price for Winston gaining an everlasting historical name as a war leader. That is all that has been achieved on our account and I do not believe the price has been anything like paid yet, if it ever will be.

In the next few months Londonderry's condition became progressively worse, as he found it more and more difficult to articulate. Sholto Douglas and his wife spent the following Christmas at Mount Stewart, and Douglas was very concerned by Londonderry's plight. 'However the old boy is fighting back gallantly, as one would expect, and he clearly improved while we were there,' he told Robin Castlereagh on his return to London. 'If only he could get his speech back.'

But he never did recover his speech, and his general condition continued to deteriorate. There was no question of removing him to hospital, and he died at Mount Stewart during the night of 10–11 February 1949. For three days his remains lay in a flower-covered coffin in the private chapel of the mansion. On 14 February he was buried in Tir-N'an Oge to the strains of his piper playing 'The Flowers of the Forest'.

'I am very sorry,' his friend Henry Channon noted in his diary when he heard the news; 'he was a good friend and a grand seigneur of the old school; even his appearance was almost theatrically 18th century.'

Slim, with an elegant figure and pointed features he was red in the face and dressed with distinction. He was always gay and amiable and completely sure of himself.

In the long run he will be proved right politically; he always maintained that there were only two possible courses for us: either we make friends with Germany, or, if this was impossible to re-arm. We did neither, and war was the result. But he was unpopular and much criticised at the time for his views.

Three days later a Memorial Service was held in Westminster Abbey which was attended by an unexpectedly large number of people, members of all political parties, friends and acquaintances. They included the Ulster writer Helen Waddell, whose scholarly books had been much admired by Lord Londonderry, who had actually cut three pages out of his copy of *Peter Abelard* so that he could carry them about with him. 'I didn't realise how fond of him I was till he was gone,' she wrote at the time. 'He had an extraordinary feeling for me—it came out in his letters —not amorous . . . The notices about him in *The Times* were really charming—old Winterton remembering him when he was "Charley", and the Air Force chiefs writing how he had fought for them when everybody else was against them. And they all said, which I think was true, that he never said a hard word to anybody.' Among the M.P.s were the Tory Henry Channon and the Socialist Arthur Henderson, who had been Air Minister in the then Labour Government. As they were leaving the Abbey together after the service, Henderson remarked to Channon, 'Possibly Londonderry was right all the time.'

'Of course he was,' Channon replied.[1]

---

[1] Lady Londonderry survived her husband by ten years and died on 23 April 1959 at Mount Stewart, where she is buried beside him in Tir N'an Oge. Their daughter Margaret, a noted writer and war correspondent, who died in 1968, is also buried there. The eighth Marquess and his wife, who predeceased him by four years, are both buried at Wynyard.

GENEALOGY OF THE FIRST MARQUESS OF LONDONDERRY

THERE HAS BEEN considerable controversy and some confusion about the ancestry of the noble family of Londonderry, who in the time of the sixth Marquess, almost a century ago, resumed by Royal Licence the family surname of Stewart in addition to that of Vane-Tempest, thus becoming Vane-Tempest-Stewart. In the first place, we have the categorical statement of the third Marquess in the introduction to his edition of the official correspondence and private papers of his statesman brother Castlereagh. 'The ancestor of our family was a native of Scotland,' the third Marquess wrote in 1848. 'He was one of the Stewarts of Wigtownshire.' He goes on to state that 'John Stewart, descended from Sir Thomas Stewart of Minto (ancestor of Lord Blantyre), settled in Ireland in the reign of James I, who granted to his kinsman the Duke of Lennox and to his relations that large tract of land in the County of Donegal lying between Lough Foyle and Lough Swilly, which had been forfeited during his reign and that of Queen Elizabeth.'

This land, according to the third Marquess, the King is said to have divided into eight manors, one of which called Ballylawn he granted with the adjacent territory of Ballyreach to 'John Stewart, Esq., a relative of the Duke's, and to his heirs forever; which manor, together with the whole of the land annexed, descended, in regular lineal succession to Robert first Marquess of Londonderry'. John Stewart is also stated to have built a castle on the estate which he called Stewart's Court, apparently settling the place with Protestants from Scotland, and exercising the manorial rights of free fishing in Lough Swilly and other privileges including the holding of a local court, known as a court baron. There is no reason at least to doubt the latter statement since Charles Stewart, the third Marquess, was originally raised to the peerage of the United Kingdom as Baron Stewart of Stewart's Court and Ballylawn in 1814. Unfortunately Stewart's Court was allowed to fall into ruin in the nineteenth century, but the ruins are still recognisable a few miles from Moville.

On the other hand, writing in 1871, the third Marquess's kinsman Sir James Stewart, eighth Baronet, of Fort Stewart, Ramelton, County Donegal, informed Mr P. H. McKerlie, the historian of Galloway in

Wigtownshire, that the Londonderry family 'have not any right whatever to assume the name of Stewart; they are MacGregors and a member of their own family living near this admitted that fact before a large party in my house a short time ago.'[1] What credence, if any, can be attached to this statement? At the elections which Castlereagh contested in County Down, particularly that of 1805 against Colonel Charles Meade, he was taunted with the MacGregor story. The members of the Clan MacGregor had been proscribed for treasonable acts against the sovereign at the beginning of the seventeenth century, when many of them changed their names, although the rebel tradition was to be carried on by their most famous freebooter Robert known as Rob Roy and the subject of Sir Walter Scott's novel of that name. This raises the question of the identity of John Stewart of Ballylawn. Was he a Stewart, or was he, as some claim, a MacGregor?

When Robert Stewart, whose direct descent from John of Ballylawn is incontestable, was raised to the peerage of Ireland as Baron Londonderry in 1789, he was required to register his pedigree with the College of Arms in Dublin. In doing so he cited the confirmation of the grant of the Donegal property by Charles I in 1629 to John Stewart, who is described in the letters patent as 'one entitled to bear arms' (*armiger*) and 'a native of our kingdom of Scotland'. Many years later, when Lord Londonderry, by then the first Marquess, was living at Mount Stewart, a correspondent wrote to him about his ancestry, apparently bringing up the MacGregor story again and asking Londonderry to state plainly from whom he was in fact descended. He replied as follows:

> *Mount Stewart,*
> *April 20th 1817*
>
> Sir,
>   In answer to your letter, not having leisure to examine a Multitude of Old Family Records, & Papers, engrossed in Latin, in so difficult and obscure a Hand to read, or understand, I cannot well do more than to say I have always understood that I am lineally descended, and hold my Property in Donegal, not by Purchase, but as Heir to Alex^r McCauley Stewart, the first Patentee who came from Scotland.
>   I am Sir,
>   Your Obedient Servant
>   Londonderry

[1] The member of the family referred to was obviously a descendant of Robert the first Lord Londonderry's younger brother Alexander Stewart who purchased the estate at Ards, between Creeslough and Dunfanaghy in Co. Donegal in 1782. Alexander's grandson, Alexander John Robert Stewart, was living at Ards House, which is not far from Fort Stewart, Ramelton, when Sir James Stewart wrote his letter in 1871, and the information may well have been volunteered by this member of the family who would have been a second cousin of both Frederick the 4th Marquess and Henry the 5th Marquess. Ards House later became a Capuchin monastery. It has since been demolished. See P. H. McKerlie. *A History of the Lands and their Owners in Galloway* (1906), at p. 304.

Now there is no doubt that the original grant of the Donegal property, amounting to 1,000 acres, was made by James I in the Plantation of Ulster to one Alexander McAuley, McAwley or McAulay, who added the name Stewart to his own, as did other grantees in the neighbourhood, either as a compliment to the king or to his representative the Duke of Lennox, both of whom were Stewarts.[1] It is probable that McAuley never visited the property. At all events it is practically certain that he exchanged it with John MacGregor (alias Stewart) for the latter's land in Dumbarton-shire, where the name MacGregor had been proscribed and where various members of the Clan took the name of Stewart. That these included John, the Londonderry ancestor, appears from a declaration made before the Ulster King of Arms in Dublin in 1639, which states definitely that the Donegal John Stewart was the second son of John MacGregor of Laggarie, Dumbartonshire, where the principal landlord was also the Duke of Lennox. It therefore looks very much as if John Stewart did not come from Wigtownshire nor was he descended from Sir Thomas Stewart of Minto, but that he came from Dumbartonshire and that he was born a MacGregor. Also the word 'heir' in the first Lord Londonderry's letter quoted above seems to have been used in the sense of one who receives or is entitled to receive property as the legal representative of the former owner.

The proscription of the Clan MacGregor was not lifted until 1774, and in spite of the romantic association with Rob Roy the name no doubt continued to carry a slur, as evidenced by the use of it against Robert Stewart, the first Marquess, and his son Castlereagh at various County Down elections. No doubt too by the time the third Marquess, who had married the Durham heiress Lady Frances Anne Vane-Tempest, came to edit his brother's correspondence, he preferred to overlook the correct ancestry. Anyhow he was able to find a way out of the genealogical dilemma through his paternal great-grandmother, who was a daughter of Thomas

---

[1] Captain Nicholas Pynner, who made an official survey of the Ulster Plantation lands in 1618 and 1619, recorded that Alexander McAwley alias Stewart had been granted 1,000 acres forming Ballyneigh on which he had built a house: this house subsequently became known as Ballylawn or Stewart's Court. Pynner states that there were originally eleven families on the property, two being freeholders and nine lease-holders, but none was Irish, although no doubt Irish sub-tenants were soon introduced: see Rev. George Hill. *An Historical Account of the Plantation in Ulster* (1877), at p. 510. According to Hill, McAuley, the first patentee, 'sold these lands to Alexander Stewart, probably a kinsman, and John Stewart son of the purchaser held the lands in 1629'. This statement is misleading, since there is little doubt that the lands, which accommodated the eleven families in 1619, were not sold but exchanged for other lands in Scotland as stated below and that it was John Stewart to whom they were conveyed.

Stewart of Fort Stewart, Ramelton,[1] and through him directly descended from Sir Thomas Stewart of Minto, as duly recorded at the Lyon Office in Edinburgh. Thus it is true to say that the Londonderrys are indeed descended from Stewart of Minto but through the female and not the male line.

[1] Younger brother of Alexander 2nd Baronet and great-great-great-great-grandfather of James the 8th Baronet mentioned above.

SOURCES AND NOTES

The Stewart family genealogy is described in CC, Vol. I, pp. 1–4;
Alison, Vol. I; Hyde *The Rise of Castlereagh* (1933); and article by W. A.
Stewart. 3 vols. Edinburgh, 1861.

CC = *Memoirs and Correspondence of Viscount Czstlereagh*. Edited by his
brother the Marquess of Londonderry. 12 vols. London, 1848–49.

DCRO = Durham County Record Office, Durham.

Frances Anne = Edith Marchioness of Londonderry. *Frances Anne. The
Life and Times of Frances Anne Marchioness of Londonderry and her
husband Charles Third Marquess of Londonderry*. London, 1958.

HCRO = Hertfordshire County Record Office, St Albans.

PRO = Public Record Office, Kew.

PRONI = Public Record Office of Northern Ireland, Belfast.

Retrospect = Edith Marchioness of Londonderry. *Retrospect*. London,
1938.

Wings of Destiny = Charles 7th Marquess of Londonderry. *Wings of
Destiny*, London, 1943.

Chapter I THE STEWARTS

SECTION I

The Stewart family genealogy is described in CC, Vol I, pp. 1–4;
Alison, Vol. I; Hyde *The Rise of Castlereagh* (1933); and article by W. A.
Stewart ('Pedigree of the Stewarts of Ballylawn now Marquess of London-
derry') in *The Genealogists' Magazine*, Vol. 7, No 6, June 1936. See also
Appendix above.

On the Colville family and its relations with the Stewarts, see article
by J. M. Dickson in the *Ulster Journal of Archaeology*, Vol. V (May–Sept.
1899).

Bernard Ward's letter to Judge Ward 10 Nov. 1744 is in the Castle
Ward Papers in PRONI: D.2092/1/6/94.

The letter about the Alexanders in Newtownards in 1787 is in the
Drennan Letters, at p. 237.

Alexander Stewart's failure to secure the reversion of the Belfast seat
in Parliament was due to his differences with Lord Donegall's agent

William Macartney, with whose father Isaac, Alexander Stewart had served his time as an apprentice in the linen industry in Belfast. As a quid pro quo Stewart had hoped to bring William Macartney in for Newtownards, but he was unable to do this since the borough had passed into the control of the Ponsonby family. The details are set out in a 52-page letter from William Macartney to his son Arthur, circa 1745-47, in the Ellison–Macartney Papers in PRONI under reference T.2873.

SECTION 2

Hertford's letter to Robert Stewart 25 Sept. 1766 about getting him an Irish peerage is in the Castlereagh Papers Vol. XXIV: PRONI.

Lady Frances Stewart's 'melancholy adventure' is described by Horace Walpole in his *Letters* (ed. Toynbee), xii, at p. 142; also in the *Hamwood Papers of the Ladies of Llangollen* (ed. Bell), at p. 277.

Camden's letter to his daughter about her son Charles, 5 Dec. 1784, is in the Charlemont MSS in the Royal Irish Academy, Dublin.

SECTION 3

On the elder Robert Stewart's career, see Alison, Vol. I, CC Vol. I, and Hyde *The Rise of Castlereagh*.

Dance's plans, drawings, and letters on the rebuilding of Mount Stewart, with letters from Castlereagh, his father Londonderry and John Ferguson, are in the Soane Museum in London: Slider No. 3, Set 9.

Haliday's letter about the Temple of the Winds, dated July 1795, is in the Charlemont MSS in the Royal Irish Academy.

Charles Stewart's letter to Castlereagh about their father's approaching death dated Vienna 19 Jan. 1821 is in DCRO and has been published in *Frances Anne*, at p. 58.

SECTION 4

On Castlereagh's Irish career, see particularly Hyde, *The Rise of Castlereagh*. Besides Alison, biographies and political studies have been written by Professor Sir Charles Webster (1931-34), Sir John Marriott (1936), Ione Leigh (1951), C. J. Bartlett (1966), and J. H. Derry (1976).

The question of Castlereagh's alleged blackmailing in the context of his last years is the subject of *The Strange Death of Lord Castlereagh* (1959) by the present writer.

Interesting sidelights on Castlereagh's private life have been given by the Countess Brownlow in *Reminiscences of a Septuagenarian* (1868), Princess Dorothea Lieven in *The Private Letters of Princess Lieven to*

Prince Metternich. Edited by Peter Quennell (1937), and *The Journal of Mrs Arbuthnot*. Edited by Francis Bamford and the Duke of Wellington, 2 vols. (1950).

SECTION 5

Castlereagh's private letters to his wife were formerly in the possession of the late Philip Marquess of Lothian and were preserved at Blickling Hall, Norfolk. There is a typescript of the letters in PRONI.

An interesting and most detailed account of the family jewels ('The Londonderry Jewels'), written by Edith Marchioness of Londonderry, is in PRONI: D. 3099/3/20/1A.

SECTION 6

The letters concerning Queen Victoria's refusal to accept the dedication by the 3rd Marquess of the Castlereagh *Memoirs and Correspondence* are in DCRO: D/Lo/C/124.

The Queen's letter to Lord Derby on giving the Garter to the 3rd Marquess is in *The Letters of Queen Victoria* (1908), II, at p. 391.

Chapter II   THE VANE-TEMPESTS

SECTION 1

For the life of Charles Stewart, the 3rd Marquess, see Alison and *Frances Anne*. See also R. W. Sturgess. *Aristocrat in Business: The Third Marquess of Londonderry as Coalowner and Portbuilder* (1975). There are many references to him, some far from complimentary, in *The Greville Diaries*. Edited by Lytton Strachey and Roger Fulford, 8 vols. (1939), and other contemporary memoirs, such as Henry Lord Holland's *Holland House Diaries*. Ed. A. D. Kriegel (1977); also in Dorothy G. McGuigan. *Metternich and the Duchess* (1975).

The letter from Charles Stewart to George Hardinge describing his attempt to save Lord Waldegrave from drowning at Eton in 1794 has been taken from a copy made by Horace Walpole now in the possession of Mary Countess Waldegrave.

The letters about Lady Catherine Stewart's death from Wellington and Castlereagh were found in an old bag at Plâs Machynlleth, having apparently been placed there by the 5th Marquess some time before his death in 1884. They are now in DCRO: D/Lo/C/118.

The incident of Charles Stewart pinching the Austrian Countess's daughter is mentioned in *The Greville Diaries*, ed. Strachey and Fulford, I, pp. 27–28.

On Hambletonian and the Stubbs painting, see H. Montgomery Hyde, *Londonderry House and its Pictures* (1937), pp. 17–18; also T. H. Taunton. *Portraits of Celebrated Racehorses* (1887), I, p. 227.

Frances Anne's Journal to the age of 24 is substantially cited in *Frances Anne*. On her marriage settlement, see particularly R. W. Sturgess. *Aristocrat in Business*.

SECTION 2

Mrs Bradford, the Vienna embassy chaplain's wife, has given some vivid and amusing descriptions of the Stewarts' life at this period in *More Letters from Martha Wilmot: Impressions of Vienna*, ed. Londonderry and Hyde (1935).

On the Milbanke family, Lord Byron and Seaham Hall, see the *Yorkshire Post*, 13 May 1922, and the *Newcastle Chronicle* 28 May 1922. See also Malcolm Dillon. *Seaham and Seaham Harbour 1828–1928* (1928), and Sturgess. *op. cit.*

SECTION 3

Holdernesse House (later Londonderry House) is described by the present writer in *Londonderry House and its Pictures* (1937), as also is Wynyard by Brian Masters in *Wynyard Hall and the Londonderry Family* (1976).

SECTION 4

On Disraeli's association with the Londonderry family, see *Letters from Benjamin Disraeli to Frances Anne Marchioness of Londonderry 1837–1861*. Edited with an introduction by the Marchioness of Londonderry (1938).

The 3rd Marquess's account of his visit to Russia with Frances Anne was published by him as *Recollections of a Tour in the North of Europe in 1836–1837*, 2 vols, 1838. Frances Anne's journal of the visit, *Russian Journal of Lady Londonderry 1836–37*, edited by W. A. L. Seaman and J. R. Sewell, was published in 1973 from the original manuscript in DCRO. Both Frances Anne and her husband also published accounts of their visits to Portugal, Spain and Africa and to Vienna and Constantinople: see Bibliography below.

Londonderry's letter on the Ashley Act was republished as a 145-page pamphlet. The manuscript of the review in Charles Dickens's handwriting is at present in the George Rylands Fletcher Library of Manchester University. See the library *Bulletin* Vol. 18 (Jan. 1934) for the full text of the review together with a facsimile reproduction of the first page of the MS, which proves it to be the work of Dickens.

Harriet Martineau's notice of Londonderry in the *Daily News* was reprinted in her *Biographical Sketches* (1869) at pp. 188–92.

SECTION 5

The account of the duel between Count de Mélcy and the 4th Marquess (then Lord Castlereagh) is taken from a press cutting dated 15 June 1836 and is stated to have appeared in the *Morning Post*. It is in a family press cutting book in the possession of the present Marquess of Londonderry.

Castlereagh's travels are described by him in *A Journey to Damascus*. 2 vols. London, 1847. The illustrations are engraved from drawings made on the spot by A. Schranz. The originals together with many others done in the course of the journey, formerly at Powerscourt, are now at Mount Stewart.

Mr Rodney Searight has proved that the nobleman in the well known picture by John Frederick Lewis, *Frank Encampment in the Desert of Mount Sinai*, painted in 1842 and exhibited in 1856, is Lord Castlereagh (later 4th Marquess). See 'An Anonymous Traveller Discovered' by Rodney Searight in *Country Life*, 4 May 1978.

The letter from Castlereagh to Hillsborough is in the Downshire Papers in PRONI: D.671/c/12/500.

The letters from Castlereagh to his step-mother Frances Anne, dated respectively 14 July, 31 October and 30 November 1854 and 23 March 1855 are in DCRO: D/Lo/C/543. Edward Cooke's letter on the intrigue in the Cabinet to remove Castlereagh as War Minister in 1809 was published by Sir Charles Webster in the *Cambridge Historical Journal*, III, No 1 (1929).

The 4th Marquess's sporting interests have been described by his step-son the 7th Viscount Powerscourt in a typescript *History of the Stags' Heads, Pictures &c at Mount Stewart* in the present writer's possession.

The extracts from Elizabeth Lady Powerscourt's correspondence with Cardinal Manning and others were transcribed by the present writer during a visit to Powerscourt in 1935.

The 4th Marquess's death certificate is in the Register of Births, Marriages and Deaths, St Catherine's House, London, W.C.

SECTION 6

The details of the 3rd Marquess's sepulchral chamber at Wynyard are in Alison, III, at p. 305.

On Lady Susan Clinton and Lord Adolphus Vane, see Virginia Surtees. *A Beckford Inheritance. The Lady Lincoln Scandal* (1977), at pp. 131–32.

The Duchess of Argyll's letter to Lord Dufferin is in the Dufferin and Ava Correspondence in PRONI: Reel 7 Vol XVIII.

SECTION 7

The biographies by 'Jehu Junior' of the 5th Marquess and his son Lord Castlereagh (later 6th Marquess) appeared in *Vanity Fair* with accompanying cartoons on 11 November 1876 and 7 June 1879.

Cornelia Lady Londonderry's letters to Lord and Lady Hardwicke are in the Hardwicke Papers in the British Library: Add MSS 35791 f. 192, 35798 ff. 396–97, and 35799 f. 39.

The description of Consuelo Marlborough's meeting with Duchess Fanny is in Consuelo Balsan. *The Glitter and the Gold (1953)* at p. 56.

Chapter III   VICTORIAN SUNSET
AND EDWARDIAN AFTERGLOW

SECTION 1

The quotations from Theresa Lady Londonderry's 'Political Notes' dated 14 August 1915 are taken from a typescript in the present writer's possession, also her letters to her sisters circa 1873.

The fact of Theresa Lady Londonderry's affair with Lord Helmsley was admitted by Edith Lady Londonderry to Henry Channon, according to the latter's diary; see *Chips. The Diaries of Sir Henry Channon* (1967), at pp. 424–25.

The 6th Marquess's and his wife's letters to Edmund Gosse are in the Gosse Papers in the Brotherton Library, Leeds University.

SECTION 2

Besides Anita Leslie's account of the Lady de Grey–Lady Londonderry affair, there is a different version in Channon *loc. cit*. Both state that Londonderry never spoke to his wife again except in public, but this is not borne out by Theresa Londonderry's correspondence in the Londonderry Papers.

There is much material about Mrs Ethel Grenfell, later Lady Desborough, in Nicholas Mosley's *Julian Grenfell* (1976). Her letters to Lord Castlereagh, later 7th Marquess of Londonderry, are in PRONI, and his to her are in HCRO.

The 6th Marquess's letter to Herbert Gladstone 19 June 1903 is in the Gladstone Papers in the British Library: Add MSS 46060.

Margot Asquith's letter to Lady Leslie is quoted by Anita Leslie in her *Edwardians in Love*, at p. 137.

SECTION 3

On the 6th Marquess's Irish viceroyalty and the Dublin Castle administration generally, see M. O'Connor Morris, *Dublin Castle* (1889); Charles O'Mahony, *The Viceroys of Ireland* (1912); Elizabeth Countess of Fingall, *Seventy Years Young* (1937); and R. B. McDowell, *The Irish Administration* (1964). Also PRO: Irish Office, Cabinet Papers 1886–90, Vol. 37, ff. 19, 20, 22, 23 and 24 on the National League, Plan of Campaign, Secret Societies in Ireland and America, Crime Reports from the Irish Constabulary, etc. Particulars of the names and salaries of the Lord Lieutenant's household, with effect from the date of the 6th Marquess's appointment, are also in PRO: CO 904/171/1.

SECTION 4

Details of the 7th Marquess's youth have been given by him in an article which he wrote for *TP's and Cassell's Weekly*, 21 March 1925 ('In the Days of my Youth.')

The suggestion for Theresa Lady Londonderry's article for *The Anglo-Saxon Review* Vol. V (June 1900), later expanded into a short biography published in 1904, came from Sidney Low, who was helping Lady Randolph Churchill to edit the review, and was made in the first instance to Edmund Gosse. See letter from Low to Gosse 30 January 1899: Gosse Papers, Brotherton Library; also papers in DCRO: D/Lo/F/1125.

Particulars of the 7th Marquess's career at the Royal Military College, Sandhurst, have been communicated by the Librarian.

The 7th Marquess's undated letter to his mother from Hyde Park Barracks is in DCRO: D/Lo/C/628.

Both the 7th Marquess's letters to his wife and hers to him, about 600 in all, are in PRONI: D.3099/13.

Lord Reginald Stewart is the subject of a well researched article by Brian Masters ('The Secret Room') in *Vogue*, December 1976,pp.146–53. Theresa Lady Londonderry's letter to Cecil Rhodes is in the Rhodes Papers in the Rhodes House Library, Oxford.

The 6th Marquess's letter to Edward Carson on Reginald's death is in PRONI: Carson Papers D. 1507/1/1899/2.

SECTION 5

Edith Castlereagh's description of her visit with her husband to Queen Victoria is in *Retrospect*, at p. 28.

The 7th Marquess's letters to his mother between 1895 and 1919, some 356 in all, are in DCRO: D/Lo/C/682. His wife's letters to her mother-in-law, between 1902 and 1918, some 143 in all, are in DCRO: D/Lo/C/683.

SECTION 6

The Prince of Wales's letter from Wynyard in 1890 is in *Personal Letters of King Edward VII*. Ed. J. P. C. Caswell (1931) at p. 29.

The Privy Council held at Wynyard in 1903 is described by Sir Almeric Fitzroy in his *Memoirs*, I, at pp. 161–62.

Theresa Lady Londonderry's MS account of her visit to Windsor Castle for Ascot Races dated 17 June 1902 is in the possession of the present Marquess.

Theresa Lady Londonderry's experience at the Coronation of King Edward VII is described by Philippe Jullian in *Edward and the Edwardians* (1967), p. 190.

SECTION 7

Theresa Lady Londonderry's account of the Royal Visit to Mount Stewart and Belfast in July 1903 is in DCRO: D/Lo/F/1127.

SECTION 8

The account of the Maidstone election is based on a typescript by the chairman of the local Conservative Association, Mr Edward Hills, *Maidstone Parliamentary Election 1906*, in the present writer's possession. Castlereagh's letters to his mother during the election are in DCRO: D/Lo/C/682.

On the election petition see *Retrospect*, at p. 77 *et seq*.

SECTION 9

Castlereagh's letter to his son Robin 21 September 1911 is in DCRO: D/Lo/C/682.

The anti-Home Rule struggle in the context of Carson's letters to Theresa Lady Londonderry is described by the present writer in *Carson. The Life of Lord Carson of Duncairn* (1953) (new edition 1974).

Castlereagh's letters to his wife are in PRONI: D.3099/13/140–44.

Theresa Lady Londonderry's MS Log of the *Red Rose*, etc. is in the possession of the present Marquess.

The 7th Marquess's letter to Lady Desborough on his father's death is in HCRO.

Theresa Lady Londonderry's letter to her grandson Robin in 1915 is in the possession of the present Marquess.

Chapter IV   WAR AND IRISH POLITICS

SECTION 1

The 7th Marquess's letters to his wife during the First World War are in PRONI, as are General Sir William Pulteney's letters to her.

SECTION 2

Asquith's account of his visit to the front in May 1915 is in *The Life of Lord Oxford and Asquith* (1932) by J. A. Spender and Cyril Asquith, II, at p. 173.

Londonderry's letter to Edmund Gosse 2 June 1915 is in the Gosse Papers in the Brotherton Library, Leeds University.

Londonderry's letters to Lady Desborough are in HCRO.

SECTION 3

The Blues in action when Londonderry was second-in-command and later acting C.O. are described by Herbert Buckmaster in *Buck's Book* (1933).

Balfour's letter of 8 May 1917 to Lady Londonderry is in PRONI.

SECTION 4

On the Women's Legion see *Retrospect*: Chapter V, and letters and papers in PRONI: D.3099/3/1.

The papers on the 'Ark' are in PRONI: D.3099/3/11.

On the history of the Irish Convention see R. B. McDowell. *The Irish Convention of 1917–18* (1970): also Fingall, *op. cit.*; PRONI:D.3099/2/4–5.

The quotations from Theresa Lady Londonderry's diary are from a typescript copy in the present writer's possession.

Colonel Repington's tribute to Theresa Lady Londonderry on her death is in his *The First World War* (1920), II, at pp. 508, 511.

The 7th Marquess's letter to Edmund Gosse on his mother is in the Gosse Papers in the Brotherton Library, Leeds University.

SECTION 5

Londonderry's first term of office at the Air Ministry as Finance Member of the Air Council and Parliamentary Under-Secretary of State is described in *Wings of Destiny* and more fully in the present writer's *British Air Policy Between the Wars 1918–1939*. His correspondence with Trenchard is in the Trenchard Papers in the possession of Viscount Trenchard.

SECTION 6

On the visit by King George V and Queen Mary to open the first Northern Ireland Parliament in Belfast see *King George V* by Harold Nicolson and *Craigavon Ulsterman* by St John Ervine (1949).

Lavery's letter to Churchill and other contemporary details are in his autobiography *The Life of a Painter* (1940), at pp. 210–12.

The 'Treaty' negotiations have been admirably recounted by Frank Pakenham (Lord Longford) in *Peace by Ordeal* (1935), and from the Unionist point of view by W. Alison Phillips in *The Revolution in Ireland* (1923).

SECTION 7

The aftermath of the 'Treaty' is described by Thomas Jones in his *Whitehall Diary* Vol. III *Ireland 1918–1925*. Edited by Keith Middlemas (1971).

Michael Collins's letter to Lady Londonderry is in PRONI. Londonderry's opinion of Collins and their meeting is in a letter from Londonderry to Frank Pakenham dated 30 October 1935 and is taken from a typescript in the possession of the present writer.

Londonderry's private papers as Minister of Education in the Northern Ireland Government, particularly dealing with the Education Act, are in PRONI: D.3099/5/1–11.

Chapter V   THE RAMSAY MACDONALD SYNDROME

SECTION 1

Ramsay MacDonald's letters to Lady Londonderry, over 400 extending from 1924 to 1937, are in PRONI: D.3099/3/10. Her letters to him, approximately 90, are in the MacDonald Papers in the PRO at Kew: 30/69/32–46. Lady Londonderry has described MacDonald and their friendship in *Retrospect*, at pp. 223–28.

SECTION 2

On the Irish Boundary Commission see the *Report*, edited with an introduction by Geoffrey J. Hand (1969). The subsequent Anglo-Irish negotiations are described by the present writer in his *Baldwin* (1973), at pp. 257–65.

SECTION 3

Londonderry's letter to Baldwin dated 13 April 1926 has been published by Thomas Jones in his *Whitehall Diary* Vol. II, at p. 10.

Londonderry's letters to Churchill are in the Churchill Papers at present in the custody of Churchill's official biographer Dr Martin Gilbert in Oxford.

SECTION 4

The letters of Robin Castlereagh (later 8th Marquess) to Adrian Holman are in PRONI.

Earle's tribute to Londonderry as Minister of Works is in PRONI. See also *Turn Over the Page* (1935) by Sir Lionel Earle.

SECTION 5

Londonderry's letter of 11 October 1930 and his other letters to Baldwin are in the Baldwin Papers, Vol. 171, in the Cambridge University Library.

Londonderry's letters to Lord Stamfordham and King George V are in the Royal Archives in Windsor Castle under reference L.2314, 43 and 44.

SECTION 6

On the formation of the National Government, see Nicolson, *op. cit.*, *Wings of Destiny*, the present writer's *Baldwin*, and David Marquand's *Ramsay MacDonald*.

SECTION 7

Ramsay MacDonald's diaries are in the MacDonald Papers in the PRO at Kew: 30/69/8/1.

SECTION 8

Thomas Jones's descriptions of his meetings with Lady Londonderry are in his *A Diary with Letters* (1954), at pp. 99–101.

On the Disarmament Conference at Geneva, see the present writer's *British Air Policy Between the Wars 1918–1939* (1976); also G. M. Gathorne-Hardy. *A Short History of International Affairs*. Revised edition (1938).

Chapter VI FINALE

SECTION 1

Londonderry's term as Air Minister has been described in the light of his official departmental correspondence by the present writer in his *British Air Policy Between the Wars*. Londonderry's private papers on air matters are in PRONI: D.3099/6/1–7; D.3099/6/40, 48–52, 55–56; and D.3099/2/8. His own account of his office is in *Wings of Destiny*.

Sir Frederick Ponsonby's letters to Londonderry, 2 and 10 November 1933, are in PRONI.

SECTION 2

MacDonald's diary entry about the Air Ministry for 10 May 1935 is in the PRO at Kew: Ramsay MacDonald Papers 30/69/8/1.

SECTION 3

Londonderry's correspondence with Baldwin about his resignation is in the Baldwin Papers, Vol. 171, in the Cambridge University Library. There is also some further relevant material in PRONI: D.3099/2/8.

Robin Castlereagh's account of his interview with Baldwin is taken from a copy of a memorandum which Castlereagh gave the late Earl Baldwin of Bewdley and which the latter gave the present writer.

Lord Hailsham's letter to Londonderry dated Xmas 1935 is in PRONI.

SECTION 4

Londonderry's account of his visits to Germany, based on a diary he kept at the time, is in his book *Ourselves and Germany* (1938).

Harold Nicolson's letter to his wife about Londonderry's visit to Germany is in his *Diaries and Letters 1930–1939*, edited by Nigel Nicolson (1966), at p. 245.

The letter from Londonderry to a friend about Halifax dated 26 Nov. 1946 was addressed to Dr F. W. Pick. Communicated by Mr Michael Pick.

Londonderry's letters from Baldwin and others about his air policy are in PRONI: D.3099/2/8.

SECTION 5

Baldwin's opinion of Ramsay MacDonald is in the Castlereagh Memorandum mentioned *supra* under Section 3. Bernard Shaw's letter to Lady Londonderry on the same subject is in PRONI.

Mrs Simpson's letter of 6 November 1936 to Lady Londonderry is in PRONI.

SECTION 6

The history of the Mount Stewart gardens has been written by Lady Londonderry in *Mount Stewart*. Privately printed, 1956.

The letters from Sean O'Casey to Lady Londonderry are in PRONI: D.3099/3/6. His visit to Mount Stewart is described in his autobiography *Rose and Crown* (1952). See also *Letters of Sean O'Casey*, edited by David Krause. Vol. I (1975).

SECTION 7

Lady Londonderry's letters to Ribbentrop and Goering and their replies are in PRONI.

Londonderry's visit to Munich with Ward Price is described in *Wings of Destiny*.

SECTION 8

The files on Lady Londonderry's work for the Red Cross and the Women's Legion during the Second World War are in PRONI: D.3099/14/31-51.

James Lees-Milne's references to Londonderry and Londonderry House in his diary are in *Prophesying Peace* (1977), at pp. 93, 94, 110 and 123.

Londonderry's letter to the present writer about his gliding accident is in the author's possession.

Henry Channon's description of Londonderry and his Memorial service is in *Chips*, at p. 434. Helen Waddell's is in Monica Blackett's *The Mark of the Maker* (1973), at pp. 206-7.

APPENDIX

See authorities cited under Chapter I, Section 1, above.

The first Marquess's letter of 20 April 1817 to an unknown correspondent about his ancestry is in PRONI.

BIBLIOGRAPHY

A MANUSCRIPT SOURCES

Broadly speaking the Londonderry archive is divided into two main parts, located respectively in the Public Record Office of Northern Ireland in Belfast and the Durham County Record Office in Durham City. The Castlereagh Papers belonging to the second Marquess, on which his published correspondence, edited with a memoir by his brother the third Marquess, is based, were purchased by the Government of Northern Ireland and are now in the N.I. Record Office in Belfast. The second Marquess's (Lord Castlereagh's) letters to his wife, also letters to her from various other correspondents, were formerly in the possession of the late Philip Marquess of Lothian at Blickling Hall, Norfolk; there are typescript volumes of these letters in the N.I. Record Office.

Also in the Public Record Office of Northern Ireland are the papers of the seventh Marquess and his wife, together with some correspondence of the eighth Marquess and the fifth Marquess's wife, which like the Castlereagh Papers were formerly at Mount Stewart, the Irish family home in County Down, and have been deposited in the N.I. Record Office by Lady Mairi Bury as her parents' literary executrix.

The more extensive Durham portion of the archive, formerly at Wynyard Hall, was deposited in the Durham County Record Office by the ninth Marquess in three batches between 1969 and 1974. It consists largely of the papers, diaries and private correspondence of the third Marquess and his wife, born Lady Frances Anne Vane-Tempest. In addition the Durham portion includes important papers of the second, fifth, sixth and seventh Marquesses and their wives not in the Belfast collection, as well as the correspondence of Lord Adolphus Vane (1825–1864); also much material concerning the Londonderry estates in England, Wales and Ireland, as well as the collieries and harbour at Seaham. Indeed there are many papers relating to Northern Ireland in the Durham collection, just as there are numerous documents concerning Durham in the Belfast part of the archive. It is unfortunate in some ways that the two collections became separated. However there are useful typescript and printed catalogues with cross-references in both the Record Offices.

There are a few of the fourth Marquess's papers in both Belfast and Durham, but many were no doubt kept at Powerscourt in County Wicklow, where the fourth Marquess lived for much of the time with his wife, formerly Elizabeth Lady Powerscourt, and his step-children. Unfortunately efforts to trace them since the destruction of Powerscourt house by fire some years ago have been unsuccessful.

Sir Edward Carson's letters to Theresa Lady Londonderry are in the N.I. Record Office, as also are the Carson, Castle Ward, Downshire, Perceval-Maxwell and Ellison-Macartney Papers, all of which contain references to various members of the Londonderry family. Theresa Lady Londonderry's letters to Cecil Rhodes are in the Rhodes Papers in the Rhodes House Library, Oxford.

The letters of the sixth Marquess, his wife Theresa, and their son the seventh Marquess, to Sir Edmund Gosse are in the Gosse Papers in the Brotherton Library of Leeds University.

Theresa Lady Londonderry's MS account of her visit to Windsor for Ascot race week in 1902 is in the possession of the present Marquess. Her typescript account of the visit of King Edward VII and Queen Alexandra to Mount Stewart and Belfast in July 1903 is in the Durham County Record Office under reference S/Lo/F/1127.

The seventh Marquess's correspondence with his cousin Winston Churchill is in the Churchill Papers at present in the custody of Churchill's official biographer Dr Martin Gilbert in Oxford.

The seventh Marquess's letters to Ethel Lady Desborough are in the Hertfordshire County Record Office at St Albans. Her letters to him are in the Londonderry Papers in the N.I. Record Office under reference D.3099/2/2. His private letters to Stanley Baldwin, first Earl Baldwin of Bewdley, are in the Baldwin Papers (Vol. 171) in the Cambridge University Library. A few letters from Baldwin to him are in the N.I. Record Office under reference D.3099/2/8.

The seventh Marquess's official correspondence as Finance Member of the Air Council, Parliamentary Under-Secretary for Air and Secretary of State for Air is in the Air Ministry and Air Staff files in the Public Record Office at Kew; also his correspondence with various Prime Ministers which is under reference Premier 1. His correspondence with Sir Hugh Trenchard, when the latter was Chief of the Air Staff, is in the Trenchard Papers in the possession of the present Viscount Trenchard.

Edith Lady Londonderry's letters to Ramsay MacDonald are in the MacDonald Papers, also at Kew, mostly under reference 30/69/3/46. His letters to her are in the N.I. Record Office under reference D.3099/3/10.

The letters of the eighth Marquess (then Lord Castlereagh) to Adrian Holman are in the N.I. Record Office.

An interesting MS account by the eighth Marquess of his interview with Baldwin in March 1936 about Baldwin's relations with his father was formerly kept with his private papers at Wynyard, but no trace of the original has been discovered with his other papers either there or in Durham. It is known that he lent it to Baldwin's son the second Earl, but the latter subsequently returned it after he had photocopies made, one of which he gave the present writer after the eighth Marquess's death.

A few other MS sources such as the Charlemont Papers in the Royal Irish Academy in Dublin are noticed separately in the Sources and Notes above.

B PRINTED SOURCES

The following are the principal secondary authorities which have been consulted:

Alison, Sir Archibald: *The Lives of Lord Castlereagh and Sir Charles Stewart*. 3 vols. Edinburgh: William Blackwood, 1861.

Arbuthnot, Harriet: *Journal of Mrs Arbuthnot*. Edited by Francis Bamford and the Duke of Wellington. 2 vols. London: Macmillan, 1950.

Asquith, Margot: *Autobiography*. Edited by Mark Bonham Carter. London: Eyre & Spotiswoode, 1962.

Balsan, Consuelo Vanderbilt: *The Glitter and the Gold*. London: Heine-mann, 1953.

Benson, E. F.: *As We Were. A Victorian Peep-Show*. London: Longmans, Green, 1930.

Blackett, Monica: *The Mark of the Maker: A Portrait of Helen Waddell*. London: Constable, 1973.

Blake, Robert: *The Unknown Prime Minister. The Life and Times of Andrew Bonar Law*. London: Eyre & Spotiswoode, 1955.

Brown, David B.: *The History of the Guild of Air Pilots and Air Navigators 1929–1969*. London: Privately printed, 1967.

Brownlow, Emma Sophia Countess of: *The Eve of Victorianism*. London: John Murray, 1940.

Buckmaster, Herbert: *Buck's Book*. London: Grayson & Grayson, 1933.

Callwell, Maj.-Gen. Sir C. E.: *Field Marshal Sir Henry Wilson. His Life and Letters*. 2 vols. London: Cassell, 1927.

Castlereagh, see under Londonderry.

Channon, Sir Henry: *Chips. The Diaries of Sir Henry Channon*. Edited by Robert Rhodes James. London: Weidenfeld & Nicolson, 1967.

Churchill, Lady Randolph: *Reminiscences*. London: Edward Arnold, 1904.

— Winston S. *Lord Randolph Churchill*. London: Odhams Press, 1951.

— *The Second World War*. Vol. I. London: Cassell, 1948.

See also under Gilbert.

Crawford, W. H. and Trainor, B. *Aspects of Irish Social History 1750–1800*. Belfast: H.M.S.O., 1969.

Davidson, J. C. C.: *Memoirs of a Conservative 1910–37*. Edited by Robert Rhodes James. London: Weidenfeld & Nicolson, 1969.

Dictionary of National Biography 1941–50. Article on Charles, seventh Marquess of Londonderry by H. Montgomery Hyde.

Disraeli, Benjamin: *Letters from Benjamin Disraeli to Frances Anne, Marchioness of Londonderry*. Edited by Edith Marchioness of Londonderry. London: Macmillan, 1938.

Doyle, Arthur Conan: *The British Campaigns in Europe. 1914–1918*. London: Geoffrey Bles, 1928.

Drennan, William: *Correspondence of William Drennan*. Edited by D. A. Chart, Belfast: H.M.S.O., 1931.

Durham County Record Office. *The Londonderry Papers*. Catalogue of the documents deposited by the 9th Marquess, with a Foreword by him. Durham County Council, 1969.

Earle, Sir Lionel: *Turn Over the Page*. London: Hutchinson, 1935.

Edward VII, King: *Personal Letters of King Edward VII*. Edited by Lieut.-Col. J. P. C. Caswell. London: Hutchinson, 1931.

Ervine, St John: *Craigavon Ulsterman*. London: Allen & Unwin, 1949.

Esher, Reginald Viscount: *Journals and Letters*. 4 vols. 1870–1930. Edited by Maurice Brett. London: Ivor Nicholson & Watson, 1938.

Feiling, Keith: *The Life of Neville Chamberlain*. London: Macmillan, 1946.

Fingall, Elizabeth Countess of: *Seventy Years Young*. London: Collins, 1937.

Fitzroy, Sir Almeric: *Memoirs*. 2 vols. London: Hutchinson, 1925.

Gilbert, Martin: *Winston S. Churchill*. Vols. III, IV and V. London: Heinemann, 1971–76.

Greville, Charles: *The Greville Diaries*. Edited by Lytton Strachey and Roger Fulford. 8 vols. London: Macmillan, 1938.

Heesom, A. J.: 'Entrepreneurial Paternalism: The Third Lord Londonderry (1778–1854) and the Coal Trade' and 'Problems of Patronage: Lord Londonderry's Appointment as Lord Lieutenant of County Durham, 1842' in *Durham University Journal*, June 1974 and June 1978.

Holland, Henry Lord: *The Holland House Diaries, 1831–1840*. Edited by A. D. Kriegel. London: Routledge & Kegan Paul, 1977.

Hyde, H. Montgomery: *The Rise of Castlereagh*. London: Macmillan, 1933.

— *More Letters from Martha Wilmot: Impressions of Vienna* (with the Marchioness of Londonderry). London: Macmillan, 1935.

— *Londonderry House and its Pictures*. London: Cresset Press, 1937.

— *Princess Lieven*. London: Harrap, 1938.

— *Carson. The Life of Lord Carson of Duncairn*. London: Heinemann, 1953. New ed. Constable, 1974.

— *The Strange Death of Lord Castlereagh*. London: Heinemann, 1959.
— *Strong for Service. The Life of Lord Nathan of Churt*. London: W. H. Allen, 1968.
— *Baldwin. The Unexpected Prime Minister*. London: Hart-Davis, McGibbon, 1973.
— *British Air Policy Between the Wars 1918–1939*. London: Heinemann, 1976.
— *Neville Chamberlain*. London: Weidenfeld & Nicolson, 1976.
See also under *Dictionary of National Biography*.
Irish Boundary Commission. *Report of the Irish Boundary Commission 1925*. Edited by Geoffrey J. Hand. Shannon: Irish University Press, 1969.
James, Robert Rhodes: *Victor Cazalet*. London: Hamish Hamilton, 1976.
Jones, Thomas: *Whitehall Diary*. 3 vols. 1916–30. Edited by Keith Middlemas. London: Oxford University Press, 1969–71.
— *A Diary with Letters 1931–1950*. London: Oxford University Press, 1954.
Jullian, Philippe. *Edward and the Edwardians*. Translated from the French by Peter Dawnay. London: Sidgwick & Jackson, 1967.
Lavery, John: *The Life of a Painter*. London: Cassell, 1940.
Lawrence, Sir T.: *Sir Thomas Lawrence's Letter Bag*. Edited by G. S. Layard. London: George Allen, 1906.
Lees-Milne, James: *Prophesying Peace*. London: Chatto & Windus, 1977.
Leslie, Anita. *Edwardians in Love*. London: Hutchinson, 1972.
Lockhart, Sir Robert Bruce: *The Diaries of Sir Robert Bruce Lockhart* Vol. I. 1915–1938. Edited by Kenneth Young. London: Macmillan, 1973.
Londonderry, Robert Second Marquess of: *Memoirs and Correspondence of Viscount Castlereagh*. Edited by the third Marquess. 12 vols. London: Colburn, 1848–53.
— Charles Third Marquess of: *Tour of the Northern Courts*. 2 vols. London: Bentley, 1838.
— *Tour of Constantinople etc.* 2 vols. London: Colburn, 1842.
— Frances Anne Marchioness of: *Three Months Tour in Portugal, Spain and Africa*. Privately printed, 1843.
— *Visit to the Courts of Vienna, Constantinople, etc.* London: Colburn, 1844.
— *Russian Journal 1836–37*. Edited by W. A. L. Seaman and J. R. Sewell. London: History Book Club, 1973.
— Frederick Fourth Marquess of (Viscount Castlereagh). *A Journey to Damascus*. 2 vols. London: Colburn, 1847.
— Theresa Marchioness of: *Robert Stewart Viscount Castlereagh*. London: Arthur Humphreys, 1904.

— Charles Seventh Marquess of: *Ourselves and Germany*. London: Robert Hale, 1938; Penguin Books, 1938.
— *Wings of Destiny*. London: Macmillan, 1943.
— Edith Marchioness of: *Henry Chaplin. A Memoir*. London: Macmillan, 1926.
— *Character and Tradition*. London: Macmillan, 1934.
— *Retrospect*. London: Frederick Muller, 1938.
— *Mount Stewart*. Privately printed, 1956.
— *Frances Anne*. London: Macmillan, 1958.
— Alastair Ninth Marquess of: *The Londonderry Album*. London: Blond & Briggs, 1978.
See also under Disraeli, Hyde and Sturgess.
McDowell, R. B.: *The Irish Administration 1801–1914*. London: Routledge & Kegan Paul, 1964.
— *The Irish Convention 1917–18*. London: Routledge & Kegan Paul, 1970.
See also Stanford.
McGuigan, Dorothy Gies: *Metternich and the Duchess*. New York: Doubleday, 1975.
Magnus, Philip: *King Edward the Seventh*. London: John Murray, 1964.
Manchester, Louise Duchess of: *'My Dear Duchess' Social and Political Letters to the Duchess of Manchester 1858–1869*. Edited by A. L. Kennedy. London: John Murray, 1956.
Marquand, David: *Ramsay MacDonald*. London: Jonathan Cape, 1977.
Masters, Brian: *Wynyard Hall and the Londonderry Family*. Hartlepool, 1976.
— 'The Secret Room', *Vogue*, December, 1976.
Morris, M. O'Connor: *Dublin Castle*. London: Harrison, 1889.
Mosley, Nicholas: *Julian Grenfell*. London: Weidenfeld & Nicolson, 1976.
Nicolson, Harold: *King George V*. London: Constable, 1952.
— *Diaries and Letters 1930–1939*. Edited by Nigel Nicolson. London: Collins, 1966.
O'Casey, Eileen: *Sean*. Edited with an Introduction by J. C. Trewin. London: Macmillan, 1971.
— Sean: *Rose and Crown*. London: Macmillan, 1952.
— *The Letters of Sean O'Casey*. Vol. I. 1910–1941. Edited by David Krause. London: Cassell, 1975.
O'Mahony, Charles: *The Viceroys of Ireland*. London: John Long, 1912.
Pakenham, Frank: *Peace by Ordeal*. London: Jonathan Cape, 1935.
Phillips, W. Alison: *The Revolution in Ireland 1906–1923*. London: Longmans, Green, 1923.
Ponsonby, Sir Frederick (Lord Sysonby). *Recollections of Three Reigns*. London: Eyre & Spotiswoode, 1951.

Pulteney, Lieut.-Gen. Sir William: *The Immortal Salient*. London: John Murray, 1925.

Repington, C. à Court: *The First World War*. 2 vols. London: Constable, 1920.

Roskill, Stephen: *Hankey Man of Secrets*. Vol. III. London: Collins, 1974.

Searight, Rodney: 'An Anonymous Traveller Rediscovered.' *Country Life*, May 4, 1978.

Sencourt, Robert: *King Alphonso*. London: Faber, 1942.

Smyth, Sir John: *Sandhurst*. London: Weidenfeld & Nicolson, 1961.

Spender, J. A., and Asquith, Cyril: *Life of Lord Oxford and Asquith*. 2 vols. London: Hutchinson, 1932.

Stanford, W. B., and McDowell, R. B.: *Mahaffy*, London: Routledge & Kegan Paul, 1971.

Stroud, Dorothy: *George Dance Architect 1741–1825*. London: Faber, 1971.

Sturgess, R. W. *Aristocrat in Business. The Third Marquess of Londonderry as Coalowner and Portbuilder*. Durham: Durham County Local History Society, 1975.

Surtees, Virginia: *A Beckford Inheritance. The Lady Lincoln Scandal*. London: Michael Russell, 1977.

Wheeler-Bennett, John W.: *King George VI*: London: Macmillan, 1958.

Wilson, Sir Henry. See under Callwell, Sir C. E.

INDEX